WE, THE JURY

We, the Jury

THE JURY SYSTEM AND THE
IDEAL OF DEMOCRACY

Jeffrey Abramson

BasicBooks
A Division of HarperCollinsPublishers

Portions of chapter 3 previously appeared in *The Journal of Political Philosophy* 1, no. 1 (1993). Reprinted by permission of Basil Blackwell, Inc.

Tables in chapter 6 are adapted from David C. Baldus, George Woodworth, and Charles A. Pulaski, Jr., *Equal Justice and the Death Penalty: A Legal and Empirical Analysis* (Boston: Northeastern University Press, 1990), pp. 315, 327. Reprinted by permission.

Designed by Ellen Levine

LIBRARY OF CONGRESS CATALOGING-IN-PUBLICATION DATA
Abramson, Jeffrey, 1947–
    We, the jury : the jury system and the ideal of democracy / Jeffrey Abramson.
      p. cm.
    Includes bibliographical references and index.
    ISBN 0–465–03698–8 (cloth)
    ISBN 0–465–09116–4 (paper)
    1. Jury—United States. 2. Justice, Administration of—United States. I. Title.
KF8972.A727 1994
347.73'752—dc20
[347.307752]
                                           94–11580
                                             CIP

95 96 97 98 ❖/RRD 9 8 7 6 5 4 3 2 1

For Sarah and Anna, that they should know

Contents

Acknowledgments

AT LAST I CAN THANK in print those who have helped me write this book. Thanks first to the National Endowment for the Humanities for a generous fellowship during the Constitution's bicentennial year of 1987 that enabled me to begin the research. Friends everywhere collected jury stories for me or listened to mine. Thanks especially to my brothers and to Kiku Adatto, Dennis Aftergut, Mark Hulliung, Sally Merry, and Jonathan Tobis. The staff of the National Center for State Courts and the NAACP Legal Defense Fund kept me supplied with contemporary information. Michael Paris was my indispensable research assistant. The Brandeis University librarians helped me gather material from near and far. Most especially, my parents formed a two-person newspaper-reading service, clipping every important article on the jury appearing in several newspapers over the years.

One of my most pleasant surprises in writing this book was to find that I could count on the help of scholars who were personal strangers to me but intellectual companions in the study of the jury. John Murrin patiently answered my questions about the colonial jury. David Baldus was uncommonly generous in walking me through his own research on race and the death penalty, as well as commenting line by line on earlier versions of chapter 6. Thomas Munsterman, Brian Ostrom, and David Rottman of the National Center for State Courts worked with me in developing much of the statistical information included in the appendix.

For many years, I was fortunate to be an assistant to Massachusetts

Attorney General Scott Harshbarger, going back to his days as district attorney for Middlesex County. From every prosecutor in his offices, but especially from Margot Botsford, Edward Rapacki, and James Sahakian, I learned that evidence, not tricks, wins jury trials.

Elizabeth Bussiere, Robert Goodin, Lawrence Fuchs, Jacqueline Jones, James Kloppenberg, Susan Moller Okin, Judith Shklar, and Michael Sandel read all or portions of the manuscript and forced me to sharpen what I wanted to say about the jury and democratic theory. Dita Shklar died in 1992; like so many of her former students and colleagues, I sorely miss the stern critic who would always level with me for my own good.

Special thanks go to Kathryn Preyer, for immersing herself so fully in reading earlier drafts, and drawing upon her unsurpassed command of legal history to keep me busy reading about jury property qualifications, Aaron Burr, and jury nullification.

Trudy Crosby, Elaine Herrmann, and Erin Dunham made the processing of the manuscript as painless as such matters possibly can be. At Basic Books, I received editorial help and encouragement from former and current presidents Martin Kessler and Kermit Hummel, and from Sally Jaskold, Dana Slesinger, and Matt Shine.

Writing a book is always partly a family matter. In my own case, having historian Jacqueline Jones in the family makes this book especially a joint enterprise. Jackie read every word of the manuscript, queried, quarreled, edited, supported, and supported some more. As to Sarah and Anna, my children, what can I say except thanks for asking about the jury, thanks for joking me through the crises, and thanks for not watching too much television.

Finally, I would like to thank the students over the years who enrolled in Politics 192b, my seminar on the jury and democratic theory at Brandeis. Every fall, I could count on fresh insights into old matters from fifteen students skeptical about hoary jury legends. In writing this book, I hope to have given the jury system the kind of defense these forever-young idealists demanded.

Introduction

TRIAL BY JURY is about the best of democracy and about the worst of democracy. Jurors in Athens sentenced Socrates to death for religious crimes against the state, but in England jurors went to prison themselves rather than convict the Quaker William Penn. Juries convicted women as witches in Salem, but they resisted witch hunts for communists in Washington. Juries in the American South freed vigilantes who lynched African-Americans, but in the North they sheltered fugitive slaves and the abolitionists who helped them escape. One jury finds the Broadway musical *Hair* to be obscene, another finds Robert Mapplethorpe's photographs to be art. The names of the Scottsboro Boys and of Emmett Till, Viola Liuzzo, Lemuel Penn, and Medgar Evers mark the miscarriages of justice perpetrated by an all-white jury system that was democratic in name only. The names of John Peter Zenger, John Hancock, Angela Davis, Father Philip Berrigan, and the Oakland Seven mark the courage of jurors willing to protect dissenters from the orthodoxies of the day. In short, the drama of trial by jury casts ordinary citizens as villains one day, heroes the next, as they struggle to deal justly with the liberties and properties—sometimes even the lives—of their fellow men and women.[1]

Today, the jury continues both to attract and to repel us precisely because it exposes the full range of democratic vices and virtues. No other institution of government rivals the jury in placing power so directly in the hands of citizens. Hence, no other institution risks as much on democracy or wagers more on the truth of democracy's core claim that the people make their own best governors. The jury's democratic gamble is striking in comparison with the hedged bet that most of our institutions of representative democracy make on the people.

Elections for president, governor, senator, or other office give power of a sort to the people by making those who are elected accountable to their constituents through the ballot box. But this is a far cry from empowering the people themselves with the daily responsibility for governing. Voting and elections, even at their best, activate popular sovereignty only periodically and for passing moments. However loudly we speak during an election, the activity of governance is still ceded to the few. Between elections, concerned citizens may write letters, sign petitions, march in the street, lobby, or contribute to interest groups. But as active as they are in these respects, they still do not directly possess the power of, or responsibility for, government.

By contrast, the jury version of democracy stands almost alone today in entrusting the people at large with the power of government (the only other example that comes to mind is the town meeting, but this hardly rivals the jury on a daily or national basis). I do not mean to suggest for a moment that jury selection in actual cases always lives up to the ideal of recruiting members from all walks of life; in practice, excuses, challenges, and changes of venue often skew the representative nature of juries. Still, for most of us the jury remains our only realistic opportunity to participate in governing ourselves. We hold no elections for jury service but instead draft people by essentially drawing lots. Although technological advancement has made the lottery system computerized today, the noble principle remains that every citizen is equally competent to do justice. So long as selected persons meet minimal qualifications of age, citizenship, literacy, and residency, they take turns as jurors, randomly rotating on and off the jury wheel.

The contemporary democratization of jury service stands in marked contrast to the discriminatory practices that dominated centuries of jury history. In England, it wasn't until 1972 that the property qualification for jurors was abolished.[2] At the time of the American Revolution, the colonies restricted jury duty to white male property holders. No African-American served on any trial jury in the United States, North or South, until 1860 during a criminal trial in Worcester, Massachusetts.[3] Women were ineligible for jury service in every state until 1898, when Utah allowed them to be jurors.[4] Up until 1968, federal jury selection in the

United States openly worked to limit jury service to supposedly elite individuals recommended by community leaders. That year, Congress officially abandoned the "blue-ribbon" jury in favor of the "cross section of the population" jury for the federal system.[5] The Supreme Court extended the cross-sectional requirement to state juries, as a matter of constitutional law, only in 1975.[6] Thus, we are the first generation in U.S. history that can regard jury verdicts as a fair test of democracy's faith in the collective wisdom of all the people.

Ironically, this very democratization of jury selection has provoked a crisis of confidence in the quality and accuracy of jury verdicts. Few in the United States advocate abolishing the jury system, but many favor following England in restricting the kind of cases civil juries may resolve.[7] On the criminal side, the violence that left thirty dead in the wake of the first jury trial for the white policemen accused of beating black motorist Rodney King in 1991 tells a story in itself about collapsed faith in the jury. All in all, the grounds for skepticism about jury justice are familiar and, at first blush, telling:

- Justice requires distance and insulation from the pressure to do whatever is popular. That, after all, is why we appoint, not elect, federal judges and grant them life tenure. The jury vision of democracy insists to a fault that what we want is popular justice, the "conscience of the community." But justice is not always popular, and the conscience of the community is not always pure. Today's juries therefore substitute the rule of people for the rule of law.

- The gap between the complexity of modern litigation and the qualifications of jurors has widened to frightening proportions. The average jury rarely understands the expert testimony in an antitrust suit, a medical malpractice case, or an insanity defense. Nor do most jurors know the law or comprehend the judge's crash course of instructions on it. Trial by jury has thus become trial by ignorance. For instance, in 1992 a Texas jury found that AT&T had infringed on a small company's patent covering modularization of digital switching equipment. The jury awarded $35 million to the plaintiff. Lawyers for AT&T complained that the jury "was unemployed laborers and housewives [who] didn't understand that stuff."[8]

- The search for representative juries bogs down jury selection over issues of demographic balance, creating the impression that justice precariously depends on the race, gender, religion, or even national

origin of jurors. The message of the cross-sectional ideal is that different groups have different perspectives on justice. This teaches us that
cases are won or lost not on the basis of evidence but on the basis of
who the jurors are.

- Justice requires living under settled laws that treat like cases alike.
  But jury verdicts are notoriously unpredictable, ad hoc, arbitrary, idiosyncratic, whimsical. Like cases are not treated alike. For instance, in
  1992, an Arkansas jury found the Ford Motor Company's Bronco II
  vehicle unsafe and awarded $7 million to an injured plaintiff, but in a
  similar case one year later, a St. Louis jury found for Ford.[9] Death
  penalty cases exhibit a more appalling arbitrariness—one jury will
  sentence a convicted defendant to die for crimes no different from
  those that lead another jury to sentence another defendant to life
  imprisonment.

- Juries decide cases according to emotion, prejudice, and sympathy
  more than according to law and evidence. They turn trials into circuses
  where the verdict is determined by defendants' way of dressing or by
  their race or ethnicity.

- Jury democracy is really pseudodemocracy because it invites, or at
  least permits, an anonymous group of unelected people to spurn laws
  passed by a democratically elected legislature. Whenever this occurs,
  the jury becomes a lawless institution, rendering decisions for which
  the jurors will never be held accountable.

In this book, I examine the pros and cons of the jury's great experiment
with democratic justice. Both the civil jury and the criminal jury are part
of that experiment, but I will concentrate on the criminal jury as the premier body translating democratic ideals into everyday practice. My concern in part is a lawyer's concern for how juries actually decide cases.
Like any zealous lawyer, I am eager to know whatever tricks of the trade
might help my client's fate before a jury. I want to know how much stock
juries put in eyewitness identifications, why they rarely buy an insanity
defense, and whether recently they have become more willing to excuse
violent acts committed by victims of sexual abuse.[10] I am curious to know
why Clarence Darrow stereotyped the Irish as "always the best jurymen for
the defense" and the Scandinavians as having "too strong a respect for law
as law."[11] And I wonder what truth, if any, there is to "scientific" experiments purporting to show that black jurors are more likely than whites to
favor acquittal[12] and that jurors are "less forgiving of their own than of the

opposite sex."[13] Ultimately, however, this is not another manual on "How to Win Cases and Influence Jurors." To write or read such a manual is to buy into the assumption that jurors are easily manipulated—that jury justice is a fragile affair, ever vulnerable to the connivances of lawyers.

My own experience—as a law clerk on a state supreme court reviewing jury verdicts, as an associate in a corporate law firm, as an assistant district attorney, and as a teacher of law and political theory—has convinced me that jurors are smarter than assumed by lawyers working from manuals. I have observed cases where judges have done their best to treat jurors as children, refusing to let them take notes during trial or to have written copies of the legal instructions they are supposed to follow. Yet time and again jurors overcome the silly obstacle course such bizarre prohibitions make them run.

We have all witnessed a jury surprise the prognosticators by accepting the insanity defense of a defendant as unpopular as John Hinckley charged with attempting to assassinate a president as popular as Ronald Reagan.[14] Then there are all the jurors we never read about, who toil out of the limelight every day, crossing all kinds of racial and ethnic lines to define a shared sense of justice—these examples convince me that the jury, far from being obsolete, is more crucial than ever in a multiethnic society struggling to articulate a justice common to U.S. citizens. Though the jury system is a grand phenomenon—putting justice in the hands of the people—we still have lessons to learn about how to design an institution that gathers persons from different walks of life to discuss and decide upon one justice for all.

I do not argue that juries always get their verdicts right. Who ever promised that there would be no risks to democracy? But to get at the good, we must risk the bad. To get the jury that resists the tyranny of the state, we must risk our freedom on the jury that practices its own petty tyranny. My ultimate concern, therefore, is what the jury teaches us about ourselves and our capacity for self-governance. What can we learn about winning democracy, not just about winning cases, from studying the jury?

Let me begin by telling a story told to me by a Philadelphia lawyer when I first started practicing law. Early in his own career, this lawyer was defending a large corporation being sued by a smaller company on charges of civil fraud. It was a classic David-versus-Goliath lawsuit. The lawyer researched the case for months and had no doubt that the facts and the law were on his client's side. Shortly before the case was due for trial, the judge called the parties in for a pretrial conference to explore grounds for settlement. The lawyer stressed the strength of his legal position and his confidence in going forward to trial. The judge patiently listened to this recital, nodding his apparent agreement with the force of the points. But when the lawyer finished, the judge focused a knowing glance on him and said simply, "But you know if this case ever goes to a jury, you'll lose." A short time later, the client agreed to settle the case for a large cash amount.

I tell this story to illustrate two points. First, the influence of the jury on the conduct of litigation in the United States goes far beyond the jury trials that actually take place. For the case I am describing, merely the threat of a jury trial controlled the outcome. So it is across the board. In the civil area, jury trials take place in fewer than 1 percent of cases disposed of in state courts and in only 2 percent of cases terminated in federal courts.[15] In criminal litigation, two-thirds of all cases are disposed of in state courts through guilty pleas.[16] But it is the background existence of the right to a jury trial, and predictions about how juries would decide cases were they to get them, that drive parties to settle or plea bargain in the first place. Those who argue that the jury is unimportant because jury trials are infrequent thus mistake the tip of the iceberg for the whole.[17]

I learned a second lesson from my lawyer friend's experience in the judge's chambers that day. Evidently, the law was one thing and jury justice was another; I remember being outraged by the difference. In my law school, there were no courses on jury forecasting. In fact, there were no courses on the jury at all. If juries introduced a disturbance into the legal system such that verdicts were not predictable from the law, then that disturbance was a proper study for psychology but not for law school courses. I was therefore able to graduate from law school and pass the bar examination without once having considered the role of the jury in our legal system.

To me, as a young lawyer, the jury signified the rule of emotion over reason, prejudice over principle, whim over written law. With the passage of years, however, I have come to take a more positive position. After all, there would be little point to a jury system if we expected jurors always to decide cases exactly as judges would decide them. The whole point is to subject law to a democratic interpretation, to achieve a justice that resonates with the values and common sense of the people in whose name the law was written. In my lawyer friend's story, the judge was asking him to consider what the people, through the jury, would eventually say about justice in his case, how the equities would seem from the commonsense point of view. And the judge's experience with prior trials put him in a position to say that the commonsense view of justice favored the plaintiff in the matter.

To resent the intrusion of such popular conceptions of justice into the judicial process now strikes me as a resentment against democracy. In a democracy, the legitimacy of the law depends on acceptance by the people. And the jury today remains our best tool for ensuring that the law is being applied in a way that wins the people's consent.

Recently, I had occasion again to consider what a jury was likely to do with a case. A woman, eight months' pregnant, had smashed her car into a utility pole while she was driving legally drunk. She survived, but her fetus did not. In the district attorney's office where I was then working, the question was whether to indict the woman for vehicular homicide. Previous decisions by the state supreme court had made clear that drunk drivers responsible for the death of a viable fetus could be charged with motor vehicle homicide. Under those decisions, we already had convicted drunk drivers who killed the fetus of another. But no one had yet charged, let alone prosecuted or convicted, a drunk woman with the crime of killing her own fetus while driving.

The question was hotly debated, even among those of us who were not assigned to prosecute the case. My own view was that, although the law permitted us to prosecute for vehicular homicide, justice would be better served by forgoing this charge and indicting the woman for driving under the influence of alcohol. I defended my argument about what the district attorney should do by considering what any jury was certain to do. "There is not a jury in this county that is going to convict a woman for killing her own fetus simply because she drove drunk and had an accident," I argued. And that was all that I argued. It seemed apparent to me that we had no business prosecuting this woman as a kind of murderer when we could predict that no jury in our community would ever ratify such a prosecution. In sum, I had come around to the judge's position in the fraud case of my friend's story. The district attorney, I thought, ought to decide how to exercise his discretion by considering how a jury was likely to exercise its discretion.

I could go on telling war stories, but my purpose here is to move beyond anecdote to sustained study of the changing democratic ideals and values embedded in our jury practices. In particular, I aim to show how changes in jury practice capture or reflect larger changes in the way we practice democratic life. I will emphasize the crucial difference between two understandings of the jury's role in a democracy. The first envisions the jury as essentially a representative body, where jurors act as spokespersons for competing group interests. Such a view comfortably fits the jury to prevailing models of interest group behavior; it assumes that jurors inevitably favor their own kind and vote according to narrow group loyalties. Like other representative institutions, therefore, the democratic jury is said to give fair and balanced representation to the competing perspectives of community groups. The description comes close to implying that jurors have constituents to represent, that their mission is to hold fast to their group's perspectives, even as other juror-representatives remain allegiant to their group's preconceptions. This view of the jury is much in vogue today, but it is a description that ultimately undermines any defense of the jury as an institution of justice. Surely the jury has not survived all these centuries only to teach us that democracy is about brokering justice among irreconcilably antagonistic groups.

I will argue for an alternative view of the jury, a vision that defends the jury as a deliberative rather than a representative body. Deliberation is a lost virtue in modern democracies; only the jury still regularly calls upon ordinary citizens to engage each other in a face-to-face process of debate. No group can win that debate simply by outvoting others; under the traditional requirement of unanimity, power flows to arguments that persuade across group lines and speak to a justice common to persons drawn from different walks of life. By history and design, the jury is centrally about getting persons to bracket or transcend starting loyalties. This is why, ideally, voting is a secondary activity for jurors, deferred until persons can express a view of the evidence that is educated by how the evidence appears to others.

Although the deliberative model of democracy survives in the jury, even there it is in serious decline. Every chapter of this book will tell part of the story of the eclipse of the deliberative ideal and the reduction of the jury into a mere mechanical fact-finder warned to leave deliberations about law and justice to the judge. I tell this story not just for its own sake but to retrieve the fading (yet not lost) deliberative ideal. As a road map to the book's themes, I offer the following summary.

In the first part of the book I focus on the question of democratic knowledge—what ordinary citizens are presumed to know to be capable of rendering accurate verdicts. The lead story, told in chapter 1, is of a sea change from the jury as an intimate institution of small-town justice, where members were expected to bring their own local knowledge of the facts to bear on their deliberations, to the jury as a distant institution of impartial justice, where jurors are expected to know as little as possible about the matters and persons on trial. But what should we make of an ideal of impartial justice that prefers ignorance to knowledge in jurors? Modern law unnecessarily undermines the fullness of jury deliberation, even about the facts of the case, by posing a false opposition between well-informed jurors and fair-minded jurors. The spectacle of jury selections that eliminate vast numbers of would-be jurors solely because they follow the news about important events in their communities can only undermine public confidence in the accuracy of jury verdicts.

In chapter 2, I continue the story of what the jury teaches us about democratic knowledge by turning to what ordinary persons know about the law. In colonial America, an understanding of law was seen as accessible to the average man of property. Hence, juries were crucially instructed that they had the right to decide questions of law as well as of fact. The judge's instructions on the law were advisory only, not mandatory. Juries could disobey those instructions, construe the law independently, or even set aside the law entirely to render verdicts according to conscience.

Jury trials today often provoke cynicism about the ability of ordinary citizens to understand the law. Law is massive and mysterious, inaccessible to the uninitiated; it takes professional study, not just natural reason, to understand its intricacies and details. Hence there must be a basic division of labor between jury and judge (juries decide questions of fact, judges answer questions of law). According to this division, jurors are duty-bound to abide by the judge's legal instructions. I explore the implications of this historical decline in the rights of juries to judge the meaning, even to contest the validity, of laws. From a system that once granted juries substantial independence from judges on questions of law, we have narrowed the jury function, in theory, to the more passive task of applying to the facts whatever the judge says is the law.

Such a mechanical description of the jury's task raises two central questions. First, do real jurors actually follow the judge's instructions or even comprehend them in the way the division of labor theory requires? Second, what happens to the jury's historic right to follow conscience rather than law? If juries must accept and abide by the judge's instructions, is there room any longer for juries to function as the conscience of the community? I argue for reviving the jury's authority to nullify unjust laws or unjust applications of law, even while acknowledging the racism and other forms of prejudice that have tainted the history of jury nullification.

In part II, I focus on what the jury teaches us about the nature of democratic representation. In particular, I concentrate on the surprisingly recent shift, starting in 1968, from selecting elite, or blue-ribbon, juries to drawing jurors from a representative cross section of the community. This shift requires us to review the long and sordid history of discriminatory jury selection practices in the United States. It also raises, in the context of the jury, all the familiar questions about color-blind justice, racial quotas, and racial balance that Americans struggle with elsewhere. Consider, for instance, the list of controversial trials just in the last few years where the racial mix of the jury was a crucial concern: the Reginald Denny and Rodney King trials, the police brutality trials in Detroit and Miami, the Crown Heights trial, the Central Park jogger rape case, the Bensonhurst and Howard Beach trials, and the Bernhard Goetz trial. Each of these involved defendants of one race charged with violence against victims of another race. Against such explosive scenarios, belief in color-blind justice is hard to maintain, and we fret considerably during jury selection over the race of jurors.

But what are we saying about jury justice when we insist on making juries fairly representative of the races, as well as of the sexes, ethnic groups, and other cognizable groups in our heterogeneous society? How do we reconcile the ideal that justice is blind to a defendant's demographic features with realities of prejudice that make it obvious that the demographic composition of the jury matters? These questions are among the most serious we ask about jury trials today, and I take them up in chapter 3 by considering the rise of the cross-sectional ideal for the jury and the vision of justice suggested by that ideal.

I offer a defense of the cross-sectional ideal, but only by insisting on some crucial clarifications. Jurors are not disembodied angels; each hears the evidence from perspectives rooted in personal experience as well as in the experiences of others in the jury. This is why democratic deliberation requires that jurors be recruited from a cross section of the community. Whenever any group is intentionally excluded from the jury, the fullness and richness of jury debates are compromised. Lost is the distinctive knowledge and perspective that persons from the excluded group may have contributed to the collective effort. Let loose into the deliberations are the prejudices that people more freely express about a group in its absence. For these reasons, the practice of drawing jurors from a cross section of the community is absolutely vital to enforcing the rational, knowledgeable, and deliberative behavior we seek to inspire in jurors.

We do not want to encourage jurors to see themselves as irreconcilably divided by race, selected only to fill a particular racial or gender slot on the jury. Yet we do want to encourage jurors to draw upon and combine their individual experiences and group backgrounds in the joint search for the most reliable and accurate verdict. The difference is subtle but real. Teaching jurors to think of themselves primarily as representatives is to give up on the ideal of impartial justice, to see the jury system as nothing better than a way for different groups to register their views on justice in a particular case. Juror-representatives might as well not meet and deliberate at all; they could just as well mail in their verdict. Encouraging jurors to think of themselves primarily as deliberators is to hold on to basic ideals of blind, or impartial, justice even while acknowledging shortcomings. Deliberating jurors are human beings who start from different places. But, so long as juries are selected without discrimination from a cross section of the community, their different views can enrich and round out the conversation. They add to the thoroughness and accuracy of deliberation.

Long ago, Aristotle suggested that democracy's chief virtue was the way it permitted ordinary persons drawn from different walks of life to achieve a "collective wisdom" that none could achieve alone. At its best, the jury is the last, best refuge of this connection among democracy, deliberation, and the achievement of wisdom by ordinary persons.

Even as I write, the cross-sectional ideal is forcing changes in centuries-old jury practices—most notably, the former right of lawyers to use peremptory challenges to strike prospective jurors for any reason. Beginning in 1986, the Supreme Court rewrote the rules to prohibit prosecutors (and now defense lawyers) from using peremptories to eliminate would-be jurors solely because of their race.[18] In 1994 the Court went one step further and announced a similar prohibition on using a person's sex as the sole reason for striking him or her from the jury.[19]

This cutback on peremptory challenges, which I consider in chapter 3, is but one example of the way changes in our understanding of democracy play out at the level of jury practice. Still to be resolved by the Supreme Court is whether to impose a ban on peremptory challenges based on religion, national origin, or even age. Indeed, sooner or later, the Court will have to confront the tension between the very existence of peremptory challenges and the ideal of the cross-sectional jury. Lawyers often use their peremptory challenges on the basis of some suspicion that young or old, rich or poor, white-collar or blue-collar, Italian or Irish, Protestant or Jewish jurors will be favorable to the other side. The effect of such peremptory challenges may be to lessen the representative nature of the jury actually seated. Why should lawyers be able to undermine the cross-sectional nature of the jury at all? Such a question forces us to explore, at a more philosophical level, what theory of representation we are trying to practice when we reform juries to be cross sections of the community.

In the third part of the book I look more closely at the nature of jury deliberation. I focus first on perhaps the most peculiar aspect of jury democracy—the traditional requirement that juries in criminal cases reach unanimous agreement. After all, most democratic institutions make do with majority rule; why did the jury historically take such a different route? And why, since 1972, has the Supreme Court permitted states to abandon the unanimous verdict requirement? Exploring the future of unanimous verdicts will require us to look at the kind of society that could expect jurors to deliberate and reach a shared view on justice. Today, when we reform jury selection to represent the diversity of social groups, there can be no surprise that the aspiration for unanimity seems out of place. Here, too, changes in long-standing jury practices reflect the changing understandings of democracy in an increasingly heterogeneous society. I argue, however, that the loss of unanimous verdicts would be a serious blow to the survival of the criminal jury as a deliberative body. It would signal its conversion into a body that functions by registering and tallying up group differences.

I turn finally from theory to practice and consider the outcome of jury deliberations in death penalty cases. When juries deliberate a death sentence, all the imperfections of the conscience of the community are under a magnifying glass. Death penalty cases are not typical, but they require us to attend to the limits of what we can sensibly ask jurors to deliberate about. In 1972, the Supreme Court declared a moratorium on the death penalty in the United States, finding that existing laws gave jurors no standards for deliberating about death sentences. In 1976, the Court permitted states to reinstitute the death penalty, so long as they specified what jurors were supposed to deliberate about when recommending execution versus life imprisonment. But substantial questions remain today about whether preoccupations with race are a determining factor in how jurors deliberate about the death sentence. Evidence that the death penalty falls disproportionately on defendants who murder whites rather than nonwhites is today the most serious indictment of the jury system. Those of us who are defenders of the jury system have special responsibility to speak out against its apparent breakdown over the death penalty.

Most of us do not see ourselves as "doing philosophy" when we fiercely debate about whether jurors are color-blind in death penalty cases, about where to find impartial jurors in highly publicized cases, or about how to make juries representative of multiethnic communities. But we could not enter into the fray without implicitly committing ourselves to some theory of how to make democracy work. My goal in writing this book is to make explicit the arguments over democratic values we are already having when we argue about whether the jury's peculiar marriage of justice and democracy works for better or for worse.

PART I

DEMOCRATIC KNOWLEDGE

Certainly, if the common law be so hard to be understood, it is far from being very common.

—William Penn, on trial, 1670

The law presumes intelligence in jurors.

—Massachusetts Supreme Judicial Court, 1829

The jury want to know whether that ar what you told us, when we first went out, was raly the law, or whether it was only jist your notion.

—Illinois jury foreman to the judge, 1830

You will . . . apply the law which I will give you. . . . You must follow that law whether you agree with it or not.

—Federal criminal jury instructions, 1992

CHAPTER ONE

Juries and Local Justice

CONSIDER TWO PORTRAITS of the ideal juror. The first and more familiar one highlights the impartiality of the juror and the ignorance that, ironically, makes impartial judgment possible. In this view, the primary qualification of good jurors is that they themselves know nothing beforehand about the case they are about to judge. Precisely because they bring no personal knowledge or opinions to the case, they can judge it with the distance and dispassion that marks impartial justice. These jurors can with integrity swear the sacred oath to decide the case solely "upon the evidence developed at the trial."[1] Their great virtue is that their minds "should be as white Paper, and know neither Plaintiff nor Defendant, but judge the Issue merely as an abstract Proposition, upon the Evidence produced" in open court.[2] A federal judge once described this tabula rasa of the impartial juror:

> The entire effort of our [trial] procedure is to secure . . . jurors who do not know and are not in a position to know anything of either [the] character [of the parties] or events [on trial]. . . . The zeal displayed in this effort to empty the minds of the jurors . . . [is a sign] that the jury, . . . like the court itself, is an impartial organ of justice.[3]

In contrast, the second portrait of the ideal juror emphasizes the closeness of the juror to the case on trial: the juror as peer and neighbor. As neighbor, the juror will likely have heard of the case prior to trial and may even know the parties or witnesses or at least know of their reputations. "What is meant by [the defendant's] peers?" asked Patrick Henry. He answered that they were "those who reside near him, his neighbors, and who are well acquainted with his character and situation in life."[4] This so-called local knowledge of the neighborhood qualifies the juror to understand the facts of the case and to pass judgment in ways that a stranger to the community could not. Local jurors more accurately get at what happened because they are familiar with, say, the grade crossing where a certain railroad accident occurred.[5] In addition, such jurors can judge cases better than strangers because they know the conscience of the community and can apply the law in ways that resonate with the community's moral values and common sense.

Of course, there is considerable tension between these two portraits. The local knowledge that gives competence to the juror as neighbor and peer destroys the impartiality of the juror as neutral arbiter of events. Indeed, what qualifies a person to serve as a juror in one model (an understanding of the conscience of the community) disqualifies the person in the other model (an embodiment of the prejudices of the community).

Moreover, the different qualities we want in a juror lead to different geographies for justice. If we want impartial jurors who know nothing of the case beforehand, then we should import them from a great distance— the greater the distance, the more likely the jurors will never have heard of the case. But if we want jurors who can represent the conscience of the community and judge a case according to local standards, then we should seek jurors close at hand—the closer the juror, the better the inside knowledge.

One of the central dilemmas of modern jury selection is how to reconcile these competing visions of the jury. How can we impanel a jury that has enough knowledge to be competent but enough ignorance to be impartial? To express the dilemma another way, how can the jury be at one and the same time an instrument of justice (with all the insulation from popular pressure and local gossip that doing the "just thing" often requires) and an instrument of democracy (with all the exposure to public opinion that doing the "democratic thing" often requires)? The jury immediately inspires but confuses us because it wants matters both ways: to insulate justice from popular prejudice and yet to leave justice in the hands of the populace.

Two brief examples will illustrate the way this tension plays out in real cases. In 1987, Eddie Crawford went on trial for his life before a jury in

Spalding County, Georgia. In fact, as many in the county knew, this was Crawford's second trial for the same crime. A prior jury had already found Crawford guilty of murder and sentenced him to death. However, the state supreme court set aside that conviction and ordered a new trial, on the grounds that the jury might have convicted Crawford not of murder but of felony murder, a crime not charged in the indictment.[6]

Prior to the start of the second trial, Crawford's lawyers moved for a change of venue, arguing that an impartial jury could no longer be found in a county where so many persons knew the results of Crawford's first trial. The motion was denied and jury selection commenced with a pool of ninety persons. Fifty-seven acknowledged that they were aware of the prior proceedings, fifty indicated that they knew Crawford had been convicted, and thirty-two knew that Crawford had been sentenced to death. Of the twelve jurors finally selected, eight knew generally about the prior trial, five knew Crawford had been convicted, and three knew that he had been sentenced to death. This second jury likewise convicted Crawford of murder and sentenced him to death. The United States Supreme Court denied Crawford's petition for review, and in early 1994 he was still awaiting execution.[7]

Crawford's case seems a clear instance where failure to grant a change of venue resulted in an extreme denial of impartial justice. It is particularly difficult to believe that Crawford's jurors could grant him his presumption of innocence, knowing that their fellow citizens had once sentenced him to die for the same crime. In the circumstances of this case, holding the trial locally was dramatically at odds with the most elemental notions of blind justice.

In many jury trials, the opposite problem occurs: granting a change of venue blinds justice by relying on strangers to view events from afar that people in the community would have put in clearer perspective. The first trial in 1992 of the four Los Angeles police officers accused of beating Rodney King provides a compelling example of this complaint. In the name of protecting the defendants' right to an impartial jury, a California appeals court ordered the trial judge to move the trial out of Los Angeles County. Press accounts mistakenly reported that the change of venue was ordered to find impartial jurors who had not seen the notorious, incriminating videotape of the alleged beating made by a bystander and shown repeatedly on television prior to trial. But the court understood there was no place it could move the trial where the videotape had not been aired. What, then, could be accomplished by a change of venue? Los Angeles jurors alone were likely to treat this as a political trial, a virtual referendum on forcing out Police Commissioner Daryl Gates and reforming the entire Los Angeles Police Department (LAPD). By moving the trial, the appeals court hoped to insulate the jury from matters of electoral politics.[8]

So directed by the appeals court, the trial judge chose Ventura County as the new place of trial—geographic neighbor to Los Angeles but demographic stranger. In a case involving white officers and a black victim, it was significant that African-Americans constituted a far smaller percentage of the Ventura County population than of the Los Angeles County population.[9] No African-Americans made it onto the jury of ten whites, one Asian, and one Hispanic that acquitted the officers of virtually all charges (they hung on one charge of one of the officers).[10]

In the aftermath of the verdict, there was near unanimous agreement that the Ventura County jurors were not well situated to judge the events accurately or democratically.[11] The King confrontation took place in a context far removed from the conditions in which the mostly suburban Ventura County jurors lived. They no doubt judged the events partly in light of their knowledge about police work and police treatment of minorities in their own area, but this was the wrong local knowledge. Rodney King and the LAPD officers met elsewhere, in a different racial climate and prepared by a different set of expectations and prior events in the neighborhood. A Los Angeles jury would have better understood the specific, concrete background against which the confrontation took place. This is true not only because the jury would have been more likely to have African-Americans on it to compare Rodney King's experience with their own knowledge of police behavior toward blacks but also because even the Anglos and Hispanics on the Los Angeles jury would have been more likely to be conversant with and concerned about local conditions. The Ventura County jurors suffered from having to view the events out of context and from a distance.*

The cases of Eddie Crawford and Rodney King show that the tensions

---

*On August 5, 1992, a federal grand jury returned new indictments against the four officers, charging them with violation of Rodney King's civil rights through the use of unreasonable force during arrest. Trial was held this time in the federal judicial district for Los Angeles County, and on April 17, 1993, a racially mixed jury, including two blacks and one Hispanic, convicted two officers and acquitted the other two. Seth Mydans, "2 of 4 Officers Found Guilty in Los Angeles Beating," New York Times, April 18, 1993, sec. 1, p. 8; Amy Stevens, "Verdict in King Case Owes Much to Lesons of State-Court Trial," Wall Street Journal, April 19, 1993, p. A1.

between impartial justice and local justice are deep and abiding. In this chapter I trace how the tension is gradually being resolved in U.S. history in favor of the impartial stranger ideal. I will focus on the criminal jury, although a similar shift has affected civil jury trials as well.

To look at the history of juries in the United States is to see that insistence on disqualifying prospective jurors for knowing or caring too much about a case prior to trial was not always typical of jury selection. Although the decline of communal-based justice dates from before the American Revolution, still the jury that was given protection by the Bill of Rights was the local jury; knowing about a case and about the community asked to judge it qualified rather than disqualied a person for jury duty. In the United States, the eventual shift away from the local knowledge model of the jury has been dramatic. The shift brings the jury in line with prevailing notions that distance puts justice in perspective, but it also contributes to a growing crisis of confidence in the competence of juries.

Too often, especially in highly publicized cases, the search for impartial jurors leads to the elimination of all persons who are normally attentive to and hence knowledgeable about the happenings around them. A remarkable level of inattention and apathy become the necessary conditions for impartiality as a juror.[12] For example, before New York subway vigilante Bernhard Goetz could be tried, a special prescreening of three hundred persons took place in the judge's chambers for over three months prior to trial; only those who had not followed the case closely in the media were kept in the pool of eligible jurors.[13] In 1986, this kind of spectacle was carried to a high-water mark in the trial of Lt. Col. Oliver North on charges arising from the Iran-contra scandal. Any resident of the nation's capital who had been enough of a concerned citizen to follow the lead story of the day or to have watched some of North's own televised testimony before the Senate was automatically disqualified.[14] The only persons whose impartiality was intact were those rarities who could say that they "saw North on television but it was just like watching the Three Stooges or something" or that all they remembered was that "it was about something overseas."[15]

A similar tension between impartial jurors and knowledgeable jurors surfaced during jury selection in the 1990 obscenity trial of a Cincinnati art museum and its director, charged with showing the provocative photographs of Robert Mapplethorpe. The trial judge dismissed the only potential juror "who had seen the Mapplethorpe exhibit, the only one who said she attended museums regularly." Her "knowledge of the entire exhibition," and not just the particular photographs alleged to be obscene, was thought to put "an unnecessary burden" on her. Among those who survived challenges was a panel member who "never went to museums."[16]

When impartiality gets defined as ignorance, the gnawing question is this: Why should anyone believe that juries are capable of rendering accurate verdicts? It becomes a paradox, with the search for impartial jurors setting off in a different direction from the search for competent jurors. This predicament justifies our revisiting the local knowledge model of the jury. A visit to the jury's past is fascinating in its own regard, but I go to retrieve a vision of jury deliberation enriched by the ability of local jurors to know the context in which events on trial took place.

THE LOCAL JURY AT THE TIME OF THE CONSTITUTION'S RATIFICATION

When the U.S. Constitution was sent to the thirteen states for ratification in 1787, a remarkable debate ensued about the kind of criminal jury system the new nation was to have. Crucial to the debate was the question of whether local juries were an asset or a hindrance to impartial justice. As originally drafted, the Constitution guaranteed trial by jury in all federal criminal felony trials (except those involving impeachment) but left the federal government free to hold those trials anywhere in the state where the crime occurred.[17] Anti-Federalist opponents of the Constitution pointed out that the common law had long required a narrower, more local geography for justice.[18] Juries were to be selected from the "vicinage" where the crime occurred—a term that the jurist Sir William Blackstone interpreted in the 1760s to require jurors to be "of the county where the fact is committed."[19] "To the safety of life, it is indispensably necessary the trial of crimes should be in the vicinity; and the vicinity is construed to mean county," remarked an opponent of ratification in Massachusetts.[20] "[The] idea which I call a true vicinage is, that a man shall be tried by his neighbors," echoed a delegate to the Virginia convention.[21]

Patrick Henry charged that by adopting the more "extensive provision" of holding a trial anywhere in the state where the crime occurred, the proposed Constitution perverted trial by jury from a protection for the accused into an instrument for tyranny.[22] Just as the British government end-ran the purpose of jury trials by bringing colonists across the Atlantic to be tried by hostile jurors in the mother country, so too the new federal government possessed the power to "shop" for a jury of its liking anywhere in the state, carry an accused "from one extremity of the state to another," and try the accused before a jury that might have been biased against him or her. Another Anti-Federalist in Virginia concurred: "They can hang any one they please, by having a jury to suit their purpose."[23] Juries "from the vicinage being not secured, this right is in reality sacri- ficed," Henry concluded; it would have been better that "trial by jury were struck out altogether."[24] Anti-Federalist pamphlet after pamphlet measured out the miles, the distances, the inconveniences, and the disad- vantages that an accused would suffer when the federal government had free choice of both venue and jury anywhere within a state.[25]

The Anti-Federalist case for preserving local juries grew directly from colonial experience in using juries to resist the Crown. During the Stamp Act Crisis of 1765–66, the great complaint (alongside "no taxation with- out representation") was that trials would be held without juries in admi- ralty courts for those accused of failing to pay the new taxes. Likewise, in 1774, George Mason of Virginia drafted the Fairfax County resolves, protesting "the taking away our Trials by Jurys, the ordering Persons upon Criminal Accusations, to be tried in another Country than that in which the Fact is charged to have been committed."[26] By 1776, Virginia (which up until 1750 had displayed only a weak commitment to jury tri- als) responded to British threats to local jury trials by including the right to "Trial by an impartial jury of his Vicinage" among the criminal defen- dant's rights guaranteed by the state Declaration of Rights.[27] The Decla- ration of Independence also placed threats to local trials and local juries on the list of grievances sparking revolution ("For transporting us beyond Seas to be tried for pretended offenses [and for] depriving us in many cases, of the benefits of Trial by Jury").

Perhaps more than in any other colony, Massachusetts juries func- tioned as resistance bodies in high-profile cases.[28] Town meetings con- trolled jury selection and used that power openly to select jurors hostile to local enforcement of British customs laws.[29] By 1765, "a Bostonian could boast that the Whigs 'would always be sure of Eleven jury men in Twelve.'"[30] In 1769, during a charge to a Suffolk County jury, the royal Chief Justice Thomas Hutchinson lamented that town meetings were sending jurors who were willing to convict ordinary criminals but who "connive at and pass over in Silence and entirely smother other Crimes of an alarming Nature."[31] Hutchinson might well have had in mind the many cases involving merchant and suspected smuggler John Hancock, in which local juries effectively outranked Parliament when it came to announcing what the law was in Massachusetts. As historian John Phillip Reid points out, local control over grand juries "meant that it was impossible for the king's officials to obtain indictments against persons accused of . . . violating imperial statutes such as the revenue laws."

In 1768, Hancock refused to permit a customs official to go below deck to inspect a discharge of cargo from his brigantine *Lydia*. The applicable statute gave customs officials the right "freely to go and remain on Board until the Vessel is discharged of the Lading." Sensing the futility of seeking a grand jury willing to indict Hancock, the customs officials prodded the attorney general to proceed by the alternative method called filing an "information." But the attorney general refused as well. Practically speaking, the inability to proceed against Hancock through either the grand jury or the filing of an information operated as a veto of the inspection statute in Boston Harbor.[32]

Hancock profited from other methods of jury defiance. Royal authorities seized one of his ships for importing more goods than had been declared during loading at a Scottish customs port. Because the case involved enforcement of laws on the high seas, British procedure entitled officials to prosecute Hancock in admiralty court without a jury. The admiralty court decreed the seizure lawful and ordered the vessel and its cargo to be condemned and turned over to customs agents. But Hancock then turned the tables and sued the customs officers for trespassing on his vessel—a lawsuit that entitled him to a jury trial. At trial, the jury was dutifully instructed that the decree of the admiralty court could not be "traversed" or challenged in this way. But the jury ignored the instructions and rendered a verdict for Hancock, ordering the customs agents personally to bear the costs of repaying Hancock for the value of his ship and cargo. When the customs officials appealed to the king in council, Hancock withdrew his lawsuit. But the political point had been made: customs officials enforced the trade acts in Massachusetts at peril of being found by local juries to be guilty of trespass. Even if such jury verdicts would ultimately be overturned, the customs agents would be out of pocket the personal expenses involved in defending at the jury trial. "A few actions of this type," notes Reid, "and Hancock and his fellow merchants could expect the customsmen to proceed more cautiously in the future."[33]

The Hancock trials became part of jury lore for the colonists. Hancock's jurors took their place among other jury heroes who resisted tyrannical laws, such as those who struck a blow for freedom of the press in 1735 by refusing to imprison New York printer John Peter Zenger simply for publishing criticisms of the Crown.[34] The most famous jury of all was in London in 1670—it refused to convict William Penn of unlawful assembly simply for preaching Quaker doctrine on the street, even though the Court instructed the jury that such preaching did violate the law.[35] These legendary cases cannot be regarded as typical, but they demonstrate the way jury trials gave local residents, in moments of crisis, the last say on what the law was in their community.

Juries had this raw, democratic power over the law only so long as the Crown could not decide where to try the likes of a Hancock or whom his jurors would be. The power of the jury to defend against tyranny depended vitally on the principle that a central government would have to leave enforcement of its laws in the hands of the local population—a principle that the Anti-Federalists found sorely lacking in the proposed Constitution of 1787.

Federalists, as defenders of the Constitution, denied any conspiratorial motive in not specifically protecting the "jury of the vicinage" in the Constitution. The reason for the absence of such protection, maintained Governor Samuel Johnston at the North Carolina ratification convention, was far more mundane. If "vicinage" simply referred to the vicinity where the crime occurred, then the term was impossibly vague to use in a written constitution. The vagueness was insurmountable because state practice had never achieved a consensus on what the term meant.[36] From early colonial days, diversity was the rule. At one extreme of localism, the seventeenth-century Fundamental Laws of West Jersey required all trials to be decided by the verdict of "twelve honest men of the neighborhood."[37] At the other extreme, early Virginia for a time held all cases involving loss of life and limb in one location (Jamestown), summoning jurors from court bystanders.[38] Even at the time of the ratification debates, Virginia procedure still called for trying cases with loss of life or limb in the state capital, with jurors summoned from the county where the crime occurred.[39]

Citing such examples, the Federalists explained the practical difficulties that stood in the way of specifying in the Constitution an exact locale for federal jury trials. But at times the Federalists went beyond reciting practical difficulties to challenging the very ideal of local justice. In Massachusetts, delegate Christopher Gore put the case against neighborhood juries elegantly and succinctly:

The idea that the jury coming from the neighborhood, and knowing the character and circumstances of the party in trial, is promotive of justice, on reflection will appear not founded in truth. If the jury judge from any other circumstances but what are part of the cause in question, they are not impartial. The great object is to determine on the real merits of the cause, uninfluenced by any personal considerations; if, therefore, the jury could be perfectly ignorant of the person in trial, a just decision would be more probable.[40]

Capturing the Federalist preference for enlarging the geography of justice, this passage is remarkable because it anticipated modern views on impartiality and the benefits of finding jurors "perfectly ignorant of the person in trial." But this is not an isolated example of the Federalists' preference. In North Carolina, Governor Johnston responded to critics of the Constitution's jury provisions who said that

this clause is defective, because the trial is not to be by a jury of the vicinage. . . . We may expect less partiality when the trial is by strangers; and were I to be tried for my property or life, I would rather be tried by disinterested men, who were not biased, than by men who were perhaps intimate friends of my opponent.[41]

Taken together, the Gore and Johnston remarks show that the debate over the Constitution's criminal jury provisions was at times explicitly about the inherent tensions between doing justice impartially and doing justice locally. James Madison, the Constitution's preeminent architect, was grappling with this tension when he pointed out during the Virginia ratification debates that there was no "safe" way to honor the tradition of local jury trials. Forces of disunion and rebellion still existed in the country; the new federal government would be hamstrung if it had to try alleged rebels in the home base of their rebellions:

It might so happen that a trial would be impracticable in the country. Suppose a rebellion in a whole district; would it not be impossible to get a jury? . . . This is a complete and satisfactory answer.[42]

Madison had legitimate reason to fear disunion (recall Shay's uprising in 1786 in western Massachusetts). The logic of the Federalist argument for preferring the impartiality of strangers to the intimacies of neighbors when it came to jury trials was strong. But it is remarkable that the Anti-

Federalists won, or at least partly won, this debate. In four different states, demands were made for amending the Constitution to protect the jury of the vicinage.[43] In time, those demands bore partial fruit in the adoption of a Sixth Amendment that required criminal juries to be selected from the "district" within the state where the crime occurred (I will discuss shortly what it meant to require juries to be drawn from the district of the crime). The Anti-Federalist success in forcing amendment of the Constitution, shrinking the geography of jury justice to some area smaller than the state, shows the vitality of the local jury ideal in 1789.

Anti-Federalist arguments in favor of local juries were of two kinds. One argument centered on the fact-finding mission of juries, a mission that local jurors with personal knowledge of the case could accomplish more accurately. "In all criminal prosecutions, the verification of facts, in the vicinity where they happen, is one of the greatest securities of the life, liberty and property of the citizens," read the Massachusetts Declaration of Rights of 1780; similar language appeared in the Maryland Constitution of 1776 and the New Hampshire Constitution of 1784.[44] The advantage of local jurors, said Patrick Henry, was that they were "neighbors . . . acquainted with [the defendants'] characters, their good or bad conduct in life, to judge of the unfortunate man who may be thus exposed to the rigors of government."[45]

By contrast, jurors from afar did not know whether the accused was "habitually a good or bad man," said James Winthrop, the Anti-Federalist who wrote under the pseudonym "Agrippa." Agrippa offered the specific example of a trial where the defendant's guilt turned on whether his acts were done "maliciously or accidentally."[46] Local jurors had a decided leg up on strangers in making such a judgment about an acquaintance.*

In Virginia, Edmund Pendleton, a supporter of the Constitution, arose

---

*An interesting example of the neighbor versus stranger issue is recorded for the year 1694 in the colony of West Jersey, when Janet Monroe went on trial for her life, charged with infanticide. Given an opportunity to challenge the jurors, Monroe noted that they "are strangers to her." Her preference, she said, would have been for jurors who knew her and could vouch for her decency. Larry D. Eldridge, *A Distant Heritage: The Growth of Free Speech in Early America* (New York: New York University Press, 1994), pp. 81–82. In his study of one Puritan county in Massachusetts during the 1600s, the historian David Konig also described an early system of local community justice in which arbitrators chosen to settle disputes "were well-acquainted with the facts of the problem, and great efforts were made to find those who were familiar with the dispute." David Thomas Konig, *Law and Society in Puritan Massachusetts: Essex County, 1629–1692* (Chapel Hill, N.C.: University of North Carolina Press, 1979), p. 109.

to correct Agrippa's assumption that juries of the vicinage would have personal knowledge of the accused's character. That might be true in cases where defendants commit crimes in their own neighborhood, but when outsiders commit the crimes, the juries that try them come from the neighborhoods of the crime, not from the defendants' home. Hence the knowledge that a jury of the vicinage brings to a case is "knowledge of the fact, and acquaintance with the witnesses who will come from the neighborhood," and not always a knowledge of the accused.[47] Knowledge of the witnesses and their reputations, Pendleton agreed, is a great asset in the search for the truth. British statesman Edmund Burke once remarked, in another context, that such knowledge makes jurors the best at distinguishing perjured from truthful testimony. And as James Wilson, another supporter of the Constitution, put it at the Pennsylvania ratification convention:

> When jurors can be acquainted with the characters of the parties and the witnesses . . . they not only hear the words, but they see and mark the features of the countenance; they can judge of weight due to such testimony.[48]

In the final analysis, the Anti-Federalist defense of the local jury was not primarily a brief for its superior fact-finding ability. The most sophisticated defense of the local jury began with this concession:

> When I speak of the jury trial of the vicinage, or the trial of the fact in the neighbourhood,—I do not lay so much stress upon the circumstance of our being tried by our neighbours: in this enlightened country men may be probably impartially tried by those who do not live very near them.[49]

Instead, another point of view made local juries "essential in every free country." The jury served freedom not only by getting the facts right but also by getting the people right. Local citizens were empowered to control the actual administration of justice—thus, the jury was our best assurance that law and justice accurately reflected the morals, values, and common sense of the people asked to obey the law. Functioning as the conscience of the community, the jury, according to the Anti-Federalists, was as much a "political" institution as it was a judicial body; it brought democracy alive, made it possible for "common people . . . [to] have a part and share of influence, in the judicial as well as in the legislative department."[50]

The democratizing features of local jury service were likely to grow in importance under the proposed Constitution, where avenues for direct

participation in the federal government were limited for the citizen. Theoretically, the new Constitution held open all offices of government to the
people. But this could not "answer any valuable purposes for [the person
who was] not in a situation to be brought forward and to fill those offices;
these and most other offices of any considerable importance, will be
occupied by the few."[51]

Nor would election of representatives secure to the people a real voice in
government. The Anti-Federalists constantly pointed out that the proposed
republic was too large and the numbers of representatives too small to provide genuine dialogue between most citizens and their representatives.[52] As
the colonial historian Gordon Wood writes, the Anti-Federalists recognized
by 1787 that diversity of interests in the republic required giving ordinary
persons more actual representation than they were likely to receive in the
executive and legislative branches of the new national government.[53]

In the "extensive empire" of the new Constitution, Congress and its
laws would dependably reflect the voices and interests of "the few, the
well-born."[54] By contrast, trial by jury could remain an oasis of genuine
democracy, if practiced on a scale small enough to "secure to the people
at large, their just and rightful controul in the judicial department."[55]

Anti-Federalists were impeccable localists. But which local citizens
did the jury empower? Colonial practices were more restrictive than the
Anti-Federalist references to the people at large serving on juries
implied. Not only was jury eligibility limited to white males but, as in
England, property and religious qualifications kept large numbers of the
adult white male population from voting or serving on juries.[56] In his
study of Plymouth, Massachusetts, historian William Nelson found that
about 28 percent of the adult male population served on juries between
1748 and 1774; only 3 percent of county jurors could be identified as
ever belonging to a dissenting congregation.[57]

The prevailing view throughout the colonial period was that property
gave persons a stake in society and thus made their decisions more
responsible.[58] Restricting jury service to the propertied was also seen as a
way of securing the jury against temptations of bribery.[59]

I have not found evidence that the Anti-Federalists objected to prevailing restrictions on jury service. Nor did they specifically argue, in
1787, for broadening the suffrage.[60] But, even though they were not perfect populists, the Anti-Federalists stood against traditional notions of
elite politics; they saw in the jury an embodiment of local people representing local values. However limited their own vision of who "the peo-

ple" were, it was farsighted enough to appreciate that juries gave more
voice to the common freeholder than did other institutions of government. Anti-Federalists agreed with Jefferson when he wrote, "Were I
called upon to decide, whether the people had best be omitted in the legislative or judiciary department, I would say it is better to leave them out
of the legislative. The execution of the laws is more important than the
making them."[61]

Although they differed on the issue of the jury's geography, both Federalist and Anti-Federalist agreed on the jury's overall importance. Here,
however, we must note that the jury they extolled was one that enjoyed
the right to decide questions of law as well as of fact. Today, the absence
of the familiar division of labor between jury and judge (juries decide the
facts, judges decide the law) seems odd, but throughout the eighteenth
century the prevailing view remained that jurors "could ignore judges'
instructions on the law and decide the law by themselves in both civil and
criminal cases."[62] In Massachusetts at that time, there was no practical
alternative to permitting juries to decide questions of law because virtually all cases were tried before a panel of at least three judges, each of
whom delivered separate and often contradictory instructions. Add to this
the privilege of opposing counsel to argue the law, and the jury heard up
to five different versions of the law.[63] By default if not design, the jurors
had to decide the law.

In 1771, John Adams wrote in his diary about the right of Massachusetts juries to disobey judicial instructions. "Every intelligent Man,"
Adams began, "will confess that cases frequently occur, in which it would
be very difficult for a jury to determine the Questions of Law." Still, what
should a juror do if the judge's statement of the law runs counter to fundamental principles of the British Constitution? Must the juror abide by the
instructions?

> Every Man, of any feeling or Conscience, will answer, no. It is not only his
> right, but his Duty, in that Case to find the Verdict according to his own
> best Understanding, Judgment, and Conscience, tho in Direct opposition
> to the Direction of the Court. . . . The English Law obliges no Man . . . to
> pin his faith on the sleve of any mere Man.[64]

That juries decided questions of law meant that "the law applied in the
towns . . . on a day-to-day basis was not the product of the will of some
distant sovereign."[65] In his study of Massachusetts law at the close of the

eighteenth century, William Nelson concluded that "the representatives of local communities assembled as jurors generally had effective power to control the content of the province's substantive law."[66] An in-depth study of the civil jury in seventeenth-century Connecticut showed jurors deciding legal issues by reference to "community norms" and to "a template of common beliefs and expectations as to how neighbors should treat one another."[67] Indeed, until the seventeenth century's end, historian Bruce Mann found "no indication that [Connecticut] judges instructed juries on the law" at all. To be sure, Mann documented Connecticut juries losing their lawmaking authority considerably earlier than did Massachusetts juries, a fact that helps illuminate why the Anti-Federalists were fighting for a lost ideal of local justice. But early Connecticut juries still embodied that communal ideal when they "decided for themselves how the law should apply—a process that is inextricably linked with, and at times indistinguishable from, deciding what the law is."[68]

In Rhode Island, a 1677 code directed the charging of jurors, but as the eighteenth century was about to dawn, a contemporary report noted that judges "give no directions to the jury."[69] The situation was similar in New Hampshire and Vermont, where a large percentage of the judges were laymen, "lacking the professional qualifications which would have made their instructions convincing."[70] As Nelson summarized the Massachusetts situation through the eighteenth century, juries possessed an "ultimate power" that enabled the colony to achieve a substantial degree of self-governance, rendering judgments "on a day-to-day basis [that] were a reflection [less] of law set out in statute books and in English judicial precedents [than] of the custom of local communities."[71] The historian J. R. Pole goes so far as to conclude that, practically speaking, in several colonies the court and jury outranked legislative and executive institutions when it came to "settl[ing] many of the issues that affected the life of town and county."[72] For those who qualified for jury duty, jury service became what Jefferson called the "school by which [the] people learn the exercise of civic duties as well as rights."[73]

With this colonial legacy of decentralized justice in mind, the Anti-Federalists made the case at several ratification conventions that only local trials could preserve the jury as a "democratic institution of self-governance." Far from being troubled by the prospect of different juries applying different laws, the Anti-Federalists embraced the fracture of unity. "The body of the people, principally, bear the burdens of the community; they of right ought to have a controul in its important concerns, both in making and executing the laws, otherwise they may, in a short time, be ruined."[74]

Uniform justice was no friend of impartial justice, in the Anti-Federalist view, if the uniformity was achieved by empowering an elite judicial class to dictate the law to the people. Such an arrangement promised objectivity but in fact invited "secret and arbitrary proceedings."[75] The black robes merely masked "severe and arbitrary" conduct by judges and left abuse of the law unchecked by any popular authority.

In fact, if bribery was the mortal enemy of impartiality, then a network of local juries rotating anonymous persons through its ranks was far more bribery-proof than standing panels of known judges ever could be. As one Anti-Federalist put it, "Judges once influenced, soon become inclined to yield to temptations, and to decree for him who will pay the most for their partiality."[76] By contrast, jurors were bribery-proof by reasons of character as well as opportunity. In terms of opportunity, "it is not, generally, known till the hour the cause comes on for trial, what persons are to form the jury." In terms of character, jurors possess the "honest characters of the common freemen of a country, . . . untaught in . . . affairs [of corruption]."[77]

The Anti-Federalists conceded that citizens will not come to the jury with "minute skill . . . in the laws, . . . [but] they have common sense in its purity, which seldom or never errs in making and applying laws to the condition of the people."[78] Here once again local knowledge of the condition of the people compensated for the lack of formal legal training. Not only was formal legal training unnecessary, but jurors did not even need to rely on a judge's instructions to know the common law of the land, rooted as it was in fundamental principles of natural justice. Even John Adams, no populist, noted:

> The general Rules of Law and common Regulations of Society, under which ordinary Transactions arrange themselves, . . . [are] well enough known to ordinary Jurors.[79]

Thus, members of a Massachusetts grand jury in 1759 were told that they "need no Explanation" as to most legal matters because "your Good Sence & understanding will Direct ye as to them."[80]

Moreover, the Anti-Federalists continued, those who argued that people of the neighborhood were too ignorant to do justice missed the crucial civic education and moral transformation jury service worked on the common man. Jury duty was a crucial "means by which the people are let into the knowledge of public affairs—are enabled to stand as the guardians of each others [*sic*] rights."[81] Said another Anti-Federalist on the theme of civic education: "Their situation, as jurors and representatives, enables them to acquire information and knowledge in the affairs and government of the society."[82] Or, as an Anti-Federalist who wrote under the pen name of a "Maryland Farmer" put it:

> Why shall we rob the Commons of the only remaining power they have been able to preserve. . . . I know it . . . will be said . . . that they are too ignorant—that they cannot distinguish between right and wrong—that decisions on property are submitted to chance; and that the last word, commonly determines the cause:—There is some truth in these allegations—but whence comes it—The Commons are much degraded in the powers of the mind:—They were deprived of the use of understanding, when they were robbed of the power of employing it.—Men no longer cultivate, what is no longer useful. . . . *Give them power and they will find understanding to use it.*[83]

In retort, the Federalists accused those who wanted to maintain the local jury of fighting old battles. Prior to the Revolution, colonies had to obey laws passed by a distant Parliament that did not represent them. In that situation, local juries provided the best available avenues for community control over the law's application. But the proposed relationship between Congress and the states according to the Constitution did not recreate the relationship between colony and mother country, argued the Federalists. Congress was to be composed directly of representatives chosen by the people or by the state legislatures. The representation of local views would be accomplished democratically in the legislature, undercutting both the need for and legitimacy of jury interpretations of the law.

THE LOCAL JURY AND THE
BILL OF RIGHTS

At the end of the ratification process, six states were specifically on record as concerned, even alarmed, about the absence of constitutional protection for local criminal jury trials. Virginia and North Carolina passed twin resolutions calling for a Bill of Rights that would specifically recognize "trial by an impartial Jury of his [that is, the defendant's] vicinage."[84] New York called for an amendment guaranteeing "an impartial Jury of the County where the crime was committed." Rhode Island, the last of the original thirteen colonies to ratify, made a similar proposal, but only after Congress had sent the first ten amendments to the states for ratification. Massachusetts and Pennsylvania debated the vicinage issue but took no specific action.[85]

Given the nature of the ratification debates, it was clear to the first Congress that it was wise policy as well as wise politics to amend the Constitution to include a Bill of Rights. In the House, Madison took the lead in resolving the vicinage problem by suggesting that the body of the Constitution itself be amended to guarantee, in Article 3, that the "trial of all crimes . . . shall be by an impartial jury of freeholders of the vicinage." The only exception would be that "in cases of crimes committed within any county which may be in possession of an enemy, or in which a general insurrection may prevail, the trial may by law be authorized in some other county of the same State, as near as may be to the seat of the offence."[86] During July 1789, Madison's proposals were submitted to the Committee of Eleven—a select committee composed of one representative from each of the eleven states that had by then ratified the Constitution. The Committee of Eleven kept intact the general guarantee that trials would be local. It dealt with trials in areas of rebellion by amending Madison's language to permit removal of the case to "some other place within the same State" and not necessarily to a place "as near" as possible to the seat of the offense.[87]

In August, the House made the decision to collect and submit to the Senate its proposed changes to the Constitution in the form of a Bill of Rights.[88] The language concerning "juries of the vicinage" became part of a proposed Ninth Amendment, later to be what we now know as the Sixth Amendment of the Bill of Rights. In that form, it was submitted to the Senate for action.[89]

Unlike the House, the Federalist-controlled Senate proved hostile to the idea of local juries. In a letter dated September 23, 1789, Madison noted the following:

> They are equally inflexible in opposing a definition of the *locality* of Juries. The vicinage they contend is either too vague or too strict a term, too vague if depending on limits to be fixed by the pleasure of the law, too strict if limited to the County.[90]

By "too vague" the Senate apparently meant that "vicinage" had no precise legal meaning and meant different things in different states. By "too strict" it no doubt echoed Madison's fear of local juries promoting disunion by shielding local rebels from federal prosecution. For these reasons, the Senate voted to delete the House language regarding vicinage from the Bill of Rights.[91]

When the House received the Senate revision of the proposed amendments, it ultimately voted to accept all but three changes. One point of resistance was renewed House insistence on the importance of local juries to the scheme of justice.[92] But given Senate stubbornness against the term "vicinage," the House sought compromise language. From the House's point of view, the body of the Constitution dangerously empowered the central government to pick and choose trial locations and juries from anywhere within the state where the crime occurred. According to the Senate, requiring federal trials to be held in the county where the crime occurred was too strict, an invitation for disunion. On September 24, the House proposed that the language of the future Sixth Amendment be changed to the following:

> In all criminal prosecutions, the accused shall enjoy the right to a speedy and public trial, by an impartial jury of the State and district wherein the crime shall have been committed, which district shall have been previously ascertained by law.[93]

Available records do not tell us who proposed the new language or why. But the language about districts most probably refers to the Judiciary Act of 1789, which Congress was simultaneously debating with the proposed Bill of Rights. The Judiciary Act created federal courts inferior to the Supreme Court and mapped out judicial districts over which these courts would have jurisdiction.[94]

The language of the Sixth Amendment requiring criminal trials to be tried before a jury that hailed not only from the state where the crime occurred but also from the district within the state was a genuine compromise that both supporters and opponents of local juries could accept. To opponents, the important thing no doubt was that the districts actually created by the Judiciary Act were exactly synonymous with the boundaries of the states. As originally drafted, the Judiciary Act created eleven judicial districts—one each for the eleven ratifying states. Prior to the act's passage, the number was enlarged to thirteen—a twelfth district was

added in that part of Virginia which became the state of Kentucky, and a
thirteenth was added in that part of Massachusetts which later became
Maine.[95] Thus, the language in the Sixth Amendment regarding districts
had virtually no immediate practical significance. Because the boundaries of the districts "ascertained by law" were the same as those of the
states, the federal government still had the right to hold trials and draw
jurors from anywhere within those boundaries.

For supporters of the tradition of local juries, the compromise could
also be counted as a partial victory. First, the Constitution itself had been
amended to recognize the principle that juries had to be drawn from discrete districts within a state. Congress retained authority to ascertain by
law what these districts were, but anytime it legislated new districts that
were smaller than a state's boundaries, the Sixth Amendment kicked in to
shrink the geography of justice.

In the Judiciary Act itself, the ideal of local juries received more
immediate, practical vindication. Although attempts to require all federal
juries to "be drawn from the county in which the offense was committed"
were defeated,[96] the act was successfully amended on the floor of the Senate to require that

> in cases punishable with death the trial shall be had in the County where
> the offence was committed, or where that cannot be done without great
> inconvenience, Twelve petit Jurors at least, shall be summoned from
> thence.[97]

Here the local jury, expressly defined as coming from the county where
the crime occurred, received protection in arguably the most important
kind of cases: those in which a jury must pass on the life of the accused.
To be sure, "great inconvenience" would justify removing the venue of
trial from the county. But, remarkably, even then the law required at least
twelve jurors to be summoned from the county where the crime occurred
to the place of trial.

THE DECLINE OF THE LOCAL JURY AND THE
RISE OF THE IMPARTIAL JUSTICE IDEAL

Local juries never again enjoyed the reputation for doing justice that they
held during the country's founding period. Within a generation of the
Constitution's ratification, two lines of cases combined to sap the historic

powers of the local jury. The first solidified an ideal of impartiality that presumed bias in local jurors who were familiar with the facts, parties, or witnesses to a case. The second stripped the local jury of its historic right to decide questions of law as well as of facts.

The presumption of bias in persons who know about a case prior to a trial was not new to the nineteenth century—it was part of the jury's previous evolution from a self-informing body to a neutral body that listened to witnesses. However, the banishment of local knowledge from the jury room continued over the last two centuries until today the ban stands history on its head—disqualifying jurors for having precisely the acquaintances or information that once qualified them to judge their community's events in context. One wonders why trials should be held locally anymore, when we go to such lengths to eliminate local knowledge from the jury box.

The second line of cases (depriving the jury of its lawmaking function) led to a steep decline in jury power. In contrast to the Revolutionary period, by the end of the nineteenth century jurors were presumed to be ignorant of the law and obligated to abide mechanically by the court's instructions on legal matters. This decline did not take place overnight or without a struggle.[98] Jacksonian democracy brought with it the era of the "common man" and concepts of egalitarianism that supported a broad role for the lay jury. But the before and after pictures are clear. The jury entered the nineteenth century as a body authorized to resolve contested points of law on its own, even to refuse enforcement of laws considered unjust.[99] The jury exited the century duty-bound to follow judicial instructions and to enforce the law whether it agreed with it or not.[100]

Together the two lines of cases rationalized the juror's function at trial, sharply distinguishing it from that of a witness to the facts and that of a judge of the law. But though these changes brought the jury in line with emerging notions of impartial justice uniformly and blindly dispensed, they also produced unwelcome consequences. An ideal of jury impartiality that can be practiced only by disqualifying the most well-informed members of the community does not inspire confidence in the accuracy of jury verdicts. It naively defines an impartial mind as an empty mind. Confidence in jury verdicts is further sapped by treating jurors as so ignorant of the law that they must mechanically obey the judge's instructions to the letter.

In the remainder of this chapter I will trace the way that the local knowledge model of the jury gradually gave way to the impartial juror

ideal. In chapter 2 I will complete the story of our declining faith in local
justice by discussing the loss of the jury's right to judge the law in ways
that represent the conscience of the community.

THE IMPARTIAL JUROR AT THE BEGINNING OF THE NINETEENTH CENTURY: THE TRIAL OF AARON BURR

In 1807, former vice president of the United States Aaron Burr was
arrested on suspicion of treason against his country. The specific acts
constituting the treason were said to have taken place in 1806 on
Blennerhassett's Island in the County of Wood, Virginia.[101] Here Burr
supposedly arranged for roughly thirty armed men to set out in nine boats
down the Ohio and Mississippi Rivers to seize New Orleans. Even prior
to Burr's arrest, Thomas Jefferson issued a presidential proclamation
warning of rebellion, Congress debated whether the danger warranted a
suspension of the writ of habeas corpus, and the partisan Republican
newspapers in Virginia saturated the state with details of Burr's planned
insurrection and of his grandiose plans to invade Mexico, detach the
southwest from the United States, and form an empire stretching from the
Mississippi Valley to Mexico City. Key depositions and documents even
found their way into the pages of the *Alexandria Expositor* and other
papers.[102]

In such an atmosphere, a federal grand jury convened in Richmond in
1807 to consider indicting Burr. The difficulty of getting a fair hearing in
a local hotbed of partisan Republican passions must have been immediately apparent to Burr from the names of the twenty-four freeholders summoned for grand jury duty. They included Sen. William Giles, Jefferson's
floor leader in the Senate, and Col. William Cary Nicholas, the president's
choice for floor leader in the House.[103] Jefferson's personal hostility
toward Burr was well known, born of Burr's cooperation with Federalists
who threw the election of 1800 into the House and almost made Burr
president. The presence of Jefferson's political allies on the grand jury
hardly seemed accidental. To add to the suspicions, the federal marshal
who summoned the grand jury had acted illegally by choosing substitutes
at his own discretion for any persons excused; the proper procedure for
making up any shortfall in the original panel was to choose from among
the bystanders at court. The presiding judge—none other than Chief Justice John Marshall sitting as a circuit judge, himself no friend of Jefferson—agreed with Burr that the federal marshal's procedure smacked of

handpicking the grand jury. He ordered the substitutes removed and replaced from among the bystanders.[104]

Burr proceeded to make the novel argument that he had a right to challenge individual grand jurors for bias or "favor."[105] This is a right that American law does not often recognize even to this day,[106] and it was certainly unheard of at common law. As one reporter of Burr's trial noted at the time, "At most the authority goes no further than this: that a grand juror may be challenged for incompetency, or for being irregularly or improperly returned. This is a very different thing from a general right to challenge for 'favor.'"[107] But Burr saw no reason why his right to impartial justice should not include the privilege of challenging biased grand jurors. His objection to Senator Giles was especially significant in this regard. Burr went out of his way to make clear that he did not think Giles was biased or prejudiced in the sense of bearing him any ill will. In fact, Burr conceded that Giles's mind was "as pure and unbiased" as possible in the circumstances. But absence of ill will was not enough to secure impartiality. "It would be an effort above human nature for this gentleman to divest himself of all prepossessions."[108] The problem was not personal animus but personal knowledge. After all, Giles was so impressed by the information Jefferson sent to Congress that he advocated suspension of the writ of habeas corpus because of threats to public safety. Having essentially prejudged the matter as a senator, Giles could not possibly still have an open mind about whether Burr deserved to be indicted.

The reactions of Giles, the prosecutor, and Marshall to Burr's challenge provide a revealing look at the emerging understanding of impartial justice. Despite having precedent on his side, the prosecutor only briefly resisted Burr's challenge and in fact urged that "every one who has made declarations expressive of a decisive opinion should be withdrawn from the [grand] jury."[109] No doubt the government had a political motive to seem indifferent "whether A, B and C, or D, E and F composed a part" of the grand jury. But there was also genuine confusion about how to make grand jury practice fit the new constitutional language guaranteeing impartial juries. Once the government acquiesced to Burr's claimed right to challenge grand jurors, Marshall was spared the necessity of making a ruling and simply endorsed the suggestion "that if any gentleman has made up and declared his mind it would be best to withdraw."[110] Only Giles himself resisted. Although "it was by no means agreeable to [him] to have been summoned on this grand jury,"[111] it was even more disagreeable to be branded as biased. Giles judged himself fully capable of

appreciating the difference between judicial evidence and the kind of
information he had as a senator. Eventually, however, he agreed to withdraw, as did Nicholas, and the dispute was over.

In the end, sixteen grand jurors were impaneled. Keeping score on the
sidelines, Jefferson counted "2 Fed[eralists], 4 Quids, and 10 Republi-
cans."[112] He privately complained that this did "not seem a fair representation of the state of Virginia" but others put the number of Republican
grand jurors at fourteen.[113] Whatever the exact figure, those keeping
track of juror backgrounds clearly expected local politics and local justice to rub elbows during the grand jury sessions.

The grand jury indicted Burr for treason and lesser offenses on June
24, 1807, specifying only one "overt act" of rebellion: the gathering of
armed men on Blennerhassett's Island. Now charged with a capital crime,
Burr was entitled, under Section 29 of the Judiciary Act, either to be tried
in Wood County, where the acts allegedly occurred, or, if great inconvenience prevented trial in that location, to have at least twelve jurors summoned from there. Reports of the case do not make clear whether Burr
ever sought trial in Wood rather than Richmond or whether the required
certification regarding great inconvenience was ever made. But Marshall
did postpone the start of trial in Richmond until the marshal could sum-
mon forty-eight potential jurors from the county where the crime
occurred.[114]

When jury selection commenced on August 3, the arguments about
impartiality that were rehearsed at the grand jury stage now broke out in
full. Burr and his lawyers argued that the "public mind has been so filled
with prejudice against him that there was some difficulty in finding
impartial jurors."[115] Indeed, of the forty-eight persons examined during
the first day, only four could be immediately seated.[116] Virtually everyone
else admitted to reading and being influenced by the newspapers. James
G. Laidly was a typical member of the venire. He stated

> that he had formed and expressed some opinion unfavorable to Colonel
> Burr; . . . that he had principally taken his opinions from newspaper state-
> ments; and that he had not, as far as he recollected, expressed an opinion
> that Colonel Burr deserved hanging; but that his impression was, that he
> was guilty.[117]

Laidly and persons of similar mind were struck from the jury without
much dispute. The controversy centered on those members of the jury

pool who expressed an opinion, from reading the papers, that Burr intended treason but who were not certain whether he ever acted on his designs, at least as charged to have occurred on Blennerhassett's Island.

Nathaniel Selden was typical of the jurors whom Burr wished to strike as having their minds "made up on one half of the guilt." Selden stated that he "had formed an opinion . . . that the intentions of the prisoner were hostile to the United States," but that he had seen no evidence to satisfy him that Burr had been guilty of an overt act.[118]

According to precedents, persons such as Selden were acceptably impartial. This had been laid down, not without controversy, only seven years earlier in the famous trial of James Callender, accused of seditiously libeling President John Adams in a pamphlet entitled "The Prospect Before Us." Jurors who had read the pamphlet and were convinced it was libelous were nonetheless found qualified to serve as jurors so long as they had not concluded that Callender was the author of the pamphlet.[119]

The prosecution urged Marshall to apply the same logic to the Burr case and strike only those jurors who had decided the entire issue of guilt or innocence. If Burr were permitted to strike potential jurors who merely had opinions on some aspects of the case, then the prosecutor

> would venture to predict that there could not be a jury selected in the state of Virginia, because . . . there was [not] a single man in the state, qualified to become a juryman, who had not, in some form or other, made up, and declared an opinion on the conduct of the prisoner.[120]

This particular legal dispute called forth an opinion from Marshall interpreting the Sixth Amendment guarantee of trial before an "impartial" jury. Marshall resolved the dispute in favor of Burr. If a person had expressed a decisive opinion on any "essential" element of the crime (such as intent), then he was disqualified. However, Marshall was careful not to go too far, noting that persons with a good deal of information and opinions on the case would be welcome on the jury so long as they fell short of prejudging any essential element of the charge:

> It would seem to the court that to say that any man who had formed an opinion on any fact conducive to the final decision of the case would therefore be considered as disqualified from serving on the jury, would exclude intelligent and observing men, whose minds were really in a situ-

ation to decide upon the whole case according to the testimony, and would perhaps be applying the letter of the rule requiring an impartial jury with a strictness which is not necessary for the preservation of the rule itself.[121]

The immediate upshot of Marshall's ruling was to enlarge vastly the number of potential jurors Burr could challenge. The defendant proceeded to do so successfully over a two-week period, exhausting the first panel and requiring a second venire to be summoned.[122]

But the specifics of jury selection in Burr's case are of far less historic significance than the general principles laid down for defining the meaning of impartial justice. It is here that Marshall sounded the death knell of the local knowledge model and outlined the portrait of the impartial juror we still try to sketch today. Yet, as I shall be at pains to point out, Marshall's vision of impartiality was markedly different from the tabula rasa version that triumphed later.

In interpreting what the framers of the Constitution meant by an impartial jury, Marshall referred to the work of the great eighteenth-century codifier of common law William Hawkins. Hawkins noted that it was good grounds to challenge a juror "that he has declared his opinion beforehand that the party is guilty, or will be hanged or the like. Yet it hath been adjudged, that if it shall appear that the juror made such declaration from his knowledge of the cause, and not out of any ill will to the party, it is no cause of challenge."[123]

Here, in one of the last hurrahs for the local knowledge model of the jury, Hawkins sharply distinguished between the knowledgeable juror and the spiteful juror. Opinions spiked by personal hatred of the defendant served to prejudice the mind and destroy impartiality. But opinions born of personal knowledge of a defendant for whom a prospective juror bore no animosity were entirely consistent with bringing an open and informed mind to court.

Marshall was not prepared to reject outright Hawkins's reconciliation of pretrial knowledge and impartiality. The episode with Senator Giles at the grand jury stage indicated that Marshall had already moved beyond the common-law notion that only an ill-willed juror could be a biased juror. But still, Marshall puzzled carefully over the circumstances in which pretrial knowledge should be equated with pretrial bias. He adopted a new approach, reflecting the shifting sources of local knowledge in modern society:

> Without determining whether the case put by Hawk . . . be law or not, it is
> sufficient to observe that this case is totally different. The opinion which
> is there declared to constitute no cause of challenge is one formed by the
> juror on his own knowledge; in this case the opinion is formed on report
> and newspaper publications.[124]

A juror whose opinions stemmed from firsthand knowledge of events in
his neighborhood was arguably of assistance in giving accurate verdicts.
But Marshall cast a jaundiced eye on those who made up their minds
prior to trial based simply on the newspapers. If this was the kind of local
knowledge a prospective juror brought, then it was far more likely to be
expressive of prejudice and rumor than of truth. What did it say about the
virtues of the potential juror, asked Marshall, if that juror conceded that
he knew nothing directly about the case and yet had made up his mind on
an important part of it simply from what he read in the papers? Such
behavior "manifests a bias that completely disqualifies himself from the
functions of a juryman."[125]

In this way, the problem of pretrial knowledge became the problem of
pretrial publicity. But Marshall was careful to stress that a person did not
lose his ability to be an impartial juror simply because he had read the
papers. Bias was not some kind of contagious disease people caught from
reading inflammatory articles. Each juror had to be questioned individually to determine whether he had crossed the line from having "light
impressions which may fairly be supposed to yield to the testimony that
may be offered" to expressing "those strong and deep impressions which
will close the mind against the testimony."[126] In other words, the focus of
the voir dire must not be on the nature of the newspaper articles but on
the nature of the opinions expressed by the would-be juror prior to trial.
Here, Marshall accepted the common-law principle, reflective of small-
town life, that a juror could be disqualified for bias only if he had
expressed and bandied his opinions about town. Until it was publicly
aired, an opinion was neither decisive nor conclusive.

The gist of Marshall's reasoning is that having pretrial information does
not disqualify a juror, but a predisposition against considering the facts
undermines impartiality.[127] It is thus the task of the judge during voir dire
to separate those whose minds are opened by attending to the papers from
those whose minds are closed and enslaved by what they read.

When Marshall applied these standards to Burr's case, the results were
not consistent with the passing local knowledge jury nor the tabula rasa

jury that was to come. Contrary to the common law, Marshall permitted Burr to challenge not only ill-willed jurors but well-informed jurors who expressed conclusive opinions about any essential element of the case. As opposed to our contemporary standards, however, Marshall seated a number of informed jurors who admitted to generally unfavorable opinions about Burr's character after reading of his intrigues in the papers.

For instance, Richard Parker "had, like every other person, formed an opinion . . . on newspaper statements, . . . [and he had] declared that if these newspaper statements were true, Colonel Burr had been guilty of some design contrary to the interest and laws of the United States." Edward Carrington "had formed an unfavorable opinion of the views of Colonel Burr, but these opinions were not definitive." Likewise, Hugh Mercer confessed that "an opinion which he had for some time past entertained of the character of Colonel Burr was unfriendly to a strictly impartial inquiry into his case."[128] All three were seated on the jury.

In the end, twelve men were found sufficiently impartial to try Burr. They acquitted him of treason, virtually compelled to reach a not guilty verdict after Marshall granted Burr's motion to exclude most of the evidence the government wished to present. The government conceded that Burr was in Kentucky on the day he was charged in the indictment with fomenting rebellion hundreds of miles away, on Blennerhassett's Island. For this reason, Marshall ruled that most of the government's proposed evidence was irrelevant to proving the only overt acts of treason alleged against Burr.[129]

From a contemporary point of view, the lesson of Burr's case lies not in the result but in the procedures articulated for selecting jurors in highly publicized cases. During a time of legal transition, Marshall expressed a preference for jurors who knew less rather than more about their assigned case. He astutely understood that small-town justice, with jurors contributing firsthand knowledge to deliberations, was no longer characteristic of Virginia society. Burr's potential jurors knew about him secondhand, their information funneled through the newspapers. Already in 1807, Marshall approached such secondhand knowledge with suspicion. The classical arguments about jurors' pretrial knowledge being a boon to informed deliberation no longer worked; newspaper coverage was as likely to inflame as it was to inform.

Hence Marshall set American law along the course it has been following ever since—searching for jurors who are as free as practically possible from local information, which came to be better described as local prejudice. Marshall himself did not define "impartiality" in ways that disqualified all persons whose opinions were influenced by the press. He thought a sensible line could be drawn between "light" and "strong" impressions, eliminating only those persons whose opinions on a crucial issue affecting guilt or innocence had become "fixed." We now need to see how well Marshall's approach to reconciling jurors' impartiality with some amount of pretrial knowledge has held up over time.

THE IMPARTIAL JUROR TODAY: THE PROBLEM OF PRETRIAL PUBLICITY

Mark Twain was no authority on the law, but sixty-five years after the Burr trial his satirical talents made him among the first to ridicule the relentless progress of jury selection toward identifying ignorance with impartiality. In 1871, Twain reported that a "noted desperado killed Mr. B, a good citizen, in the most wanton and cold-blooded way." Not surprisingly, "the papers were full of it, and all men capable of reading read about it. And of course all men not deaf and dumb and idiotic talked about it." The odd lot—the "fools and rascals" who neither read nor talked about the case—was sworn in as the jury. Twain recounted the relentless way "the system rigidly excludes honest men and men of brains":

> A minister, intelligent, esteemed, and greatly respected; a merchant of high character and known probity; a mining superintendent of intelligence and unblemished reputation; a quartz-mill owner of excellent standing, were all questioned in the same way, and all set aside. Each said the public talk and the newspaper reports had not so biased his mind but that sworn testimony would . . . enable him to render a verdict without prejudice and in accordance with the facts. But of course such men could not be trusted with the case. Ignoramuses alone could mete out unsullied justice.[130]

A century later, we are still selecting jurors in the manner that Twain mocked. Communications lawyers and scholars Newton Minow and Fred Cate estimate that during the 1980s at least thirty-one hundred defendants claimed that pretrial publicity made it impossible to impanel an impartial jury locally.[131] Defendants throughout that decade and into the 1990s, from mobsters like Gennaro Anguilo and Samuel Granito to bigtime tax evaders like hotel magnate Leona Helmsley,[132] complained about the corruption of public opinion through the sheer barrage of sensational and inflammatory articles in local media outlets bent on creating a circus atmosphere in the vicinity.*

Some pointed to damaging revelations about their prior criminal records, others to reports of their suppressed confessions—all information legally inadmissible at their trial and yet sneaking through the back door straight into the jury room.[133] When local media create a fire storm over a cause célèbre, how can impartial jurors still be found locally? Marshall previewed this dilemma, but in an age of electronic media the sheer saturation possibilities are beyond what he ever encountered.

Trial judges remain reluctant to grant changes of venue as a way to escape local prejudices and local publicity.[134] But the justifications for keeping trials at home reveal just how weak the old ideals of community justice are today. Judges seldom defend their refusal to move a trial by identifying the positive advantages of convening a local jury to decide the case. They simply limit the contamination that comes from holding trials locally, using strategies such as continuing the case until the community loses interest in it or sequestering the jury during voir dire and weeding out persons whose impartiality is destroyed by having knowledge of the case and being prejudiced.

In theory, judges do the weeding by applying Marshall's distinction between light and fixed opinions.† In practice, however, judges find it dif-

---

*Typical of the complaints about local juries and pretrial publicity were those made by Pamela Smart in her celebrated 1991 New Hampshire trial for conspiring with her high school students to murder her husband. In arguing unsuccessfully for a change of venue, Smart stressed the sheer number of articles about her in the print press (nearly twelve hundred), in addition to blanket radio and television coverage. She derided the inflammatory nature of newspaper headlines such as "Smart Wanted Key Witness Killed, Police Say." She objected to the "circus-like" atmosphere surrounding the court during jury selection that was created by the "overpowering physical presence" of reporters, equipment, satellite trucks and the like. The combined effect of the media barrage reduced the trial process to a "Roman circus" acted out in the "white heat glare of media scrutiny." *State of New Hampshire v. Pamela Smart,* 136 N.H. 639 (1993).

†The current Supreme Court has reiterated that "mere familiarity with the petitioner or his past" is not disqualifying; there must be an "actual predisposition against him." *Murphy v. Florida,* 421 U.S. 794, 800–801, n. 4 (1975). The relevant question, the Court noted in 1984, "is not whether the community remembered the case but whether the jurors . . . had such fixed opinions that they could not judge impartially the guilt of the defendant." *Patton v. Yount,* 467 U.S. 1025, 1035 (1984). See also *Irvin v. Dowd,* 366 U.S. at 722–723; *Holt v. United States,* 218 U.S. 245 (1910); *Spies v. Illinois,* 123 U.S. 131 (1887); *Reynolds v. United States,* 98 U.S. 145, 156–57 (1878); *Yount v. Patton,* 710 F. 2d 956, 972 (3rd Cir. 1983) (Stern, J., concurring) (*Burr* has been standard for 175 years), rev'd., *Patton v. Yount,* 467 U.S. 1025.

ficult to mark the degree to which a potential juror's opinions are fixed.[135] Moreover, Marshall's seating of jurors who were lightly predisposed to finding Burr guilty no longer seems reconcilable with the presumption of innocence. Thus, Federal District Judge John G. Davies greeted prospective jurors in the federal civil rights trial of the four police officers accused of beating Rodney King by "remind[ing] them of their obligation to set aside *any* [emphasis added] impressions they had of the case or of the four officers."[136] Nothing less accorded with the presumption of innocence, Judge Davies warned, despite the herculean effort it would have taken for Angelenos to clear their minds of all preconceptions formed during the first King trial or subsequent riots.

Beyond these problems, the *Burr* standard more or less required judges to take jurors at their word. But, as one federal district judge wryly puts it, it is hard to treat as meaningful a juror's promise that, for example, he or she can lay aside an opinion, gained from reading the papers, that "the high school teacher brutally killed one of his students."[137]

Moving beyond *Burr*, contemporary law has added the concept of inherent, or presumed, bias as a way of disqualifying potential jurors. Media coverage occasionally reaches such levels of revelation and inflammation that bias may simply be presumed in anyone exposed to it; there is no need to uncover particular evidence of prejudice through voir dire questions. Rather, as the Supreme Court put it, "adverse pretrial publicity can create such a presumption of prejudice in a community that the jurors' claims that they can be impartial should not be believed."[138]

The notion of presumed bias has given the Supreme Court a great deal of trouble over the years. The concept came into the law in the early 1960s as an apparent reaction to fears about television's power to control local opinion. In 1961, a television station in a small Louisiana parish (population 150,000) aired a film made by police of a defendant's murder confession. The station ran the film three consecutive nights, to audiences of twenty-four thousand, fifty-three thousand, and twenty-nine thousand, respectively. For this case, *Rideau v. Louisiana*, the Court ruled that pervasive bias could be presumed in the jury venire as a whole and that the defendant's motion for a change of venue should have been granted. There was no need to produce evidence of actual prejudice in particular jurors because it was believed that there was no way a person could witness the televised confession and still keep an open mind for trial. In fact, the Court noted, the spectacle of a defendant confessing on television reduced the actual trial to a "hollow formality."[139]

Rideau was a decision compelled by the facts; presuming bias in jurors who see a defendant confess on television was easy. Left undecided by *Rideau* was the question of what else persons could learn from the media without losing their capacity to serve as impartial jurors. In a case preceding *Rideau*, the Court had "given little weight" to jurors' affirmations of their own impartiality after they had been exposed to media reports that the defendant had confessed to six murders and twenty-four burglaries and had offered to plead guilty.[140] In two subsequent cases in the mid-1960s, the Court carried forward the message that media coverage could reduce local courts to local carnivals, so entirely undermining the "solemnity and sobriety" of trials as to degrade jury verdicts into a "verdict of the mob."[141]

By the end of the 1960s, the oft-repeated comparison of local trials to circuses and carnivals showed how tarnished was the once proud reputation of the jury of the vicinage as an informed and deliberative body. According to the doctrine of presumed bias, jury selection standards mapped the uphill battle judges needed to wage against the negative consequences of local jury trials. In particular, jury selection became wed to a flawed understanding of impartiality in jurors—as if the only open minds were empty minds. An impartial jury is supposed to represent all segments of the community. But, as former U.S. attorney for the District of Columbia Jay Stephens complained, the categorical elimination of "people . . . who have read something, heard something, watched something, seen something, or talked to somebody" does not produce impartial juries. Such exclusionary standards "prejudice . . . the case against the government at the start" by disqualifying the very persons "who are an integral part of the community, who participate in the community, who are aware of what is going on in the community and who stay informed."[142]

Within a decade of its leading decisions on pretrial publicity and inherent bias, the Supreme Court began to have second thoughts. In a 1977 decision, the Court repudiated any proposition "that juror exposure to information about a state defendant's prior convictions or to news accounts of the crime with which he is charged alone presumptively deprives the defendant of due process."[143] A 1984 case followed up by refusing to find that jurors were necessarily prejudiced by media accounts prior to retrial of the defendant's conviction, confession, and plea of insanity at the first trial.[144] Most recently, a 1991 case found no inherent bias in jurors even though there was massive publicity about the defendant's alleged confession to killing a woman after escaping from a prison work detail.[145]

In part, these cases reflect a simple, political shift in a conservative Supreme Court's reluctance to reverse criminal convictions. But the change from presuming bias in news-following members of the public also speaks to a widely shared sense that prior cases had pushed the demands for impartiality in jurors to an absurd point where only the most inattentive citizens could readily qualify for jury service. Ignorance was becoming a virtue in jurors, and knowledge was becoming a vice.

Although recent Supreme Court cases suggest a retreat from the selection standards Mark Twain once lampooned, in practice trial procedures indicate that there is still a preference for jurors with empty minds. I turn to detailed accounts of two recent trials—one famous, the other not—to illustrate the problematic understanding of impartiality that drives jury selection today.

The Trial of Oliver North

Like Aaron Burr, Oliver North was a colonel charged with high crimes against the federal government. The scandal known as Iran-contra cast North in the leading role of diverting funds from weapons sales to Iran to aid for the contra forces fighting the Sandinista regime in Nicaragua. At the time, Congress had cut off funding for the contras. North went to trial in 1989 on a dozen charges of obstructing Congress, making false statements, destroying documents, conspiring to defraud the government, and receiving illegal gratuities and traveler's checks.[146]

Jury selection for North's case was particularly problematic because a national television audience had seen him testify before the Senate, which had granted him immunity for his testimony (meaning it could not be used against him in a court of law). For this reason, the presiding trial judge, Gerhard Gesell, understandably eliminated jury panel members who retained intimate recall of the immunized testimony. But Judge Gesell went considerably further in purging pretrial knowledge from the jury.[147] First, a written questionnaire was used to prescreen the initial pool of 235 persons. The 156 venire members who acknowledged seeing or reading about North's testimony were automatically eliminated, without being individually questioned at all about their level of exposure or reactions. Next, during voir dire, the trial judge dismissed another 56 for having "rudimentary prior knowledge" of North's Senate testimony.[148] The judge even excused a venire member who said she only listened to the hearings "with one ear."[149]

Those making the first cut included the eventual forewoman of the jury, who told the court, during jury selection, "I don't like the news. I don't like to watch it. It's depressing."[150] Also eligible were jurors who "never read the newspapers except to see the comics and horoscope," those who recalled only that North was a "head of soldiers, or something like that," and those who "didn't understand . . . whatever I heard about this case."[151]

Those who had to select a jury were left in a terrible quandary. Who were these jurors who knew next to nothing about North's appearance before the Senate, and why should we entrust the conscience of the community and the hard work of justice to them? Such an "extreme application of the impartiality requirement," one commentator lamented, was "in direct conflict with the notion of a trial by a representative panel of one's peers."[152] It skewed jury selection "toward the disaffected and disinterested." Lost was the idea that some knowledge of Iran-contra, some concern for the doings of government during those years, might be helpful to the jury's task. Instead, as had happened in Watergate-related trials a decade earlier, "a well informed student of public affairs [was], for that very reason, disqualified from sitting on a jury in matters of public moment."[153] To anyone following the jury selection, the integrity of the jury was itself drawn into question.

In the end, the twelve chosen jurors performed their task admirably, as almost all jurors do. But the jury was lenient toward North, acquitting him of all nine charges of lying to either Congress or federal investigators and convicting him on only three charges. The verdicts arguably reflected the jury's agreement with defense suggestions that all politicians lie and that North was a scapegoat for superiors.[154] We can never know whether there was any connection between the verdicts (with their implicit mistrust of government) and the elimination of engaged citizens from the jury. But the possibility is there.[*]

---

[*] In an epilogue that underscored the tension between impartiality and knowledge in the *North* case, the United States Court of Appeals vacated even the three convictions against North, and remanded the case to the District Court for a hearing to ensure that the government made no use of North's immunized Congressional testimony. North was never retried. *United States v. North*, 910 F. 2d 843, *mod.* and *reh'g. den.* 920 F. 2d. 940 (1990). The diffi-

A Child Sexual Abuse Trial

In 1986, Gerald Amirault went to trial on charges of sexually abusing and raping dozens of children at his mother's day-care center in Malden, Massachusetts.[155] For months prior to trial, local and Boston newspapers and TV and radio stations had blanketed the community with graphic coverage of alleged abuse in the basement of the center, where Amirault, playing "Tookey the Clown," would escort children.

A third of the initial jury pool was immediately disqualified after noting that they had formed impressions of the case from the media and would find it difficult to lay them aside. Subsequently, the judge's voir dire examination focused on those persons who thought they could be impartial, despite following the case in the news. One prospective juror thought he could be fair but remembered reading press accounts of statements made by the defendant to the police. These statements were not admissible at trial, and the judge considered it unlikely that the person, if seated, could put his knowledge of the statements out of his mind.

In contrast, the judge was more likely to certify as fair and impartial those persons who could remember virtually nothing of what they read. Typical of the surviving candidates was a woman who did not read the local paper and who, if she saw anything about the case at all in the Boston papers, didn't pay any attention to it. Another panel member was deemed impartial because she remembered reading something about the day-care center but "it was so long ago I don't remember what I read."

The voir dire also attempted to detect general attitudes about sexual crimes. An alarming number of prospective jurors apparently confided that they or people close to them had been the victims of sexual abuse as children. The judge excused all such persons from serving, on the

---

culty of finding impartial jurors in highly publicized cases was front-page news again in 1993, when Erik and Lyle Menendez came to trial on charges of killing their wealthy parents. The story made for sensational news because the state alleged that the brothers killed for the inheritance, whereas the brothers claimed fear of a sexually abusive father. Jury selection started in June with a phenomenal 1,017 persons—more than usual not only because of pretrial publicity but because separate juries were needed for the brothers. By July 7, only 180 jurors remained eligible. Struck for cause was a juror who said media reports made him think of the defendants as "wealthy, spoiled kids." Acceptable was the person who read "only *Cosmopolitan* and *Water Ski Magazine*." After five months of trial testimony, both juries deadlocked. Alan Abrahamson, "Menendez Brothers' Murder Trial Opens," *Los Angeles Times*, June 15, 1993, p. B3; Alan Abrahamson, "Lyle Menendez Case Ends in Mistrial; D.A. to Retry Brothers," *Los Angeles Times*, Jan. 29, 1994, p. A1.

grounds that they could hardly be expected to be disinterested in a case of this sort.

A number of parents and grandparents also confessed to having certain "feelings" at the start of the case because their children or grandchildren were roughly the same age as the alleged victims; these people were likely to be dismissed. A grandfather of six, including two at day-care centers, confessed to thinking of his own grandchildren when he first heard of the case. Still, he thought he could listen objectively to the evidence. But the judge dismissed him when he conceded that it would be hard to put his grandchildren "a hundred percent" out of his thoughts.

The judge's greatest concern during jury selection was with prospective jurors who hailed from Malden itself. The list of scheduled witnesses included several of the city's doctors, social workers, and police officers. To know any of them cast a shadow of suspicion over a person's qualifications for jury duty. For example, several prospective Malden jurors had sent their own children to a pediatrician who was scheduled to testify. The judge thought that these jurors would be biased in favor of believing whatever the doctor said because they already trusted him enough to place their children in his care.

The contrasting fates of two local Malden residents sum up the way jury selection worked to eliminate pretrial knowledge. Disqualified was a longtime resident who thought he could be impartial but had come into contact with a number of persons on the witness list through his job at the Malden YMCA. The contact was infrequent and involved merely the recreational facilities. Nevertheless, the judge thought it wiser to excuse anyone "tainted" by personal knowledge of trial witnesses. Qualified as an impartial juror was a person who had lived in Malden only two years, who never read the local paper, who did not even know her neighbor across the hall let alone the names on the witness list.

At the end of voir dire, the search for impartial jurors had substantially altered the composition of the jury pool. The remaining panel contained a smaller percentage of Malden residents and no one who had personal knowledge of the witnesses or parties to the case. The average age of the jurors was older than that of the venire group, and they were less likely to have children currently at a day-care center. The percentage of college-educated jurors dropped dramatically.

It seems plausible that there was another major difference between the excused jurors and those who remained. Massachusetts law strikingly uses the word "indifferent" to describe the mental posture of the impartial juror. But it is odd to demand indifference in a child rape case. A juror of Asian background was excused for saying that his culture did not tolerate behavior of this sort. The judge explained that Massachusetts law did not tolerate it either, and that the question for trial was merely whether the defendant did the reprehensible things charged. The prospective juror seemed to understand the point, but the judge excused him anyway because his remarks betrayed a moral passion at odds with the indifference welcomed as a sign of objectivity.

The North and Malden cases illustrate what we might call a process of deselecting well-informed citizens, as if civic engagement, concern for the issues on trial, and interest in reading the papers were enemies of fair-mindedness. The Malden case in particular shows just how far we have come from colonial times, when having local knowledge brought a juror praise and being informed made one an ally of justice.

When jury selection works overtime to eliminate persons who follow events closely in the news, judges are assuming that the media have power over people's opinions. Fortunately, recent jury verdicts have called this assumption into question. In 1984 the CBS show "60 Minutes" broadcast an FBI videotape of John DeLorean in a hotel room with a convicted cocaine smuggler and a suitcase full of drugs.[156] In 1990, District of Columbia's mayor Marion Barry was captured on tape, using cocaine in the Vista Hotel.[157] In 1991 there was the surefire incriminating videotape of four officers delivering eighty-odd blows to a prostrate Rodney King.[158] Finally there were the riveting televised pictures of truck driver Reginald Denny being beaten in the riot that followed the first King verdicts.[159] In all these instances, virtually everyone forecast convictions. Yet the juries acquitted DeLorean, acquitted or deadlocked on the King police officers during the first trial, convicted Barry of only one minor misdemeanor drug charge and deadlocked on twelve other charges (including the one based on the Vista Hotel tape), and acquitted the Denny defendants of the most serious charges against them. Whatever one thinks of these verdicts, they certainly explode the myth that pretrial publicity—even of a dramatic sort—makes it impossible for defendants to get a fair trial locally.*

---

*Newton N. Minow and Fred H. Cate point out that "regular exposure to media" may be preferable in jurors because it inculcates the same habits of "evaluating the barrage of . . . rhetoric" that are necessary in the jury room. Newton N. Minow and Fred H. Cate, "Who Is an Impartial Juror in an Age of Mass Media?" *American University Law Review* 40 (1991): 631–64, p. 658. They quote former CBS law correspondent Fred Graham to

JACK RUBY, PRETRIAL PUBLICITY, AND THE LIMITS OF IMPARTIALITY

One case above all tested the limits of banishing pretrial knowledge from the jury room in the name of securing impartiality. On November 24, 1963, in Dallas, Texas, Jack Ruby shot Lee Harvey Oswald dead before a national television audience. Few Americans escaped seeing the event, reruns of the shooting, or photos of the scene.

As trial approached, Ruby's motion for change of venue from Dallas was denied.[160] Jury selection began on February 17, 1964. Ninety-five percent of the venire acknowledged seeing the November 24 shooting live or on rerun.[161] The defense challenged each of these prospective jurors for cause. But the judge rejected challenges of any panel member so long as the person agreed that he or she could "lay aside" what was read and seen on television about the case and render a fair and impartial verdict. Jury selection was completed on March 3. The jury returned a verdict of guilty on March 14, rejecting Ruby's defense of insanity and sentencing him to death.[162]

On October 5, 1966, the Texas Court of Criminal Appeals reversed Ruby's death sentence and conviction, ruling both that a change of venue should have been granted and that an inadmissible oral confession was improperly introduced into evidence.[*]

Jack Ruby never was retried. He died in prison of cancer in January 1967.[163] In 1976, in a little-noticed footnote, the Supreme Court picked up on the trial before an impartial jury Ruby never had. The Court expressed skepticism that an impartial jury could have been found any-

---

similar effect: "I was assigned by CBS to cover a series of some of the most sensational trials of the century [Watergate, Hinckley, Connelly, DeLorean]. It became absolutely clear to me that *jurors were absolutely unphased* [sic] by all of that broadcasting that my colleagues and I had been doing on television. . . . As citizens, [jurors] were given responsibility over the high and the mighty. They were not going to let someone like me tell them what to think because I had been on television two and a half minutes on a few nights when they had sat through six weeks of trial; it was so clear to me that we were not affecting that process." Ibid., p. 659.

[*]*Jack Rubenstein v. The State of Texas*, 407 S.W. 2d at 795. The Court did not claim moving the trial from Dallas would solve the problem of jurors who had seen the fateful events. But holding trial in Dallas was uniquely prejudicial. The Court noted that "Dallas was being blamed directly and indirectly for President Kennedy's assassination and for allowing the shooting of Oswald by Ruby. . . . It is fair to assume that the citizenry of Dallas consciously and subconsciously felt Dallas was on trial and the Dallas image was uppermost in their minds to such an extent that Ruby could not be tried there fairly."

where in the United States.[164] Had Ruby lived, the only impartial jury would have been the absurd group of the few misfits who missed the major events of the day.

A twist of fate kept the Ruby case from beating the bushes for the rare juror who never saw the television coverage of Oswald's shooting. But recent cases—including those of Oliver North, Erik and Lyle Menendez, and Bernhard Goetz—bring us to a sorry state of affairs where we seek empty minds and consider them impartial. We need to change the standards of jury selection that make ignorance a virtue in jurors. Change is necessary for practical reasons—highly publicized cases do not leave many persons uninformed about the events to be tried. But abandoning overly strict definitions of impartiality would also free jury selection from the folly of preferring jurors who somehow missed hearing what everyone else was talking about.

Two hundred years after the Constitution was amended to protect the local jury, our basic commitment to impartial justice leaves us skeptical that neighbors render more accurate verdicts than strangers. If ever there was anything to the claim that local jurors are likely to know what's going on around town, it died when jurors themselves had to read the papers to find out what was going on. The idea of local knowledge as an asset in jurors was replaced by an ideal of impartiality that strangers could best fulfill. Indeed, the pejorative sound of "local," "community," or "popular" justice is the sound of a jury system in crisis.

In 1791, when the Sixth Amendment bestowed constitutional status on the local jury, there was an answer to why ordinary persons were competent for the hard work of deliberation—they came to the task knowledgeable about the events on trial or the reputation of the parties and witnesses. Although the model of the self-informing jury is no longer available to us today, we can achieve a better balance between the ideals of the impartial juror and those of the informed juror. There is no reason to let Mark Twain have the last laugh on the law.

CHAPTER TWO

Juries and Higher Justice

DURING THE SPRING OF 1989, members of the antiabortion group Operation Rescue attempted to shut down several abortion and family planning clinics in the San Diego area. Describing their mission as the rescue of unborn children, group members entered onto the private property of the clinics, forming a human blockade at entrances and exits. Police arrested thirty-two protesters, charging them with trespassing and resisting arrest.

In January 1990, three separate trials began for the defendants, one of whom was James Holman, publisher of the weekly newspaper the *San Diego Reader*. On January 25, with Holman's trial under way and others about to start, his newspaper ran an advertisement urging jurors and potential jurors to use a little-known right called "jury nullification" to find the defendants not guilty. Jury nullification is a controversial doctrine that claims jurors have the right to refuse to enforce the law against defendants whom they believe in good conscience should be acquitted. Jurors should know, the ad headline announced, that "you can legally acquit anti-abortion 'trespassers' even if they're 'guilty.'" This is because jurors always have discretion to find that justice is better served by ignoring the law and setting a defendant free.[1]

The ad portrayed the Operation Rescue defendants as especially worthy candidates for an act of jury nullification. By having trespass laws enforced against them, the defendants would be treated as ordinary lawbreakers when in fact they were engaged in an act of civil disobedience. The real issue at trial was not whether the defendants trespassed and blocked access to abortion clinics—they proudly admitted as much. The deeper issue the jury verdict would resolve was what judgment the conscience of the community made about those who claimed that the immorality of abortion justified the trespass.

Of course, the ad warned, the judge would deny that there was any such right and would instruct jurors that they had a duty to apply the law whether they agreed with it or not. It went on to point out that it was "unjust and illegal" for the judge to deny jurors their historic right to disregard the law to uphold higher justice. The ad urged would-be jurors to hide their knowledge of jury nullification: "The most important rule is, don't let the judge and prosecutor know that you know about this right." It might even be necessary for potential jurors to "lie" to the court, to make a "mental reservation":

> Give them the same answer you would have given if you were hiding fugitive slaves in 1850 and the "slave-catchers" asked if you had runaways in your attic. Or if you were hiding Jews from the Nazis in Germany.[2]

The advertisement correctly predicted the response of the judges presiding over the Operation Rescue trials. A judge in one trial admonished jurors to "pay no attention to the ad, to ignore it." A judge at a second trial criticized the ad because it told "potential jurors to disregard the law in the state of California, . . . to hide their true feelings and intentions from the judge . . . [and] to disregard the oath that they take." The deputy city attorney said that his office was considering banning the *San Diego Reader* from being distributed in courthouses—"to have hundreds of these papers dumped in the laps of prospective jurors worries us. . . . It distresses us that [the *Reader*] pulled this stunt at all."

The deputy city attorney went on to characterize "the history of jury nullification [as] as an ignoble one. . . . [The] only time he knew of its having been used was in the South, at a time when Ku Klux Klan members were on trial for having murdered blacks. . . . The jury decided, in essence, that Klan members could do whatever they wanted. . . . [But] law isn't a case of 'who wins is who we like.'" Jury nullification, the city attorney continued, "is asking jurors to ignore evidence, to ignore law. As a juror, you look at the law and the facts, and to do otherwise is to ignore your sense of duty and promise as a citizen."[3]

The ad apparently failed to sway the jurors. Holman was convicted and sentenced to thirty days in county jail; other convictions followed. But the episode revived interest in the doctrine of jury nullification. In fact, an entire organization—the Fully Informed Jury Association (FIJA)—was founded in the summer of 1989 to lobby for laws protecting the right of nullification. The FIJA membership cuts across political lines, drawing together National Rifle Association members, antilogging environmentalists, advocates for the legalization of marijuana, tax protesters, and bikers opposed to mandatory helmet laws. These persons, despite ideological differences, are all involved in disobeying some law. They turn to nullification as a way of authorizing the jury to determine whether the disobeyed laws ought to be enforced.[4]

In 1990, Operation Rescue raised the issue of jury nullification from the conservative side of the aisle, but a generation earlier, opponents of the Vietnam War turned to jury nullification to make their defense at trial. Resisting the war on moral grounds, protesters often engaged in open and notorious acts of lawbreaking. In 1969, nine persons, including five members of the Catholic clergy, broke into and ransacked the offices of Dow Chemical to protest the company's manufacture of napalm.[5] Four years later, twenty-eight protesters went on trial in Camden, New Jersey, for destroying draft records at their local selective service office.[6] In both instances, the defendants conceded that their conduct was unlawful. Nonetheless, they asked the jury to acquit them because the higher justice of opposing the war necessitated their violations of the law.

The judge in the Camden trial permitted the defendants to mount a jury nullification defense.[7] In his closing argument, the defense counsel argued that the term "nullification"

> describe[s] the power of a jury to acquit if they believe that a particular law is oppressive, or if they believe that a law is fair, but to apply it in certain circumstances would be oppressive. Now, the second situation might be something like the Boston Tea Party. No one would say that breaking into a ship shouldn't be . . . a crime. But in those particular circumstances, should people be convicted of doing that? That's the question. This power that jurors have is the reason why we have you jurors sitting there instead of computers. Because you are supposed to be the conscience of the community. You are supposed to decide if the law, as the Judge explains it to you, should be applied or if it should not. . . . You decide, considering the circumstances of the case, should you brand the defendants as criminals. . . . Are they deserving of the community's scorn? That's what the question is.[8]

The jury acquitted all twenty-eight defendants, even though the FBI had caught them red-handed inside draft offices destroying records.

By contrast, the judge in the Dow Chemical trial refused defense requests that he inform jurors about their powers of nullification. Instead the judge instructed the jury that

> the law does not recognize as a defense to ... these charges [of burglary and malicious destruction of property] that the defendants were motivated ... by sincere political, religious or moral convictions or in obedience to some higher law. Individuals who believe that the Vietnam War is illegal or immoral ... have the right ... to ... protest ... by any lawful means. ... But the Constitution ... does not protect ... the destruction of private property and the violation of valid laws. . . .[9]

The jury convicted all nine defendants.

Did the nullification defense make the difference in the outcomes of these two Vietnam War trials? Because the jurors did not explain their verdicts, it is impossible to say. But, presumably, jurors instructed about the right to nullify laws deliberate differently than those told they have a sworn duty to apply the law to everybody. One jury is being asked for its substantive judgments about justice, the other is warned to check such judgments at the jury room door. In the trial of Dr. Benjamin Spock and others for organizing draft resistance during the Vietnam War,[10] three jurors acknowledged after trial to having misgivings about the law they were asked to apply; they joined in the guilty verdict only because they thought they had no choice but to follow the letter of the law.[11] Had they been instructed about nullification rights, they may well have voted to acquit.

In this chapter I defend a return to the tradition of jury nullification, although, as we will see, this requires acknowledging the prejudice and racism that contaminated that tradition. My major concern is to enlarge the space for rich jury deliberation, which will not be easy, given the obvious dangers and historic failings involved. But my task may become somewhat simpler once we realize that jury nullification endures underground,[12] however much it is officially condemned, and that there are compelling arguments in its defense.

By history and design, the jury is more than a mechanical fact-finding body; it is a body where ordinary citizens cobble a common justice out of their different backgrounds. I suggested earlier that the modern preference for jurors with "empty minds" diminishes the jury's capacity to deliberate by disqualifying the most attentive citizens. Now I discuss the loss of the jury's right to deliberate as judges of the law's justice.

TWO SIDES OF JURY NULLIFICATION

Philosophically, jury nullification is a close cousin to the theory of civil disobedience.* In our own time, Martin Luther King, Jr., was a leading advocate for the view that individuals have a "moral responsibility to disobey unjust laws." But King accepted the state's authority to punish his acts of lawbreaking. In fact, willingness to accept punishment was a sign that the disobedience was a challenge to a particular unjust law and not to the state as a whole.

Jury nullification takes the classic theory of civil disobedience one step further by inviting the jury not to punish justified acts of lawbreaking. If the jury agrees that the broken law is unjust, then, say proponents of nullification, it should acquit rather than convict the defendant. The jury should also acquit when it finds the broken law just but agrees that enforcing it against the particular defendant on trial would be unjust.

Jury nullification is an appealing doctrine, promising to give meaning to the sometimes empty phrase "verdicts rendered according to conscience." Authorized to nullify, a jury might move from merely finding that the defendant violated the law to further deliberation about the ethical claims raised by acts of civil disobedience; instead of mechanically convicting because the law has been broken, the nullifying jury would have to consider the justice of the cause for which the law was violated. Sometimes the causes are grand, as was the case when juries deliberated whether to enforce the Fugitive Slave Law against those who helped runaway slaves attain freedom. At other times, the tension between law and conscience concerns lesser matters, such as enforcing liquor laws during Prohibition. But, for anyone who takes seriously the jury as a bridge between community values and the law, jury nullification is a strong plank. In essence, nullification empowers jurors to appeal to fundamental principles of justice over and above the written law.[13]

There is, however, a vicious side to jury nullification that Americans know all too well. The moral case for this right foundered and sank over the issue of race. In the South especially, all-white juries repeatedly refused to convict whites charged with murdering blacks or civil rights workers of any race. Few bothered to use the word "nullification" to

---

*I do not mean to suggest that jury nullification is itself an act of civil disobedience. This depends, as discussed later, on whether state procedures authorize juries to nullify.

describe the horror of the not guilty verdicts for Emmett Till's or Viola Liuzzo's murderers, but it was also no secret that the verdicts flew in the face of both the evidence and the law. As the sociologist Gunnar Myrdal noted in his classic study of American racism, the Southern all-white jury became a shield for local racism and a prime obstacle to enforcement of national civil rights legislation.[14] The obstacle was all the more solid because, in our trial system, a not guilty verdict is final and unreviewable.

This is not just a story about the distant past. In Mississippi in the late 1960s, a former Ku Klux Klan leader accused of plotting to murder a black leader reportedly told an associate, "Don't worry. . . . No jury in Mississippi would convict someone over killing a nigger." The KKK leader was tried twice, the jury deadlocking each time.[15] In 1979, Ku Klux Klan gunmen opened fire on marchers in an anti-Klan rally in Greensboro, North Carolina, organized by the Communist Workers' Party. Five marchers died. An all-white jury (including one juror who said, "It's less of a crime to kill communists") found the gunmen not guilty on all charges. The not guilty verdict barred any state retrial of the Klansmen on the same charges. (The Klansmen were subsequently tried in federal court on separate federal civil rights charges, but an all-white jury acquitted the defendants again in 1984.)[16]

Episodes such as the Greensboro and Mississippi trials undercut any innocent faith in nullification to pardon defendants. Once we grant jurors the right to set conscience above law, we have to live with consciences we admire as well as those we despise. As one critic put it, an "invitation to jurors to vote their consciences is inevitably an invitation to greater parochialism. . . . Local biases . . . are legitimated and activated . . . , immuniz[ing] criminal acts visited upon members of society's 'discrete and insular minorities.' "[17]

Stripped of moral stature by its service to racism, the doctrine of nullification is in virtual eclipse today. Only two states, Indiana and Maryland, recognize the doctrine and require judges, upon the request of a defendant, to apprise the jury of its right to disregard the law in favor of an acquittal.*

---

*In both Indiana and Maryland, the state constitutions provide that criminal juries have the right to determine the law as well as the facts. Indiana Constitution, art. 1, sec. 19 (1993); Maryland Declaration of Rights, art. 23 (1993). Because of this constitutional provision, a Maryland judge instructs jurors that "whatever I tell you about the law while it is intended to be helpful to you in reaching a just and proper verdict in the case, it is not binding upon you as members of the jury and you may accept it or reject it." Alan W. Scheflin and

In every other state and in the federal system, the doctrine has passed into history. In California, Operation Rescue jurors heard, as all California jurors hear, that they had "a duty to apply the law as I give it to you to the facts as you determine them."[18] The Massachusetts *Trial Juror's Handbook* states that the jury "decides the facts . . . [but] does *not* decide the rules of law to be applied to the facts in the case. . . . The judge tells the jury the proper rules of law required to resolve the case."[19] Pennsylvania's *Handbook for Jurors* is similar: "It is the jury's function to determine what facts are established by competent evidence [but it] is the judge's responsibility to tell . . . the jury the proper rules of law required to resolve the case. . . . [The] judge instructs the jury on the law which must guide and govern." During deliberations, "the jury is free to determine the procedures it will follow . . . as long as the judge's instructions are followed."[20]

In some federal courts, the jury is greeted with an even more explicit statement of its duty to follow the law:

> Ladies and gentlemen: You now are the jury in this case and I want to take a few minutes to tell you something about your duties as jurors. . . . It will be your duty to decide from the evidence what the facts are. You, and you alone, are the judges of the facts. You will hear the evidence, decide what the facts are, and then apply those facts to the law which I will give to you. That is how you will reach your verdict. *In doing so you must follow that law whether you agree with it or not* [emphasis added].[21]

These instructions illustrate the strict division of labor between judges deciding questions of law and juries deciding questions of fact. But, for all its familiarity, the idea that jurors must have nothing to do with the law marked a fundamental shift, a deep decline, in the democratic functions the jury once exercised in England and America. Well into the nineteenth century, criminal juries frequently (and civil juries occasionally) were instructed that the judge's statement of the law was not binding on them,

---

Jon M. Van Dyke, "Jury Nullification: The Contours of a Controversy," *Law and Contemporary Problems* 43 (1980): 83. Similarly in Indiana, the trial judge may "declare the law to the jury, but . . . [it] must not be done in a manner calculated to bind the conscience of jurors and restrict them in their right to determine the law for themselves." *Burris v. State*, 218 Ind. 601, 34 N.E. 2d 928 (1941). For a brief period between 1971 and 1973, trial judges in Kansas gave jury nullification instructions. Jon Van Dyke, *Jury Selection Procedures: Our Uncertain Commitment to Representative Panels* (Cambridge, Mass.: Ballinger Publishing, 1977), pp. 241–42.

that they could determine for themselves what the law was.[22] Juries in England used this authority to become the first to extend legal protection to Quakers assembled in peaceable worship.[23] Juries in the American colonies found that newspapers had a lawful right to print "true" criticisms of government long before legislatures recognized truth as a defense in seditious libel cases.[24] And up until the Civil War, defendants charged with violating the Fugitive Slave Law appealed to juries to judge the law invalid.[25] Well-known examples such as these illustrate the substantial contributions that juries, equipped with the right to decide questions of law, once made to upholding civil liberties.

The fact/law distinction, so starkly posed in judges' instructions to juries today, is, however, a fiction that seldom corrals the behavior of actual jurors. Even critics of jury nullification concede that criminal juries have the raw power to pardon lawbreaking because there is no device for reversing a jury that insists on acquitting a defendant against the law. Opponents of jury nullification therefore fall back on a technical distinction between the conceded power to nullify and the denied right to nullify. They insist on this distinction because it has one major practical implication: judges should not instruct juries about nullification because it is not a power jurors have any lawful right to exercise.

Much of the debate over jury nullification is about this formal issue of whether to instruct or not. Defenders of jury nullification argue in favor of open instruction; anything less misleads the jury about the full extent of its powers and may produce convictions a jury knowing about nullification would have rejected as unjust. Jurors who grudgingly convict because they mistakenly believe that they have no choice may feel deceived if they learn after trial that they had the power to acquit.[26]

Critics retort that nullification instructions conflict with instructions to jurors that they are duty-bound to apply the law whether they accept it or not.[27] Officially informing jurors that they have the power to nullify would confuse them; it would also threaten the impartiality of justice with the anarchy of conscience, as jurors pick and choose against whom to enforce the law. Open instruction might even encourage jurors to nullify, by portraying nullification as a right rather than a power. The present arrangement of keeping mum about nullification may be hypocritical, but it ensures that jurors will nullify only in extreme cases of conflict between law and conscience.

The debate over nullification instructions is important, but it sometimes obscures the overriding fact that jurors continue to nullify, whether officially instructed about their options or not. Ultimately, I think all sides must admit that verdicts according to conscience are so deeply entwined with popular images of the jury that jurors follow their conscience rather than the law in a good many cases, and the more visible cases at that.*

Before turning to the history of jury nullification, I pause to offer three illustrations of the subterranean life that jury nullification continues to live today.[28]

In 1994, a Detroit jury acquitted Dr. Jack Kevorkian of violating a Michigan law that made it illegal to assist persons to commit suicide. In the few years prior to trial, the infamous "suicide doctor" had by his own count helped twenty persons to end their lives, but this was the first time Dr. Kevorkian had come to trial.

The law that Dr. Kevorkian was accused of breaking contained an exemption for acts that were done with the intent of relieving pain and suffering, even if the person performing the acts knew they would hasten death. In interviews after trial, several jurors indicated that they believed Dr. Kevorkian acted only to relieve the person's suffering, but this was hard to believe in light of the fact that Dr. Kevorkian had placed a mask over the person's face and released carbon monoxide into his lungs for twenty minutes. The more likely explanation for the jury verdict is that they nullified the law insofar as it prohibited a physician from assisting a suicide.[29]

On August 10, 1990, a Washington, D.C., jury convicted Mayor Marion Barry of one misdemeanor charge of cocaine possession, acquitted him of another, and deadlocked on the remaining twelve narcotics charges.[30] Speaking to a law school audience after sentencing Barry to six months in jail for the one conviction, the trial judge said he had "never seen a stronger Government case" against a defendant. He rated the evidence "overwhelming" on at least eleven of the thirteen charges on which the jury either acquitted Barry or deadlocked. Among the charges on which the jury hung was one based on an FBI sting at the Vista Hotel, where

---

*In its research on the American jury in the 1950s, the University of Chicago Jury Project found that jury sentiments on the law were one factor, among others, mentioned by judges as helping to explain 50 percent of the cases where the judge disagreed with the jury verdict. In 22 percent of judge/jury disagreements, jury sentiments on law were cited as the major explanation for the disagreement. Harry Kalven, Jr., and Hans Zeisel, *The American Jury* (Chicago: University of Chicago Press, 1970), pp. 111, 113. In general, the project authors did not find the jury in full-scale revolt against any law. But they did find the jury to be at "modest war" with a number of laws considered "too severe," including gambling laws, drunk driving laws, liquor laws, and game laws. Ibid., pp. 286–87.

Barry was lured by a woman friend and videotaped smoking cocaine. The likely explanation for the jury verdicts was a deliberate decision to nullify the law. The judge singled out four jurors as having lied during jury selection to get on the jury, determined to acquit the mayor from the start.[31] But, the judge continued, "the jury is not a minidemocracy or a minilegislature. They are not to go back and do right as they see fit. That's anarchy. They are supposed to follow the law."[32]

Others found value in the jury's relatively lenient treatment of Barry. Columnist William Raspberry wrote in the *Washington Post* that "it would surprise me not at all to learn that all 12 jurors secretly believed the mayor guilty on virtually all the counts." Letting the mayor simply walk, after his own lawyer at trial described him as a casual cocaine user for over a decade, would send the "wrong message" about drugs. The jury therefore convicted on one minor charge. But beyond that, Raspberry speculated, the jury behaved as if Washington were a "federal colony" with a black population and a white power structure. The jury, Raspberry thought, bridled at the years-long vendetta of the U.S. Attorney's Office and the FBI to bring down a popular black mayor. They refused to convict, beyond the one charge, out of a sense that "occupying forces" had pulled out all the stops to topple a powerful black man for merely personal sins.[33] There may have been no legal basis for some jurors' refusal to convict on the most serious charges, but Raspberry congratulated them for using their nullifying powers to send a powerful message to federal authorities about the nature of life in Washington, D.C.

The split jury verdicts in the Iran-contra trial of Oliver North also raised suspicions of jury nullification. The judge clearly instructed the jury that following orders did not excuse criminal acts. Yet the jury convicted on only three of twelve charges, acquitting North of all charges of lying to Congress and all but one of obstructing Congress.[34] Of the three charges where the jury convicted, the evidence indicated that North acted alone, without authorization from superiors. On all charges where North credibly argued that his superiors knew of his false statements to Congress and his other steps to cover up the illegal contra-funding activity, the jury acquitted. After trial, one juror described North as "a scapegoat blamed unfairly for following the instructions of his superiors, and that is why [we] voted to acquit" him of the charges of lying. The jury foreperson said that "North was the subordinate. . . . He wasn't running the show." Another juror agreed: North "had people over the top of him. . . . [His superiors] put him out in the cold and closed the door on him."[35]

The jurors' words, as well as the verdict pattern, suggest that they decided, against the judge's instructions, that it would be unjust to convict someone for carrying out government policies approved at the very top, even if North had to lie to Congress to carry on. One juror even characterized North's lying to Congress as an act of civil disobedience: "He was living for the Constitution of America and to save people, and felt that he could do this."[36]

The Kevorkian, Barry, and North trials show us that jury nullification lives on, even when officially banished from the approved list of jury rights.* But its life is secret because jurors are discouraged from openly deliberating about the justice of enforcing the law and are no doubt forced frequently into smuggling their views on the justice of law into "approved debate" about the evidence or facts. But, if jurors continue to nullify on the sly, would we not do better to recognize in theory what jurors do in practice? Would not the quality of the debate about law versus justice be better if jurors were told that such debate was part of their function, that we cherish trial by jury precisely because we expect ordinary citizens to repudiate laws, or instances of law enforcement, that are repugnant to their consciences? These are the questions I wish to pursue, by revisiting the history of jury nullification.

NULLIFICATION'S RISE AND FALL

Jury nullification grew out of a general claim that jurors have the right to decide all questions of law necessary to reach a verdict. According to this broad claim, jurors have the right to disregard judicial instructions and arrive at their own resolution of all contested matters of law at trial.[37]

Jurors' right to decide questions of law gives them considerably greater authority than jury nullification itself requires. The right to nullify is narrow, permitting jurors only the right not to apply the law.[38] The crucial significance of this restriction is that juries can nullify only to acquit, never to convict. By contrast, the right to decide questions of law entitles

---

*For other cases where jury nullification arguably occurred, see "Law: Dallas County Official Is Acquitted in Trial with Racial Overtones," *Wall Street Journal*, May 12, p. B7 (in aftermath of Rodney King acquittals, jury finds black county commissioner not guilty of assaulting white carpenter); Carlyle C. Douglas and Mary Connelly, "The Goetz Case: Jury Sees Justification, Some See Injustice," *New York Times*, June 21, 1987, p. D6.

heir own interpretation of the law to either the detriment
defendant.

speaking, it is possible to defend jury nullification while
...ng the notion that juries have any general right to decide questions
of law.[39] After all, it is one thing for a judge to tell the jury what the
applicable law is; it is quite another for the judge to require the jury to
apply the law. But historically, jury nullification was debated as one
example of the broader claim that jurors decided questions of law. The
classic arguments came into English law in the middle of the seventeenth
century, made by dissenting groups such as Levellers or Quakers on trial
for treason, seditious libel, unlawful assembly, or disturbance of the
peace. Defendants appealed to the jury to be "judges of the law," never
quite specifying whether they were calling upon the jury to reject English
law as unjust (to nullify it) or simply to find them innocent under existing
laws (despite judicial instructions to the contrary). At any rate, the right
of juries to decide questions of law became a rallying cry for political and
religious minorities throughout the seventeenth century; in the colonies it
turned local juries in times of crisis into centers of resistance to parlia-
mentary law.[40]

I turn now to the rise and fall of jury nullification. Early, legendary
cases showcase juries struggling over conflicts between law and justice.
They capture juries doing the hard work of deliberating over contestable
points of law. Later cases cede that work solely to the wisdom of judges.

JURIES AND FREEDOM OF RELIGION: THE TRIAL OF WILLIAM PENN AND WILLIAM MEAD

On September 1, 1670, the Quakers William Penn and William Mead
entered Old Bailey Courtroom in London to stand trial on charges of
unlawful assembly and breach of the peace. The charges grew out of
events on August 14 of that year, when Penn addressed a group of Quaker
worshipers standing outside the Friends' Meeting House on Gracechurch
Street. Persecution of the Quakers was at its height, with soldiers standing guard over locked meetinghouses. The recently renewed Conventicles
Act forbade worship other than that performed according to Anglican
form. Penn therefore knew he was courting arrest when he began speaking. In fact, even before he uttered his first word, a warrant had been
drawn up charging him with "preaching seditiously and causing a great
tumult of people on the royal street to be there gathered together riotously

and routously." Armed with this warrant, two London constables arrived at Gracechurch Street, arrested Penn and fellow Quaker William Mead, and dispatched the pair to Newgate prison.[41]

Trial began on September 1, on an indictment that did not charge the defendants under the Conventicles Act but instead with the common-law crimes of unlawful assembly and disturbance of the peace. The indictment alleged that, with Mead's help, Penn "did take upon himself to preach and speak . . . in the street, . . . by reason whereof a great concourse and tumult of people . . . a long time did remain and continue, in contempt of the . . . king, and of his law, to the great disturbance of his peace."[42]*

To prove the facts alleged in the indictment, the government called three witnesses. The first, the constable James Cook, testified that he tried to disperse the meeting but could not get at Penn because of the large crowd of three to four hundred people. Cook saw Penn speaking to the people but could not hear what he said because of the noise.[43] A second constable corroborated Cook's testimony, stating that he "endeavored with my watchmen to get at Mr. Penn to pull him down, but . . . could not, the people kicking my watchmen and myself on the shins."[44] This constable stated that he "heard Mr. Penn preach to them" but then added that he did not actually hear what was said. A third witness saw Penn "make a motion with his hands . . . [and] suppose[d] he was speaking . . . [but] could not understand what he said." This third witness did not see Mead at all.[45]

The defense for Penn and Mead was more legal than factual. Penn freely "confessed" to preaching and praying to a crowd on the street. Far from wishing to deny evidence of his preaching, Penn trumpeted his "indispensable duty" to worship God. But he denied that any law of England made it a crime for people to assemble with a design to worship God. Thus, when the court asked him whether he pleaded guilty to the indictment, Penn saucily shot back that the question was not "whether I am guilty of this Indictment but whether this Indictment be legal." Penn then

---

*As proceedings began, the Lord Mayor of London, sitting as one of the judges, was irked to find that an officer had removed Penn's and Mead's hats; Quaker custom dictated wearing hats and the Lord Mayor was gleefully looking forward to holding the pair in contempt of court as soon as they appeared in hats in the courtroom. "Sirrah, who bid you put off their Hats?" the Mayor bellowed at the officer. "Put on their Hats again." As soon as their hats were fetched and donned, the Mayor then fined Penn and Mead forty marks each for disrespect to the court. Howell's *State Trials* 6:956 (1670).

asked the court to "produce" for the jury the law upon which the indictment was based, so that the jury could judge for itself whether Quaker
meetings constituted unlawful assemblies. The court summarily stated
that the "common law" formed a sufficient and lawful basis of the indictment. Penn was not satisfied:

PENN: Where is that common law?
REC: You must not think that I am able to run up so many years, and over so
     many adjudged cases, which we call common-law, to answer your curiosity.
PENN: This answer I am sure is very short of my question, for if it be com-
     mon, it should not be so hard to produce.[46]

When the court reiterated that it could not tell Penn "in a
moment . . . [what] many have studied 30 or 40 years," Penn again
retorted that "if the common law be so hard to be understood, it is far
from being very common."[47] The court grew increasingly irritated by Penn's
attempt to invite the jury to go "behind" the indictment and assess for
itself what the common law meant by unlawful assembly and disturbance
of the peace. The indictment's validity was a matter of law for the court to
resolve, and the bench was satisfied that the alleged facts, if proven, constituted the crime of unlawful assembly and disturbance of the peace.
"Therefore, you are now upon matter of fact, which fact you have heard
proved against you; you are to answer it."[48] When Penn persisted in asking what law he had broken, the bench labeled him a "pestilent" fellow
and removed him from the courtroom to the bale dock; he was still
exclaiming to the jury, as his sole judges, to use their consciences to
maintain the fundamental laws of England.[49]

Exiled from the courtroom, Penn never finished his defense. But in a
pamphlet written after trial, he stated the essence of the legal question he
was trying to put before the jury:

Because to worship God, can never be a crime, no meeting or assembly,
designing to worship God can be unlawful. . . . That is properly an unlawful assembly, according to the definition of the law, when several persons
are met together, with design to use violence and to do mischief, but that
dissenters meet with no such intention, is manifest to the whole world,
therefore their assemblies are not unlawful.[50]

In other words, a conviction for the common-law crime of unlawful assembly required the jury to determine, among other things, that the defen-

dants met with an intent to do violence or harm to persons and property. Penn sought to put this question of unlawful intent squarely before the jury; by contrast, the court's view was that the act itself of preaching in the street and drawing a large and tumultuous crowd was enough to establish guilt. In its charge to the jury, the bench instructed the jury as follows:

> You have heard what the Indictment is, It is for preaching to the people, and drawing a tumultuous company after them, and Mr. Penn was speaking; if they should not be disturbed, you see they will go on; there are three or four witnesses that have proved this, that he did preach there; that Mr. Mead did allow of it: . . . now we are upon the matter of fact, which you are to keep to, and observe, as what hath been fully sworn at your peril.[51]

After deliberating an hour and a half, eight jurors returned to court, stating that they had agreed on an apparently guilty verdict but that the four others balked. The court harangued the holdouts and sent all twelve back to agree upon a verdict. After "some considerable time," the jury returned to the court with a verdict:

> CLERK: Is William Penn Guilty of the matter whereof he stands indicted in manner and form, or Not Guilty?
> FOREMAN: Guilty of speaking in Gracechurch-street.
> COURT: Is that all?
> FOREMAN: That is all I have in commission.
> REC: You had as good say nothing.
> MAYOR: Was it not an unlawful assembly? You mean he was speaking to a tumult of people there?
> FOREMAN: My Lord, This is all I had in commission.[52]

The exchange makes clear the jury's initial attempt to give a partial verdict, pronouncing Penn "guilty" of preaching on Gracechurch Street, but leaving unresolved the issue of whether this made Penn guilty of unlawful assembly. However, the court required a definitive verdict and sent the jury back to reach one. A little more than half an hour later, the jury returned with a written verdict repeating that Penn was "Guilty of speaking or preaching to an assembly, met together in Gracechurch-street. . . . And that William Mead is Not Guilty." Furious at the repeated nonverdict as to Penn, the court ordered the jury locked up without "eat, drink, fire, and tobacco" until it reached a proper verdict; the court rejected the not guilty verdict as to Mead on the separate ground that the jury could not resolve the guilt of one coconspirator without resolving the guilt of the other.[53]

The next morning, the same scenario was repeated—the jury informing the court that it had no other verdict to render than the one already given. Again the jury was discharged, and again they came down to say Penn was guilty of speaking on Gracechurch Street. The bench's insults to the jury grew in passion; threats were made to starve the jurors and cart them about the city. When the jurors balked at retiring yet another time to reconsider their verdict, the sheriff forcibly escorted them back to their deliberations. Finally, the next morning, the jury avoided its attempt to walk a tightrope and rendered a verdict of not guilty for both Penn and Mead. The court accepted the verdicts but then promptly fined the jurors for rendering a decision the court found contrary both to the evidence (the jury itself determined that Penn did preach on Gracechurch Street as charged) and to the judicial instructions that such preaching made Penn and Mead guilty under the law.[54]

We can never know for sure what reasons lay behind the jury's decision to acquit Penn and Mead. As historian Thomas Andrew Green points out in his study of the case, it is possible that the jurors followed the judge's instructions on the law but simply concluded that the evidence did not establish any tumult. But their continued holdout against pressure to convict makes it likely that they rebuffed the court's statement of the law and followed Penn in concluding that "the Crown had . . . to prove an unlawful intent, especially where the law of criminal trespass was being applied to a man of God preaching His Word to those gathered to hear him."[55] For Penn, Green continues, "the message of his acquittal was unmistakable: the jurors had made their own assessment of the law, or at least had rejected that put forth by the court [and] rebuffed the tyranny of the judiciary and vindicated their own true and historical and moral purpose."[56]

Penn's trial changed the course of jury history. Rather than pay his fine and be done with it, juror Edward Bushel refused to pay, accepted imprisonment, and appealed his incarceration. Three fellow jurors joined in his suit to the royal justices of the Court of Common Pleas. In a landmark decision agreed to by all the justices of England save one, Chief Justice Sir John Vaughn flatly ruled that jurors may never be fined or imprisoned for their verdicts.[57] Vaughn's opinion stopped well short of endorsing the view that Penn's jurors had a right to decide questions of law. Instead he reasoned that judges could never conclude for certain that Penn's jurors had gone against their instructions on the law because the judges were not privy to the jury's conclusions about the facts and the evidence. It was possible that the jurors followed the law but acquitted Penn simply because they viewed the facts in evidence differently than did the judges or because they knew facts that the judges did not know. Because courts do not second-guess jurors on facts, they have to accept acquittals as proper and final.[58]

Although Bushel's case did not recognize any official right of juries to decide questions of law, the upshot of the decision was that juries could never be punished for acquitting a defendant. In this sense the case established the power of the criminal jury to disregard the bench's instructions on law.[*]

JURIES AND FREEDOM OF THE PRESS: THE TRIAL OF JOHN PETER ZENGER

The 1735 trial of John Peter Zenger became the defining moment for the American jury in the colonies, as Penn's trial had been for the English jury. Zenger, printer of New York's *Weekly Journal*, was charged with

---

[*]It is interesting to compare Penn's defense with that of Operation Rescue defendants in their antiabortion trials. Penn was not as willing to concede that he had broken any law as the Operation Rescue defendants were to concede that they had. But, to the extent that he was asking his jurors to find English law on unlawful assembly unjust, Penn was asking jurors to pardon his civil disobedience, just as Operation Rescue defendants asked their jurors to excuse their disobedience of trespass laws. Still, there is a difference. Penn never urged his jurors to acquit him because they happened to agree with Quaker doctrine. What the jurors thought of Quaker theology was irrelevant to the principle of justice for which Penn was willing to break the law. That principle was that persons gathered with an intent to worship God in peace could never be guilty of unlawful assembly. Any law of England, or any judicial interpretation of English law, that provided otherwise was inherently unjust and should never have been enforced by any jury against any religious group. Penn's dispute with the law, therefore, was not narrowly self-serving. He sought to change the law equally for all. And in time, English law did respond to the position taken by Penn's jurors.

The Operation Rescue argument cannot be similarly generalized. The defendants never disputed the justice of the law of trespass under which they were tried. Presumably, they were content to have other juries convict other defendants for breaking a concededly just law. Their appeal to their jurors' conscience was really a narrowly partisan or political pitch: jurors should refuse to enforce a just law against antiabortion defendants because the jurors happened to agree with the politics that motivated the lawbreaking. There was nothing in the Operation Rescue argument about jury nullification that welcomed discretion in juries to refuse to enforce trespass laws against proabortion demonstrators. In the end, the antiabortion protesters pleaded to be exempt from a law that they themselves considered just and that they presumably wanted to remain on the books without change.

the infamous crime of seditious libel after publishing articles complaining that the colony's royal governor had dismissed the chief justice of the New York Supreme Court for ruling against him in a personal equity case. The charges against the governor apparently were true, but the court instructed the jury that, as a matter of law, truth was not a defense to charges of seditious libel. The law, as stated by Blackstone, made it criminal to publish "written censure upon any public man whatsoever for any conduct whatsoever, or upon any law or institution whatever."[59] Because there was no factual dispute that the articles did constitute written censure of the governor, the court concluded that the publications were libelous as a matter of law. The jury was left with the meager task of determining whether Zenger had in fact published the articles at issue and whether they referred to (that is, carried an "innuendo" about) the governor. Practically speaking, this came close to directing a verdict of guilty.[60]

Zenger's lawyer—Andrew Hamilton, the foremost American attorney of his day—urged the jury to disobey the instructions of the court and to determine for themselves whether the laws of England made it a crime to punish truthful criticism of government. He reminded the jurors that they "have the right beyond all dispute to determine both the law and the fact, and where they do not doubt of the law, they ought to do so."[61] Thus, jurors ought

> to see with their own eyes, to hear with their own ears, and to make use of their consciences and understanding in judging of the lives, liberties or estate of their fellow subjects.[62]

Hamilton blended two arguments about how the jury might exercise its right to decide questions of law. At times, he appeared to argue that the court had stated the law of seditious libel correctly but that the existing law was unjust, at least when applied to truthful criticisms of government. Therefore, the jury as "judges of the law" ought to nullify it by appealing to higher law. "Nature," Hamilton implored, gave every man "a right— the liberty—both of exposing and opposing arbitrary power (in these parts of the world at least), by speaking and writing truth."[63] At other times, Hamilton suggested that the law was just but that the judges construed it incorrectly as applying to truthful criticisms of government. The jury should disregard the incorrect judicial instructions and find on their own that the common law of England recognized truth as a defense to charges of seditious libel.[64]

On either argument, the jury had the right to resolve for itself a legal question that the court wished to reserve for itself: whether the newspaper articles met the definition of libel. The jury returned a verdict of not guilty. The *Pennsylvania Gazette* praised the verdict by saying that "if it is not law it is better than law, it ought to be law, and will always be law wherever justice prevails."[65]

It is possible to see Zenger's jurors as behaving in a purely partisan and political manner. Certainly, this was the way the verdict was dismissed in England, with no one doubting that colonial jurors would have been more than willing to convict Tory printers of libeling local favorites. But, whatever the motives behind the verdict, the acquittal rested on a principled claim about freedom of the press and the right to print truthful criticism of government. The effect of the jury's nullification was to vindicate that principle as fundamental to liberty in the colonies; even prior to the Bill of Rights, many states recognized truth as a defense in seditious libel actions.[66] What started out nullifying the law became the law in the states of the emerging new nation. Ever since, the Zenger case has stood as a proud reminder of the contribution jury nullification can make to reconciling law and justice.

AFTER THE REVOLUTION: THE STRUGGLE TO MAINTAIN JURY POWER

The law-finding rights of colonial juries survived the Revolution. This is somewhat surprising because the immediate political/oppositional need to rely on juries for local input into the law abated with independence. Certainly, from 1800 on, some federal judges already pressed the argument that the new republic no longer needed to use the jury system as a device for representing popular views on the law; representative legislatures now discharged this democratic function. Still, in most state jurisdictions and many federal cases, the criminal jury's prerogative to decide questions of law lasted well into the nineteenth century. Not until 1895 did the Supreme Court definitively resolve the argument against the federal criminal jury's authority.

The civil jury, generally speaking, lost its lawmaking rights much earlier, but even here cases go back and forth on the issue. In 1794 we still find Supreme Court Justice John Jay instructing a civil jury, while riding circuit, that "you have . . . a right to take upon yourselves to . . . determine the law as well as the fact in controversy." Jay noted for the jury the "good old rule, that on questions of fact, it is the province of the jury, on questions of law, it is the province of the court to decide." But this amounted to no more than a presumption that the judges were correct about the law. Ultimately, "both objects [the law and the facts] are lawfully within your power of decision."[67]

Several state constitutions, including the Georgia Constitution of 1777 and the Pennsylvania Constitution of 1790, specifically provided that "the jury shall be judges of law, as well as fact."[68] As to Pennsylvania practice in the early years of statehood, Supreme Court Justice James Wilson noted, in his Philadelphia law lectures of 1790, the obligation of the jury to "pay much regard" to what the court said about the law. Still, when "a difference of sentiment takes place between the judges and jury, with regard to a point of law, . . . the jury must do their duty, and their whole duty; they must decide the law as well as the fact." Wilson qualified his remarks only by noting that the doctrine was "peculiarly applicable to criminal cases."[69] As late as 1879, the Pennsylvania Supreme Court noted that "the power of the jury to judge of the law in criminal cases is one of the most valuable securities guaranteed by the Bill of Rights."[70]

In Massachusetts, an 1808 statute codified the petit jury's right to "decide at their discretion, by a general verdict, both the fact and the law, involved in the issue." At the Massachusetts Constitutional Convention of 1820, delegates found it unnecessary to include protection of the jury's law-finding power in the Constitution because "that the jury have the right of deciding on the law as well as the fact, is a part of the common law of the country."[71] In 1825, the state's highest court approved a charge to the jurors in a libel case that they need not follow the judge's instructions if "they knew the law to be otherwise."[72]

In Vermont in 1849 the state's highest court specifically reversed a trial judge for instructing the jury in a criminal case that it was bound to take the law from him. The court stressed that the "opinion of the legal profession in this state, from the earliest organization of the government . . . has been almost if not quite uniform in favor of the . . . right of the jury" to decide questions of law.[73]

As noted, federal cases fall on both sides of the issue from early in the nineteenth century. In an 1817 piracy prosecution in Richmond before Chief Justice John Marshall sitting as a trial judge, the justice expressed his opinion about the law but "conclude[d] his charge to the jury by telling them that, as it was a criminal case, they were not bound to accept his opinion, but had the right to decide both the law and the fact."[74] Likewise, in a prosecution for treason in Maryland, the presiding federal judge gave his opinion on the law of treason but noted that "the jury are not bound to conform to this opinion, because they have the right, in all criminal cases, to decide on the law and the facts." The defense counsel was even permitted to argue to the jury that "the opinion which the Chief Justice has just delivered is not, and I thank God for it, the law of this land."[75]

The strength of the tradition permitting juries to act as judges of the law was ironically demonstrated in 1808 when a federal judge tried to go against it. Samuel Dexter, a well-known Massachusetts lawyer, was defending his client on charges of violating the Embargo Act. Local resistance to the act was high and reminiscent of colonial attitudes toward the British revenue acts. To capitalize on local sentiments, Dexter sought to argue the act's unconstitutionality to the jury. Judge Davis of the federal district court instructed the jury, as a matter of law, that the act was constitutional. When the defense "persisted in arguing the question of constitutionality to the jury, notwithstanding the remonstrances of the Bench, . . . Judge Davis . . . said to Mr. Dexter, that if he again attempted to raise that question to the jury, he should feel it his duty to commit him for contempt of Court." On the following morning, Dexter arose and stated that he had

> reflected very solemnly upon the occurrence of yesterday. . . . No man cherished a higher respect for the legitimate authority of [the court]; but he entertained no less respect for his moral obligations to his client. He had arrived at the clear conviction that it was his duty to argue the constitutional question to the jury . . . , and that he should proceed to do so regardless of any consequence.[76]

Dexter made his argument and secured an acquittal from the Massachusetts jury, "despite the very obvious fact that the defendant had violated the terms of the statute."[77]

JURIES AND THE SLAVE TRADE: THE TRIAL OF JOHN BATTISTE

In a famous trial in 1835, a federal judge succeeded in denying the jury's right to construe or nullify the law. In *United States v. Battiste,*

Supreme Court Justice Joseph Story went to great lengths in rejecting the entire notion that juries may decide questions of law.[78] Significantly, the issue that brought debate over the jury's control over the law out into the open was slavery. From *Battiste* on, the debate over slavery and the debate over jury control of the law would march together.

While riding circuit in the Massachusetts federal district, Justice Story presided over the prosecution of a sailor for illegally engaging in the slave trade. An 1820 Congressional law made it a crime for any crew member of an American ship to seize or forcibly bring aboard the ship any Negro or mulatto, not already bound for service, with the intent of making that person a slave. John Battiste was a mate on an American ship on a voyage along the African coast. The brig stopped at Portuguese colonies and, for a fee, transported shackled slaves held by the Portuguese from one colony to another. The Americans were not involved in the original seizure of the Negroes as slaves, but Battiste and other crew members did physically board them in fetters and transport them in this condition. The Americans had no financial interest in the slaves other than the pay they received for transporting them. Nor did they have any power or control over the future status of these slaves.[79]

In his charge to the jury, Justice Story noted that it could convict Battiste only if it found that he had transported Negroes with the intent required by the statute—namely, the intent to make them slaves. The question arose as to what Congress meant by the words "to make a slave." Here Story paused to confront the defense counsel's argument that the jury had the final right to decide what the law meant.

Battiste's lawyer—none other than Daniel Webster—had strenuously argued to the jury that the 1820 law could not possibly apply to the boarding of Negroes who were already slaves. For, unless the Negroes were previously free, Battiste could not be said to have intended to make them slaves.[80]

Story rejected this interpretation of the law, claiming it would empty the 1820 law of any significance. Congress surely knew that slave traders customarily bought and boarded Negroes who had already been kidnapped and enslaved by others; they did not mean to exempt Americans who traded in slaves simply because the Negroes they bought, transported, and resold as slaves may have been slaves already. Instead, for Story the focus of the law was the intent of the accused as to the future status of the Negroes brought on board. A defendant was guilty under the 1820 law if and only if he had the intent of making the Negroes slaves in the future. Where a defendant merely transported other person's slaves for hire, with no control over or financial interest in the future status of those transported, then the law did not apply.

This disagreement over the law provoked Story to instruct the jurors that they had no "moral right to decide the law according to their own notions, or pleasure."[81] Instead, Story laid down the strict division of labor that soon would whittle down the jury's power:

> I hold it the most sacred constitutional right of every party accused of a crime, that the jury should respond as to the facts, and the court as to the law. It is the duty of the court to instruct the jury as to the law; and it is the duty of the jury to follow the law, as it is laid down by the court.[82]

Story emphasized one particular reason why juries should not be trusted to decide legal questions. Such a system would threaten the accused's right to be tried according to fixed and certain rules of law. The judge well knew that the popular imagination portrayed the jury as the accused's best protection against government. But popular lore had it backwards, Story dared to say. Could sailors such as Battiste, accused of slave trading, really expect fair trials before Northern juries entitled to have the last say about what constituted slave trading? In the throes of antislavery sentiment, would jurors carefully consider the kind of intent that differentiated a slave trader from a mere sailor?

Story considered it far more likely that juries would interpret the law according to the latest shifts in public opinion, leaving defendants exposed to local prejudices and parochialism. If the jury were left free to announce what the law was, "the law itself would be most uncertain, from the different views, which different juries might take of it." By contrast, the "truest shield against oppression and wrong" is the right of every citizen to be "tried by the law, and according to the law." Judges are that true shield, applying the law in evenhanded fashion to popular and unpopular defendants alike.[83]

Clearly, by 1835 Story was one federal judge ready to invert conventional wisdom about the criminal jury. If democracy is fundamentally about participation in self-government, then the model of a criminal jury deciding questions of law fits democracy well. But if democracy is more keenly about receiving the equal protection of the laws, then, Story thought, judges ought to replace jurors in deciding legal questions consistently, uniformly, and predictably.

JURIES AND THE FUGITIVE SLAVE LAW: THE TRIAL OF FREDERICK JENKINS'S LIBERATORS

With the passage of the Fugitive Slave Law of 1850, slavery emerged again as the single greatest issue driving the debate about whether criminal jurors should be able to decide questions of law and to nullify the law in the name of higher justice. Among its other purposes, the Fugitive Slave Law was designed to avoid jury trials requiring a slaveholder to prove his property in an alleged runaway slave. Instead, the law provided for a summary process before federal magistrates, where the owner or agent could appear ex parte, present "satisfactory proof" of ownership, and receive a certificate permitting him to remove the slave from the free state. Testimony was not allowed at these proceedings from or on behalf of the slave.[84]

Jury trials typically took place, however, for those arrested and charged with aiding fugitive slaves to escape. These were ordinary felony trials triggering the constitutional rights to jury trial. In these cases, Northern defense lawyers put the Fugitive Slave Law itself on trial.

One of the most famous appeals to a jury to nullify the Fugitive Slave Law occurred in the case of *United States v. Morris* in Boston.[85] In 1850, a man known as Shadrach escaped from slavery in Norfolk, Virginia, and made his way to Boston. Under the name of Frederick Jenkins, he worked as a waiter at the Cornhill Coffee House until an agent of his former master discovered him in February 1851 and began summary proceedings before a federal magistrate to remove him back to Virginia and slavery. Jenkins's fate seemed sealed until a large crowd burst into the courtroom and "invited Shadrach to accompany them. . . . [They] hurried him through the square into Court Street, where he found the use of his feet, and they went off toward Cambridge, . . . the crowd driving along with them and cheering as they went." Eventually, Jenkins made his way safely to Canada, but eight of his alleged rescuers, four blacks and four whites, were arrested and charged with violating the Fugitive Slave Law by aiding, abetting, and assisting the escape of a fugitive slave.[86]

In May 1851, jury trial began for the first three defendants. The defense went beyond disputing evidence of the defendants' participation in the escape to appealing to the jury to refuse enforcement of the hated Fugitive Slave Law. In his closing argument, the defense attorney

> stated the proposition that, this being a criminal case, the jury were right-fully the judges of the law, as well as the fact; and if any of them conscien-

tiously believed the act of 1850 . . . , commonly called the "Fugitive Slave Act," to be unconstitutional, they were bound by their oaths to disregard any direction to the contrary which the court might give them.[87]

This was an extraordinary line of argument, openly inviting the jury to disregard the judge's instructions, act as its own constitutional court, and declare a duly passed act of Congress null and void. The argument made clear what most Northern jurors sitting in fugitive slave cases must already have sensed: it would not be easy to follow both the law and one's conscience in such cases. What should a dutiful juror do when justice points one way and the law points the other?

The defense counsel suggested a way out of the dilemma. Criminal juries should consult the higher law of the Constitution to judge whether the Fugitive Slave Act was a valid law at all. Criminal juries were not bound by the judge's opinion on the validity or applicability of the law. They were judges of the law themselves—a function that required them to consider and interpret the Constitution as the highest law of the land.

The logic of the closing argument depended on making no distinction between ordinary legal questions and questions of constitutional law— the defense claimed the jury could answer both. Of course, if a jury could judge the constitutionality of a law, then a jury could nullify the law. The defense argument amounted to a bold claim that juries, like courts, had the power of judicial review.

But the closing argument seemed so extraordinary to the presiding judge, Benjamin Curtis of the Supreme Court riding circuit, that he stopped the defendants' lawyer from finishing it. To Curtis, it was clear that the notion that juries could decide questions of law was now being put to extreme lengths. Despite precedents to the contrary, he therefore warned the jurors that they "have not the right to decide any question of law." Rather, it was "their duty and their oath . . . to apply to the facts, as they may find them, the law given to them by the court."[88]

According to Curtis, the possibility that the jury would disagree with the law was no reason to ignore it; the law was the law. In a written opinion justifying his refusal to permit the defendants to argue the validity of the Fugitive Slave Law to the jury, the judge dwelt on the practical consequences that would flow from making "every jury, impannelled in every court of the United States . . . the rightful and final judge of the existence, construction, and effect of every law which may be material in the trial of any criminal case." Federal law and the Constitution itself

would become hydra-headed monsters, having as many different interpretations as there were juries. Worse, juries might apply the Fugitive
Slave Law in some sections of the country and not in others, against
some defendants but not all.

The judge posed a thorny question: Would juries be bound by a definitive Supreme Court ruling upholding the constitutionality of the Fugitive
Slave Law, or would the defendants believe that juries might "revise and
reverse" opinions of the Supreme Court every bit as much as they might
disregard instructions of the trial judge?[89] He concluded by recalling Story's opinion in *Battiste* and challenging the silent premise of the defense
argument: that the rights of defendants were better served when juries
had the right to decide questions of law. To the contrary, jury control of
the law was likely to leave defendants exposed to the shifting tides of
public opinion:

> To enforce popular laws is easy. But when an unpopular case is a just
> cause, when a law, unpopular in some locality, is to be enforced there,
> then comes the strain upon the administration of justice; and few unpreju-
> diced men would hesitate as to where that strain would be mostly firmly
> borne.[90]

Notwithstanding the judge's warning, the jury nullified the Fugitive
Slave Law by acquitting all three defendants. Cases against the remaining
five defendants were dropped, and no one was ever convicted of aiding in
the escape of Frederick Jenkins.

THE MASSACHUSETTS CONSTITUTIONAL CONVENTION OF 1853

Two years after the *Morris* decision, delegates to the Massachusetts
Constitutional Convention renewed the debate over the proper division of
labor between jury and judge in criminal cases.[91] The Fugitive Slave Law
was a frequent topic at the convention,[92] but the immediate occasion for
debating the judge/jury boundary was the considerably less grave issue of
liquor. In 1845, a defendant charged with violating state liquor license
laws attempted to argue the invalidity of the law to the jury. The trial
judge disallowed such argument, saying that the jury was bound to accept
the judge's statement that the law was valid. On appeal, in *Commonwealth v. Porter*, the state's highest court agreed with the trial judge that

the jury had no right to decide questions of law in disregard of judicial instructions. (Illogically, the court went on to find error in the judge's refusal to grant counsel the customary privilege of arguing the law anyway and remanded for a new trial.)[93]

At the convention, an amendment was proposed precisely to overrule that part of the *Porter* decision which stripped the jury of law-finding authority. The amendment read as follows:

> In all trials for criminal offenses, the jury, after having received the instruction of the court shall have the right in their verdict of guilty or not guilty, to determine the law and the facts of the case.[94]

Supporters of the amendment referred to two different, if overlapping, rights at stake. The first was the right of criminal juries to interpret and construe existing laws on their own. For example, the Fugitive Slave Law made it a crime to knowingly harbor runaway slaves. The amendment would restore to the jury its right to decide what the law meant by "harbor" and what state of mind must be shown. The second right secured by the amendment was the jury's right to nullify laws, such as the Fugitive Slave Law or liquor legislation, outright.

As to the jury's right to interpret the law, amendment supporters emphasized that criminal law rested on simple principles of common law and natural justice known to the average man:

> The common law is the science of reason and justice; and a man who can tell what justice is, can tell what the common law is, in almost all cases, and therefore he is just as competent to decide the case as the judge.[95]

Critics of the amendment responded that professionals alone were qualified to decide questions of law. Said delegate John Gray, "The common law is not always common sense," as anyone knows who asks "exactly what [the law of] murder is?"[96] Critics also stressed that jury decisions on legal matters would leave law without the certainty and predictability that ought to be valued most. One jury after another would resolve the same legal issue over and over again, back and forth, and no jury verdict would ever be a binding precedent on the next jury.

As to nullification, the term itself was not used at the convention. But jury advocates revived the argument, rejected in *Morris,* that the criminal jury's right to decide questions of law necessarily included the right to

decide whether the law before it was just and valid. Jurors were competent to make these judgments because they could, on their own, consult
the standards of natural justice, most of which had been codified in the
Constitution. Referring explicitly to the Fugitive Slave Law, delegate
James Allen of Worcester argued:

> Whenever the rights which we reserve to the people are invaded by any
> law, . . . a jury coming from the people may be allowed to come in and
> give their judgment, and rescue the people, in the name of their declared
> rights, from an unconstitutional law, or from an unconstitutional interpre-
> tation of that law.[97]

Amendment supporters thought judges were too much themselves
creatures of "power and authority," too distant from the people, to be a
safeguard against governmental oppression. Delegate Benjamin Butler
thought he had "seen quite as many errors on the bench as in the jury-
box." He continued:

> Which is the best tribunal to try [a] case? This man who sits upon the
> bench, and who . . . has nothing in common with the people; who has
> hardly seen a common man in twenty years. . . . Is he the better man to try
> the case than they who have the same stake in community, with their
> wives, and children, and their fortunes, depending on the integrity of the
> verdicts they shall render?[98]

Opponents rejected this view of the jury as romantic hogwash. Jury
decisions on the law were "more apt to reflect current prejudice" than
natural justice. Unpopular but innocent defendants suffered the oppressive force of public opinion being substituted for the rule of law. By contrast, the judge was "*of counsel for the accused*," said delegate Increase
Sumner, extending the same rules of law evenhandedly to popular and
unpopular defendants alike.[99]

In the end, the convention included the amendment guaranteeing the
criminal jury's right "to determine the law and the facts of the case" in
the new draft Constitution submitted for voter approval.[100] In November
1853, voters rejected the entire new Constitution, for reasons that apparently had little to do with its jury trial provisions.[101] But in 1855, the legislature passed a statute tracking the language of the defeated amendment and recognizing the criminal jury's right to decide questions of
law.[102]

Once more, this apparent victory for the criminal jury's historic prerogatives was snatched away the same year by an odd decision of the Massachusetts Supreme Judicial Court in *Commonwealth v. Anthes*.[103] The defendant was indicted for violating the state liquor law by being "a common seller of spiritous and intoxicating liquors." The trial judge ruled that the new statute permitted the jury to determine the proper meaning of the liquor law, but not its constitutionality. On appeal, Chief Justice Lemuel Shaw went even further. Despite the statute, Shaw found that the jury had no right to resolve any legal question whatsoever and that the trial judge had erred in permitting such questions to go to the jury. Shaw dismissed the statute as merely a "declaratory act, making no substantial change in the law" as he had fixed it ten years earlier in his 1845 *Porter* decision. Shaw could only reach this conclusion by ignoring clear legislative history documenting the legislature's intent to overturn the result in *Porter*. But Shaw noted that, if the statute were interpreted as permitting juries to decide questions of law in criminal cases, then it would be unconstitutional—a violation of the state constitutional right to be tried by standing laws before an impartial judge.[104]

In Massachusetts, *Anthes* put an end to the judge/jury debate that had gone back and forth since the beginning of the century. By 1855, the romantic stories about John Hancock and jury resistance to tyrannical laws had become narratives unfit for instructing juries of their role vis-à-vis the law in a democracy.

THE OFFICIAL END OF LAWMAKING JURIES: THE TRIAL OF SPARF AND HANSEN

In time, the criminal jury suffered the same decline in other states and in federal trials as it had in Massachusetts during the decade before the Civil War. By the end of the century, the right of juries to decide questions of law had been repudiated virtually everywhere; in place of the older, more expansive understanding of jury functions rose the modern, narrow view of the jury as competent to find the facts but little more. The Supreme Court's 1895 decision in *Sparf and Hansen v. United States* provides a fitting conclusion to this historical narrative.[105]

In 1893, the second mate of the American ship *Hesper* disappeared and was presumed to have been murdered while the ship voyaged through the Pacific a thousand miles from Tahiti. Sparf, Hansen, and a third sailor were arrested and tried for the murder. At Sparf and Hansen's trial, the defense counsel asked the judge to instruct the jury that, in an indictment charging murder, it was not limited to a guilty or not guilty verdict on murder alone; it could also consider convicting the defendants of manslaughter because that crime was a "lesser included offense" within the meaning of murder. The trial judge refused this instruction, instead guiding the jury as to the legal definition of murder. He then briefly described the law of manslaughter but said that he did not "consider it necessary . . . to explain it further, *for if a felonious homicide has been committed, of which you are to be the judges from the proof, there is nothing in this case to reduce it below the grade of murder.*" It is interesting that the judge alerted the jury that "it may be in the *power* of the jury" to find the defendants guilty of manslaughter, but again he repeated that such a finding would be inappropriate in this case because "if a felonious homicide has been committed at all . . . there is nothing to reduce it below the grade of murder."[106]

After the jury had been deliberating for some time, it sought clarification of its instructions. Apparently, there was some sentiment in the jury for avoiding the mandatory sentence of death that would follow murder convictions. Two jurors desired to know whether the law permitted them to consider a verdict of manslaughter. The judge repeated that "in a proper case, a verdict of manslaughter may be rendered, . . . and even in this case you have the physical power to do so; *but as one of the tribunals of the country, a jury is expected to be governed by law, and the law it should receive from the court.*"[107] The jurors thought this clarified matters satisfactorily; subsequently, the jury returned with a verdict of guilty of murder.

On appeal, the defendants argued that the judge erred in telling the jury that a verdict of manslaughter would be legally indefensible. This deprived the jury of its right to decide questions of law as well as fact; here the jury should have been left to resolve not only whether a homicide occurred on the high seas but also whether the killing (if it occurred) amounted to murder or manslaughter.

The Supreme Court affirmed Hansen's conviction (Sparf's was reversed on other grounds), taking the opportunity to decisively reject the right of criminal juries to judge the law. In a case where no evidence had been introduced to support a verdict of manslaughter, the judge rightly withdrew this option from the jury, as a matter of law. The only possible "true" verdicts were guilty of murder, if the jury believed the state's evidence, and not guilty of murder, if the jury disbelieved the evidence. A verdict of manslaughter would have been "false" because it would have reflected the jury's judgment that a homicide occurred but that the prescribed legal punishment for murder was too severe in this case. A manslaughter verdict "would have been the exercise by the jury of the power to commute the punishment for an offense actually committed, and thus impose a punishment different from that prescribed by law."[108]

In scholarly fashion, running scores of pages in the official reports, the Court reviewed the century-long debate over the federal criminal jury's right to decide questions of law. Acknowledging that prior cases went both ways on the issue, the Court sided with the logic of *Battiste* and *Morris*, reiterating that each jury could not be allowed to become "a law unto themselves." It noted that placing law-deciding authority in jurors' hands would render futile the whole enterprise of reversing convictions and remanding the case for new trial—because the jury could simply disregard the appellate court's answer to the legal issue.

Moreover, the Court wondered whether those who advocated the jury's right to decide contested points of law would go so far as to allow jurors to resolve questions about the legal admissibility of evidence. In examples such as these, the Court pejoratively portrayed the right of juries to decide questions of law as threatening the "protection of citizens against unjust and groundless prosecutions."[109] With juries "uncontrolled by any settled, fixed legal principles," the Court feared, a "government of laws" would be reduced to the mere "government of men"—twelve unelected, unaccountable men at that.[110]

These arguments summarize the sweeping sea change that had transformed official attitudes toward the jury in the years since the Constitution's ratification. For the revolutionary and founding generations, the criminal jury reliably stood between the individual and government, protecting the accused against overzealous prosecutions, corrupt judges, and even tyrannical laws. Crucial to the jury's ability to shield liberty against tyranny was the jury's right to control the local application of law, to bring its enforcement into harmony with local values and sentiments. Jury control over the law no doubt decentralized justice, politicizing it to some extent by inviting jurors to consult the conscience of the community in rendering verdicts. But these were welcome features of jury trials, basic to the ability of jurors to be involved as people at large in the administration of justice.

At the dawn of the twentieth century, the *Sparf* Supreme Court preferred to put its faith in judges to protect the accused against government.

The greater tyranny and threat to the accused resided in juries that substituted the whims of public opinion for the fixed principles of law. Far better to strip the jury of its right to judge the law and to entrust judges to apply the law uniformly to popular and unpopular defendants alike.

THE JURY, THE COMMUNITY, AND THE TRANSPARENCY OF LAW

In hindsight, the jury's loss of its expansive, law-deciding rights seems to have been inevitable. By the beginning of the twentieth century, basic shifts in the nature of American law and democracy doomed the decentralized, local control model of justice implicit in granting juries the right to decide questions of law.

In regard to the nature of law, two fundamental shifts required a weaker jury. In eighteenth-century America, law was still seen as having its source in natural reason. Criminal law especially was "elementary and simple, and easily understood by jurors taken from the body of the people."[111] As even John Adams put it, "The great Principles of the [English] Constitution, are intimately known, they are sensibly felt by every Briton—it is scarcely extravagant to say, they are drawn in and imbibed with the Nurses' milk and first Air."[112] Jefferson agreed: "The great principles of right and wrong are legible to every reader: to pursue them requires not the aid of many counsellors."[113] The people know "very well what violated decency and good order."[114]

Few today would follow Adams or Jefferson in their confidence that law is transparent to the ordinary person. Modern law is complex and variable, rooted in the shifting politics of a legislature, not necessarily rational, and certainly not traceable to eternal laws of nature. This basic, overwhelming change in our views about the nature of law has carried with it fundamental changes in the nature of the jury. From an institution that once presumed ordinary citizens were competent to make independent judgments about the law, the jury changed to reflect the assumption that jurors knew precious little about the law. From an institution that valued decentralized justice and local control over law's interpretation, the jury became exclusively a fact-finding body, leaving judges to enforce a more uniform and consistent body of legal rules. These changes were so monumental that it is scarcely an exaggeration to say that the jury praised by America's founders no longer survives today.

The second great shift was in the law's relation to communities. As

William Nelson points out in his study of the jury in colonial Massachusetts, the homogeneity of the politically enfranchised part of the population permitted towns to express an "ethical unity" regarding the values they wished to articulate in the law. With jury duty limited to white male freemen likely to share the same background and values, jury verdicts could represent that ethical consensus in fairly consistent manner from case to case. But in the nineteenth century, increasingly heterogeneous conditions fractured the ability of law to capture shared moral values (Adams's remark referring to Americans as "Britons" is jarring to the modern ear).

With the growth of heterogeneity, the function of the legal system itself changed. From seeking to embody shared values and natural justice, law came to express the clash and compromises of competing interest groups. In such a legal world, juries deciding questions of law were no longer anchored to one another or to a common community consensus on fundamental values; the only way to know laws that were subjective and constantly changing was to make a profession of it. Thus, even as modern notions of due process were emerging that put the highest value on the certainty, predictability, and uniformity of legal rules, the jury was less able to serve these values.[115]

The loss of the jury's law-deciding function also reflected changing conceptions of democracy. For all its inconveniences and, within the restricted world of white male freemen, the jury emerged, at the time of the American Revolution and through the early decades of the nineteenth century, as a premier institution of local self-government, empowering the enfranchised with an effective voice to interpret and enforce the laws in their community. The lawmaking jury partly presumed that citizens had the knowledge and virtue it takes to find the law justly; but the lawmaking jury also served as a hands-on school where citizens learned the virtues of self-government by actively participating in constructing their community's laws. That different communities might then interpret national laws differently and fit them into a local context was not a threat to republican government; it was the welcome result of decentralizing power over the law down to the local level and into the hands of citizens.

When the Constitutional Convention drafted a document that failed to protect the common-law requirement that criminal juries be drawn from the "vicinage" where the crime occurred, opponents sensed that the new blueprint for republican government was a serious departure from the ideal of local control. Power was shifting to the national level, and the tra-

ditional design of the jury—locally situated with power to revamp or veto
laws distantly enacted—threatened the nationalizing design of the Constitution. Defenders of the passing order of decentralized justice sounded
the alarm at various ratification conventions and demanded amendment
of the Constitution to protect the local jury. They only partially succeeded, with a Sixth Amendment that required jurors to be drawn from
"districts" within a state.

The fight over the jury's right to decide questions of law was another
front in the battle over the geography of democracy in America. The great
complaint of federal judges was that juries gave local communities too
much control over the law. In a republican government, law could not rule
unless its application was uniform. Juries, armed with the right to decide
questions of law, threatened these core legal values by giving too volatile
an expression to popular sovereignty.

When power over the law shifted from jury to judge, democracy shifted
in its nature as well. From *Battiste* to *Morris* to *Sparf,* federal judges
worked out a political theory that severed the classical connection
between liberty and self-government. In this new theory, too much popular participation in the judiciary was a decided threat to freedom. Liberty
was a matter of receiving equal protection from the law, not necessarily a
matter of making the law oneself. And the federal bench concluded that
judges, not juries, would do a better job of giving to every accused person
equality before the law—better because judges were more insulated from
the pressure to do what was popular.

THE FACT/LAW DISTINCTION AND THE DECLINE
OF JURY NULLIFICATION

This chapter has traced the steady erosion of the jury's lawmaking function. In place of the expansive, inspiring deliberations about law and its
relation to justice that characterized the work of the Penn and Zenger
juries, modern law invokes the distinction between facts and law to provide jurors with a frequently deadening description of their mission. In
virtually every jurisdiction's handbook for jurors, the same mechanical
description appears: find the facts, and reach a verdict by applying whatever the judge says about the law to those facts.

But the search for a strict division of labor between jury and judge creates a number of practical problems for trials today. First, as we saw in
the Jack Kevorkian, Marion Barry, and Oliver North trials, the division of

labor does not hold up well in practice. The more we emphasize the remoteness of law from the experience of the average juror, the less credible it is that jurors receive sudden enlightenment on legal matters simply by listening to the judge's furious, quick-paced, jargon-laced set of instructions.

For instance, if I do not understand what differentiates murder from manslaughter in Massachusetts, I am unlikely to suddenly understand it because a judge instructs that murder requires malice and that malice does not require any ill-will toward the victim but includes a deliberate purpose to injure without legal excuse or palliation. Nor were jurors in the Bernhard Goetz trial likely to understand from the judge's instructions whether Goetz acted lawfully in self-defense, if he *mistakenly* thought he was facing deadly attack. In a Philadelphia racketeering trial in 1993, several jurors said that they did not believe the defendant guilty but voted to convict because they mistakenly thought a hung jury was unacceptable.[116]

Legal realist critics have pointed out since the beginning of the century that modern jury procedures mask a charade: we have judges go through the motions of instructing jurors on the law and tell them they must abide by the instructions, but we suspect that jurors do not fathom the instructions and fall back on their own gut reactions or common sense in deciding how the case should come out.[117] To anyone who has ever witnessed a judge instructing a jury, it is clear that our system does not even pretend that the instructions are meaningful. Rarely are jurors even provided with written copies of the instructions; little attempt is made to translate jargon into common language. Most annoying of all, juror questions about the instructions are usually rebuffed with verbatim rereadings of the same instructions.

The second difficulty, as our predecessors appreciated, is that the world outside the courtroom does not neatly divide questions of fact from questions of law. When we ask jurors to decide, as a matter of fact, whether the defendant acted with malice, we are asking them to make a complicated assessment of the nature of the defendant's mental state—an inquiry far different from finding facts in the who did what, when, and where sense. To label the defendant's behavior malicious is partly to find the historical facts, but it is also to render a judgment about its blameworthiness. Juries are constantly presented with these mixed questions that jump the artificial law/fact boundary. This is true in negligence cases, where juries decide the fact of whether a defendant's behavior fell below the behavior expected of a reasonable person. It is true in obscenity cases, where juries apply "contemporary community standards" to decide the fact of whether the work in question is pornographic. So here too, against official theory, we have to admit that juries do what we say they are not equipped to do: they decide what the law means by "negligence" or "obscenity" or even "murder."

The practical impossibility of abiding by the fact/law distinction casts a new light on the earnest attempts of American law to stamp out the tradition of jury nullification. History teaches us that jurors escape from all kinds of legal straitjackets designed to restrain conscientious acquittals in criminal trials.*

And this is the way it ought to be. Many of the arguments that the Supreme Court laid down in *Sparf,* stripping juries of any right to decide legal questions, have no relevance to what jury nullification is about—the right to set aside the law only to acquit, never to convict. As a doctrine, jury nullification poses no threat to the accused; it is in fact the time-honored way of permitting juries to leaven the law with leniency.

To permit juries to show mercy by not enforcing the law in a given case is hardly to destroy the fabric of a society under law. Indeed, putting pressure on jurors to convict against their conscience would seem to threaten the integrity of the law far more seriously. Our current system, in which we tell jurors they must apply the law in every case no matter how unjust the results seem to them, opens the chasm between law and popular beliefs that the jury system exists to prevent.

This is not to deny that jury nullification sometimes goes badly. Even if limited to acquittals against the law, it gives us the Emmett Till jury along with the William Penn jury. There is no denying, as the Supreme Court said in another context, that "the power to be lenient is the power to discriminate."[118] It is for this reason that the Massachusetts affiliate of the American Civil Liberties Union (ACLU) took a firm stance against a bill,

---

*A recent book on Clarence Darrow recovers a neglected case in which the legendary lawyer was brought to trial on charges of attempting to bribe two jurors. The charges stemmed from a case in which Darrow represented labor union officials accused of dynamiting the *Los Angeles Times* building in 1911 and of killing twenty-one people. In his closing argument to the jury in the bribery trial, Darrow suggested nullification was the appropriate response to the charges. "Suppose I am guilty of bribery," he said. "Is that why I am prosecuted in this court? Is that why, by the most infamous methods known to the law, these men, the real enemies of society, are trying to get me inside the penitentiary?" After deliberating for forty minutes, the jury found Darrow not guilty. Geoffrey Cowan, *The People v. Clarence Darrow* (New York: Times Books, 1993).

introduced in the state legislature in 1991, that would have amended the jury trial handbook to inform jurors that they could acquit "according to their conscience" if they felt "the law as charged by the judge is unjust or wrongly applied to the defendant(s)." The ACLU chapter believed that "jurors often manage to control their own strong prejudices because the judge tells them they must."[119] Its fear was that jury nullification would be an open invitation for jurors to unleash their prejudices in the name of conscience.

The ACLU affiliate's stance against jury nullification is a succinct expression of the collapsed faith in the virtue of jurors that drives the declining role of jurors at trial. In that group's judgment, jury nullification encourages jurors not to rise above law to consult fundamental justice but to fall below law into brute bias. One is left to wonder whether the rejection of jury nullification is not a rejection of the idea of the jury altogether.

Suppose we were to inform jurors that nullification is an option. Is the Massachusetts chapter of the ACLU right to fear dire consequences—a sudden bursting of prejudice through legal dikes? In the two states that do instruct about nullification—Indiana and Maryland—judges have not detected any dramatic rise in the frequency of nullification.[120] Alan Scheflin and Jon Van Dyke, the leading scholars of jury nullification, reported recently on an empirical study where the effect of jury nullification instructions on mock jurors depended on the issue involved. Juries given nullification instructions were not more likely to acquit a college student charged with driving drunk and killing a pedestrian; in fact, they were less likely to acquit than juries given standard instructions. On the other hand, receiving a nullification instruction did increase the number of mock juries that acquitted a nurse charged with the mercy killing of a terminally ill cancer patient.[121] It is encouraging that nullification instructions left the mock jurors able to distinguish the merits of pardoning the nurse and not acquitting the drunk driver.

In 1983, a California murder trial demonstrated the dwarfing of deliberation that comes from denying juries the right to nullify. A seventeen-year-old shot and killed a marijuana-growing farmer during a botched attempt to rob crops from the farm. In accordance with the felony murder rule, the judge instructed the jury that a killing committed during armed robbery was to be considered first-degree murder. After deliberating some time, the jury returned to ask the judge whether it was compelled to find the defendant guilty of first-degree murder if it found that the killing occurred during an armed robbery. At this point, there was only one forthright answer; the jury should have been apprised of its power to nullify.

Clearly, the jury was struggling with the issue of the harsh consequences of the felony murder rule and was searching for a way to convict the defendant of less than first-degree murder. In reacting this way to the felony murder rule, the jury was not behaving strangely but rather in tune with sentiments that had caused many other states to abandon the rule by 1983. But the judge remained silent about nullification and simply repeated the instruction that felony murder is first-degree murder. Even if the judge was not originally obliged to volunteer information about nullification, surely he answered incorrectly when the jury broached the issue on its own. An entire line of deliberation was cut off, or at least it appears to have been cut off, because the jury returned a first-degree murder conviction.[122]

Whether such a verdict represented the jury's considered and independent judgment of justice in the case, we will never know. We do know that the California Supreme Court upheld the conviction but reduced the punishment to that for second-degree murder, finding the punishment of first-degree murder to be so "grossly disproportionate to the offense" in the case as to constitute cruel and unusual punishment. Thus, the Court ended up reaching exactly the judgment the jury was not permitted to make.

I close with a story about an act of disguised jury nullification that occurred over six hundred years ago. In fourteenth-century England, an inquest jury found that "Robert Bousserman returned home at mid day, to find John Doughty having sexual intercourse with his wife. Bousserman forthwith dispatched Doughty with a blow of his hatchet."

At trial, the petit jury found the facts to be dramatically different and acquitted Bousserman:

John Doughty came at night to the house of Robert in the village of Laghscale as Robert and his wife lay asleep in bed in the peace of the King, and he entered Robert's house; seeing this, Robert's wife secretly arose from her husband and went to John and John went to be with Robert's wife; in the meantime Robert awakened and hearing noise in his house and seeing that his wife had left his bed rose and sought her in his house and found her with John; immediately John attacked Robert with a knife . . . and wounded him and stood between him and the door of Robert's house continually stabbing and wounding him and Robert seeing that his life was in danger and that he could in no way flee further, in order to save his life he took up a hatchet and gave John one blow in the head.[123]

Why should the facts have changed so drastically from inquest to trial? The trial jury would have known the consequences of finding the same facts as the inquest: Bousserman would be sentenced to die. To avoid what seemed an unjust or harsh verdict, the jury apparently concocted an elaborate story that justified acquitting Bousserman on grounds of self-defense.

The jury did not explicitly reject or dispute the severity of English law on murder—a severity that recognized no degrees of murder and left the jury with a stark choice between finding Bousserman guilty or not guilty of a capital crime. Instead, it conveniently found the facts to support a not guilty verdict under the law of self-defense.

The remarkable aspect of this story, as law professor Richard O. Lempert points out, is how familiar the fourteenth-century jury seems to us.[124] Either openly displayed or hidden, nullification remains a timeless strategy for jurors seeking to bring law into line with their conscience. This reconciliation is what the jury system is about, for better or worse. Official disapproval of jury nullification may drive it underground, seeking disguise in fact-finding, as was the case with Bousserman's jury. But, as long as we have juries, we will have nullification and verdicts according to conscience. Some of those verdicts will outrage us, others will inspire us. But always nullification will give us the full drama of democracy, as citizen-jurors assume on our behalf the task of deliberating about law in relation to justice.

PART II

DEMOCRATIC
REPRESENTATION

If the accuser and the accused be both foreigners, then the jury shall be made up of foreigners only. If there be no foreigner on either side, then there shall be no foreigner on the jury. If there be a foreigner on one side and a native on the other, then in forming the jury, half shall be foreigners and half natives.

—First Jury Statute in Kingdom of Hawaii, 1842

The kingpins of the trial-by-jury system—the impartial juror, the representative panel, and the challenge method—are filled with ambiguities and at war with one another. It is possible that the legal fiction of the "impartial" juror should be disposed of as a "cultural lag" hopelessly out of tune with reality. A juror without any significant biases relevant to a case . . . growing out of a confrontation between a black militant and a white policeman would have to be a person of apathy, ignorance, even stupidity, or at least someone who is not living in today's social world.

—Robert Blauner, commenting on the Huey Newton trial in 1968

CHAPTER THREE

Jury Selection and the Cross-Sectional Ideal

IN THE UNITED STATES TODAY, it is common to describe the ideal jury as a "body truly representative of the community."[1] To practice this ideal, all jurisdictions rely on a computerized version of the oldest and most direct of democratic selection methods: the random drawing of names by lot. The basic principle behind the lottery is that the pool of persons from which actual juries are drawn must approximate a fair, representative cross section of the local population. Because of the luck of the draw, as well as uneven patterns of excuses and challenges, the particular jury a person gets may not itself form a cross section of the community. But so long as jurors are summoned randomly from an initially representative list, the democratic nature of jury membership is said to be preserved.

The cross-sectional jury is so familiar to us today that we forget how modern is its triumph. As recently as 1960, federal courts still impaneled blue-ribbon juries. The theory was that justice required above average levels of intelligence, morality, and integrity.[2] In place of random selection, therefore, jury commissioners typically solicited the names of "men of recognized intelligence and probity" from notables or "key men" of the community. A 1967 survey of federal courts showed that 60 percent still relied primarily on this so-called key man system for the names of jurors.[3]

In 1968, with the Jury Selection and Service Act, Congress abandoned this system for federal courts, declaring it henceforth to be "the policy of the United States that all litigants in Federal courts entitled to trial by jury shall have the right to grand and petit juries selected at random from a fair cross section of the community."[4] In 1975, the Supreme Court extended the ideal of the cross-sectional jury to state courts as well, ruling that the very meaning of the constitutional guarantee of trial by an impartial jury required that the jury pool be a mirror image or microcosm of the eligible community population.[5]

Both Congress and the Court justified the new theory as a remedy for the discrimination practiced under the guise of searching for elite jurors. The slippery and subjective standards for jury eligibility under the elite model provided convenient cover for systematic exclusion of certain people, African-Americans in particular; they also allowed for the perpetuation of the all-white jury in the South nearly a century after the Supreme Court outlawed, in theory, such juries. The immediate task of the cross-sectional reform was to strip away such discrimination, making all persons equally eligible for jury duty who met minimum and objective standards of citizenship, age, residency, and literacy.

But the ideal of the cross-sectional jury speaks to more than the abolition of intentional discrimination in jury selection. To say, as the Supreme Court did in its landmark 1975 decision, that only "representative" juries are "impartial" juries is to suggest a new way of thinking about how to make jurors capable of impartial justice—a way that stands the classical view of impartiality on its head.

As discussed in chapter 1, common law defined an impartial juror as genuinely capable of bracketing his own interests and preconceptions and of deciding the case solely upon evidence presented in open court.[*] In the words of the great common-law jurist Lord Coke, "He that is of a jury, must be *liber homo*, that is, not only a freeman and not bond, but also one that hath such freedome of mind as he stands indifferent as he stands unsworne."[6] This is a demanding notion of impartiality, requiring jurors to be independent not only from the dictates of others but also from their own opinions and biases. It requires jurors to achieve "a mental attitude of appropriate indifference."[7]

The ideal of the cross-sectional jury rejects this common-law view of impartial deliberation. It sees individual jurors as inevitably the bearers of the diverse perspectives and interests of their race, religion, gender,

---

[*]I say "his own" advisedly here because the common law's disqualification of women as jurors was almost total. The issue of gender discrimination in jury selection will be taken up later in this chapter.

and ethnic background. Deliberations are considered impartial, therefore, when group differences are not eliminated but rather invited, embraced, and fairly represented. To eliminate potential jurors on the grounds that they will bring the biases of their group into the jury room is, we are told, to misunderstand the democratic task of the jury, which is nothing else than to represent accurately the diversity of views held in a heterogeneous society such as the United States.[8] If the jury is balanced to accomplish this representative task, then as a whole it will be impartial, even though no one juror is. The jury will achieve the "overall" or "diffused" impartiality that comes from balancing the biases of its members against each other.[9]

In this chapter I trace the rise of the modern view of the jury as a representative body, paying special heed to an unacknowledged and unfortunate shift that courts have made over time in their arguments about what or whom jurors are supposed to represent. In the earliest cases describing the jury as a representative body—cases dating to 1940—the drive to democratize jury membership was justified in terms of the contribution persons from different walks of life would make to realizing the traditional goal of informed and impartial deliberation.[10] The worthy vision was never one of the races and sexes voting their preconceived preferences through their juror representatives. Rather, the democratic aim of the cross-sectional jury was to enhance the quality of deliberation by bringing diverse insights to bear on the evidence, each newly evaluating the case in light of some neglected detail or fresh perspective that a juror from another background offered the group.[*]

The noble purpose of such a jury was also to silence expressions of group prejudice and to ratchet up the deliberations to a higher level of generality. Jurors wishing to be persuasive would now have to abandon arguments that depended on the particular prejudices or perspectives of their own kind. Their arguments would have to resonate across group lines.[11]

---

[*]In 1990, Han Tak Lee, a Korean-born defendant, was found guilty of murdering his daughter by arson. No Asian-Americans served on the jury and several jurors indicated that they were swayed by the prosecutor's emphasis on Lee's lack of emotion when firefighters led him and his grieving wife to the charred cabin where their daughter's body was recovered. Following the guilty verdict, Asian-American groups rallied in support of Lee, pointing out that "his behavior during and after the fire was inexplicable to most Americans and appeared to convey his guilt—but it was perfectly in tune with Korean custom." The Rev. Joon Soo Choe, an organizer of the rally, said that "Korean fathers, even when they are feeling extreme sorrow, they can't cry." Jennifer Lin, "Was Jury Confused by Culture—or Did He Kill His Daughter?" *Philadelphia Inquirer*, April 28, 1992, p. A1.

   More recently, courts have begun to sever the connection between the
deliberative and representative features of the jury and to justify the
cross-sectional jury in terms borrowed from the world of interest group
politics. Cases and law reviews are full of language about the mythical
nature of impartial deliberation as the common law conceived it and
about the ubiquitous presence of subtle bias embedded in group identity
in America.[12] The new purpose of the cross section becomes to give voice
or representation to competing group loyalties, almost as if a juror had
been sent by constituents to vote their preferred verdict. Such a description of the representation we expect from jurors might explain why we call
the jury a democratic institution. But it is a vision of democracy so tied to
different groups voting their different interests that it cannot inspire confidence in the jury as an institution of justice. This is the predicament we
find ourselves in today.

The debate over forging representative juries is important in its own
regard. But it also joins the broader debates about the meaning of justice
in a multiethnic society. On one side of this debate stand those who hold
fast to the ideal of a color-blind Constitution and a world in which race,
sex, and national origin are irrelevant to legal rights and responsibilities.[13] On the other side are those who argue that justice requires more
than prohibiting discrimination, that it requires affirmative results. Those
on the latter side stress that democracy does not reach its ideals if blind
procedures leave significant groups underrepresented in our schools,
police forces, and elected and appointed offices. Beyond ending discrimination, they impose upon government and government-assisted programs
an obligation to achieve representation for minority and other groups in
proportion to their numbers in the population.[14]
   These arguments over group-blind versus group-conscious assignments spill over into the world of the jury. The leading question is
whether we have democratized jury selection by accomplishing the so-
called negative goal of not discriminating. Or does the principle of the
cross-sectional jury go beyond traditional color-blind norms, to impose on
jury commissioners the affirmative duty to achieve demographic balance
on the jury rolls? The difference between these two approaches is crucial.
In the first, it does not matter, for example, what race jurors are; justice is
satisfied so long as selection procedures make all persons equally eligible
for jury duty.[15] In the second, "proportional representation" view, an all-
white jury cannot possibly do justice to a black defendant, black victim,

or black civil litigant (or vice versa) no matter how color-blind the procedures are for selecting the jury.[16]

In 1992 two trials, a continent apart, did much to spawn cynicism
about the capacity of jurors to deliberate across racial lines. First, in the
Crown Heights section of Brooklyn, violence erupted between African-
Americans and Jews in 1991 after a car escorting a Hasidic rabbi struck
and killed a four-year-old black child. The violence left Yankel Rosenbaum, a visiting Hasidic student, dead. Lemrick Nelson, Jr., a black
teenager, was arrested for the murder, on the strength of the dying Rosenbaum's identification of his assailant and the fact that the murder weapon,
a knife, was found in Nelson's possession. Nonetheless, in what many
regarded as a verdict of racial loyalty, a jury of six African-Americans,
four Hispanics, and two whites acquitted Nelson of all charges.[*]

Meanwhile, in Los Angeles, many drew the same despairing conclusion about juries and racial justice from the notorious failure of a state
jury, which included no African-Americans, to convict four Los Angeles
police officers of beating Rodney King. The "universal assumption was
that ten whites, one Asian, and one Hispanic could not fairly decide a
case in which white police officers were accused of beating a black man,
or at least that a verdict of acquittal rendered by such a jury could never
be accepted as fair."[17]

What the King and Crown Heights cases did to spark cynicism about
race-conscious juries the 1994 Menendez verdicts did for gender-con-
scious juries. Erik and Lyle Menendez were jointly tried for the murder of
their parents before separate juries hearing evidence admissible only
against each brother. Their defense was sexual abuse by their father. Both
juries deadlocked, but the jury for Erik Menendez apparently split along
sexual lines, with six women holding out for voluntary manslaughter and
five of the six men voting first-degree murder (the sixth came in for second-degree murder). Media accounts stressed that the split "was not a

[*]Robert D. McFadden, "Teen-Ager Acquitted in Slaying During '91 Crown Heights Melee,"
New York Times, Oct. 30, 1992, p. A1; "Black Teenager Cleared in Jew's Death," *Philadelphia Inquirer*, Oct. 30, 1992, p. C1. The jury may not have been entirely wrong. In December 1993, witnesses provided new evidence suggesting that Nelson handed the knife to a
second man, now in prison on unrelated charges, who did the fatal stabbing. Partly on the
basis of this new information, Attorney General Janet Reno announced on January 25,
1994, that she would seek federal indictments in the Crown Heights case. Craig Wolff,
"Another Suspect Named in Slaying in Crown Heights," *New York Times*, Dec. 31, 1993, p.
A1; Stephen Labaton, "Reno to Take Over Inquiry into Slaying in Crown Heights," *New
York Times*, Jan. 26, 1994, p. A1.

coincidence" but was typical of the difference between "victim-sensitive women" sympathetic to sexual abuse charges and "cold-blooded men" more impressed by the brothers' money motives to murder.[18] Moreover, the six women on Erik Menendez's jury portrayed the men as "sexist," "homophobic," and incapable of entering into arguments with women. The message was clear—on real juries, men and women filter the evidence through different preconceptions, even different prejudices.

The cynicism prompted by the Crown Heights, King, and Menendez trials was unfortunate. I acknowledge the many empirical studies showing that race especially, but other demographic factors as well, influence jurors.[19] But just because jurors start from different places does not mean that they are doomed to deadlock; in fact, only about one in twenty juries fails to reach a unanimous verdict.[20] Nor do the empirical studies show that jurors are so captivated by narrow group loyalties that they typically vote in blocs, with conversation powerless to change views and deliberation a meaningless sideshow. Indeed, research indicates that "when jurors of different ethnic groups deliberate together, they are better able to overcome their individual biases."[21]

From personal experience as an assistant district attorney, I can add my own testimony that jurors cross demographic boundaries to reach unanimous verdicts in cases every day. The crossing is far from perfect, and in some areas—notably, death penalty cases—a breakdown in color-blind justice continues to haunt the system.*

But it would be wrong to ignore the considerable progress American juries have made from the openly bigoted deliberations reported for all-white juries of the 1950s[22] or to sour on continued efforts to devise a jury system that defines our common values, not just our different interests. The aspiration for jury behavior may outstrip the reality, but it is still an aspiration within our reach.

The story of how American society has struggled, failed, forgotten, and struggled again to create representative juries is a long one, and I turn to it now. My purpose is to defend the rise of the cross-sectional ideal insofar as it speaks to enriched deliberation across group lines and to criticize it insofar as it recommends mere proportional representation for group differences.

---

*Chapter 6 will take up the difficulties of juries deliberating on death.

JURY SELECTION PRIOR TO THE
CROSS-SECTIONAL IDEAL: THE CASE OF
THE ALL-WHITE JURY

In 1880 two cases came before the Supreme Court involving black men convicted of murder by all-white juries. In the case of *Strauder v. West Virginia*, exclusion of blacks from the jury was mandated by a state law restricting jury service to "white males."[23] In the case of *Virginia v. Rives*, Virginia law itself did not discriminate against blacks as jurors, but the actual pool of persons from which the jury for Burton and Lee Reynolds was drawn included no blacks. And it also appeared that no blacks had ever served on a jury in that county "in any case . . . in which their race had been in any way interested."[24] In deciding the *Strauder* and *Rives* cases, the Supreme Court distinguished between them in ways that still influence the course of jury selection.

On one level, the Court distinguished the cases in terms of the familiar contrast between de jure and de facto discrimination. The defendant Strauder proved that the absence of blacks from his jury was attributable to the deliberate design of the state and not to chance. For the majority of the Court, such legal discrimination was incompatible with the Fourteenth Amendment's guarantee of equal protection of the laws to black citizens.[25] By contrast, the Reynolds defendants in Virginia failed to convince the Court that the absence of blacks from their jury was due to a deliberate intent on the part of the state to exclude blacks. On its face, Virginia law made citizens between the ages of twenty-one and sixty eligible for jury duty, without regard to race. The only evidence cited to prove that state officials administered the law in a discriminatory fashion was the fact that no black persons were available to be selected as jurors in the Reynolds case or in any case in which their race was an interested party. But the 1880 Court was not yet prepared to treat such results as conclusive proof of an intent to exclude blacks.[26]

This was no doubt a stingy evidentiary decision by the Court that immediately defanged *Strauder*'s otherwise biting condemnation of de jure exclusion of blacks from juries. Still, even if one granted the possibility that the all-white jury in Virginia was the result of nondiscriminatory selection procedures, this would not have decided the *Rives* case. For the defendants' complaint was that they suffered prejudice from having to defend themselves before an all-white jury, no matter whether the whiteness of the jury came about through chance or design. They alleged "that a strong prejudice existed in the community of the county against them, independent of the merits of the case, and based solely upon the fact that they are negroes, and that the man they were accused of having murdered was a white man." On account of this prejudice, "they could not obtain an impartial trial before a jury exclusively composed of the white race."[27]

As a remedy, the defendants moved prior to their trial to have the panel of available jurors modified so that it would be one-third black. Such a motion, the Supreme Court rightly noted, went beyond a *Strauder*-like claim for neutral procedures in selecting jurors. The motion for a jury that was one-third black was premised on the existence of an affirmative right to have blacks actually included on the jury (that is, to have blacks represented in rough proportion to their population in the county). In other words, the focus of the defendants' motion was on whom the jurors were, not on how they came to be there.

The Virginia defendants were asking for a variant of the common-law mixed jury—a jury composed half and half of peers of both parties to a case. The mixed jury had enjoyed a long and ancient history, dating back at least to thirteenth-century England and still alive in the United States at the time of the *Rives* case.*

Typically, the right to a mixed jury was extended to marginal groups that lacked full legal equality in a society and who therefore could not easily be swept into a homogenized concept of trial by one's peers. One of the oldest examples of the mixed jury was the English Crown's requirement that Jews be present on the jury deciding lawsuits brought by a Christian against a Jew. More generally, the Crown sought to attract alien merchants to the realm by guaranteeing them trial by a jury of six aliens and six citizens.[28]

Understood against this background, the Virginia defendants' motion for a jury that was one-third black was a claim that society was so cleaved along racial lines that the jury had to be also. But the Supreme Court emphatically rejected the implied analogy between the legal status of blacks and aliens. Aliens might need the device of a mixed jury because they themselves were not citizens legally entitled to be jurors. But the

---

*In May 1867, a mixed jury of six blacks and six whites was impaneled to try Jefferson Davis for treason. This was the first time blacks ever were selected for a jury in the South. The government elected not to proceed with the trial, and Davis was released from custody in 1868. "The First Integrated Jury Impaneled in the United States, May, 1867," *Negro History Bulletin* 33 (October 1933): 134.

whole point of the Civil War amendments, according to the Court, was to abolish those forms of discrimination that made blacks legal aliens in their own state. Blacks were now eligible to be on the jury, and Virginia had recognized that eligibility. Because this was so, a "mixed jury [was] not essential to the equal protection of the laws."[29]

But why was the Court so opposed to any concept of proportional representation for the races on the jury? After all, if one started with *Strauder*'s refreshing acknowledgment of the depth of racial division in 1880, it would seem to follow that there was no such thing as an impartial all-white jury, no matter how fairly the particular whites were chosen. But this was exactly the skeptical conclusion, implicit in the idea of a mixed jury, that the Court staved off in *Rives*. In *Strauder*, the Court saw itself serving the traditional ideal of impartial justice across racial lines, by insisting that the state no longer deliberately pack the jury with members of only one race. West Virginia was not content to be neutral as to the race of jurors. It openly made white skin a qualification, thereby signaling to jurors that the state expected them to judge black defendants as their inferiors. By ending such racially discriminatory selection procedures, the Court was doing no more than forcing the state to practice the theory that justice is color-blind.

But if the Court were to order the remedy of a jury that was one-third black, it would be implicitly abandoning the ideal of color-blind justice. It would be acknowledging that racial prejudice was so deep that the only solution was to represent it—to include blacks on the jury so they would counterbalance the prejudices of whites. The significance of *Virginia v. Rives* was the Court's adamant refusal to admit that racial justice required such a racially conscious jury.*

---

*In a companion case to *Rives*, Supreme Court Justice Stephen Field expressed that refusal as follows: "The position that in cases where the rights of colored persons are concerned, justice will not be done to them unless they have a mixed jury, is founded upon the notion that in such cases white persons will not be fair and honest jurors. If this position be correct, there ought not to be any white persons on the jury where the interests of colored persons only are involved. The jury would not be an honest or fair one, of which any of its members should be governed in his judgment by other considerations than the law and the evidence, and that decision would hardly be considered just, which should be reached by a sort of compromise, in which the prejudices of one race were set off against the prejudices of the other." *Ex Parte Virginia*, 100 U.S. 339, 369 (1880) (Field, J., dissenting).

RACIAL DISCRIMINATION AFTER
STRAUDER: THE ELITE JURY

Strauder's promise to end racial discrimination in jury selection proved stillborn.[30] From 1880 to 1909, cases steadily came before the Supreme Court in which black defendants throughout the South drew the Court's attention to the fact that the Southern jury remained de facto all white. But, with alarming regularity, the Court invoked the authority of *Virginia v. Rives* to hold that the mere absence of blacks from a jury did not establish an intent to discriminate on the basis of race. Some typical cases include the following:

- In 1896, a black man indicted by an all-white grand jury in Washington County, Mississippi, for the murder of a white man complained that though there were "7000 colored citizens competent for jury service in the county . . . and 1500 whites qualified to serve as jurors . . . there had not been for a number of years any colored man ever summoned on the grand jury of said county court." The Supreme Court's response to this was only to say that "these facts, even if they had been proved and accepted, do not show that the rights of the accused were denied by the Constitution and laws of the state."[31]
- In 1903, a South Carolina black man appealed his murder conviction on the grounds that the grand jury indicting him was all white, even though blacks accounted for four-fifths of the population and of the registered voters in the county. The Supreme Court's decision fit the pattern: the mere disparity between the racial composition of the county and the racial makeup of the jury was not evidence that the state was purposely excluding blacks from the jury.[32]
- The story continued in Texas in 1906: although the county was one-fourth black, the Supreme Court found no evidence of a purpose to discriminate just because the grand jury indicting a black defendant was all white.[33]

By 1909, the Court's record of rebuffing equal protection challenges to jury selection methods was so unbroken that cases simply stopped coming the Court's way on the subject.[34] For an entire generation, the Court remained silent on jury selection. Then, in 1935, the Court reentered the fray in a more enlightened posture. In that year, for the first time, the Court looked beyond the face of the law and ruled that defendants could make out a prima facie case of discrimination through evidence of "long-continued, unvarying, and wholesale exclusion" of members of their race.[35] In the particularly odious case before it, the Court set aside a black teenager's conviction of rape by an all-white jury, relying on testimony from some of the county's elderly lifelong residents that no one could remember a black ever serving as a grand or trial juror in either the county where the defendant was indicted or the county where he was eventually tried. County officials' mere recitals that they did not consider race in selecting jurors were not sufficient to overcome the presumption that only discrimination could account for the absence of blacks, especially because the evidence in one county further showed that the abbreviation "col." appeared next to the names of all black males on the jury list.[36]

This new "systematic exclusion" theory marked progress in putting teeth back into *Strauder*, but it came nowhere close to ending the era of lily-white juries in the South.[37] Jury scholar Jon Van Dyke estimates that, from 1935 to 1975, the Supreme Court decided on average one case per term regarding discriminatory jury selection, usually ruling in favor of the challenge.[38] But the steady stream of cases requiring reversal indicated that, at ground level, the discrimination continued. A large part of the problem was that jury commissioners were under no affirmative obligation to make jury lists representative of the population, and so many kept on with attempts to fob off as coincidental the racial disparities in their jury lists. The best the courts could do, under the systematic exclusion theory, was to review cases on a one-on-one basis, to see whether the underrepresentation was of such a magnitude as to suggest intentional discrimination.

But it took egregious patterns of fact to satisfy the systematic exclusion standard of proof. In 1938, the Court found discrimination when no blacks had been summoned for grand or petit jury service in one Kentucky county from 1906 to 1938, even though eight thousand of the county's population of forty-eight thousand were black.[39] In 1939, the Court found blacks were systematically excluded from jury service in a Louisiana parish (county) for twenty years running.[40] In 1947, the Court reversed a Lauderdale County, Mississippi, death penalty conviction of a black man sentenced to death by an all-white jury; out of an adult black population of 12,511 in the county, only roughly 25 blacks met the jury requirement of being a qualified elector, and no black had served on a county jury in the previous thirty years.[41] In 1953, the Court found that

Fulton County, Georgia, commissioners drew names of jurors out of a box, but only after printing names of prospective white jurors on white tickets and names of prospective black jurors on yellow tickets.[42]

One common defense offered by jury commissioners when they were questioned as to why blacks were underrepresented on their jury lists was that it was a legitimate side effect of recruiting blue-ribbon juries.[43] Consider this 1959 episode from the federal district court in Georgia. In that year, federal jury commissioners added 559 new names to the court's pool of qualified jurors. Only 4 of the newly approved jurors were black, leaving the total percentage of blacks on the jury list at 5.9 percent in a district where 34.5 percent of the population was black. When asked to account for such a dramatic underrepresentation of blacks in the jury pool, one jury commissioner pled ignorance: the problem was that neither he nor any of the "key men" in the community with whom he consulted happened to know many qualified blacks personally.[44]

There was a second, more sinister reason why the blue-ribbon ideal so readily permitted the state to discriminate against blacks. The same jury commissioner who pled ignorance also testified that,

> unfortunate as it may be, I think the Negro community . . . does not qualify on the very grounds that we set up, of intelligence, integrity and ability to serve on those grounds alone. . . . I think anybody who reads the papers and knows about the educational levels of our State would have to admit, reluctantly if he wants, that there is no question but that there . . . aren't numerically as many of them that are qualified in terms of the same educational standards.[45]

It should come as no surprise that juries selected through prejudice deliberated with prejudice. In the 1950s, the University of Chicago undertook a massive empirical study of the American jury. In regard to black defendants, the study suggested two conclusions about jury verdicts. First, all-white juries had trouble taking seriously violence within the black community, especially within the black family. They treated black defendants in such cases as parents treat children, dismissing their crimes as "what one expects from a Negro."[46] Second, all-white juries reacted with severity to black defendants charged with violence against whites, convicting them in disproportionate numbers.[47]

In his classic study of American racism, the Swedish sociologist Gunnar Myrdal singled out the all-white jury for giving racial prejudice its safest harbor in the South. The jury system, Myrdal noted, was a form of "extreme democracy" that worked tolerably for cases involving only members of the majority group, which "controls the court. . . . [But it] causes . . . the gravest peril of injustice in all cases where the rights of persons belonging to a disfranchised group are involved." Myrdal found that grand juries refused to indict "when the offender is a white man and the victim a Negro." "It is notorious," he added, "that practically never have white lynching mobs been brought to court in the South, even when the killers are known to all in the community and are mentioned by name in the local press." By contrast, "when the offender is a Negro, indictment is easily obtained and no such difficulty at the start will meet the prosecution of the case."[48]

Two of the most infamous cases of all times bear out Myrdal's portrait of the all-white jury's extreme version of democracy. On March 25, 1931, two groups of young drifters, one white and one black, were riding a freight train across northern Alabama. A fight broke out, ending with all but one of the whites thrown off the train. By the time the train pulled into the depot at Paint Rock, a sheriff and posse were waiting. The posse rounded up nine black youths from the forty-two car train, and also came across two young white women, wearing men's caps and overalls. When one woman said she had been raped by the blacks, the nine blacks were whisked off to Scottsboro, indicted within a week and brought to trial for their lives before two weeks had passed. Eight of the nine "Scottsboro Boys" were found guilty and sentenced to death by all-white juries in four separate trials lasting less than a day each (a mistrial was declared for the ninth defendant, a thirteen-year-old, when several jurors held out for the death penalty even though the prosecutor sought only life imprisonment). Although the Scottsboro Boys were indigent and illiterate, the trial judge made no serious attempt to appoint counsel for them, first appointing all members of the local bar to assist them and then placing the defense in the hands of a lawyer from Chattanooga, Tennessee, who had met the defendants only minutes before the first trial began. It took the intervention of the United States Supreme Court to stay the Scottsboro executions and grant new trials with adequate representation. Subsequently, one of the two women admitted to lying about being raped.[49]

The Emmett Till case is perhaps the single worst instance of the all-white jury's quickness to acquit whites charged with crimes against blacks. Fourteen-year-old Till was shot through the head and dumped in the Tallahatchie River with a fan tied to his neck, by two men who thought Till had talked freshly to the wife of one of the men. At trial, Moses Wright identified the two defendants as the men who came to Wright's house and kidnapped Till the night of the murder. But it took the all-white jury only one hour and seven minutes to acquit the defendants. Said one juror, "If we hadn't stopped to drink pop, it wouldn't have taken that long."[50]

SEX DISCRIMINATION IN JURY SELECTION

The history of discrimination against women in the selection of juries runs deep into the common law. Sir William Blackstone thought it obvious that women were disqualified from jury service *propter defectum sexus* ("on account of the defect of sex").[51] But the common law did impanel a "jury of matrons" when a possible pregnancy affected an inheritance claim or the scheduling of a prisoner's execution. Loath to hang a pregnant woman, authorities turned to all-female panels to certify that the pregnancy was real rather than feigned.[52]

Early colonial records from Virginia make clear that a jury of matrons was known in the New World. In 1633, Margaret Hatch was "sentenced to be hanged; pleads pregnancy; and jury of Matrons find 'her not pregnant.'" In 1679, in Accomack County, an infant "bastard child" was found dead as a result of circumstances indicating foul play. The coroner's inquest jury was composed entirely of women, who watched for any telltale changes in the corpse's appearance when each of three suspects touched it.[53]

Into the eighteenth century, witchcraft proceedings also occasioned another exceptional circumstance where all-female juries or committees were charged "to inspect and search [the defendant's] body whether any suspicious signs or marks did appear that were not common or that were preternatural."[54]

Outside of such special issues calling for so-called women's wisdom, or a woman's perspective, females remained disqualified from jury service in the colonies and then the United States until late in the nineteenth century. The suffrage movement included jury eligibility among the rights of political participation it sought for women.[55] The movement's first, momentary success occurred in 1870 when the Wyoming Territory granted women the right to vote and hold office; a few local trial courts thereafter permitted women to serve on juries because, theoretically, voter eligibility and jury eligibility went together.

   The very first jury to include men and women appears to have served in Laramie City, Wyoming, in March 1870.[56] In their history of the suffrage struggle, Elizabeth Cady Stanton, Susan Anthony, and Matilda Joslyn Gage reported that newspapers from New Orleans to Philadelphia criticized the Wyoming example as defying the "laws of delicacy," and threatening "all distinctions of sex . . . with swift obliteration."[57] A rhyme captured the counterreaction: "Baby, baby, don't get in a fury; Your mamma's gone to sit on the jury."[58] Women were needed at home, women were too delicate for the vulgar world of trial testimony, women were too emotional to abide by the disciplines of evidence: all these rationales stood behind the barrier against women on juries.[59] By September 1871, women disappeared from Wyoming juries.[60]

   In 1898, Utah became the first state to break the sex barrier and authorize women to serve on juries.[*] Washington followed in 1911, Kansas in 1912, Nevada in 1914, California in 1917, and Michigan in 1918.[61] The ratification of the Nineteenth Amendment in 1920 spurred additional states to qualify women for jury service, but it was not until the 1940s that a majority of the states made women eligible as jurors.[62]

   But making women legally eligible for jury duty was not the same as treating them equally. As late as 1975, several states continued to run a two-track system of jury selection. Men were drafted but women had to volunteer.[63] The different recruitment procedures for the sexes was justified in terms of women's "special responsibility" for the family.[64] As recently as 1961, Supreme Court cases approved of such self-exemption programs for women, even if they resulted in virtually all-male jury lists.[65] Not until 1975 did the Constitution begin to definitively require that the jury pool represent women as equally as men.[66]

   As with exclusion of black jurors, the absence of women on the jury marred the impartiality of deliberations, especially in cases involving rape and domestic violence. The University of Chicago Jury Project found that the 1950s, when rape cases were decided by predominantly male juries, was an era of leniency toward rape defendants. In trials of aggravated rape, involving violence extrinsic to the act of rape itself, juries

---

[*]*Taylor v. Louisiana*, 419 U.S. 522, 533, n. 13. Until 1957, federal jurors were to have the qualifications required by the states in which the federal court was sitting. Thus, as long as state law disqualified women, federal juries impaneled in that state remained all male. It was not until the Civil Rights Act of 1957 that Congress made citizens eligible to serve on federal juries without regard to sex.

were willing to convict. But in cases of so-called simple rape, jurors agreed on the "contributory fault" of the victim or her "assumption of risk" and acquitted defendants of rape charges in thirty-seven of forty-two cases studied (although in nine of these cases the jury did convict of a lesser charge). In explaining why juries acquitted when they would have found the defendant guilty of rape, presiding judges sounded similar themes. One speculated that the jury "probably figured the girl asked for what she got," after being raped following a beer-drinking party; another judge thought the jury unwilling to find rape "where [a] woman involved went to public dance and was picked up by defendant."[67]

There were also telltale signs of sex-biased deliberations in regard to women as defendants. In 1957 Gwendolyn Hoyt bludgeoned her husband to death with a baseball bat, following a failed attempt to save their marriage. Florida law at the time still exempted women from jury duty unless they volunteered. The result was that women constituted only 0.1 percent of the jury list, even though they accounted for 52 percent of the county's population and 40 percent of registered voters. Predictably, Hoyt's jury included no women, and she was convicted of second-degree murder.[68]

In her appeal to the Supreme Court, Hoyt argued that "the nature of the crime of which she was convicted peculiarly demanded the inclusion of persons of her own sex on the jury." This was so because her defense at trial was temporary insanity brought on during a fight with her husband over his infidelity and his rejection of her efforts at reconciliation. Women jurors, Hoyt argued, would have been more understanding or compassionate than men in pondering her insanity defense.*

The Supreme Court dismissed Hoyt's complaint as "misconceiv[ing] the scope of the right to an impartially selected jury." The right did not include "a jury tailored to the circumstances of the particular case, whether relating to the sex or other condition of the defendant, or to the nature of the charges to be tried." The Court went on to affirm the right of Florida to grant exemptions to women on account of their special responsibilities at home, even if this left defendants like Hoyt with all-male juries. Before the Supreme Court would overrule *Hoyt* and end open dis-

---

*Echoes of this Florida case could be heard in Lorena Bobbitt's acquittal in 1994, when a jury of seven women and five men agreed that a history of prior abuse had driven Bobbitt temporarily insane when she picked up a knife and severed part of her husband's penis. David Margolick, "Lorena Bobbitt Acquitted in Mutilation of Husband," *New York Times*, Jan. 22, 1994, p. A1.

crimination against women in jury selection, the ideal of the cross-sectional jury would have to be promoted.

THE RISE OF THE CROSS-SECTIONAL IDEAL

In the 1940 case *Smith v. Texas*, the Supreme Court for the first time referred to the need to make the jury a "body truly representative of the community."[69] Such a phrase suggested a reform of jury selection procedures going beyond a simple ban on racial discrimination. It suggested what *Virginia v. Rives* had rejected—inclusion of blacks on juries in proportion to their numbers in the eligible adult population. And it suggested that this right of representation extended not just to the races but to all groups in the community.

But the looming battles over exactly what it meant to revamp the jury into a representative body had not yet come into focus. The concern of the *Smith* court was still with racial discrimination of a familiar, if abysmal, sort. On its facts, the *Smith* case once more presented the Court with clear evidence that "chance and accident alone could hardly have brought about the listing for grand jury service of [only five] negroes from among the thousands shown by the undisputed evidence to possess the legal qualifications for jury service."[70] It was only in this context that Justice Hugo Black, writing for the Court, could say almost in passing that it was "part of the established tradition in the use of juries as instruments of public justice that the jury be a body truly representative of the community."

So long as what was meant by a "representative" jury was a jury selected without discrimination, the emerging ideal could coexist with the traditional practice of using supposedly elite juries. For instance, in 1942 a committee of federal judges issued a report on the federal jury system, detailing instances of discrimination and calling on courts to impanel more racially representative juries. But the same report explicitly endorsed the key man system, noting that "nothing in the concept [of representative juries] opposes the tradition of federal courts that jurors should be men of recognized intelligence and probity."[71]

However, these early attempts to stave off the tension between elite jurors and representative jurors proved short-lived. Soon debate spilled over from the legal periodicals to the popular journals concerning what kind of juror was wanted. To federal judge Jerome Frank, the choice was obvious: we could have a democratic jury or we could have a knowledge-able jury but we could not have both. Frank therefore urged reforms that would make the jury less representative of the community.[72] Taking up his cry, a whole school of elitist critics of the concept of a representative jury arose during the 1940s and 1950s, urging that jurors be carefully screened by being subjected to newly available psychological tests for intelligence and lack of prejudice.[73]

In the midst of this debate, the Supreme Court hesitated about how far to push the mass democratic implications of the representative ideal. For instance, in 1946 and 1947 two cases came before the Court raising the issue of whether a jury pool had to fairly represent the laboring popula-tion. In the case involving a federal jury, the Court invoked its inherent supervisory power over the federal courts to prohibit one court's practice of deliberately excluding all persons known to work for a daily wage from the jury list, on the assumption that jury service would be a financial hardship for them. No matter how well intentioned the exclusion, the Court feared that such an open departure from the cross-sectional ideal "would encourage whatever desires those responsible for the selection of jury panels may have to discriminate against persons of low economic and social status." It would "breathe life into any latent tendencies to establish the jury as the instrument of the economically and socially priv-ileged." Moreover, the Court was emphatic that "jury competence is not limited to those who earn their livelihood on other than a daily basis. One who is paid $3 a day may be as fully competent as one who is paid $30 a week or $300 a month."[74]

But when it came to reviewing the lack of representation of laborers on a state jury the following year, the Court refused to apply the representa-tive ideal.[75] At issue was the long-standing practice in New York of impaneling so-called special juries in cases of unusual intricacy, impor-tance, or publicity. Special jurors were chosen after personal interviews that were alleged by defendants to imbalance the jury against fair repre-sentation of manual laborers. In the particular case before it, the Court refused to find that such underrepresentation had been proven. But even if it had been proven, the Court emphasized that the Constitution did not prohibit New York from preferring elite over representative jurors:

All were subjected to the same tests of intelligence, citizenship and understanding of English. The state's right to apply these tests is not open to doubt even though they disqualify, especially in the conditions that prevail in New York, a disproportionate number of manual workers. A fair application of literacy, intelligence and other tests would hardly act with proportional equality on all levels of life.[76]

Matters stood in this mixed position until the civil rights movement of the 1960s caught up with the jury. As we saw earlier, Congress formalized the cross-sectional requirement for federal juries in the Jury Selection and Service Act of 1968.[77] Abolishing the elite jury and the key man selection system, the law mandated random selection procedures, beginning with the use of names from voter registration lists or lists of actual voters.[78] These lists could be supplemented with other sources whenever their exclusive use failed to serve the overall policy of achieving proportionate representation on the jury rolls for all "distinct," or "cognizable," groups in the community.*

Under the new law, a jury plan did not meet the test for cross-sectionality merely because it was nondiscriminatory. The law's novelty was that government now bore the additional, affirmative obligation to include members of cognizable groups, in proportion to their percentage of the voting population or population registered to vote. Federal jury selectors were to start with the voter registration list or actual voter list for their judicial district and then pick an "interval number" (arrived at by calculating what percentage of voters on the source list would be needed for jury duty over a given period of time). Next, they were to choose names from the assigned intervals and place them on the master jury wheel for the jurisdiction. Questionnaires were then to be mailed to a random sample of people whose names were on the master wheel, to determine whether these persons were qualified for jury service.

At this stage of selection, the new congressional law removed all discretionary authority from the jury commissioners. All persons returning the qualification form were deemed qualified unless it appeared from the form or other competent evidence that the person was (1) not a U.S. citizen eighteen years of age who has resided in the judicial district for at

---

*A cognizable group is any "recognizable, distinct class, singled out for different treatment under the laws, as written or applied." *Castanada v. Partida*, 430 U.S. 482, 494 (1977). Courts have found cognizable groups to include those based on race, sex, national origin, religion, and economic status. Cf. *United States v. Sanchez-Lopez*, 879 F. 3d 541 (9th Cir. 1989) (Hispanics); *United States v. Black Bear*, 878 F. 2d 213 (8th Cir. 1985) (Native Americans). The young have not been found to be a cognizable group for jury selection purposes. *Barber v. Ponte*, 772 F. 2d 982, vacated, 772 F. 2d 996, 1000 (1st Cir. 1985), overruling *United States v. Butera*, 420 F. 2d 564 (1st Cir. 1970).

least one year; (2) unable to read, write, or understand English sufficiently to fill out the qualification form; (3) unable to speak English; (4)
incapacitated by mental or physical infirmity so as to be unable to render
jury service; or (5) a convicted felon or facing pending felony charges.
Names of all persons found to be qualified then went into the qualified
jury wheel. As needed, names were then publicly drawn at random from
the wheel. Those whose names were drawn were sent summonses to
appear in court as part of the pool of persons from which grand or trial
juries would be chosen.[79]

The final labor for the representative ideal came in the 1975 case of
Taylor v. Louisiana. Here, the Supreme Court elevated the cross-sectional
requirement from statutory to constitutional law by holding that the very
meaning of the Sixth Amendment guarantee of trial by an "impartial" jury
required that the jury be drawn from a representative cross section of the
population.[80] The *Taylor* Court did not go so far as to say that the jury
finally seated had to be a representative sample of the community.* The
defendant's rights were adequately protected so long as jury lists and jury
venires were fair cross sections of the community. As long as this were
true, government could not tilt jury verdicts by reserving jury eligibility to
favored classes.

THE SHIFTING MEANING OF A REPRESENTATIVE JURY: A COMPARISON OF TWO CASES

Between the time of the Court's first mention of the representative ideal in
1940 and its constitutionalization of the concept in 1975, there occurred
a subtle, unacknowledged but unmistakable, shift in the arguments the
Court made to justify the cross-sectional ideal. That shift can be documented by comparing two cases, separated by a generation, in which the
Court worked out the implications of the cross-sectional ideal for the right
of women to serve as jurors.

---

*"We impose no requirement that petit juries actually chosen must mirror the community
and reflect the various distinctive groups in the population. Defendants are not entitled to a
jury of any particular composition." *Taylor v. Louisiana,* 419 U.S. at 538. See also *Lockhart
v. McCree,* 476 U.S. 162, 173 (1986) ("We have never invoked the fair cross-section principle . . . to require petit juries, as opposed to jury panels or venires, to reflect the composition of the community at large"); *Batson v. Kentucky,* 476 U.S. 79, 85 (1986) (defendant has
no right to a "petit jury composed in whole or in part of persons of his own race," quoting
Strauder v. West Virginia, 100 U.S. at 305).

BALLARD V. UNITED STATES

In California in 1943 Edna Ballard and her son were convicted of conducting a fraudulent religious scheme through the federal mails. At that time, California was among the majority of states that had moved to qualify women for jury service. According to then prevailing federal law, the fact that women were eligible to serve as state jurors in California made them eligible as well to serve on the juries of any federal court sitting in that state. Nonetheless, the federal district court sitting in southern California conceded that it had intentionally excluded women from both the grand jury that had indicted Ballard and her son and the trial jury that convicted them. The rationale for the exclusion was the court's feeling that the courthouse lacked sufficient accommodations for women jurors.[81]

Exercising its supervisory powers, the Supreme Court declared that such a deliberate exclusion of women (in a jurisdiction where they were legally eligible to serve) violated the obligation "to make the jury 'a cross-section of the community' and truly representative of it."[82]

But why were women necessary to make the jury pool representative of the community? Exactly what were women to represent that men did not already represent? Here, the Court confronted the "sameness versus difference" question that was hotly debated, then as now, among advocates of gender equality.[83] The sameness argument stressed the irrelevance of gender to the work of juries and, for that very reason, the right of women to serve on the same terms as men. The difference argument placed emphasis on the unique contributions women would make to the quality of justice, drawing on their fundamentally different station in life and experiences about which men knew little.[84] *Ballard* gingerly expressed the difference argument in this way:

It is not enough to say that women when sitting as jurors neither act nor tend to act as a class. Men likewise do not act as a class. But, if the shoe were on the other foot, who would claim that a jury was truly representative of the community if all men were intentionally and systematically excluded from the panel? The truth is that the two sexes are not fungible; a community made up exclusively of one is different from a community composed of both; the subtle interplay of influence one on the other is among the imponderables. To insulate the courtroom from either may not in a given case make an iota of difference. Yet a flavor, a distinct quality is lost if either sex is excluded.[85]

This is a tense passage in which the Court walked a fine line between two opposing points of view. On the one hand, the Court shunned the view that women jurors were there to represent women as a class. There was no evidence, the Court noted, that women jurors vote as a bloc any more than men vote as a bloc. There was no reason to believe that sex somehow prejudiced and predetermined female views, but not male views, on a case.

On the other hand, the Court also shied away from the view that, because women and men do not vote as separate blocs, the sex of jurors is irrelevant to the group's deliberations. The Court found it difficult to explain how sexual difference matters—it was "among the imponderables," a matter of "subtle interplay of influence" between the sexes, a "flavor, a distinct quality" lost to the jury when either sex is excluded. Using phrases such as these, the Court struggled to carve out its middle ground. I believe that the Court was trying to say that we can best understand the contribution women make as jurors by concentrating not on the act of voting but on the act of deliberating. The presence of women changes and enriches the deliberations for men and women alike. The "subtle interplay" pushes each sex to consider facts they might have ignored in the absence of the other or to consider them from a new point of view.*

But looking at facts from a new point of view has nothing to do with looking at them from a self-interested or group-interested point of view. The purpose of having a woman's perspective on events is to elicit the richer and more rounded conversation that occurs when that perspective

---

*A compelling 1917 short story by Susan Glaspell centers on differences in the way women and men perceive and judge a woman's murder of her husband. A neighbor discovers the husband strangled to death with a rope. The neighbor and sheriff, their wives, and the city attorney return to the house to search for evidence of a motive. The men skip the kitchen as a place that might harbor murder clues and concentrate their search on places such as bedrooms and the barn. Left alone in the kitchen, the women's attention is drawn to domestic items such as sewing; they quickly notice that the woman's usually careful stitching went terribly awry at one point, as if she had suffered some shock. Eventually, their affinity with a homemaker's world leads them to a sewing box, in which they find a dead canary, its neck broken in quite the same way as the husband's.

Not only do the women find facts the men overlook, but they judge the murder differently, going so far as to suppress the evidence. To them, the canary was the woman's only relief from a severe and harsh husband. They sympathize with her desperation but know that she will not get a jury of her peers. Susan Glaspell, "A Jury of Her Peers," in *The Best Short Stories of 1917*, ed. E. J. O'Brien (Boston, Mass.: Small, Maynard and Co., 1918), pp. 256–82.

challenges the settled but perhaps parochial understanding men alone have of the issue, and vice versa. Thus it is a matter of reaching a common understanding of events that no one person and no one sex could reach alone. The fact that, in the end, the sexes do not vote as blocs is a sign that the deliberation has worked to produce a verdict persuasive across gender lines.

Ballard itself is a textbook example of the difference women might have made to the content of jury deliberation. When a mother and son were being prosecuted for promoting an allegedly fraudulent religious movement, the Court considered it quite possible that exclusion of women from the jury was "highly prejudicial" to the defendants. The jury was being called upon to make a fine judgment: were Mrs. Ballard and her son guilty of fraud because they themselves did not believe in the religion but were only using it to bilk people through the mail? The Court quoted at length from the opinion of an appellate judge who, in dissenting from his court's upholding of the Ballards' conviction, noted the different conversation that might have taken place in the presence of women jurors:

> The souls of children . . . receive the first and most lasting teaching of religious truths from their mothers. . . . In the churches of all religions the numbers of women attendants on divine service vastly exceed men. The one large and vital religious group created in America since Joseph Smith is that of the Christian Scientists, founded by a woman, Mary Baker Eddy. . . .
>
> It matters not from my viewpoint [the defendants were justly convicted]. I am not a woman juror sitting in the Ballard trial, who is the mother of five children at whose knee have been instilled in them the teachings of Jesus as interpreted by Mrs. Eddy. . . . Well could a sensitive woman . . . rationalize all the money income acquired by Mrs. Ballard as being devoted to the teachings of the same Jesus as are the profits of the trust created by Mrs. Eddy for the Christian Science Monitor.[86]

The point of this illustration is to show that the absence of women from the *Ballard* jury undercut confidence in the ultimate verdict. As the reference to Christian Science indicated, every new religion is heavily involved in soliciting funds, and the faithful who give those funds do not see themselves as victims of fraud. Women, according to the Court, would have been more likely than men to push this line of inquiry during the deliberation, forcing everyone to define more clearly the line that separates fraud from faith.[87]

TAYLOR V. LOUISIANA

Billy J. Taylor was a man tried, convicted, and sentenced to death by a Louisiana jury for the crime of aggravated kidnapping. The death sentence was set aside, but Taylor appealed his conviction to the Supreme Court in 1975, claiming that his constitutional right to "trial by a jury of a representative segment of the community" was denied to him by the systematic underrepresentation of women on the jury list.[88]

Taylor's appeal presented the Supreme Court with the intriguing question of how a male defendant could be claiming prejudice from the absence of a fair number of women in the jury pool. Taylor could hardly be understood as claiming that as a man he suffered prejudice at the hands of a virtually all-male jury panel. Nor was it plausible for a person charged with kidnapping to suggest that the state had an interest in excluding women from the trial of a kidnapper! Given the absence of any showing of bias or prejudice to the defendant, a minority of the Court would have upheld Taylor's conviction and dismissed the underrepresentation of women as harmless error in his case.

Interestingly enough, the Court majority never disputed the fact that Taylor was unable to show any actual bias to himself. Nonetheless, the Court held that Taylor was denied his constitutional right to an impartial jury because, by definition, no jury was impartial unless it was drawn from sources representative of all segments of the community.[89]

But what did the *Taylor* court mean by so conflating the meaning of "impartiality" and "representativeness"? Traditionally, the first term referred to the mental state of an individual juror—the person's ability to hear the evidence with disinterested and dispassionate neutrality. But in *Taylor*, the term came to mean something quite different, almost opposite. The claim that only a representative jury was an impartial jury rested on the argument that, because we live in a community of "diversely biased people," a jury achieved impartiality only by representing the full range of the people's prejudices. In other words, impartiality was accomplished by turning the traditional search for disinterested jurors on its head: we should realistically admit that jury deliberation is but the interplay of group biases. Paradoxical as it sounds, the *Taylor* court was committed to the notion that the most impartial jury was the jury that most accurately reflected the mix of popular prejudices. The Court itself quoted with approval this passage in a House report urging passage of the 1968 Jury Selection and Service Act:

It must be remembered that the jury is designed not only to understand the case, but also to reflect the community's sense of justice in deciding it. As long as there are significant departures from the cross-sectional goal, biased juries are the result—biased in the sense that they reflect a slanted view of the community they are supposed to represent.[90]

The revealing aspect of this quotation is how it connected one view of an impartial jury (the jury that understands the case) to another view (the jury that understands the community). The implication was that there is not one but many ways to understand cases. In the critical words of Sen. Sam Ervin, the cross-sectional principle could easily degenerate into "suggest[ions] that the search for truth . . . is . . . a partisan operation, [that] justice is one thing for the hyphenated American, another for the New England Yankee."[91] Or as Van Dyke, a sympathetic commentator, summarized the shifting sense of impartiality implicit in the cross-sectional ideal:

[A] randomly selected jury will not necessarily be "impartial" in the strict sense of that term, because the jurors bring to the jury box prejudice and perspectives gained from their lifetimes of experience. But they will be impartial in the sense that they will reflect the range of the community attitudes, which is the best we can do.[92]

Perhaps the clearest statement of the new theory of impartiality driving the need to construct cross-sectional juries came from a California Supreme Court opinion in 1978. The Court started out with a noncontroversial statement that it would be "unrealistic to expect jurors to be devoid of opinions, preconceptions, or even deep-rooted biases derived from their life experiences in such groups." Given these deep roots of bias in prospective jurors of this race or that religion,

the only practical way to achieve an overall impartiality is to encourage the representation of a variety of such groups on the jury so that the respective biases of their members, to the extent they are antagonistic, will tend to cancel each other out.[93]

This reference to canceling out the competing biases built into identity in America was striking. Absent was any sense that members of different groups brought much of value to the conversation; the cross-sectional requirement lost the high ground it deserved and became a weak prophylactic attempt to "balance the biases." Philosophically, such a checks-and-balances program for the jury was reminiscent of Madisonian solutions to interest group politics elsewhere in America. But to hear juries conceived of in interest group terms, one group's juror checking another group's juror, was jarring. The cross-sectional ideal, which promised so much in the way of enriching jury deliberation, instead became wed to a cynic's view of juries, in which there was not one justice for juries to represent but multiple justices reducible to whom a juror happened to be by race, sex, national origin, religion, occupation, income, educational level, and on and on.

In *Ballard*, the chief justification for the cross-sectional requirement remained the contribution that people from different walks of life made to the deliberative process—a contribution that sometimes took the form of silencing the prejudice of others and at other times of bringing more knowledge to bear on the problem. Because the *Ballard* Court was still a believer in the classical ideal of informed and impartial deliberation, it felt compelled to show how the deliberations in the particular case before it might indeed have been enriched by the arguments (not biases) of women jurors.

In *Taylor*, the Court continued to refer to the contribution the cross-sectional requirement made to impartial deliberation. But this was no longer the chief rationale behind the ideal. Instead, the principal virtue of a representative jury was its contribution to the jury's political function.

"Political function" is the Supreme Court's exact term in *Taylor*.[94] And the justices were, to their credit, frank about the politics of justice. The jury's political function, according to the Court, was to legitimize the verdict to the population at large and to preserve public confidence in the justice of the verdict. The jury best played this role of "selling" the verdict when all parts of the community saw the verdict as its own. But this legitimizing function of the jury, the Court warned well before the world ever heard of Rodney King, was threatened any time the jury failed to represent adequately a particular group in the community. As one federal judge explained:

> Our jury system has often fallen short of the mark. Its deficiency has inhered not in the quality of the verdicts individual juries have reached, which in the main have reflected understanding and judgment, but in the failure of the institution to include all segments of the community in its operation, thereby . . . jeopardizing that appearance of justice which . . . is as important as the actuality of justice.[95]

This attempt to justify the cross-sectional ideal by reference to its contribution to the appearance rather than the actuality of justice is disturbing. It makes the purpose of the cross-sectional theory a nakedly political one, bent on popularizing the verdict, and divorces the concept wholly from what in the earlier cases was the contribution it indeed would make to insulating justice from popular prejudice.

When the cross-sectional ideal is justified in terms of its ability to sell the verdict, the representative jury is brought into line with the general theory of representative government. Just as Congress helps keep the peace among competing interest groups by giving each group the opportunity to participate in making the politics of the nation, so the jury keeps the peace among competing groups by giving each of them the opportunity to participate in making the justice of the community. But now there is no longer anything special about the jury as an institution of justice that exempts it from the normal barter and compromises of representative democracy. The way to justice, we are told, is not through some mythic course of impartial deliberation floating free of racial, gender, ethnic, and economic bias. Justice, alas, is reached by miring the jury in representing those subtle, imponderable but inescapable biases and preferences we all imbibe along with our group identities.

THE CROSS-SECTIONAL IDEAL VERSUS PROPORTIONAL REPRESENTATION: EMERGING CONFLICTS

Has the Supreme Court proved willing to carry through with the full implications of its 1975 decision equating a jury's impartiality with its representativeness? Logically speaking, *Taylor* pushes toward the conclusion the Court most wishes to disown—namely, that groups need to be proportionately represented on the trial jury itself. After all, as numerous commentators have pointed out, if balancing group perspectives is as important to achieving impartiality as the *Taylor* decision says it is, then the place to represent groups is not just on the jury list or jury pool; the desired interaction takes place only in the jury room.[96]

A number of practical considerations explain the Court's hesitancy to play out the full logic of the cross-sectional ideal. Americans are divided into so many different and overlapping groups that there would not be room on the jury to represent all groups in the community.[97] Moreover, in the United States, "groups" means many things; it is a fluid term. In one case, the issue might be whether white ethnics constitute a group needing to be represented as such; in another case, any requirement to make the jury a mirror of the community might raise the question about whether African-American women are a distinct group from African-American men or Norwegian-Americans are a distinct group from Swedish-Americans.[98] There would be no end to the calculations. Thus, for sufficient practical reasons, the *Taylor* Court drew the line where it did.[99]

Still, the line drawn where it is lacks sense. *Taylor* and the 1968 congressional reform law suggest one theory—proportional representation—for drawing up master jury lists, yet they are not posed to maintain any balance for group views on actual juries.*

That the Court balks at following through with the logic of proportional representation tells us much about the instability of the Court's starting point. At its best, the cross-sectional principle represents the common sense that "different groups have different contributions to make to the jury."[100] But *Taylor* went awry by adopting a skeptic's account of the "something" that diversity contributes to jury deliberations: group identity was reduced to the baggage of bias and prejudice, one group's bias necessary only to counter another group's bias. Such a description of the cross-sectional jury could quite easily suggest to those chosen that "he or she is filling some predetermined 'slot.'"[101]

The Court's flight from such implications of cross-sectional analysis shows the need for going back to cases such as *Ballard* and regaining our

---

*Some commentators, and a few jurisdictions, do accept the logic of guaranteeing some level of group representation on actual juries. In 1992 the district attorney for Hennepin County, Minnesota, recommended assigning two seats on every twenty-three-member grand jury to eligible members of a racial minority. In 1985, law professor Sheri Lynn Johnson argued that black, Hispanic, and Native American defendants have a constitutional right to "racially similar jurors." She suggested three as a practical number of reserved seats. Johnson, "Black Innocence and White Jury," pp. 1695–70. See also Johnson, "Unconscious Racism and the Criminal Law," *Cornell Law Review* 73 (1988): 1024 ("what black defendants need is not purification of voir dire procedures, but black jurors").

In 1970, the *Yale Law Journal* published "The Case for Black Juries," in which the authors suggested that "every jury be proportionately representative of the black *population* in the vicinage." Actually, this proposal for proportional representation was limited to "Black Belt counties of the rural South," where the black population was sufficiently large to ensure "juries that are at least three-quarters black [in] most cases." In the North, where black and white populations were less interspersed, the authors preferred to solve the problem of black representation on juries by deliberately redrawing judicial districts "so that each black community would constitute a jury district." This would result in "all-black juries" for cases arising within the bounds of the black community. "The Case for Black Juries," *Yale Law Journal* 79 (1970): 546–50.

bearings. There, the purpose of the cross-sectional jury was not to recruit jurors to represent the "deep-rooted biases" of their section of town; it was to draw jurors together in a conversation that, although animated by different perspectives, still strove to practice a justice common to all perspectives. This is a noble justification for the cross-sectional ideal and one that defends the aspiration for jurors who render verdicts across all the fault lines of identity in America.

FROM THEORY TO PRACTICE: USE OF VOTER LISTS TO GENERATE MASTER JURY LISTS

Contemporary debates over the cross-sectional ideal are of more than theoretical interest. At the practical level, two major changes are taking place today, as jury selection makes itself over in the cross-sectional image. The first change is at the initial stage of recruiting jurors, where long-approved use of voter lists and registration lists as a source of juror names has come under attack for leaving minorities underrepresented. Debates over use of the voter lists to generate the master jury list raise the question of how mathematically exact the representation of groups on the jury rolls must be. There is also the issue of whether a perfectly neutral and nondiscriminatory plan for selecting jurors is invalid nonetheless if it fails to achieve the desired demographic balance among prospective jurors. Obviously, these issues about balanced results versus blind selection are ones that Americans fiercely debate elsewhere, in school assignments, affirmative action programs, and the creation of minority voting districts.[102] The voter list controversy is a case study of a society struggling to mesh the directives of cross-sectional justice (to monitor the demographics of the jury list) with the older imperatives of color-blind justice (to ignore the identity behind the name).

The second stage at which the cross-sectional principle is forcing change is in the final moments of selection, when lawyers exercise so-called peremptory challenges to eliminate unwanted persons from the jury pool. Historically, lawyers could exercise these challenges for any reason at all. In particular, prior to 1986, lawyers could peremptorily strike persons on the basis of race alone. Prior to 1994, lawyers could still use a juror's sex as a reason for exercising a peremptory challenge. Obviously, such practices cannot readily be reconciled with the effort to recruit representative juries, and the Supreme Court is currently struggling to reconfigure the peremptory challenge in light of the cross-sectional ideal. (I will discuss this trouble spot in the next section.)

Turning first to controversies over the construction of a master jury list, I start with federal practice. As we have already seen, in the 1968 Jury Selection and Service Act, Congress specified the voter registration list or voter list as the source from which names of prospective jurors would be taken.[103] But voters or registered voters hardly constitute a fair cross section of the community. Blacks, Hispanics, the young, and the poor register to vote and vote at rates significantly lower than the rest of the population.*

Despite these problems of underrepresentation, Congress settled on voter lists as a neutral, nondiscriminatory source of juror names. It then attempted to cure the discrepancy between the goal of the legislation (drawing jurors from a fair cross section) and the vehicle (voting lists that do not represent a cross section) by providing that voter lists should be supplemented, though not supplanted, when necessary to meet cross-sectional goals.[104]

Defending the choice of voter lists as a source for jury names, House sponsors of the proposed jury reform bill pointed to the provisions for supplementing the voter list, though they failed to specify how great a deviation from proportional representation needed to occur before the obligation to supplement voter lists was triggered.[105] More revealing was the House Judiciary Committee's defense of drawing juror names from voter lists whether or not this method achieved proportional representation for groups:

> In a sense the use of voter lists as the basic source of juror names discriminates against those who have the requisite qualifications for jury service but who do not register or vote. This is not unfair, however, because anyone with minimal qualifications . . . can cause his name to be placed on the list simply by registering or voting. No economic or social characteristics prevent one [from becoming eligible] for jury service.[106]

---

*Of the eligible voting-age population in the 1992 presidential election, 68.2 percent registered to vote; 70.1 percent of the white population registered; 63.9 percent of the black population registered; and 35 percent of the Hispanic population registered. Of eighteen- to twenty-year-olds, 48.3 percent registered to vote. In the same presidential election, 61.3 percent of the voting-age population reported actually voting. The figures once again varied by race, with the percentages as follows: 63.6 percent of whites; 54 percent of blacks; and 28.9 percent of Hispanics. Of eighteen- to twenty-year-olds, 38.5 percent voted. Bureau of the Census, U.S. Department of Commerce, *Statistical Abstract of the United States* (Washington, D.C.: Government Printing Office, 1993), p. 283 (Table 454).

In fact, the chair of the committee of federal judges who drafted an earlier version of the jury selection bill testified that use of voter registration lists as a source of jury names was commendable precisely because it filtered out certain elements of the population:

> I call to your attention that the use of voter lists supplies an important built-in screening element. It automatically eliminates those individuals not interested enough in their government to vote or indeed not qualified to do so.[107]

This legislative history shows that congressional commitment to the cross-sectional ideal was more qualified than the bold policy declaration with which the statute opens might otherwise have indicated.

In the quarter-century since the cross-sectional requirement went into effect for federal courts, literally hundreds of litigants have challenged the validity of jury selection plans that rely exclusively on voter or registration lists and fail to supplement. There does not appear to be a single decided federal case where the claim prevailed.[108] Every federal court of appeals that has ruled on the issue has held that federal courts are "not required to supplement simply because an identifiable group votes in a proportion lower than the rest of the population."[109] For instance, in 1990, a federal jury selection plan survived challenge, despite uncontradicted evidence that Hispanics constituted only 1 percent of the master jury wheel in a district where they made up 15.7 percent of the adult population.[110] In a North Dakota case, only 17 percent of eligible Native Americans who lived on reservations voted in the election; this led to only one Native American from the reservation being summoned out of 174 jurors that year, although Native Americans who lived on reservations constituted 2 percent of the population. The Court refused to find that the district was obligated to supplement the voter list with another source of names, such as tribal rolls.[111]

Looking at this line of cases, the actual federal judicial enforcement of cross-sectional principles is rather weak. But federal judicial decisions do not tell the whole story of how the cross-sectional requirement has changed jury selection since 1968. According to a 1993 survey by the National Center for State Courts, a majority of states has abandoned voter lists as an exclusive source for master jury lists. Over thirty states now supplement the voter lists with names taken from driver's license lists, using some technology for avoiding duplication. Other source lists include telephone directories, city directories, tax rolls, town resident lists, and utility customer lists.[112] In short, at the state level, as a practical matter, there is a shift toward using more exact proportional representational strategies. For instance, one respected jurist notes that, in Georgia, the "good faith of the commissioners for compiling the list is not the important factor; the proportional representation of distinctive, identifiable groups is determinative of the jury list."[113]

How far this trend will carry, how mathematical the concept of jury representation will become, is up for grabs. Some years ago, the Fifth Circuit Court of Appeals eloquently stated the inevitable tension between cross-sectional selection and color-blind selection. Under the cross-sectional principle, jury commissioners are obliged to compile master jury lists that give a "true picture of the community and its components." Obviously, discharging this responsibility requires the commissioners to "be conscious" of those components and to measure the master list against the community's makeup. Thus, the Fifth Circuit thought it "inevitable" that cross-sectional selection had to be, among other things, race-conscious selection.[114]

Writing in the *New Republic* in 1992, legal scholar Andrew Kull described the quota-like approach that jury commissioners in DeKalb County, Georgia, take to constructing a master jury list. The commissioners still rely on the voter registration list as a source of names, but to avoid charges of underrepresentation,

> the entire voting-age population of the county is broken down into those groups treated as "cognizable." The relevant groups at present are black males, black females, white males, white females, "other" males and "other" females, each subdivided into age groups 18 to 24, 25 to 34, 35 to 44, 45 to 54, 55 to 64, and 65 plus. Taken together, these categories yield a grid of thirty-six squares: each square is assigned "requested quota totals" by percentage and, for a jury list of given magnitude, by head count. The computer fills the quotas by a random draw from the list of registered voters in the various categories.[115]

Kull presents DeKalb County as typical of the way the cross-sectional requirement pushes jury commissioners to balance the spaces given to each "cognizable" group on the jury list. But this conclusion overstates the tidiness of the change taking place. The story line, as we have seen, is far more tentative. On the one hand, traditional color-blind norms retain a strong hold on our ideals for the law. But the realities of prejudice make us keenly aware that not even the appearance of justice can be delivered by a jury selection process that continually underrepresents minorities. Hence the need to move beyond abolishing discrimination to more creative remedies aimed at actually achieving enhanced representation for minorities on jury rolls.

The cross-sectional mandate grew out of this struggle to increase minority representation without abandoning principles of color-blind justice in favor of quotas and racial balancing. But it is not easy to move from accomplishing the negative tasks (no more discrimination) to achieving specific, representational goals. When it comes to jury selection, American society is no closer to resolving the tensions between norms of blind justice and norms of effective representation than it is when the same tension breaks out over school assignments, affirmative action hiring, or race-conscious creation of electoral districts.

PEREMPTORY CHALLENGES AND THE CROSS-SECTIONAL IDEAL: JURY SELECTION LAW AT THE CROSSROADS

Peremptory challenges have proven the hardest part of existing jury selection procedures to reconcile with the cross-sectional ideal.[116] For hundreds of years, trials have featured lawyers exercising peremptory challenges to eliminate prospective jurors suspected of leaning to the other side.[117] Unlike challenges for cause, peremptory strikes require no justification, no spoken word of explanation, no reason at all beyond a hunch, an intuition. In theory, peremptories are justified as tools for fashioning impartial juries, used by both sides to eliminate "extremes of partiality." At the very least, peremptory challenges function to "assure the parties" by giving them the right to veto those members of the jury panel whom they most distrust.[118] The "law wills not," said Blackstone, that a defendant "should be tried by any one man against whom he has conceived a prejudice, even without being able to assign a reason for such his dislike."[119]

Sometimes, the lawyer's hunch about a prospective juror stems from something individual to the person—a remark during voir dire, a glance, even clothing worn. Other times, the lawyer suspects a potential juror of bias merely because the person belongs to the same group as the defendant, the victim, or a litigant in a civil suit. Many peremptory challenges rest on the unspoken assumption that jurors are incapable of doing justice across group lines, that jurors always favor their own kind. As a federal district judge surmised in 1974:

> If statistics were compiled on the basis of any particular religion, e.g., Jewish or Catholic, or any particular nationality, e.g., Italian or Chinese, . . . there is a pattern by state prosecutors to peremptorily challenge veniremen from the same genetic, religious, or national background on the unstated grounds that such persons might be partial toward a defendant of like kin.[120]

But, as ancient as the peremptory challenge's credentials are, the theory of impartiality that underlies its use (that both sides should be free to eliminate persons suspected of racial, sexual, or ethnic bias against them) is in conflict with the theory of impartiality in the cross-sectional ideal (that such bias needs to be represented on an impartial jury because there is no way to escape from it, there are only ways to balance it). As the California Supreme Court put it, "If jurors are struck simply because they may hold . . . beliefs" identified with a particular group, then this "frustrates the primary purpose of the representative cross-section requirement," namely, to achieve impartiality through the "interaction of the diverse beliefs and values the jurors bring from their group experiences."[121]

In 1978, the California Supreme Court took the lead in ruling that lawyers in criminal cases could no longer use peremptory challenges to remove prospective jurors, simply on the presumption that they were biased as members of a particular group.[122] This did not abolish all peremptory challenges; it remained lawful to strike persons suspected of harboring a personal bias.

To rule as it did, the California Court went beyond the Supreme Court's own taboo on applying the cross-sectional principle to the selection of the actual jury. Grounding its decision on the state rather than federal Constitution, the California court agreed that defendants did not have the right to have any particular group represented on their juries. The court also agreed that the persons seated in a jury box and subject to peremptory challenges may or may not be fairly representative of the community— the defendant lived with the luck of the draw and a host of other factors that caused the final candidates for the jury to be less than a representative sample of the community. But, whatever level of representativeness survived to the final stage where peremptory challenges were exercised, it was that amount of representativeness, the Court concluded, that lawyers could not whittle down by using peremptories to remove persons simply because of their group identity.[123]

The Supreme Court has been slow to respond to the problems posed by peremptory challenges. In fact, during the years that the Court was giving birth to the cross-sectional ideal in one line of cases, it was undermining that ideal in another line of cases about peremptory challenges. Those cases go back to 1965, when the Court heard the appeal of Robert Swain, a black man tried for rape, convicted, and sentenced to death by an all-white jury in Talladega County, Alabama. Six blacks had been among the eligible jurors in the venire, but the prosecution used its peremptory challenges to eliminate all of them.

At the time of Swain's conviction, the Court had not yet applied the Sixth Amendment to state criminal trials at all, let alone interpreted the Amendment as guaranteeing state criminal defendants the right to a jury drawn from a fair community cross section.[124] On appeal, Swain therefore relied on traditional Fourteenth Amendment equal protection grounds: surely a color-blind Constitution prohibited the state from removing persons from the jury box simply because they were the same race as the defendant. The Court disagreed. The prosecutor was entitled to the "presumption" that he had challenged the prospective black jurors not out of racial prejudice but for "acceptable considerations related to the case he is trying, the particular defendant involved and the particular crime charged."[125] In Swain's case, suspicion fell on black jurors because the defendant was black. But in other cases, the Court was confident that parallel suspicions cause lawyers to strike "white[s], Catholics, accountants or those with blue eyes." As Chief Justice Warren Burger was to say twenty-one years after *Swain* was decided, quoting another in support of *Swain:*

> Common human experience, common sense, psychological studies, and public opinion polls tell us that it is likely that certain classes of people statistically have predispositions that would make them inappropriate jurors for particular kinds of cases.*

Batson v. Kentucky, 476 U.S. 79, 121 (1986) (Burger, C. J., dissenting). Burger went on to quote with approval the remark that it would be "socially divisive" to spell out the stereotypes behind the use of peremptory challenges. He mentioned the hypothetical example of a prosecutor striking black males because experience reveals that black males as a class could be be biased against young alienated blacks who have not tried to join the middle class. The beauty of the peremptory challenge is that it "allows the covert expression of what we dare not say but know is true more often than not."

Of course, the *Swain* Court agreed, evidence that prosecutors in a single jurisdiction were systemically using peremptory challenges to remove blacks in case after case would be a different matter. Such evidence would overcome the presumption that the state was after impartial jurors and would suggest instead that the state was pursuing its own prejudices, in violation of the equal protection clause.

Swain was sour with cynicism about the capacity of jurors—at least black jurors—to render color-blind justice. By 1965, one expected to find the Supreme Court rigorously enforcing the principle that jurors could not be dismissed because of their race; instead the Court surprisingly sided with the argument that race was relevant to an assessment of a person's capacity for impartiality. The Court portrayed peremptory challenges as "equal opportunity" strikes against all groups. But the notion that peremptories fell upon, say, "accountants" or "blue-eyed" individuals with the same frequency or damaging effect as they fell upon African-Americans was historically naive, or worse.

Swain also rested on the fiction that peremptories were just as efficient in eliminating "white bias" from juries as they were in eliminating "black bias." But, as the Massachusetts Supreme Judicial Court noted, in using that state's constitution to prohibit what *Swain* allowed, the math almost always favors the majority. Given a small number of peremptory challenges, the side wishing to eliminate all minority members of the jury venire may frequently succeed. But rare is the case where a side has sufficient peremptories to eliminate all majority members of the venire. The result "is a jury in which the subtle group biases of the majority are permitted to operate, while those of the minority have been silenced."[126]

In the two decades following *Swain*, not a single federal court found use of peremptory challenges to violate the *Swain* standards; in practice, the evidentiary burdens regarding proof of what was going on in cases other than the defendant's own case proved insurmountable.*

In 1986, Justice Marshall summarized some of the data regarding just how alive and well the race-based peremptory was after 1965. In the

---

*Johnson, "Black Innocence and White Jury," p. 1658. In some jurisdictions, court records did not list the race of jurors challenged during voir dire; in other jurisdictions, voir dire proceedings were not transcribed at all. Even putting aside these problems, *Swain* placed on the defendant "the crippling burden" of investigating across a whole line of cases the race of persons tried, the racial composition of the venire and the petit jury, how many jurors of each race were eliminated by cause and how many by peremptories, and which peremptories were exercised by the state, as opposed to the defense. *Batson v. Kentucky*, 476 U.S. at 92–93.

Western District of Missouri, a study of fifteen criminal cases in 1974 showed that prosecutors peremptorily challenged 81 percent of eligible black jurors. In a study of fifty-three cases from 1972 to 1974 in the Eastern District of Louisiana, federal prosecutors used 68.9 percent of their peremptory challenges against black jurors, even though blacks made up less than one-quarter of the venire. In Spartanburg County, South Carolina, in thirteen criminal trials in 1970–71 involving black defendants, prosecutors peremptorily challenged 82 percent of black jurors. In 1973, the *Texas Observer* published excerpts from an instruction book used in the Dallas County prosecutor's office, advising prosecutors to conduct jury selection so as to eliminate "any member of a minority group." Ten years later, in one hundred felony trials in Dallas County in 1983–84, prosecutors were still peremptorily striking 405 out of 467 eligible black jurors.[127] My own research uncovered that, into the 1980s, the Office of the District Attorney in Conroe (Montgomery County), Texas, followed a jury manual that directed prosecutors to strike all black members of the jury venire in trials of black defendants; this advice was followed even in death-penalty cases.[128]

Use of peremptory challenges to eliminate African-Americans from juries was not limited to the South. In 1977, Federal District Judge Jon O. Newman detailed evidence regarding prosecutorial use of peremptories in the federal district of Connecticut. Over a two-year period, eighty-two blacks remained eligible into the final stages of jury selection. The state used peremptories to eliminate fifty-seven of them, or 69.5 percent. If the defendant were white, the rate of prosecutorial strikes against black jurors was 59.2 percent. However, if the defendant were black, the rate skyrocketed to 84.8 percent.[129]

In the years after *Swain*, some of the most highly publicized trials of black defendants, charged with violence against whites, showed the persistent use of peremptories by prosecutors to eliminate prospective black jurors, on the assumption that blacks would obviously favor the defense in such cases. In the 1968 murder trial of Black Panther leader Huey Newton, who was charged with killing a white police officer, the Alameda County District Attorney's office used eight of its twenty-one peremptories against blacks, leaving only one black on the jury.[130] In the 1972 trial of Angela Davis, the prosecutor eliminated the only remaining black in the venire. In 1975, in the North Carolina murder trial of Joan Little on charges of killing her jailer, the state used eight of nine peremptory challenges against blacks.

In 1986, a potentially large breakthrough occurred. In *Batson v. Kentucky*, the Court finally overruled the evidentiary requirements of *Swain* and held, for the first time, that using race as the reason for striking a juror was a violation of the Equal Protection Clause. It was a violation of the prospective juror's own right not to be dismissed solely for racial reasons and of the defendant's right not to have jurors of his or her own race systematically removed from the jury.[*]

Under *Batson* rules, a prima facie case of discrimination exists whenever a prosecutor creates a racial pattern in use of peremptories. The burden then shifts to the prosecution to offer a nondiscriminatory explanation for the pattern.

Batson marks a genuine step forward in eliminating racial discrimination in jury selection. More than one hundred years after *Strauder*, it promises to put an end to the longest-lived prop for the all-white jury. But it remains to be seen how easy it will be for lawyers to explain away a seeming racial pattern to their strikes. A few years ago, I observed a jury selection where the prosecutor was able to satisfy the judge that he eliminated the only black on the jury panel because she reminded him of the defendant's mother. If this is all it takes to rebut a prima facie case of racial use of peremptories, then *Batson* will signify little.[131]

In 1994 the Supreme Court extended the logic of *Batson* to prohibit state actors from using peremptory challenges to eliminate jurors simply because of their sex.[132] In the trial of a complaint filed by Alabama on behalf of a mother seeking a determination of paternity and child support from the putative father, the prosecutor struck nine of ten men in the venire. Apparently, the prosecutor believed that gender was an accurate predictor of juror responses to paternity suits. Lawyers for the alleged father must have agreed, since they used all but one of their peremptory challenges to strike women members of the panel. In the end, an all-female jury was seated; it found paternity and awarded child support to the mother.

Writing for a six-person majority, Justice Harry Blackmun found that

---

[*]*Batson v. Kentucky*, 476 U.S. at 86–87. Since *Batson*, the Court has ruled that the Equal Protection Clause is violated even when the jurors removed are not of the same race as the defendant. *Powers v. Ohio*, 499 U.S. 400 (1991). The Court has also prohibited defense counsel from exercising peremptory challenges on the basis of race. *Georgia v. McCollum*, 112 S. Ct. 2348 (1992). And the Court has extended *Batson* to prohibit race-based peremptory challenges in civil as well as criminal trials. *Edmonson v. Leesville Concrete Co.*, 500 U.S. 614 (1991).

"intentional discrimination on the basis of gender by state actors violates the Equal Protection Clause, particularly where, as here, the discrimination serves to ratify and perpetuate invidious, archaic, and overbroad stereotypes about the relative abilities of men and women." Blackmun found scant empirical support for the claim that "gender alone is an accurate predictor of juror's attitudes." Instead, he characterized use of gender to guide peremptory challenges as resting on "gross generalizations" that "ratify and reinforce prejudicial views of the relative abilities of men and women." Blackmun also faulted gender-based peremptories for "invit[ing] cynicism respecting the juror's neutrality" and for depriving persons of equal rights to serve on juries, regardless of gender.

The extension of *Batson* from race to gender, while significant, does not settle larger questions about the future of peremptory challenges. The next case will challenge the Court to explain why the Constitution should permit peremptory challenges exercised on the basis of generalizations about the influence of religion, national origin, or occupation on jurors.*

It is unlikely that the Court can articulate grounds for tolerating these kinds of peremptory challenges, now that it has banned race- and gender-based peremptory challenges. This is why the logic of *Batson* calls into question the very survival of peremptory challenges. Future litigants might still be permitted to challenge persons based on individualized observations, but the current practice of basing peremptory challenges on a person's group identity should be ended.

What would jury selection be like without group-based peremptory challenges? Supporters of change argue that abolition of most peremptory challenges is necessary to give juries a fair shot at being genuine cross sections of the community. Opponents retort that litigants have a fundamental right to a fair and impartial jury, even if the elimination of "group bias" means the destruction of a jury's representative nature in the final stages of jury selection.

To date, the Court has managed to avoid ruling on the overall tension between peremptory challenges and cross-sectional juries only through

---

*In Massachusetts, where state courts have limited use of peremptory challenges against any group specifically protected by state civil rights laws, an appeals court in February, 1994 threw out the conviction of a Roman Catholic priest for blocking access to an abortion clinic, after finding that the prosecution had used peremptories to strike the only three persons in the jury panel with Irish-sounding surnames, in the apparent belief that they were Catholic. Patricia Nealon, "Conviction Overturned of Priest Who Blocked Boston Abortion Clinic," *Boston Globe*, March 1, 1994, p. 19.

some careful doctrinal maneuvering. In *Batson* itself, the petitioner originally asked the justices to find race-based peremptory challenges a violation of his Sixth Amendment right to a selection process where jurors
were drawn from a fair community cross section. The Court refused this
invitation to scrutinize peremptory challenges in terms of damage to representative goals, and instead narrowly based its ruling on traditional
equal protection principles that persons should not be excluded from jury
duty simply because of their race.

In the 1990 case of *Holland v. Illinois*, the Court did confront and
reject the argument that the tradition of peremptory challenges was
inconsistent with the post-1975 mandate to draw jurors from a representative sample of the community.[133] Holland, a white defendant, argued
that the Sixth Amendment guaranteed him the "fair possibility" of a petit
jury representing a cross section of the population. He asserted that he
lost even the chance of trial before a representative jury, when the prosecution intentionally used its peremptory challenges to strike all black
venirepersons solely on the basis of their race.[134]

In a 5–4 decision, the Court ruled against Holland, refusing to apply
the same cross-sectional mandates to the final stages of jury selection
that govern the composition of jury lists, venires or pools. Writing for the
majority, Justice Antonin Scalia reasoned that the Sixth Amendment concept of representative jury venires was a way of assuring that the state did
not initially stack the deck against a defendant, by producing a pool of
prospective jurors "disproportionately ill disposed" toward the accused.
But, "once a fair hand is dealt," Justice Scalia had no problem with
departures from representation brought about by each side's use of
peremptory challenges to eliminate prospective jurors belonging to groups
suspected of favoring the other side. In the last stages of jury selection,
when peremptory challenges are being exercised, the goal is the construction "not of a *representative* jury (which the Constitution does not
demand), but an *impartial* jury (which it does)."

Justice Scalia was quite clear about what the import of applying cross-
sectional analysis to the final stages of jury selection would be for
peremptory challenges:

> if the goal of the Sixth Amendment is representation of a fair cross section of
> the community on the petit jury, then intentionally using peremptory chal-
> lenges to exclude *any* identifiable group should be impermissible—which
> would . . . likely require the elimination of peremptory challenges.[135]

In concurrence, Justice Anthony Kennedy agreed that application of the fair cross-sectional requirement to peremptory challenges would "admit of no limiting principle."[136] Almost all peremptory challenges upset the representative balance on juries and thus would become suspect.

But should peremptory challenges survive, even if they do upset the chances that the jury finally seated will be representative of the community? In 1975, the Court initiated a line of cases stating that ideals of impartiality and ideals of representation went hand in glove. But in 1990, five justices drew back from this reasoning. Their great fear, as we have seen throughout this chapter, was that the cross-sectional principle blended into arguments for affirmative representation of groups on the actual jury. They feared that, carried full forward, the demand for representative juries would usher into jury selection all the attention to numerical balancing that characterizes American law on discrimination elsewhere. Thus, in *Holland,* they protected the peremptory challenge from fear of what lies behind its abolition. A jury system stripped of peremptory challenges would be, for the Court, a jury system that much closer to imposing proportional concepts of representation on the actual jury.

Nonetheless, the present position of American law on peremptory challenges is incoherent. Having taken the first step of prohibiting race and sex as grounds for peremptory challenges, the Supreme Court has little logical choice but to take the second and decisive step of banning all uses of peremptory challenges that target specific groups for exclusion from the jury.

TWO JUSTIFICATIONS FOR THE CROSS-SECTIONAL IDEAL

What will the future of the cross-sectional jury bring? If the only replacement for the peremptory challenge system were a jury selection system that dictated particular and proportional levels of representation for groups on juries, then the Court would be right to object, for practical and philosophical reasons. We do not want jurors to see themselves as filling reserved "slots" on the jury, nor are there enough seats on the jury to carry out any such divisive theory of representation.

But does the cross-sectional ideal have to rest cynically on the supposed incapacity of jurors to put aside their group biases? Must we concede that justice in a multiethnic society reduces in the end to balancing the biases of one group against another? The cross-sectional ideal under-stood as merely a method for balancing group bias on the jury is an invi-tation to jurors to abandon even the attempt to approach the evidence from a disinterested point of view. After all, what are jurors of diverse backgrounds to understand about their task from a description of the jury system that stresses the need to balance the inevitable prejudices built into group identity in America?

Suppose, for instance, that jurors were to begin to practice this way of representing the community. Such jurors would approach their task as the more or less mechanical job of voting or recording the preconceptions or preferences of their group. They would be less prepared to enter into the kind of independent and impartial deliberations that historically have dif-ferentiated jury behavior from voting behavior. When we vote in an elec-tion, we vote in private behind a closed curtain—the better to express freely our individual preferences. But when we serve as jurors, we talk and deliberate and argue face-to-face first and "vote" only to make offi-cial the consensus already achieved in the deliberations. The emphasis on the need to deliberate until unanimity is achieved is a sign that what we want is not the mere recording of individual opinions but the more considered and cautious judgment achieved by twelve persons acting in concert.

It takes a certain kind of moral character for a person to be able to enter into the free and independent deliberations we expect of jurors. No doubt the common law's description of the impartial juror was a naive and exaggerated view of the ability of ordinary people to achieve the kind of disinterest expected of them. The cross-sectional ideal arose to correct the common-law fiction that jurors were pure pieces of disembodied rea-son. But it is possible to carry the correction too far, as happens when cynics conclude that we should no longer even aspire to impartial delib-erations, that the best we can do is balance the biases expressed during deliberation. Such skepticism, often expressed in cross-sectional terms, leaves us without any reason to trust the competence of ordinary persons to render justice. It allows us to forget the oldest of democratic truths, which jurors are actually constantly verifying—that twelve persons of diverse backgrounds are capable of achieving a wisdom together that no one person is capable of achieving alone.

In the end, what is at stake is whether we want jurors to understand their task primarily in terms of deliberation or representation. I have argued that the deliberative ideal is preferred for the jury. Jurors recruited randomly from different corners of the community may never be able to practice perfectly the deliberations we ask of them. But we know at least why we cherish the jury when it aspires to act as the common conscience of the community and not just as the register of our irreconcilable divisions.

CHAPTER FOUR

Scientific Jury Selection

THERE IS A FAMOUS LAWYERS' QUIP about the difference between trials in England and trials in the United States: in England, the trial starts when jury selection is over; in the United States, the trial is already over. The humor is actually serious strategy to many lawyers on this side of the Atlantic. As we saw in the previous chapter, the ideal of a jury that represents different groups in the community is an ideal that fosters cynicism when it comes to the practical parameters of jury selection. All potential jurors, the manuals state, inevitably bring with them the views and biases built into their race, religion, age, and gender.[1] These preconceptions supposedly influence the eventual verdict as much, if not more than, the evidence presented at trial. The task of the lawyer, therefore, is to outsmart the system—to figure out the demographics of justice and to manipulate it during jury selection by eliminating jurors with the so-called wrong personal characteristics. Or, as social scientists put the point, in the cumbersome language that dominates discussions of jury selection today:

> The examination of jurors' demographic and socioeconomic characteristics is of great significance because each juror's psychological attributes and proclivities, which will influence a particular verdict, are closely intertwined with the juror's ascriptive characteristics (e.g., age, race, and gender) and socially achieved status (e.g., education, and income).[2]

Media accounts of jury selection bear involuntary witness to our widespread public belief that jury selection determines all. Race especially gains privileged status in popular accounts of why verdicts turn out as they do, as if it were obvious not only that justice does not cross racial lines but also that a juror's race always outweighs the competing or over-lapping influences of class, gender, or education.

Consider, for instance, this story about how jury selection supposedly influenced the outcome of a North Carolina medical malpractice suit. A thirty-seven-year-old woman sued her obstetrician for emotional distress caused by the death of her fetus, following the doctor's allegedly negligent interpretation of a fetal stress test. After settlement negotiations broke down, defense counsel determined to go to trial, believing he could convince a jury that much of the woman's psychological problems were caused by the death of her husband within the same year. The jury came back in favor of the plaintiff, awarding the woman $195,000. Commenting on the verdict, the defense counsel attributed his side's loss to jury selection. "As you know, probably the most uncertain factor in trying a case like this is the selection of the jury." The defense had sought a jury of "middle-aged white males because . . . they would be more conservative." But the defense counsel noted that the "luck of the draw" led to a jury that "had a number of young black jurors." Exactly why the racial/age composition of the jury should have had control over the deliberations of a jury on med-ical malpractice, the report of this case does not say. Even if the plaintiff was black, the story is remarkable because it demonstrates how easy it is to assume that the race of the jurors selected—not the evidence, not even whether the jurors as parents identified with the plaintiff—would be the preeminent factor at work in this trial.[3]

I suspect that most readers of this book share a suspicion that jury selection is as sovereign over verdicts as lawyers and jury consultants say it is. In 1991, veteran defense lawyer William Kunstler took on the case of Egyptian-born El Sayyid A. Nosair, charged with the 1990 murder of Rabbi Meir Kahane, founder of the Jewish Defense League and an Israeli ultranationalist. Nosair was arrested minutes later near the Manhattan hotel meeting room where Kahane was shot, after wounding a seventy-three-year-old man who attempted to block his escape and then being wounded himself in a shootout with a U.S. Postal Service police officer. Ballistics tests showed that the .357 revolver Nosair used to shoot the postal worker was the same weapon used to kill Kahane.

At first, Kunstler advised his client to plead insanity, since the evi-dence of guilt seemed overwhelming. But Nosair refused. A jury of nine women and three men eventually returned a bizarre, split verdict, acquitting the defendant of murdering Kahane but convicting him on lesser charges, including possession of the murder weapon in the assault of the postal officer.

Following the trial, Kunstler trumpeted jury selection as critical to the defense strategy, recounting how he used peremptory challenges to eliminate jurors who supported Israel and to impanel a jury of "third world people." At one point in the jury selection, six persons had been seated— five African-Americans and one Hispanic. Kunstler had targeted so many whites for elimination from the jury that the judge issued a stern rebuke.[4] The judge also barred Kunstler from asking members of the jury venire whether they were Jewish, stating that this was a "gross invasion of privacy."[5] Kunstler denied any systematic attempt to keep whites off the jury but affirmed he wanted a "third world jury of non-whites, or anyone who's been pushed down by white society."[6] For whatever reasons, the remaining six seats on the jury went to whites.[7]

Kunstler then fashioned a defense, apparently successful, aimed at arousing what he hoped would be a high level of suspicion in the jury about police willingness to arrest the nearest Arab to the scene of the crime. In this case, Kunstler suggested that members of the Jewish Defense League assassinated Kahane and then framed Nosair.[8] Commenting on the verdict, defense lawyer Alan Dershowitz said, "Kunstler knows better than anybody in America how to manipulate the ethnic prejudices and biases of a jury."[9]

In this chapter I consider the supposed dominance of jury selection over the entire trial process. During the last generation, the drama of jury selection has grown considerably as a so-called science has emerged, claiming to have unlocked the secrets of selection. Where lawyers used to rely on intuition or guesswork they now hire jury consultants offering mathematical modeling of jury behavior. The specter of science stacking juries in favor of one side now looms throughout the process.

My conclusions about this science of jury selection will be straightforward. Empirically, there is no evidence that it works.[10] There is no scientific way to predict whether an individual juror will conform, in any one case, to the general attitudes of his or her group. Moreover, even generalizations about groups are of limited use in the jury context, because the behavior of jurors, as well as the local community from which they are drawn, is so specific to the particular case on trial. In the end, we all belong to so many overlapping groups that science cannot forecast whether a juror will respond to the evidence more as, say, a woman, a white, a thirty-year-old, a Lutheran, a Norwegian, a college graduate, a member of the middle class, a Republican, or whatever.

Ethically, the failure of scientific jury selection is its saving grace. Still, its continued popularity fuels public skepticism about the fairness of jury justice and caters to a view that sees justice as a game, won by those best at stacking the jury in its favor. The overselling of jury selection's importance is itself responsible for a declining faith in the jury and the rise of cynicism about the possibility of achieving justice across group lines.

STEREOTYPES AND JURY SELECTION

Fascination with the supposed secrets of jury selection is hardly new in the United States.* Lawyers have always relied on hunches, intuition, and their ideas about stereotypes to distinguish proprosecution jurors from prodefense jurors. But, until recently, the "how to" wisdom in trial manuals hardly seemed threatening to the integrity of jury trials, trading as it did on the latest opinion fads. Thus in the 1950s and 1960s, the manual writers told attorneys to prefer men on a jury if the client was a woman.[11] The reason was that "male jurors, out of gallantry, favor women litigants."[12] But female jurors were preferable if the defendant was "a handsome young man."[13] If the defendant was an attractive female, however, lawyers were told to avoid female jurors.[14] In general, women were seen as harder on their own sex.[15†]

Other traditional folklore about jurors was equally suspect. Well-known criminal defense attorney F. Lee Bailey thought "heavy, round-faced, jovial looking persons" made the best defense jurors, whereas "the

---

*In England, lawyers rarely make an attempt to craft the jury to their liking. In criminal trials, defense lawyers are allowed a certain number of peremptory challenges and the prosecution has the right to have jurors "stand by" (thereby effectively excluding them from the jury). But voir dire is extremely restricted or nonexistent, and challenges are infrequently executed. One study of criminal trials in Birmingham found that challenges were exercised in only one trial out of every seven. John Baldwin and Michael McConville, *Jury Trials* (Oxford: Clarendon Press, 1979), pp. 91–93.

†It is surprising that much of this conventional wisdom about women jurors remains in the current "How to Select a Jury" manuals. A good example is retired Los Angeles County Superior Court Judge Robert A. Wenke's 1988 *The Art of Selecting a Jury*, which claims that "women are often prejudiced against other women they envy, for example, those who are more attractive." Robert A. Wenke, *The Art of Selecting a Jury*, 2d ed. (Springfield, Ill.: Charles C. Thomas, 1988), pp. 61–90.

undesirable juror is quite often the slight underweight and delicate type."[16] In a 1936 article for *Esquire* magazine, Clarence Darrow divided religions and ethnic groups into the prodefense and proprosecution camps. Favorable to defendants were Irish, Jews, Unitarians, Universalists, Congregationalists, and agnostics. The ideal prosecution juror had high regard for the law and a religious attitude toward sin and punishment, qualities found among Scandinavians in particular but also among Lutherans, Baptists, and Presbyterians.[17]

Similarly, a 1935 trial manual provided lawyers with a scale for rating how well emotional appeals played to various ethnic jurors. If a party's case was primarily emotional, the advice was to go with Irish, Jews, Italians, French, Spanish, and Slavs. If the strategy was to combat emotional appeals, then the nod went to Nordic, English, Scandinavian, and German jurors.[18] In medical malpractice cases, however, the plaintiff was warned away from Jewish jurors because "most Jews want their sons to become doctors, . . . and they want their daughters to marry doctors."[19]

Occupations have also been stereotyped as either favorable or unfavorable to defendants. According to lawyer Melvin Belli, farmers favored the state but waiters and bartenders were more forgiving.[20] In civil trials, good plaintiff's jurors were "cabdrivers, union members, secretaries, social workers, salespersons, [and] retired government employees." Good defense jurors included "physicians, engineers, architects, executives, supervisory administrative personnel, unemployed people, and . . . insurance adjusters."[21]

Just as lawyers traditionally select jurors partly on the basis of ethnic, religious, sexual, and occupational stereotypes, so too does race figure prominently in jury selection. The most commonly accepted wisdom is that blacks are proplaintiff in civil cases and prodefendant in criminal trials.[22] Into the 1980s, the District Attorney's Office in Montgomery County, Texas, apparently used a manual that explicitly directed prosecutors to strike blacks from the jury panel in cases involving black defendants.[23] Tidbits about other minority groups included advice that "Orientals . . . tend to go along with the majority" and that Mexican-Americans tend to be "passive."[24]

THE BIRTH OF SCIENTIFIC JURY SELECTION

In 1972, a new phenomenon known as scientific jury selection burst upon the legal world, promising to take the guesswork out of selection. The basis of this new science, it turned out, was the old and familiar techniques of public opinion polling.

Opinion polls had already made a science out of everything from predicting elections to selling a new brand of toothpaste. Scientific jury selection simply applied these tried and true survey research methods to tracing correlations between a potential juror's background (for example, race, religion, and reading habits) and his or her attitudes toward the case. Such correlations could be found by surveying a random sample of the local population from which jurors were to be drawn. Local residents would be asked about their general attitudes toward authority, government, police, racial issues, and other factors relevant to the particular case. They would also be asked case-specific questions—about whether they had heard of the case to be tried, whether they had an opinion, and so forth. Demographic data would be kept on each respondent.

Pollsters would then use computers to search for significant correlations between, say, a person's race, religion, or sex and attitudes of interest to the lawyers in the case. For instance, various groups in the population might be rated for tendencies toward an authoritarian personality (a trait unfavorable to the defense) or toward a strong belief in equity. On the basis of these correlations, profiles of desirable and undesirable jurors would be sketched.

Scientific jury selection began innocently enough. The first highly publicized use of this method came in 1972 when sociologist Jay Schulman and others volunteered their services to Catholic antiwar protesters accused of conspiring to destroy draft records during the Vietnam War.[25] The volunteers were mostly students with antiwar leanings, and the entire effort was fueled by an ethical sense that their help was merely allowing unpopular underdogs to get a fair and impartial jury. Out of this first effort came, in 1975, the National Jury Project in Oakland, California. Throughout the 1970s, the project continued to use scientific jury selection mostly for radical or political defendants; it provided services on either a free or a low-cost basis.[26]

But knowledge cannot pick its users. Defendants using scientific jury selection methods achieved a string of acquittals in the 1970s. These apparent successes included not guilty verdicts for anti–Vietnam War defendants accused of destroying draft records in Camden, New Jersey, and Gainesville, Florida; Angela Davis in her 1972 trial for murder and kidnaping; Joan Little in 1975, when the jury believed she had killed her jailer in self-defense during an attempted rape; and the automaker John

Z. DeLorean, acquitted in 1984 of selling cocaine to finance his failing company.[27]

Defendants on the political right also had apparent success with scientific jury selection when a District of Columbia jury, at the height of the Watergate affair in 1974, acquitted two of President Nixon's cabinet members accused of calling off a Securities and Exchange Commission investigation of financier Robert Vesco in return for an illegal $200,000 campaign contribution.[28] With scientific jury selection's track record growing, large corporate defendants in civil suits turned to this method in search of favorable jurors. IBM, MCI, Penzoil Company, Firestone, and the National Football League were among early, supposedly successful users of jury consultants in antitrust and product liability cases.[29]

Soon scientific jury selection was a growth industry, spawning whole new companies with names such as Litigation Sciences, Inc., founded in Los Angeles in 1979 by the former chairman of the marketing department at the University of Southern California; Leo Shapiro and Associates of Chicago; Trial Consultants, Inc., of Miami; Jury Research Institute in Walnut Creek, California; and Jury Think in Minneapolis.[30] Perhaps the most famous individual consultants to emerge were Cathy Bennett of Galveston, a prime consultant in the Wounded Knee, DeLorean, and William Kennedy Smith trials;[31] and Jo-Ellan Dimitrius, defense consultant in the first Rodney King trial and the Reginald Denny trial.[32]

In 1994, the American Society of Trial Consultants estimated that there were at least 250 jury consultants in the United States, compared with 25 in 1982.[33] Fees run about $150 an hour; in a high-profile case, Litigation Sciences's fees range from $10,000 to over $250,000 per case. The company's gross revenues in 1988 were $25 million.[34] Revenues for the jury consulting industry as a whole are about $200 million.[35] "It's gotten to the point where if the case is large enough, it's almost malpractice not to use them," remarked a New York trial attorney in 1989.[36]

The costs have spurned considerable fear that scientific jury selection will aggravate the already wide gulf between the trial resources of rich and poor. "The affluent people and the corporations can buy it, the poor radicals [in political cases] get it free, and everybody in between is at a disadvantage," remarked sociologist Amitai Etzioni, an early critic of the ethics of scientific jury selection.[37] Criticisms of the pricey services led Hans Zeisel, a dean of jury experts in the United States, to suggest that courts might require either side to disclose to the other the results of any investigation of potential jurors.[38] And Etzioni asked how we as a society should respond if the government decides to provide prosecutors with extra funding for scientific jury selection purposes.[39]

Although the heart of scientific jury selection is the community survey or poll, other methods are used as well. The Angela Davis defense team employed a handwriting expert to analyze potential jurors' handwriting on their questionnaires;[40] the Joan Little defense team included a body language expert to cull clues from posture, vocal tones, and eye contact.[41] Perhaps most alarming of all is the simple "community network," or "background check," approach. In cases where the names and addresses of potential jurors are known, some lawyers have employed field investigators or private detectives (the federal government has used the FBI) to ride through the neighborhoods of prospective jurors, interviewing acquaintances about marital problems, drinking problems, and treatment of minorities.[42] For instance, in 1990, the *Boston Globe* reported that consultants for the American Tobacco Company drove through the neighborhoods of potential jurors shortly before a lawsuit against the company was to commence in United States District Court in Boston, looking for hints about the kind of neighborhood the juror lived in (for example, bumper stickers and the like).[43]

Bennett popularized an approach to scientific jury selection that placed less reliance on survey data and more on individualized questioning during voir dire. Through her work for the defense in the Wounded Knee, DeLorean, and Smith trials, Bennett became the nation's premier jury consultant.[44] She rejected "assumptions that jurors from certain income or ethnic groups will be best for certain clients." Jury profiles based on demographic surveys were useful "as a guide [but] should not substitute for in-court observations, gut feelings, and intuition." For Bennett, jury selection remained "three quarters art and one quarter science." Still, she agreed that "jurors are products of what they have been exposed to and are thus reflections of the people, experiences, and lifestyles they have known." This makes voir dire the crucial stage of any trial. "Creative [lawyers] put as much energy into selecting a jury as they do in presenting a case." They understand that a trial is like a play: no matter how good the play, it will flop if the audience is not receptive.[45]

Bennett taught lawyers a new set of voir dire skills for finding the right juror audience. Psychological research showed the importance of establishing an attorney–juror relationship during voir dire. Lawyers could get jurors to reveal more about themselves if the lawyers would take the lead in disclosing things about themselves ("I've been in situations where I didn't think I could be totally honest. I have the sense you may be feeling that way right now. Please talk to me about this"). Bennett also advised "humanizing" the defendant by always introducing him or her to the jury or even appointing the defendant as cocounsel in certain cases. This would permit the defendant to talk directly to the jurors during voir dire, which is important because research shows that jurors find it far easier to convict persons "they have not personally encountered."[46]

Bennett's studies of voir dire showed that most judges and lawyers asked unproductive, "close-ended" questions ("Do any of you have strong feelings against drugs or people who are accused of selling drugs?"). The questions were so poorly worded that they rarely uncovered the feelings or biases jurors undoubtedly had. The key to successful voir dire was to frame open-ended questions ("Would you describe the kind of person who could not be a fair and impartial juror in a drug case?"). To uncover ethnic prejudice, for example, Bennett advised questions such as "What's the first thing that comes to mind when you find out someone is Colombian?" rather than "Is there any reason you could not be a fair and impartial juror, given that the defendant is Colombian?"[47] The key was to stimulate prospective jurors to give lengthy responses—something not easy to accomplish given most people's fear of public speaking.*

Scientific jury selection remains the most visible product of jury consulting firms. But just as dramatic and potentially influential is the emergence of what might be called scientific jury preparation.[48] The 1977 IBM and 1980 MCI antitrust suits are early examples of lawyers turning to social scientists to prepare their case. IBM was worried about how to make a complex antitrust case understandable to lay jurors. It hired a market research expert to find six persons who mirrored demographically the actual jury deciding the case. These six became a "shadow jury," paid to sit in on the actual case proceedings every day and report their reactions to the IBM lawyers. Because plaintiffs go first in civil cases, the

*Robert B. Hirschhorn, a jury consultant himself and Bennett's widower, described the voir dire of the jury venire for a case in which the defendant was accused of stabbing a sixteen-year-old girl. The first question was, "Can you look Kevin in the eyes and say, 'Kevin, I can give you a fair trial'? Some said, 'Yes.' Others said, 'I think I can.' Those equivocating words sent us a message that they doubted, and probably couldn't [provide a fair trial.] Those who said 'yes' and looked at their shoes, we got rid of. If they could not in an open and honest way answer that question, it was clear to us where that person was coming from." The jury, selected with Hirschhorn's help, acquitted the defendant. Philipp M. Gollner, "Consulting by Peering into Minds of Jurors," *New York Times*, Jan. 7, 1994, A23.

nightly debriefings enabled the IBM team to tailor the next day's cross-examination to deal with any problems and to revise their own upcoming presentations accordingly. It so happened that the judge directed a verdict for IBM at the close of the plaintiff's case, so the opportunity to use the shadow jury never fully came about.[49]

In 1980, MCI made fuller use of scientific jury preparation in its antitrust suit against AT&T. On three consecutive nights prior to trial, MCI lawyers presented an abbreviated version of their case to a mock jury, selected by jury consultants to reflect the makeup of the jury pool for trial. With the mock jurors' permission, lawyers watched their deliberations through a one-way mirror. On the first night, MCI found that surrogate jurors had a great deal of trouble accepting the fairness of legally requiring AT&T to share its long-distance lines with competitors. Accordingly, in the second simulated jury trial, MCI lawyers dwelt on the duty to apply the law whether one agreed with it or not. This second jury had far less difficulty with the law.

The MCI lawyers also used the mock jurors to refine their evidence of damages. On the first night, they specified $100 million as MCI's lost profits from AT&T's monopolistic behavior. The jury awarded exactly $100 million. The next night, the lawyers experimented with mentioning no dollar amount. The second mock jury, left to speculate about damages, awarded $900 million. Not surprisingly, at the real trial, MCI left the jury free to speculate about damages; the jury awarded $600 million. Because antitrust awards are trebled for punitive purposes, this entitled MCI to $1.8 billion in damages, the largest antitrust award ever given until that time. The mock jury preparation seemed to more than pay for itself.[*]

Similar use of mock juries was made by plaintiffs suing General Motors in 1977 for allegedly installing Chevrolet engines in Oldsmobile automobiles. GM's defense was that the engines were comparable products and that such interchange was standard in the industry. The plaintiff's lawyers planned to rebut GM's defense by establishing gas mileage differences between the two engines. But, when they ran their case by mock jurors, the gas mileage point seemed to make little impression.

---

[*]Morton Hunt, "Putting Juries on the Couch," *New York Times*, Nov. 28, 1992, sec. 6, pp. 70–72. In the end, MCI may have been too aggressive in its strategy of how to get juries to award big-money damages. An appeals court overturned the jury award as excessive; a second jury trial on the issue of damages concluded with an award of $37.8 million. Valerie P. Hans and Neil Vidmar, *Judging the Jury*, pp. 80–81.

What did get through to jurors, and arose their sense of foul play, was evidence that GM had deliberately covered up evidence of the switch.[50]

The idea for mock juries comes from the world of politics, where candidates typically pretest campaign advertisements and speeches before focus groups. The candidates find out which issues are "hot" for which kind of persons; they then tailor their campaign message to push these hot buttons. Jury consultants have simply brought these focus group techniques into the world of jury trials. At times, the scientific jury preparation can become as high-tech and gadgetry-oriented as is campaign preparation. One consulting firm provides mock jurors with hand-held computers to register their second-by-second reactions to the presentation of their client's case. Elaborate charts and color codes are generated and analyzed for correlations as to which evidence matters most to which kind of juror.[51]

Some of the scientific selection and preparation techniques I have described are rather benign. There seems little ethical difference, for instance, between rehearsing an opening argument before your partners and rehearsing before a mock jury. Bennett's advice about voir dire also seems rather tame. In defense of jury consultants, Stephen Gillers, a professor of legal ethics at New York University Law School, notes that lawyers "may not have been able to articulate it all, but they did [what the consultants now teach]." Scientific jury selection is only "intuition made manifest."[52]

On the other hand, as one New York trial lawyer puts it, the "effort is also being made to try and *cause* jurors not to decide things rationally [emphasis added]."[53] After visiting the offices of Litigation Sciences, *Wall Street Journal* reporter Stephen Adler wrote:

> Much like their cohorts in political consulting and product marketing, the litigation advisers encourage their clients to . . . provide their target audiences with a psychological craving to make the desired choice.[54]

Litigation Sciences's consultants, Adler went on, instruct lawyers that "logic plays a minimal role" in trials. The crucial thing is to find the jurors' "psychological anchors"—a few focal points calculated to appeal to the jury on a gut level.[55] Former head of Litigation Sciences Donald Vinson urged lawyers not to try to change jurors' opinions through fact and argument. Instead, they should anticipate which of the jurors' basic beliefs are consistent with, and which conflict with, various views of the case. The lawyer should adopt a view ... linked to the jurors' attitudes, ... consistent with what the jurors already believe.[56]

Jury consultants openly admit that they do not "make moral distinctions. If a client needs prejudiced jurors, the firm will help find them."[57] But they defend the ethics of their profession by pointing out that they obey the same imperatives lawyers do in our adversary system: they seek their clients' advantage within the rules of the game. The rules of the game do not permit parties to change or alter the evidence, but they do permit shopping for jurors.

Of course, the rules of the game used to seem relatively fair: neither side could seriously outguess the other about the best and worst jurors. The frightening message today is that science can rig the game without breaking the rules—if you have enough money to spend. It is as if science has discovered that "jurors are not ... free moral agents, able to assess impartially where the truth lies, but ... organisms whose emotional and mental processes are determined by 'predictor variables,' such as social status, education, age, sex, personality traits, ethnic origins and religion."[58] This amounts to a sustained attack on the worth of jury trials. For if scientific jury selection actually works, then facts and evidence play a subordinate role in trials. Crucial, if hidden, social forces are at work, predisposing different groups in the population to react to the same evidence differently. Jury trials are thus only what Etzioni called a game of "sociological dice," testing the skills of lawyers in loading the dice during jury selection.

What faith can we have in jury verdicts when in celebrated case after celebrated case the preoccupation is with how many blacks or whites, men or women, rich or poor, young or old are on the jury? Media accounts strongly reinforce the notion that jury selection is the only game in town and the game is crooked. Given this crisis in confidence, it is imperative to pause and ask whether scientific jury selection performs as advertised. Are the realities of jury behavior so far from the ideals of color-blind justice that the jury has outlived its usefulness? I approach this question by studying in detail six celebrated cases in which scientific jury selection is credited with successfully influencing the verdict.

THE HARRISBURG SEVEN

In 1972, seven members of the Catholic Resistance to the Vietnam
War went on trial, charged with conspiring to raid draft boards, destroy
draft records, blow up heating tunnels in the nation's capital, and kidnap
National Security Adviser Henry Kissinger.*

The most well known of the defendants was Father Philip Berrigan.
Already in prison for other antiwar activity, Berrigan was additionally
charged with smuggling letters out of federal prison, aided by another
defendant, Sister Elizabeth McAlister.

The government chose Harrisburg, Pennsylvania, as the site for trial.
Suspecting that the Harrisburg jury pool would be highly conservative,
the defense turned to social scientists for help in finding favorable jurors.
A quick victory was won when a telephone survey of 840 randomly
selected registered voters showed that young persons constituted a
greater percentage of registered voters than they constituted in the jury
pool supposedly drawn from voter registration lists. Because youth was
correlated with antiwar sentiment, the defense sought and gained a new,
more representative pool of local jurors.

Next the social science team conducted in-depth interviews with 252
of the original group of 840 in their homes. The interviewers asked general questions about a person's trust in government and attitudes about
the legitimacy of protesting government activities. These attitudes, it was
thought, would be highly relevant at trial. Respondents were also asked
more specifically about their knowledge and opinions of the defendants
and the case. Finally, standard demographic data (race, religion, gender,
age, national origin) were recorded for each person interviewed.

On the basis of these interviews, the social scientists provided the
lawyers with profiles of the so-called good and bad juror. A bad juror for
the defense was likely to be Episcopalian, Presbyterian, Methodist, or
fundamentalist. The bad juror was also more likely to be college educated. This was a surprise because, nationally, higher education correlated with more liberal attitudes. But the survey revealed a distinctive,
local fact about Harrisburg. Apparently, liberal college-educated persons

*The account of jury selection in this case is taken from lead jury consultant Jay Schul-
man's own report, first published in 1973 in *Psychology Today* and reprinted as "Recipe for
a Jury" in Lawrence Wrightsman et al., *In the Jury Box: Controversies in the Courtroom*
(Beverly Hills, Calif.: Sage Publications, 1987), pp. 13–47.

moved away to more urban areas, leaving behind a self-selected group of conservative college-educated persons. The bad juror was also more likely to be a Republican businessman who belonged to local civic organizations and subscribed to *Reader's Digest*. By contrast, the ideal defense juror was a female Democrat having no religious preference and working in a white-collar job or a skilled blue-collar job.

Overall, the survey revealed that the local population had higher than average trust in government. Eighty percent of the community scored high in this area, compared with a national average of 45 to 50 percent at the time. The social scientists interpreted these numbers to mean that, absent their help, a proprosecution jury would inevitably have been selected.

Jury selection began with a panel of 465 persons. Because of the large amount of pretrial publicity, the trial judge permitted extensive voir dire of individual jurors for bias. After three weeks of challenges for cause, forty-six persons had qualified for jury duty. In this case, it was necessary first to qualify forty-six persons for the jury because the judge had allotted the defense twenty-eight peremptory challenges and the prosecution six, for a total of thirty-four peremptory challenges. When the sides exhausted their peremptory challenges, the surviving twelve persons would constitute the jury.

In a felony case involving multiple defendants, a federal judge has discretion to fix the number of peremptory challenges.[59] The fact that the judge granted the defense such a large number of challenges—both absolutely and in comparison with the six allowed the government—was crucial to the defense's opportunity to "scientifically select" the jury. In essence, the large number of (and disparity in) peremptory challenges granted the defense extraordinary opportunities to strike jurors who matched the "bad juror" profile.

Prior to exercising their challenges, the defense lawyers huddled with the social scientists and defendants to rate each of the forty-six jurors from 1 (best) to 5 (worst). They rated eight jurors as 1, six as 2, fifteen as 3, and seventeen as 4 or 5. The eight top-ranked jurors included two blacks; two females who held liberal, antiwar views; a blue-collar "hippie"; and a person who considered defense lawyer Ramsey Clark one of his heroes. To no one's surprise, the prosecution used its six peremptories to strike these top-rated defense jurors from the panel.

Obviously, the defense would not use its peremptories to challenge the two remaining 1s and six 2s. Just as obvious was the decision to use eighteen of its peremptory challenges to strike all of the low-rated 4s and 5s from the jury. This left the defense with ten peremptories to use against the fifteen 3s. Which five should be left on the jury? All fifteen were reviewed for their match to demographic requirements. Because the community survey had indicated that women were more opposed to the war than were men, the defense decided to add a core group of women to the jury who, according to small group behavior studies, could be expected to compose a subgroup once on the jury. One woman was a "natural" by survey criteria: single, in her mid-twenties, a social service technician, and having studied three years at a women's liberal arts college. Nonetheless, her answers during voir dire had left the lawyers suspicious of her. At this point, scientific jury selection turned into something close to spying: "our scouts in the community learned that she had dated—among others—a black man, read a good deal of social and political philosophy, and liked elements of the counterculture." She was put on the list of five not to be struck.

For the second woman chosen, "her demography . . . was favorable," most especially her lack of religious affiliation. The third woman met the demographic criteria of young age. A fourth was selected because she was Catholic; not only did the survey show that Catholics would make better defense jurors than Protestants, it was also believed that the jury needed a Catholic to inhibit expression of anti-Catholic sentiments. The fifth juror was a man chosen over the advice of the social scientists.

Did scientific jury selection work for the Harrisburg Seven? In the end, after sixty hours of deliberation, the jury hung on the major conspiracy charges by a vote of 10 to 2 in favor of acquittal. It convicted Father Berrigan and Sister McAlister on the more minor charge of smuggling letters out of prison. On the whole, the social scientists regarded the deadlock on the conspiracy charges as a victory. After all, their preliminary polling showed that eight out of every ten registered voters held attitudes unfavorable to the defense. They had succeeded in flipping those percentages on the actual jury. "Without careful screening of prospective jurors, we have every reason to believe that the jury would have consisted of many more individuals who were strongly opposed to the defendants." The social scientists also attempted to verify the success of their jury selection by comparing the 10–2 split on the actual jury with the opinions on guilt reached by eighty-three of their original interview group. When these eighty-three were recontacted while the actual jury was deliberating, an overwhelming majority leaned toward convicting the defendants on at least one of the conspiracy charges.

Nonetheless, scientific jury selection failed the Harrisburg Seven. The two jurors who held out for conviction were rated as 2s (good) by the survey team. One holdout, Kathryn Schwartz, fit the good juror profile closely. She was a woman, a member of a "desirable" religion (the pacifist Brethren Church), and the mother of four conscientious objector sons. The other juror who held out, Lawrence Evans, did not fit the desired religious or occupational profile—he was a Lutheran and owner of two grocery stores. But he was chosen because of predictions about his behavior from his general political attitudes toward the counterculture and protest.

The behavior of Evans and Schwartz, once on the jury, showed the difficulty of moving from probabilistic statements about a group to predictions about how any one individual from that group will behave. In the case of Evans, there was apparently a simple "fluke factor" at work. Evans turned out to be something of a religious zealot who talked of doing "God's work" on the jury, was heard conversing with God in his hotel room during sequestration, and could not be engaged through rational deliberation.

In Schwartz's case, the difficulty was more subtle. Although the survey research had determined Schwartz's religion as a plus, what could not be predicted in advance was that she would form a religious bond with Evans that worked against the defense. In the end, as the social scientists admitted, they were faced with the "tragic irony" that acquittal was blocked by two of their favored jurors. The evidence of conspiracy was extremely weak, bordering on the ridiculous when the Catholic Resistance was charged with plotting Henry Kissinger's kidnapping. The 10–2 verdict was itself testimony to the weakness of the evidence and indicated that, but for the flukes surrounding Evans and Schwartz, an acquittal was likely.

Still, the social scientists credited their techniques with achieving a fair and impartial jury for the Harrisburg Seven. They suspected that the government engaged in its own form of "jury shopping," choosing Harrisburg as a place for trial likely to produce jurors uncommonly favorable to the state. The social scientists justified their use of scientific jury selection as a way to offset the government's natural advantages.

But there were two troubles with this proposed ethic for scientific jury selection. First, it strains credulity to think the defense team was after an impartial jury rather than one favorable to the defense. In our adversary system of justice, there is nothing wrong with the defense approaching jury selection in search of jurors biased in its favor. Social scientists working within the system will just have to acknowledge that their mission is partisan and one-sided, not neutral service to a balanced jury. Second, jury consultants are far too quick to assume that persons willing to presume a defendant's guilt in response to a poll question would also presume guilt if seated on a jury. The Harrisburg jury pool only seemed biased toward the state, if we make this assumption. But most people, I believe, understand that their duty as jurors is to presume innocence (whereas no such duty hems in their answers to a telephone survey). The jury consultants made things look worse for the defendants in Harrisburg than they probably were.

THE MITCHELL/STANS TRIAL

In 1974, scientific jury selection's reputation took a giant step forward when a jury surprised court watchers by acquitting John Mitchell and Maurice Stans, two former cabinet members under Richard Nixon, of Watergate-related crimes.*

At a time when Watergate fever was running high in the nation's capital, the defense's use of survey data to navigate passage through jury selection was singled out in press accounts as a secret weapon.[60] Adapting the techniques used in the case of the Harrisburg Seven, the defense compiled a portrait of "'the worst possible juror': [a] liberal, Jewish Democrat, who reads the *New York Times* or the *Post*, . . . is interested in political affairs, and is well informed about Watergate."[61] The defense then used its peremptory challenges to successfully lower the number of jurors who had a high level of education, were informed about Watergate happenings, and read the *Times*. Nonetheless, from interviews after trial, reporters learned that the jury voted 8 to 4 on their first ballot to convict Mitchell and Stans. Such a first-ballot vote shows that scientific jury selection was a flop in this case. In only 5 percent of cases does a defendant secure an acquittal from a jury that starts out 8 to 4 against him.[62]

In fact, this was a rare case where the minority of four prevailed in the end. But posttrial interviews made clear that scientific jury selection was not responsible for the turnaround. The crucial, unpredictable event was that one juror fell ill prior to deliberations; alternate Andrew Choa took that juror's seat on the panel. Choa did not fit the survey data of a good

---

*The account of this case is taken from Hans Zeisel and Shari Seidman Diamond, "The Jury Selection in the Mitchell-Stans Conspiracy Trial," *American Bar Foundation Research Journal* (1976): 151–74; and Martin Arnold, "How Mitchell-Stans Jury Reached Acquittal Verdict," *New York Times*, May 5, 1974, p. A1.

defense juror—he was college educated and extremely informed about Watergate. But he was the vice president of a major bank, and the defense used the old-fashioned word of mouth method to find out that he held political views to "the right of Attila the Hun." He also apparently lied during voir dire, withholding information that he was an acquaintance of an assistant U.S. attorney, to keep himself in the pool of eligible jurors. Knowing Choa's views and sensing that he wanted to serve, the defense did not challenge him, and he became first an alternate and then a juror.

Once on the jury, Choa emerged as the dominant personality and a quasi social director, taking jurors to see a movie in the bank's private auditorium and arranging for them to see the St. Patrick's Day Parade from a bank branch office. During deliberations, Choa was able to call upon the ties he had forged with fellow jurors to exercise considerable influence. Eventually, he was able to convert the initial majority for conviction into a unanimous verdict of not guilty.

The flukes surrounding one juror, not the science of survey data, thus account for the surprise acquittals of Mitchell and Stans. The most that can be said for scientific jury selection in this case is that it perhaps prepared the way for Choa's power broker role by surrounding him with jurors whose lower education and lower occupational status made them unduly deferential to the one person among them familiar with the world of high finance and campaign contributions. Otherwise, absent Choa, the scientifically selected jury most likely would have gone on from an 8–4 first-ballot vote for conviction to an eventual guilty verdict.

The Joan Little Trial

The famous acquittal of Joan Little in 1975 provides no better evidence that scientific jury selection works.[*]

To be sure, as a black woman accused of killing her jailer in a rural North Carolina county, Little faced an uphill battle in getting a jury to believe she had killed in self-defense, after her jailer had entered her locked cell in the women's section of the jail. Given the closed, racist attitudes in the county of Beaufort where the crime occurred, a change of

[*]The account of this case is taken from John B. McConahay, Courtney J. Mullin, and Jeffrey T. Frederick, "The Uses of Social Science in Trials with Political and Racial Overtones: The Trial of Joan Little," *Law and Contemporary Problems* 41 (1977): 205–29; and Jeffrey T. Frederick, *The Psychology of the American Jury* (Charlottesville, Va.: Michie Co., 1987), pp. 7, 20–21, 33–41, 58–71.

venue was crucial if Little was to get a fair hearing. Here social science did play a significant and ethical role, far removed from its use in jury selection per se.

Polls of Beaufort County and its neighboring Pitt County (the most likely place to where the trial would be moved) showed that pretrial publicity and bias were equally great in both areas. About 75 percent of residents in both counties had heard of the crime; two-thirds believed that black women have lower morals than white women and that black people are more violent than white people. By comparison, residents of distant Orange County, in the Chapel Hill area of the state, were equally likely to have heard of the case but not to harbor the same attitudes about black women. Partly on the basis of this data, the judge moved the trial to Wake County, home of Raleigh, the state capital, where the judge thought that impartial jurors could more readily be found.

The defense conducted further surveys in Wake County to aid jury selection. A team led by Duke University psychology professor John McConahay developed a mathematical model of the ideal juror for the defense. An "authoritarianism rating scale" was used to rate how "rigid, racist, anti-semitic, sexually repressed, politically conservative or highly punitive" individuals were. Finally, an expert on body language from the University of Nebraska was brought in to observe the prospective jurors' patterns of "kinesic and paralinguistic behavior." All this information constituted a juror profile—a "predictive equation . . . based on which background characteristics were important predictors for that subgroup."

At a cost of over $35,000, the social scientists concluded that the more desirable jurors for Joan Little would be Democrats or Independents, younger than forty-five years old, residents of Raleigh, with a college education. To an outsider, these conclusions seemed rather obvious—hardly worth the fee. Nonetheless, the profiles became a benchmark against which defense lawyers judged individual jurors during voir dire. Following the profiles, they succeeded in impaneling a jury that included some ideal defense jurors—including two health food waitresses from Raleigh with some college education and a former college drama major turned record store manager.

But did all this attention to jury selection matter to the verdict? Probably not. The jury took only seventy-eight minutes to acquit Little of all charges, following a trial lasting five weeks. The facts, not whom the jurors were personally, controlled and curtailed their deliberations. The presiding judge said that the case against Little was one of the weakest he had seen in over twenty years on the bench. In the end, there was little the state could do to counter the physical evidence of semen on the jailer's leg when his body was discovered inside a locked woman's cell, his pants and shoes outside the cell. The only hypothesis that would support Little's guilt was that she had seduced the jailer into her cell, intending to attack and disarm him. The jury found that such a hypothesis fell far short of proof beyond a reasonable doubt.

And yet popular commentaries on the Little verdict trumpeted the role of scientific jury selection and ignored the discipline of the evidence. Changes in racial attitudes in parts of North Carolina and the willingness of white jurors to acquit a black woman charged with killing a white man were given little credit. The myth of scientific jury selection was unstoppable.

THE CASE OF JOHN DELOREAN

Belief in the almighty power of jury selection took yet another quantum leap forward in 1984 when a federal jury of six men and six women stunned prosecutors by acquitting automaker John DeLorean of cocaine trafficking charges.*

Undercover federal agents had videotaped DeLorean in the apparent act of conspiring with government informants (posing as crooked bankers and drug dealers) to sell cocaine as a quick way to raise money for his failing new automobile venture. One tape, shown prior to trial on the national CBS program "60 Minutes," showed DeLorean in a hotel room sitting in front of an open suitcase filled with fifty-five pounds of cocaine, saying, "It's as good as gold." How could a jury find DeLorean not guilty after viewing such an incriminating videotape? Press accounts once again favored defense advantages gained during jury selection as the likely explanation.

In particular, the advice of jury consultant Cathy Bennett emerged as the defense's supposed secret weapon. Bennett began by commissioning a random telephone survey of some one thousand residents of the Central District of California (the place set for trial). But the focus of her efforts

---

*The account of this case is taken from "DeLorean Trial Jurors Tell Why They Voted to Acquit," *New York Times*, Dec. 10, 1984, p. B15; Jay Mathews, "New Courtroom Consultants; DeLorean Jury Selected with Expert Help," *Washington Post*, Aug. 18, 1984, p. A1; Robert Lindsey, "DeLorean Jurors Discuss Reasons Behind Verdict," *New York Times*, Aug. 18, 1984, p. 46; Judith Cummings, "DeLorean is Freed of Cocaine Charge by a Federal Jury," *New York Times*, Aug. 17, 1984, p. A1; Steven Brill, "Inside the DeLorean Jury Room," in Brill, *Trial by Jury*, pp. 229–65.

was never on predicting jury behavior from demographic profiles. The poll's main use was to convince the presiding judge that pretrial publicity had led some 72 percent of the population to believe that DeLorean was guilty of the drug charges. A forty-two-page questionnaire returned by 143 prospective jurors showed a similarly high percentage of persons leaning toward a guilty verdict.

The defense used this data to win from the judge key concessions about the conduct of voir dire. In federal courts, judges often do all the questioning; in the DeLorean case, the judge permitted the lawyers to conduct part of the voir dire themselves. Even more crucial, the judge departed from normal procedures and permitted jurors to be questioned privately, out of the hearing of fellow jurors. These changes, according to Bennett, were significant in getting honest answers during voir dire.

The defense strategy during voir dire was hardly all that scientific or manipulative. Following Bennett's well-known advice, DeLorean's chief lawyer, Howard Weitzman, stayed away from asking the normal boiler-plate question "Have you formed an opinion about this case?" He sought to relax jurors into acknowledging that, of course, they had heard things about the case. Open-ended questions like "Tell me, what do you think?" were asked instead. Bennett's advice was to be wary of jurors who flat-out denied the effects of pretrial publicity; a juror with an open mind would concede that "it's hard to put [media accounts] aside but I think I can do it."

Such an approach to voir dire was more conventional than scientific. Standard survey research would have led the defense to use one of its peremptory challenges to eliminate William Lahr, a former California Highway Patrol officer, in a trial that was going to turn largely on the testimony of law enforcement agents. But Lahr's open-minded answers during voir dire constituted a better guide to his attitudes, according to Bennett, than his "bad" background. The defense did not object to him, and he eventually became foreman of the jury.

Overall, the twelve jurors seated were politically moderate or conservative; they had voted 10 to 2 for Ronald Reagan in the previous presidential election. Three came from law enforcement backgrounds, including one retired army colonel. Two were insurance adjusters. In posttrial interviews given after the verdict, nine of eleven jurors admitted to going into the trial assuming that DeLorean was guilty. Thus, the defense did not win the case through some immediately apparent scientific edge gained during jury selection.

Media accounts reported the verdicts as if they flew in the face of DeLorean's obvious guilt—all recorded on videotape. But, according to posttrial interviews, the jurors did not find the evidence as strong as the media reported. Seven jurors concluded that there was insufficient evidence that DeLorean had ever entered into a conspiracy to deal drugs. Carefully viewed, what most of the government's tapes showed was DeLorean seeking investors in his failing auto company through a supposedly crooked banker (actually an undercover federal agent). The so-called banker told DeLorean that he had clients who needed to invest tremendous amounts of illicit drug profits. DeLorean, in the videotapes, was certainly eager to engage in some scheme for laundering this money through investment in his failing company. But apparently the jury found the tapes far from clear as to whether DeLorean went further and conspired to buy and resell drugs himself for profit.

At one point, DeLorean told the banker that he did not have $2 million to invest in drugs; the banker then concocted an arrangement whereby DeLorean could remain in the deal by putting up what the banker knew to be worthless stock in the car company. According to the final tape, where DeLorean is filmed with a real drug smuggler and an open suitcase of cocaine, there were never any arrangements made by the two for what drugs DeLorean would buy, how much he would pay, or how profits would be split. Seven jurors found that such evidence left them with reasonable doubts about whether DeLorean was actually intending to do a drug deal—as opposed to laundering a drug smuggler's profits (a crime with which he was not charged).

Five other jurors thought that DeLorean might have conspired to sell drugs but that the government had entrapped him. Acting as an undercover government informant, a convicted drug dealer who knew DeLorean made the initial contact with the auto mogul. The jury disbelieved, as probably any jury selected in any fashion would have disbelieved, the informant's story that he called DeLorean only to suggest that their children play together and that DeLorean then turned a social call into talk of a drug deal. Moreover, the jury was apparently bothered by the fact that it was the federal agent posing as the banker who kept DeLorean in the deal, even when DeLorean said he had no money to invest.

In sum, the defense had a stronger case than media accounts ever acknowledged. From posttrial interviews, a consistent picture emerged of a jury basing its decision on the evidence, or lack of it. As one juror put it, "You start with the presumption of innocence and it was never proven to my satisfaction that he'd committed those acts." But remarks such as these were not taken at face value in the considerable speculation following trial about what went wrong for the government. With images of the "60 Minutes" tape still fresh in people's minds, the work of jury consultant Bennett became the lead story of the trial.[63]

PEOPLE OF CALIFORNIA V. LEE EDWARD HARRIS

I turn next to an example of scientific jury selection that did achieve positive, if still mixed, results. In 1979, Lee Edward Harris, a young black male, went on trial for the murder of a white couple who managed an apartment complex in Long Beach, California.*

Of the eligible jurors in the jurisdiction, 16.4 percent were black and 20 percent were Hispanic. Nonetheless, an all-white jury of twelve was impaneled. The jury convicted Harris of committing a murder during an armed robbery and sentenced him to death.

The California Supreme Court reversed Harris's conviction, holding that blacks and Hispanics were systematically underrepresented in the available jury venire because the county unlawfully relied exclusively on voter registration lists as the source of potential juror names.[64] Retrial was set for July 1985; use of supplementary sources of juror names was ordered.

Harris's defense team turned to scientific jury selection in an attempt to impanel a jury that would at least spare Harris's life. The defense considered Harris's conviction of first-degree murder a foregone conclusion on retrial. They pinned their hopes on selecting a jury that would sentence Harris to a life prison term, even after learning in the penalty phase of trial that Harris had a prior murder conviction.

Obviously, the defense task was not easy. After excuses for hardship, a venire of 120 prospective jurors remained, all of whom filled out lengthy questionnaires. Defense experts codified and computerized the answers and "identified risk profiles, that is, jurors who were more likely to vote

---

*The account of this case is taken from Hiroshi Fukurai, Edgar W. Butler, and Richard Krooth, *Race and the Jury: Racial Disenfranchisement and the Search for Justice* (New York: Plenum Press, 1993), pp. 144–54. Details about the actual case come from *People v. Lee Edward Harris*, 36 Cal. 3d 36, 679 P. 2d 433 (1984) (setting aside conviction and death sentence and remanding for new trial); *People v. Harris*, 191 Cal. App. 3d 819, 824–26 (1987) (reversing conviction and life sentence due to trial court's error in preventing defendant from testifying); *People v. Harris*, 217 Cal. App. 3d 1332 (1990) (state may not seek death penalty on remand).

for death (high risk) or who were more likely to vote for life imprisonment without possibility of parole (low risk)." Their statistical analysis revealed that high-risk jurors were characterized by being old, white, and female (a surprise correlation in a death-penalty case) and having less than a high school education.

During voir dire, defense lawyers used the high risk/low risk profiles to guide their peremptory challenges. The defense exercised nine peremptories, eight of them against white members of the venire. The defense did not strike any members of racial minorities or persons under the age of thirty.* The prosecution exercised six peremptory challenges, three against non-Hispanic whites, two against African-Americans, and one against a Hispanic.

In the end, a jury of seven whites, three African-Americans, and two Hispanics was impaneled. Nine of the twelve jurors were male. No person younger than twenty or older than seventy was seated. All jurors had at least a high school education, a majority had some college education, and three had postgraduate education.

The defense was satisfied that it had won the battle over selection and gained a jury that was of adequately low risk in its attitude toward the death penalty. But the defense gave far too much credit to scientific jury selection for making the difference between the all-white jury at Harris's first trial and the more racially diverse jury impaneled for retrial. The major changes had to do first with the court-ordered recruitment of a more representative jury venire than had been available during the first trial. Second, as we saw in chapter 3, California had taken the lead in barring prosecutors from using peremptories to eliminate minority members of the venire simply on the basis of suspicion that they would favor their own race. These two legal reforms had more to do with the achievement of a racially diverse jury on retrial than did any scientific strategizing by the defense.

Moreover, the importance of having a critical mass of African-Americans on Harris's jury would have been obvious to any competent criminal lawyer, with or without the advice of jury consultants. Historically, capital

---

*At the time of Harris's retrial, California law prohibited defense counsel, as well as prosecutors, from basing peremptory challenges solely on group-based suspicions. *People v. Wheeler*, 583 P. 2d 748, 760 (1978). It is not clear whether any issue was raised about defendants using their peremptories to strike members of the jury panel solely on the basis of race. See Fukurai et al., *Race and the Jury*, pp. 148–50.

punishment has fallen disproportionately on black defendants who kill white victims.*

The Harris case itself is an unfortunate if revealing example of the undeniable gulf that separates the ideals of color-blind deliberation from the realities of jury behavior. Postverdict interviews showed that the jury split 9 to 3 on racial lines on the first ballot, in favor of the death sentence. Apart from race, none of the other demographic factors that supposedly made jurors low risks panned out for the defense on the first ballot, although arguably they might have made the jurors' attitudes soft enough to be moved by the opposition of the three African-Americans. Normally, an initial nine-person majority carries the eventual verdict. But the defense emphasis on getting more than a token black on the jury apparently paid off; the three African-Americans were able to hold together, and ultimately the assertiveness of one led the jury to recommend life without the possibility of parole.

Due deference to reality means acknowledging that Harris's fate hinged partly on the racial composition of his jury. But it does not take fancy number-crunching to teach lawyers that whites and blacks occupy different places in American society and that these differences affect attitudes toward the death penalty, police officers, and the criminal justice system.[65] Because such differences exist, we strive to recruit jurors from a cross section of the community. The problem with race-based scientific jury selection is that, if we permit both sides to use such tactics in criminal trials, the goal of racially representative juries would be undermined more often than it was realized. Harris may have narrowly won the battle over the jury's racial composition this time around, but in general, the invocation of science to justify elimination of jurors for racial reasons is bound to work in favor of the majority race.

THE MCMARTIN CHILD ABUSE TRIAL

In 1990, the longest trial in U.S. history ended in the acquittal of Raymond Buckey and his mother, Peggy McMartin Buckey, on charges of sexually abusing children at the McMartin preschool in Los Angeles.†

---

*See chapter 6 for a discussion of race and the death penalty.

†The account of jury selection in the *McMartin* trial is taken from Fukurai, *Race and the Jury*, pp. 200–208; and Lois Timnick and Carol McGraw, "McMartin Verdict: Not Guilty," *Los Angeles Times*, Jan. 19, 1990, p. A1.

After two and a half years of testimony and nine weeks of deliberation, the jury acquitted the defendants of fifty-two counts and deadlocked on thirteen other charges. Subsequently, Raymond Buckey was retried on eight of the thirteen charges; another hung jury resulted in August 1990, and the district attorney elected not to seek a third trial.

Jury consultants for the defense on the first McMartin trial credit their work with playing a leading role in achieving the favorable verdicts. Given the length of the trial, this is a remarkable claim to make on behalf of the staying influence of what occurs during jury selection. It makes a bad joke of the quip that the trial is over when jury selection is over—as if sixty thousand pages of testimony was not enough to erase the hold of group bias and preconceptions over jurors.

What edge did the McMartin defendants supposedly gain during jury selection? The defense commissioned a community survey of eligible jurors who lived in the judicial district where the case would be tried. Of the respondents, 96.7 percent had heard or read about the McMartin case; 97.1 percent of them believed that the children at McMartin had been sexually abused. Two-thirds "did not know" whether Peggy McMartin Buckey was guilty or not. But, of those who had an opinion, 86 percent thought she was guilty.

To deal with pretrial prejudice, the defense employed a consulting firm to examine the survey data and "identify the sociodemographic and behavioral characteristics of the potential jurors who were least likely to be influenced by the pretrial publicity." In addition to using the community survey, the consultants collected data from a court questionnaire filled out by the 205 prospective jurors from among whom the actual jury would be drawn. As voir dire occurred, the consultants made individual "behavioral observations," and then computers were used to evaluate the information for possible hidden prejudices among individual jurors.

Combining all their sources of information, the consultants rank ordered all 205 prospective jurors, the first being the least biased. Despite the massive pretrial publicity, the consultants purported to discover that "the *race* of the prospective jurors was one of the most crucial factors differentiating those who expressed the opinion that the defendants were guilty and those who were not sure about the trial outcome." In particular, the survey identified Hispanics and Native Americans as more likely to render a guilty verdict than were African-Americans, Asians, and whites. The consultants isolated other demographic factors that they thought made prospective jurors less biased toward guilt: young, male, college educated, and a relatively high income.

The jury of twelve consisted of one Hispanic, two Asians, three African-Americans, and six whites. It included four women and eight men, with age being skewed toward the young and middle-aged groups. The majority of jurors had a college education. These numbers indicate that the defense succeeded in hitting its demographic targets during jury selection. Eleven jury members were from racial groups found less likely to lean toward a guilty verdict; the remaining factors were likewise favorable.

The underrepresentation of Hispanics in particular was striking. At the time, Hispanics constituted 23.3 percent of Los Angeles County and 27.7 percent of the Central Superior Court judicial district where the case would be tried. However, they made up only 7.9 percent of the defense's own community survey of eligible jurors in the judicial district, 4.9 percent of the jury venire available for voir dire, and 8.6 percent (one of twelve) of the jury itself. On their own, these numbers raise some troubling questions about whether the jury that acquitted the McMartin defendants of most charges was a fair cross section of the community.

But what I want to focus on is the consultants' claim that Hispanics and Native Americans were more likely to have "already decided the verdict on the basis of the mass media reports."[66] There are serious problems with such a claim. First, it is misleading to report that the Hispanics and Native Americans surveyed had already decided on what verdict they would render as jurors. The questionnaire asked individuals only about their preconceptions about the case, based on media accounts. To describe responses to polls as verdicts is to prejudge the crucial issues at stake. Do people respond, as part of a jury group, the same way they respond to a poll question? The consultants' provocative use of the word "verdict" to describe individual answers to survey questions reveals a view that denigrates group deliberation as but the sum of individual biases.

A deeper problem surfaced when the consultants suggested explanations for why Hispanics and Native Americans were predisposed to find the defendants guilty. Their first speculation was that "the defendants were white and did not share the racial or ethnic background of the prospective jurors." The consultants offered no evidence for this familiar assumption that jurors favor their own kind. On that assumption, blacks and Asians should have been equally predisposed to find the defendants guilty—a finding not born out by the survey. Moreover, "Hispanic" is not a racial category, and the contrast between whites and Hispanics in the Los Angeles area can be quite misleading.

The consultants do offer a second, more promising explanation for why Hispanics and Native Americans should have been particularly primed to find the defendants guilty: "Child molestation may have had significant cultural and ideological meaning" to those groups. But, to the extent this is true, then a defense jury selection strategy that aimed at minimizing the number of Hispanics and Native Americans on the jury was inconsistent with the public's interest in preserving the jury as a body whose deliberations are enriched by a dialogue among various communities. It is one thing for a lawyer to establish during voir dire that a particular individual, of any group, cannot be impartial in the case due to personal attitudes or experiences.* It is quite another matter to design jury selection strategy around the inexact science that infers bias from the person's demographic profile. The science is so inexact that it blurs back into the kind of stereotypical assumptions that *Batson* and its progeny are currently trying to weed out of American law.

In the end, the McMartin case is one among many where scientific jury selection had minimal influence on the verdict. Posttrial interviews indicate that the jurors were deeply troubled by the leading and suggestive questions children were asked during their taped interviews; they reacted negatively to interview techniques that seemed to border on programming children to believe they were molested. Even so, many jurors expressed their belief that the McMartins were probably guilty; they just could not certify that the interview evidence established guilt beyond a reasonable doubt.[67] These posttrial comments indicate a jury that gave a rational verdict in light of the evidence. The fact that a second jury also deadlocked is further indication that the verdicts were the result of flawed evidence, not perfect jury selection.

---

*Many prospective jurors in the McMartin retrial were surprised at just how personal and intrusive the voir dire was. Lawyers asked individuals, "Have you ever been accused of sexual misconduct?" or "Have you ever been a victim of sexual assault?" Lawyers also probed individual bias through more general questions such as, "Do you think it is possible that children could say they have been molested when they haven't? Do you think a defendant in a criminal trial should be required to prove his innocence?" Seth Mydans, "Brevity Follows Marathon in Retrial," *New York Times*, July 6, 1990, p. A9.

THE MYTH OF SCIENTIFIC JURY SELECTION

The science of jury selection is now a generation old, and much of the bloom is off the rose. Neither the fears nor the hopes of those who thought social scientists were on the verge of predicting the verdicts of jurors have been realized. By 1994, a lawyer's use of social scientists during selection seems just another part of the routine—better than consulting a magic man, says one lawyer, but by no means the power tool once advertised. In his survey of scientific jury selection technique, sociologist Michael Saks concludes that it is a relatively "weak device."[68] He blames jury consulting firms for selling a product they know is not effective, and he takes lawyers to task for ignoring convincing evidence that "with few exceptions . . . verdicts are far more heavily influenced by the evidence and arguments presented than by the jurors' personal characteristics."[69]

At best, survey data generates probabilistic statements about the attitudes or biases of a specific group. Within limits, probabilistic theorems may be of use to lawyers, enabling them to play the odds or make educated bets. But, as jury scholar Shari Seidman Diamond puts it, scientific jury selection becomes "blatant voodoo" if it promises to sketch the ideal defense or prosecution juror for all cases and communities.[70]

Moreover, scientific jury selection cannot control for the fluid group dynamics that influence jury deliberations. Whether a prospective juror turns out to be, say, vocal or deferential, a loner or a member of a clique, depends in part on the others chosen for the jury. Astute trial lawyers thus rarely work from static formulas during jury selection, which is an unfolding drama where factors about individuals far outweigh the static significance of group identity considered alone.

Once trials start, the smallest of accidents or coincidences upset the best of selection plans. In one case, "the victim turns out to be the spitting image of the juror's deceitful Uncle Louie"; in another, "a juror suddenly remembers that she forgot to pay the mortgage bill and misses a few minutes of crucial testimony."[71] These examples may seem mundane, but they are precisely the intricate details that resist scientific forecasts.

The most recent reviewers of empirical research on jury selection agree that demographic profiles fail to provide specific enough information to a lawyer faced with sizing up a prospective juror. Psychologists Saul Kassin and Lawrence Wrightsman note that "attempts to connect demographic states, abilities, aptitudes, temperaments, and personalities of jurors to verdict differences, have met with limited success."[72] Phoebe

Ellsworth, of the University of Michigan's School of Law and Institute for Social Research, concurs: the literature is full of "overoptimistic claims that various personality or background variables are reliable indicators of a proprosecution or prodefense juror. . . . A review of the relevant research indicates that the usual hoary or trendy stereotypes are not very useful (race, class, gender, occupation, and nationality)."[73] A third review of scientific jury selection's track record indicates that "there is surely nothing surprising about [its] signal lack of success: the empirical evidence supporting the assumed link between the behavior of jurors and their background characteristics is slender and sometimes contradictory."[74]

I do not mean to suggest that scientific jury selection is made out of whole cloth. All jurors hear, or at least sit through, the same evidence. Yet they react differently, and unanimity is rare on first ballots. In this sense, it is a truism that "whom the jurors are" matters to the verdict.[75] And, if a lawyer knows nothing else about a prospective juror other than the groups to which he or she belongs, then using polling data about group attitudes may be a better approach to voir dire than pure intuition. One critic compares the science of jury selection with the science of deciding whether to pinch-hit for a batter on a single occasion.[76] In both situations, statistical averages are helpful but they fall far short of forecasting any one trip to the plate or any one juror's verdict in any one case.

In rejecting scientific jury selection, I do not mean to insist that race, gender, religion, national origin, age, and a host of other characteristics have no influence whatsoever in the jury room. The choice is not between the myth about jurors who deliberate as if they had no earthly backgrounds and the science of jurors captive to their group allegiances. The sober middle ground acknowledges that jurors will be influenced by their group backgrounds; it simply denies that these demographic factors are so strong—or static—as to overwhelm the force of evidence, make every member of an ethnic group fungible with every other member of the same group, override personal dynamics among jurors, and make a science out of forecasting jury behavior.

Take, for instance, the influence of gender on jury verdicts. As I argued in chapter 3 in discussing the Ballard case, women make distinctive contributions to jury deliberation not because of biology but because of different life experiences.[77] These differences may well be at their greatest when cases turn on allegations of rape or sexual abuse, as did the Menendez brothers' trial and the celebrated 1994 case of Lorena

Bobbitt.[78] But in general there is no evidence that women and men end up voting as blocs on juries.[79]

Research on gender and jury verdicts, observes psychologist Reid Hastie, establishes only two conclusions with any degree of certainty. First, women talk less frequently than men on juries. Second, female students on mock juries are more likely than male students to regard the defendant guilty in a rape case.[80] The most sophisticated studies show that even in rape cases, a juror's sex does not emerge as some constant, all-powerful, or isolated determinant of attitudes but rather interacts in complex ways with a host of other variables, including the race of the defendant and victim, the strength of the evidence, the kind of rape involved (by stranger or acquaintance), and, most important, personal views about rape and its causes, women, and sex-role norms.[81]

These complex conclusions are not surprising; they are implicit in the fluid ways we define who is "the same" and who is "the other." Gender does not stand alone—neither for women nor for men—in setting up these boundary distinctions.

In studies of gender and jury verdicts in cases other than those involving rape, no consistent pattern has emerged.[82] And the most commonly made generalization about women jurors—that they will be more "empathic than men in terms of guilty verdicts and in terms of considering a defendant's intentions"—is not universally supported by the evidence.[83]

Empirical conclusions about gender and jurors are difficult to reach, precisely because sex is only one factor among many that influence jurors. One study tellingly found that the influence of sex varied depending on whether the comparison was between white men and white women or between black men and black women.[84] This flags a more general problem with attempts to predict juror behavior from demographic profiles. When a defendant is a young, white, Italian Catholic woman from the middle class, is the important demographic factor about prospective jurors their age, race, ethnicity, religion, sex, or economic status? And would the answer change depending on whether the charge against the defendant were shoplifting, child abuse, or embezzlement? Or do attitudes become influential only in relation to specific facts about a case?[85]

A good example of this problem occurred in 1968 during the first trial of Black Panther leader Huey Newton, who was charged with murdering a police officer. In general, the prosecutors settled on using their peremptory challenges to strike black members of the jury venire. But they chose not to strike one particular black, David Harper, a loan officer for the Bank of America who lived in a middle-class, mostly white section of Oakland. Apparently, the prosecution thought that the loan officer would identify himself less in terms of race and more in terms of class, at least vis-à-vis Newton.[86]

But is it possible to disentangle all the competing identities that constitute a person and predict how that person will behave as a juror in a single case? Could any of us say about ourselves which of our many group identities comes to the fore and when? The verdict in the Newton case does not provide a definitive answer as to whether the prosecution guessed rightly or wrongly about Harper. He became foreman, and the jury returned a "compromise" verdict, acquitting Newton of murder but convicting him of voluntary manslaughter.

In the end, the questions raised by scientific jury selection are more of an ethical nature than an empirical nature. Scientific jury selection, as currently practiced, is not possible without the use of peremptory challenges based largely on inferences about a prospective juror from the person's group background. The suspicions are now based on polls and surveys rather than mere stereotypes. Still, scientific jury selection raises the same questions about the legitimate bounds of peremptory challenges that we discussed at the end of chapter 3.

Attorneys on each side have adversarial reasons for wanting to exclude persons of a certain group from the jury. But what public good comes from permitting lawyers to offer a scientific reason for why they struck, say, blacks, women, Jews, or Irish? The full ethical dilemma is hidden when race or sex is the basis for exercising a peremptory challenge, because these features of a prospective juror are generally visible. But a person's religion or national origin is not obvious or always detectable from a name. Should a defense lawyer be permitted, during voir dire, to ask a prospective juror what his or her religion or national origin is and then strike the person if the prospective juror acknowledges belonging to a group that the jury consultants say is statistically hostile to the defense? The spectacle of inquiring into a person's religion or national origin, only to strike the person if the answer is one way rather than another, should be enough to indicate the underlying tension between traditional norms of blind jury selection and the new science.

Scientific jury selection makes the ethical case against itself. Suppose science could predict which group identity, among the many that form a personality, would come to the fore if a particular person were chosen as a juror in a particular case. The conclusion to draw from such a break-through is not that both sides should remain free to use their peremptory challenges as aids in tilting the demographic balance in their favor. Rather, the need to disarm the parties of peremptory challenges and to preserve the full range of views on the jury would be more apparent than ever.

In short, scientific jury selection cannot have it both ways. It cannot claim that a person's group identify is a useful predictor of how that person will behave as a juror and then also claim that each side to a lawsuit or criminal trial should have the right to use that predictive power to skew the impartiality of juries. The traditional justification for peremptory challenges was that they enhanced the final impartiality of the jury by permitting parties to remove persons suspected of bias against them. But, as eminent criminal defense lawyer Herald Price Fahringer told a *New York Times* reporter, "There isn't a trial lawyer in this country who wouldn't tell you—if he were being honest—'I don't want an impartial jury. I want one that's going to find in my client's favor.'"[87]

The basic method of scientific jury selection contradicts the new ethic the Supreme Court set for jury selection, when it outlawed race- or sex-based peremptory challenges.[88] If we are serious in holding fast to the ideal that individuals are not captives of narrow group loyalty as jurors, then we should practice jury selection in a way that inspires those selected to do the best they can to live up to these ideals of blind justice. Scientific jury selection cannot carry any such inspiration for those selected or for the rest of us watching the jury trial. Far from being just a neutral device for selecting jurors, scientific jury selection is itself the kind of trial practice that undermines public confidence in the jury system and teaches each to think of the other as representing someone else's justice.

In closing, I return to the question of why scientific jury selection garners a reputation beyond what the evidence supports. The idea that jury selection can be manipulated obviously resonates with a public already skeptical about traditional ideals of impartial or color-blind justice. Indeed, scientific jury selection provides the cynic with the perfect language for rejecting talk of virtuous jurors putting aside personal opinions to find the truth. As a professor of rhetoric remarked after surveying social science literature on the jury, "No social scientist thinks that the judgment reached by a jury establishes or determines—in a deep sense—the innocence or guilt of the defendant. No social scientist thinks that the verdict is the speaking of truth."[89]

Nor are jurors described any longer as "members of a community of persons who share the same law."[90] Instead, scientific jury selection takes its cue from the new description of the jury as a "fair community cross section." An understanding of the cross-sectional jury took hold in the 1970s, casting jurors as inevitable bearers of the biases of their own kind. A jury verdict was the result of group interactions, with each juror "processing" the evidence and instructions in tune with the particular attitudes and predispositions he or she brought to the case.[91] In this scientific scenario, juries still deliberated. But the key to understanding how deliberation worked was no longer to be found in the evidence. Deliberation, scientifically speaking, was demoted to a psychological process about how pressure in small group situations permits a political resolution of the social forces represented on the jury.

Scientific jury selection grew out of, and in turn pushed further, the prevailing skepticism about juries as impartial institutions of justice. More than any other idea over the last generation, it captured the basic shift in our conception of the jury—from a group that would find common ground above individual differences to a group that divides, almost predictably, along all the fissures of identity in America.

PART III

DEMOCRATIC
DELIBERATION

Juries invest each citizen with a sort of magisterial office; they make all . . . feel that they have duties toward society and that they take a share in its government. By making men pay attention to things other than their own affairs, they combat that individual selfishness which is like rust in society.

—Alexis de Tocqueville, *Democracy in America* (1833)

Several secret votes were taken and each time there were fewer votes for a life sentence. But Ms. Daniels did not change her mind. The other jurors reminded her that she had sworn in court that she "could" impose the death penalty and implied [she] could get in trouble if [she] continued to hold out. One of the jurors said that [they] needed to go ahead and get it over with because the next day was Mother's Day.

As the pressure against her mounted, Ms. Daniels stood up and said, "You do what you have to do, but I won't vote for a death sentence." She refused to participate in further votes.

The remaining jurors then came up with an astounding solution to the apparent deadlock. According to Ms Daniels: "The other jurors decided to go and tell the judge that we had voted for a death sentence. . . ."

That was how [the defendant] was sentenced to death.

—Bob Herbert, *New York Times*, March 27 and 30, 1994

(the prisoner was executed on March 31)

CHAPTER FIVE

The Unanimous Verdict

FOR OVER SIX HUNDRED YEARS, the unanimous verdict has stood as a distinctive and defining feature of jury trials. The first recorded instance of a unanimous verdict occurred in 1367, when an English Court refused to accept an 11–1 guilty vote after the lone holdout stated he would rather die in prison than consent to convict.[1] Steadily afterward, the requirement of unanimity took hold. As legal historians Frederick Pollock and Frederic Maitland point out,

> From the moment when our records begin, we seem to see a strong desire for unanimity. In a thousand cases the jury is put before us as speaking with a single voice, while any traces of dissent . . . confessed by some only of the jurors are very rare.[2]

Some American colonies briefly authorized majority verdicts in the seventeenth century, apparently because of unfamiliarity with common-law procedures.[3] But by the eighteenth century, it was agreed that verdicts had to be unanimous. Indeed, prior to 1972, no case explicitly disputing the unanimity requirement in criminal cases ever came before the Supreme Court. Incidental references to the "obvious" requirement that criminal jury verdicts be unanimous date to the late 1800s.[4] As the Court noted in 1898, "The wise men who framed the Constitution of the United States and the people who approved it were of [the] opinion that life and liberty, when involved in criminal prosecutions, would not be adequately secured except through the unanimous verdict of twelve jurors."[5] In 1897, a case challenging the necessity of unanimous verdicts in civil cases reached the Court. But the Court readily dismissed the challenge, saying that "no authorities are needed to sustain [the] proposition" that "unanimity was one of the peculiar and essential features of trial by jury at the common law."[6]

Unquestioned acceptance of the concept of unanimous verdict abruptly came to an end, for the criminal jury, in the late 1960s and early 1970s.[*] In 1967, England authorized criminal juries to return verdicts by a margin as low as 10 to 2, so long as the jury deliberated at least two hours.[7] In 1972, in cases from Oregon and Louisiana, the Supreme Court ruled that the Constitution permits state, though not federal, criminal juries to split by a 10–2 or 9–3 margin in noncapital cases.[8]

Dismissing the unanimous verdict requirement as a historical accident lacking constitutional stature, the Court concluded that elimination of the requirement would not materially affect the essential function of the criminal jury—placing between the accused and government "the common-sense judgment of a group of laymen" drawn from a cross section of the community.[9] Specifically, the Court found that unanimity was not essential to justice because its demise would lessen neither the reliability of verdicts, still proven beyond a reasonable doubt to the overwhelming majority of the jurors,[10] nor the representativeness of jury verdicts, because deliberation supposedly would go on as before between majority and minority points of view.[11]

During roughly the same years the Court was withdrawing constitutional protection from the unanimous verdict in criminal cases, it was also finding that the twelve-person jury was not constitutionally required. As with unanimity, the Court reasoned that the number twelve was a fluke of history unrelated to the core functions of the jury.[12] In subsequent years, the Court has engaged in some elaborate line-drawing to map how far states may shrink jury size or combine smaller jury size with less than

---

[*]The chronology regarding civil juries and unanimous verdicts is different. By force of the Seventh Amendment, unanimous verdicts are still constitutionally required in all federal civil jury trials. However, since 1937, the Federal Rules of Civil Procedure have permitted the parties to waive the unanimity requirement and agree to a verdict by "a stated majority of the jurors." Fed R. Civ. Proc. 48.

Because the Seventh Amendment has never been held applicable to the states, the unanimous verdict has never been required in state civil jury trials as a matter of federal constitutional law. All but seventeen states permit nonunanimous verdicts in civil cases tried in courts of general jurisdiction. National Center for State Courts, *State Court Organization*, preliminary draft (Williamsburg, Va.: National Center for State Courts, forthcoming), table 7.

unanimous verdicts. As to jury size in nonpetty criminal cases, the Court has drawn the line at six, holding five persons too small to meet the Sixth Amendment requirement that juries be representative of the community.[13] And the Court has made clear that states may not get around the six-person minimum, by allowing 5–1 jury convictions.[14]

Today, over thirty states use juries that are made up of fewer than twelve persons to try at least some nonpetty criminal offenses.[15] But few states avail themselves of the Court's permission to experiment with nonunanimous verdicts. Louisiana and Oregon remain the only states authorizing felony convictions by less than unanimous verdicts. Florida permits juries to recommend life versus death, for persons convicted of murder, by a straight majority vote; however, the jury's recommendation is advisory only and subject to judicial override.[16] Some states permit defendants to waive their right to a unanimous verdict.[17]

Even though the Court's 1972 decisions did not open the floodgates to majority verdicts, those decisions represent a remarkable demotion of the unanimous verdict rule, stripping it of constitutional protection and leaving it up to states to accept it or not. After so much history, what lies behind this weakened stature for the unanimous verdict rule? What is the Court saying about the future of the jury—long identified as the forum where Americans define a common justice above social divisions—when it finds unanimity to be superfluous to the jury task? In short, what light does the Court's debate over unanimous verdicts shed on the future of the deliberative ideal for the jury?

I begin by considering why so many previous generations thought unanimity was fundamental to jury justice. Why did unanimous verdicts become so characteristic of jury trials, when majority rule triumphed generally in modern democracies? The Supreme Court itself decides cases through bare majority decisions; congressional legislation generally requires only a simple majority for passage; supermajorities are reserved for exceptional circumstances such as overriding a presidential veto, ratifying a treaty, or impeaching a president. Presidents are elected by a simple majority of the electoral college vote and sometimes by only a plurality of the popular vote.

Constitutional democracies, of course, recognize individual and minority rights in ways that temper and corral the will of the majority. Still, the criminal jury has long remained the odd institution out, wholly rejecting the legitimacy of majority rule as a tool for doing justice.

THE POLITICAL THEORY OF
UNANIMITY VERSUS MAJORITY RULE

History provides no clear answer as to why the ideal of unanimity found such a permanent home in the jury. There is some evidence that the ideal prevailed generally in medieval institutions. The Church placed a premium on unanimity as "the infallible sign of God's voice."[18] Fourteenth-century English Parliaments still doubted that a majority vote was sufficient to bind individuals; their hesitancy may have reflected an argument that individuals could be bound legally only by their own consent and not by what the majority decided.[19] As one medieval scholar put it, "The word consent . . . carried with it the idea of *concordia* or unanimity."[20]

In its original form, the medieval jury had its own reasons to prefer unanimity. Being drawn from the neighborhood, jurors were presumed to be witnesses to the events on trial, or at least informed about them. Disagreement therefore suggested perjury and argued for a unanimity requirement. The medieval mind was also more likely than our own to believe that reason could tolerate only one, correct, answer to what happened; there was no room for reasonable jurors to disagree.[21] But, whatever its medieval origins, the unanimous verdict requirement survived into modern times to become a pillar of popular faith in the legitimacy and accuracy of jury verdicts. By contrast, "the decision-making process in Parliament became avowedly majoritarian" by the fifteenth century.[22]

Why did unanimity retain its grasp on the jury long after other democratic institutions converted to majority rule? In political decisions generally, truth is not thought to be the goal. Nor in pluralist democracies is much emphasis placed on uniting persons to a common good. Legitimate clashes of interest occur that are not resolvable through reasoned debate but reflect merely subjective preferences and partisan allegiances. Because there is said to be no common good above the assortment of desires and interests persons happen to have, we leave individuals and groups free to assert their own interests against those of others. There is no expectation that harmony and consensus will emerge as practical tools for governing. Disagreement and dissent are the very stuff of politics—in a democracy at least.

But, in line with the basic theme of this book, it is illuminating that the jury did not develop into just another example of the politics of bargaining. The unanimous verdict rule gives concrete expression to a different set of democratic aspirations—keyed to deliberation rather than voting and to consensus rather than division. Voters pull a curtain and vote in private; jurors meet face-to-face and debate their differences. Numbers are decisive in elections, making problematic the effective representation of small or marginal groups; on the jury, the practice of unanimity represents an ideal where individual views cannot simply be ignored or outvoted. At its best, unanimity disempowers narrow and prejudiced arguments that appeal to some groups but not others. It favors general arguments persuasive to persons drawn from different walks of life.

One of the ironies of current law is that the Supreme Court withdrew constitutional protection from the unanimous verdict even as it was reading the Constitution for the first time as guaranteeing that the jury be a body truly representative of the community. But if the great reforms of jury selection in recent years are not to degenerate into the mere token presence of minorities on juries, then the Court needs to regain an appreciation of the unanimous verdict's service to cross-community deliberation. In essence, the unanimous verdict is the crucial element in the jury designed on the model of collective wisdom that Aristotle isolated as the best argument on behalf of democracy. When "the many" govern, Aristotle noted, each individual is an ordinary person considered alone. When these ordinary persons meet together, greater understanding may result than when persons must decide on their own:

> For each individual among the many has a share of virtue and prudence and when they meet together, they become in a manner one man. . . . Some understand one part, and some another and among them they understand the whole.[23]

Ultimately, the requirement of unanimity necessitates that jurors conduct extensive deliberations out of which collective wisdom flows. Each must consider the case from everyone else's point of view in search of the conscience of the community. Each must persuade or be persuaded in turn. As one contemporary political theorist summarized the argument for the unanimity principle:

> Where action can be taken under it at all there is some sort of presumption that the action taken is the wisest and most reasonable of which the deliberators are, as a group, capable. Every disputant among them must have been heard and convinced before action becomes possible. . . . Thus,

although unanimous decisions do become unanimous only by the accumulation of individual approvals, they do not owe their peculiar quality to the *number* of the approvals—or, at least, the further claim may be made for them that they are underwritten by the reasoning process itself. . . . Of decisions made under it we may say not only that they have secured general approval, but also . . . that they have been able to withstand all the criticisms urged against them.[24]

In the United States, the ideal of unanimity received one of its greatest endorsements from political leader John Calhoun, who searched for a practical solution to the sectional rivalries between North and South. He criticized majority rule ("numerical majority") as resting on the principle of force because it permitted one part of the nation to rule over, without the concurrence of, another part.[25] The solution to the tyranny of numbers was to provide each community, or each interest, with a veto power over the actions of the rest of the nation. The existence of the veto, Calhoun thought, would facilitate compromise, influence persons to reason from the same love of country, and lead to unanimity.[26]

The jury was Calhoun's primary evidence that unanimity was a practical ideal. The requirement of unanimity, he thought, created a "disposition to harmonize" or compromise among jury members. The consensus building not only permitted juries to reach verdicts rather than become paralyzed, it produced more accurate and just results than would occur under majority rule procedures:

> If the necessity of unanimity were dispensed with and the finding of a jury made to depend on a bare majority, jury trial, instead of being one of the greatest improvements in the judicial department of government, would be one of the greatest evils. . . . It would be, in such case, the conduit through which all the factious feelings of the day would enter and contaminate justice at its source.[27]

By contrast, what justifies majority rule in a democracy? In classical liberal theory, starting with the principles of John Locke, the moral basis for majority rule has been a belief in the equality of all individuals.[28] If we start from the axiom of "one person, one vote," then we are saying that the vote of each shall be counted as equal to any other. On paper, majority rule gives equal weight to each person's vote or desires; any other decision-making rule violates the principle of equality and permits a minority to rule.[29] This is emphatically true of unanimity, which permits even one person to check, block, veto, or override the desires of the rest.[*]

Today few, if any, constitutional democracies practice pure majoritarianism. Under absolute majority procedures, minorities may have formal equality, but their votes might as well not be counted if the majority votes as a bloc. This problem has led to much debate in recent years about how to generate electoral success and representation for minorities. One of the principal strategies to emerge under the Voting Rights Act of 1965 is the drawing of voting lines to create districts where minorities are in the majority. But some scholars, most notably Prof. Lani Guinier, have criticized this approach as the "triumph of tokenism": minorities elect a few representatives who are not well situated to participate effectively in the legislative process. In a now famous article that apparently cost her confirmation as President Clinton's choice for deputy attorney general for civil rights, Guinier wrote that the election of minority representatives "does not, by itself, translate into intergroup cooperation. . . . Black representatives may be perceived as tokens or marginalized in the legislative process."[30]

This problem of marginalization renewed Guinier's and others' interest in the jury and its unanimous verdict as an example of an alternative approach to structuring effective deliberation across group lines. And yet, since 1972, the Supreme Court has stuck with its incoherent mix of decisions: stressing the need for juries to be drawn from a community cross section but making it more difficult for the cross-sectional dialogue to occur by authorizing states to abandon both the twelve-person jury and the unanimous verdict.

THE 1972 DECISIONS:
AUTHORIZING NONUNANIMOUS VERDICTS

Advocates of the unanimous verdict rule presented the Court with two constitutional reasons to mandate unanimity in state criminal jury trials. In *Apodaca v. Oregon*, the defendants argued that unanimity was essential to enforcement of their Sixth Amendment right to be tried before cross-

---

[*]According to Locke, and social contract theory generally, unanimity was considered necessary only for the founding of a civil society. No one could exit the state of nature and join a community except by his or her own consent. But part of what one consented to, by joining into one body, was to be bound afterward by the decisions of that body, as given by its greater part or majority will.

sectional juries. Only the unanimous verdict rule could guarantee effective representation to minority views; anything less empowered majorities simply to outvote minorities.[31]

In *Johnson v. Louisiana,* the defendant was tried before the Supreme Court had extended the Sixth Amendment to state criminal trials.[32] But Johnson argued that Louisiana's acceptance of a 9–3 jury verdict in his case violated his due process rights under the Fourteenth Amendment to have his guilt proved beyond a reasonable doubt. By definition, no jury could reasonably find a defendant's guilt proved beyond a reasonable doubt, he argued, when some of its members continued to harbor doubts.[33]

By a narrow 5–4 margin, the Court rejected both arguments for constitutionalizing the unanimous verdict.[*]

Apodaca v. Oregon: Unanimity and Representation

To decide the Oregon case, the Court first turned to the history of the Sixth Amendment's passage for evidence of what the drafters of the amendment intended to include within the mandatory features of a jury trial. The Court noted that, as originally introduced by James Madison, the proposed amendment provided for trial "by an impartial jury . . . with the requisite of unanimity for conviction, . . . and other accustomed requisites." But the amendment as finally adopted dropped all references to unanimity and "other accustomed requisites." From this legislative history, the Court thought it possible to "draw conflicting inferences." It is possible that Congress simply thought it unnecessary to specify features as customary as unanimity because it was "thought already to be implicit in the very concept of jury." Or perhaps Congress deleted all references to accepted features of the jury in 1791 because it wished to leave specification of the jury's nature for the future.[34]

Because history alone could not resolve the meaning of the Sixth

---

[*]There was no majority opinion in the *Johnson* or *Apodaca* cases. A group of four justices found that the Sixth Amendment did not protect unanimous verdicts, *Apodaca v. Oregon,* 406 U.S. at 404–11 (opinion of White, J.). Another group of four concluded just the opposite; Ibid. at 414–15 (Stewart, J., dissenting). Justice Powell, in a separate opinion, held that the amendment required unanimous verdicts in federal, but not state, jury trials for historical reasons. He therefore provided the crucial fifth vote for the actual decision in the cases that the Constitution does not require the states to follow the unanimous verdict tradition. *Johnson v. Louisiana,* 406 U.S. at 369–78 (opinion of Powell, J.).

Amendment, the Court approached its decision from a "functional" point of view. Was the requirement of unanimous verdicts so indispensable to the jury's essential functions that it must be considered part of what the Sixth Amendment means by a "jury"? Here, five justices concluded that, for all its longevity, unanimity lacked fundamental importance and thus constitutional stature.[35]

The chief function of the criminal jury, the Court noted, was "to prevent oppression by the Government." To provide this safeguard, the jury places between the accused and the state "the commonsense judgment of a group of laymen ... representative of a cross section of the community."[36] In terms of this shielding function, five justices could "perceive no difference between juries required to act unanimously and those permitted to convict or acquit by votes of 10 to two or 11 to one."[37]

On what basis did the Court conclude that unanimity was superfluous to the jury's core functions? The defendants in *Apodaca* characterized the unanimous verdict requirement as a "necessary precondition for the effective application of the cross-section requirement."[38] They reviewed the Court's commitment in other cases to making the jury a representative body.[39] That commitment had led to sweeping reforms to end the systematic exclusion of certain groups from jury panels and to the new requirement for drawing jurors randomly from a cross section of the community.[40] But all these reforms of jury selection would be meaningless, the defendants argued, if unanimity were abandoned, leaving majorities free to ignore and outvote minorities on the jury. As the defendants' brief put it:

> While members of racial, religious, or ethnic minorities, women, poor people, young people or other previously excluded groups may now be represented on juries, a rule permitting a less than unanimous verdict makes it possible for a verdict to be rendered without their acquiescence and indeed without the consideration of their views.[41]

An amicus brief filed by the American Civil Liberties Union took a similar tact in warning that less than unanimous verdicts make it "easier—perhaps commonplace—for a jury to ignore the viewpoints of minority group members."[42]

These arguments convinced four justices of the Court that unanimous verdicts were vital to the jury's ability to grant effective representation to minority viewpoints. Justice Potter Stewart hypothesized a worst-case scenario where the jury splits along racial lines to convict a defendant "conspicuously identified" as of the same race as the dissenting jurors.* Such verdicts contradict the very purposes of recruiting jurors from a cross section of the community, Justice Stewart concluded. They corrode the community's confidence in criminal justice because they let jury verdicts follow racial or class divisions on the jury.[43]

Justice Stewart was frank in conceding that his defense of unanimity rested on a less than rosy picture of the virtues of individual jurors. Ideally, jurors should be virtuous enough to deliberate rationally across group lines, but it takes the unanimous verdict requirement to enforce the ideal. "It does not denigrate the system of trial by jury to acknowledge that it is imperfect, . . . [that there are] serious risks of jury misbehavior, . . . [that juries] sometimes act out of passion and prejudice," Stewart wrote. Human behavior is such that the requirement of unanimity is a necessary "and effective method endorsed by centuries of experience and history to combat the injuries to the fair administration of justice that can be inflicted by community passion and prejudice."[44]

On the other side of the issue, five justices rejected the need for unanimous verdicts by portraying jury behavior in a far more idealized light. With or without the unanimous verdict requirement, jurors retained the duty to deliberate and debate opposing points of view. Technically, of course, Oregon's system would permit jurors to dispense with deliberation altogether if the required majority of ten were present from the beginning. (The dissenters were particularly troubled by the decision of Apodaca's jury to terminate deliberation after only forty-one minutes and return a conviction by a 10–2 vote.)[45]

But five justices found no grounds for believing that a majority of jurors would suddenly cease to live up to the ideal of rational deliberation with the minority, once the unanimity requirement was lifted. Each individual seated on a jury had survived challenges for cause and been found capable of impartial, color-blind, ethnic-blind justice. Lacking evidence

---

*In chapter 4 we saw an actual instance of Stewart's scenario, when a 1985 California jury deliberating whether to impose the death penalty on a black man convicted of murdering a white couple split 9 to 3 in favor of death, with the three holdouts being all three black jurors. The black jurors held out, and the jury recommended life imprisonment. *People v. Harris*, 36 Cal. 3d 36 (1984); Hiroshi Fukurai, Edgar W. Butler, and Richard Krooth, *Race and the Jury: Racial Disenfranchisement and the Search for Justice* (New York: Plenum Press, 1993), p. 154. California required the jury's recommendation of death to be unanimous.

to the contrary, the Court would not "assume that the majority of the jury will refuse to weigh the evidence and reach a decision upon rational grounds, just as it must now do in order to obtain unanimous verdicts, or that a majority will deprive a man of his liberty on the basis of prejudice when a minority is presenting a reasonable argument in favor of acquittal." It may be that the minority viewpoint is outvoted in the end. But this was no evidence that the majority had cast its votes "based on prejudice rather than the evidence."[46] In short, according to the Court, there was no reason to think minority views were not being heard, discussed, and therefore adequately represented under Oregon's 10–2 verdict rule.

JOHNSON V. LOUISIANA: THE PROBLEM OF DOUBT

Under the due process clause of the Fourteenth Amendment, it had previously been settled that the Constitution required states to prove a defendant's guilt beyond a reasonable doubt.[47] In the Louisiana case, Johnson argued that the remaining, unresolved doubts of three of his jurors meant that the reasonable doubt standard had not been met at his trial.

A majority of the Court found no inconsistency between nonunanimous verdicts and proof beyond a reasonable doubt. To begin with, the Court pointed out the unquestioned practice of permitting defendants to be retried, when a jury hung and failed to agree on guilt. If Johnson were correct that the doubts of some jurors equaled a failure of proof beyond a reasonable doubt, then the proper remedy for a hung jury would be acquittal, not a second trial.[48]

Proof beyond a reasonable doubt, the Court agreed, was meant to underwrite the accuracy and reliability of jury verdicts. But rational persons may disagree in their judgments. Nine persons can conscientiously and in good faith follow their instructions to be convinced beyond a reasonable doubt, even in the face of the doubts of three of their colleagues. All that is required is that the majority listen to the arguments for acquittal, terminating deliberation and "outvot[ing] a minority only after reasoned discussion has ceased to have persuasive effect or to serve any other purpose—when a minority, that is, continues to insist upon acquittal without having persuasive reasons in support of its position."[49]

As in *Apodaca*, the Court presumed that jurors would behave according to this deliberative ideal. Indeed, if any jurors were being irrational, it was more likely to be those few who persevered in their doubts when a majority of the jury, after having considered the dissenters' views, remained convinced of guilt or innocence. The Court suggested that these dissenting jurors should be the ones asking whether their views were reasonable, when argument failed to persuade such a majority of the jury. Here the Court alluded to *Allen v. United States,* the so-called dynamite charge case authorizing judges to instruct deadlocked juries that

> if much the larger number were for conviction, a dissenting juror should consider whether his doubt was a reasonable one which made no impression upon the minds of so many men, equally honest, equally intelligent with himself.[50]

The *Allen* charge is often criticized for suggesting to jurors that they compromise simply to avoid hanging. In his concurring opinion, Justice Lewis Powell took the unanimous verdict to task on precisely this ground. For Powell, the unanimity rule put pressure on jurors to compromise, "despite the frequent absence of a rational basis for such compromise." In the end, so-called unanimity led "not to full agreement among the 12 but to agreement by none and compromise by all."[51] This meant that greater accuracy might be achieved under a system that permitted nine jurors, convinced that guilt has or has not been proved beyond a reasonable doubt, to deliver the verdict without having to compromise with a few holdouts who resist rational argument.

Justice Powell made the strongest argument against unanimity by separating it from the goal of reaching truth. But what if a compromise verdict agreed to by all jurors leads to greater popular *belief* that justice has been done? In our earlier discussions of the rise of the cross-sectional ideal, we saw the Court relying on the jury not only to do justice but to gain public confidence in the justice done. This legitimizing function, the Court stressed, was one of the main reasons for placing justice in the hands of laypersons.[52] It seems plausible to assume that a community will have greater confidence that justice has been done when these laypersons agree on the verdict. It seems especially apparent that a minority section of the community would suspect verdicts rendered over the objections of the only minority members on the panel. Thus, what Justice Powell harshly criticized as the "irrational" compromises wrought by unanimity may unfairly denigrate unanimity's important role in legitimizing verdicts in the public eye.

Of course, Justice Powell was suggesting that the public was wrong to assume a connection between unanimous verdicts and accurate verdicts. But there can be little doubt that for centuries the unanimous verdict has inspired confidence in the administration of justice. As political scientist Gary Jacobsohn points out, to jettison unanimity and ask the public to accept majority verdicts as equally reliable could well sap the legitimacy of the system.[53] Even Justice Powell accepted this historic, symbolic connection between the unanimity of jury verdicts and their legitimacy when he favored preserving the time-honored tradition of unanimous verdicts in federal trials.[54]

In dissent, Justices William Douglas and Thurgood Marshall emphatically endorsed the logical connection between unanimity and proof beyond a reasonable doubt. For Justice Marshall, the "doubts of a single juror [were] . . . evidence that the government has failed to carry its burden" of proof. This was so because no juror's doubts could ever be dismissed as a sign of "irrationality." Assuming the juror is mentally competent, the "'irrationality' that enters into the deliberation process is precisely the essence of the right to a jury trial." Each juror was there to be "a spokesman . . . simply for himself." For Marshall, unanimity was the only method for empowering the solitary dissenting voice when it came to the question of whether reasonable doubt existed.[55]

Likewise for Justice Douglas, under unanimous verdict conditions proof beyond a reasonable doubt sponsored a long and intense process of deliberation where each juror seriously wrestled with the doubts of others. Under majority verdict conditions, deliberation could be cut off before the dissenters had full opportunity to argue for their doubts. Douglas conceded that, even after they had the votes, the majority might deign to listen to the doubts of the minority. But there was all the difference in the world between deliberation entered into as "courtesy dialogue" or "polite and academic conversation" and deliberation entered into because of a necessity to convince others.[56] In the former case, deliberation was reduced to a weak matter of "majority grace," in Justice William Brennan's term.[57] In the latter case, deliberation aided the search for truth by privileging arguments strong enough to win the consent of all. Proof beyond a reasonable doubt was met only when deliberation, in this stronger form, harmonized the views of all jurors.

UNANIMOUS VERDICTS AND THE DELIBERATIVE IDEAL

The Court's dispute over unanimity raised a number of intriguing empirical and philosophical questions. From the empirical point of view, what factual evidence was there to support the majority's conclusion that nonunanimous verdicts would make "no difference" to the thoroughness of deliberation? From the philosophical point of view, what understanding of the deliberative ideal did the justices have in mind when they examined the practical importance of abandoning unanimity? In particular, what does it mean to ask persons from various groups to come together as one community to deliberate toward a shared sense of justice? I begin with the philosophical issues at stake.

Despite their sharp split over unanimity, all nine justices agreed in 1972 that the basic institutional design of the jury speaks to the paramount importance of deliberation to the jury's task. Legislators are supposed to stay closely informed about their constituents' views, but we often sequester juries to prevent members from even learning the community's opinions about a case. Surely, if the legislative model of representation were appropriate in the jury context, then sequestration would be counterproductive and we would encourage all the newspaper reading, public opinion sounding, and communication with "constituents" that go into such representation. But a practice such as sequestration clearly indicates that the jury is supposed to represent the community in a far different way than legislators represent it.

All nine justices appreciated such a difference. They extolled an ideal of face-to-face deliberation in which juries were asked to bracket narrow loyalty to their own group and join with others in search of norms whose power lies in the ability to persuade across group lines. Where the justices differed was on the question of whether unanimity mattered to the jury's ability to define a common sense of justice above community divisions.

In answering this question, the justices divided in paradoxical ways. One would have expected the defenders of unanimity to be positive about the contribution to rich, well-rounded deliberation jurors made by drawing on their personal experiences and group backgrounds. Such a defense would not have lamented that jurors of different groups approached justice differently, nor would it have regarded such differences as a sign of prejudice. Instead, echoing Aristotle's account of how democratic assemblies achieved a common wisdom beyond the grasp of isolated individuals, the best defense of the unanimous verdict would have celebrated the jury's bringing together of persons from various walks of life, each inevitably drawing on valued perspectives embedded in his or her religion and ethnic background and yet each fair-minded enough to appreciate the wisdom someone from another background brings to the discussion.

But, among the four justices in 1972 who favored unanimous verdicts, none was optimistic about jurors' capacity for open-minded deliberation. Their defense of unanimity was unsatisfyingly negative: prejudice and bias so abound among jurors that we need an institutional mechanism such as unanimous verdicts to force jurors into deliberation. Left to their own moral devices, jurors would (the dissenters feared) inevitably broker justice through all their different racial, religious, ethnic, and gender loyalties. The result would not be collective wisdom but simply a transplantation of interest group politics into the jury room. Thus the need for unanimity was a constraint on the otherwise parochial and prejudiced ways jurors would behave. For the dissenters, one question was paramount: why go to all the trouble to achieve some level of representation for minorities on a jury if the majority can always outvote the minority in the end? Without the unanimity requirement, the cross-sectional requirement would achieve only an arid, formal representation of minority points of view.

This negative defense of unanimity ceded the moral high ground to the five-justice majority, who cast themselves as believers in the jury's moral capacity for impartial deliberation, even as they dismissed the necessity of seeing the deliberation through to unanimity. These justices considered the unanimous verdict to be expendable because the civic virtue of jurors was supposedly already a sufficient guarantee that all points of view will be canvassed and confronted.

In other areas of law in 1972, these same justices were already opposed to remedying discrimination through mandates for racial balance, racial quotas, or proportional representation. Color-blind justice remained, for them, the Constitution's ideal, and they balked at approving race-conscious remedies or assignments that would violate this ideal to cure the problems of prejudice. Far better to continue to enforce colorblind norms until they took root.

The justices approached the debate over unanimous verdicts with the same concern for maintaining color-blind justice against schemes that assumed jurors were doomed to vote in racial or ethnic blocs. We should continue to pursue the goal, they thought, of individual jurors deliberating blind to their own race and group interests. We should presume that, whatever the composition of the jury, jurors have the moral capacity to represent views other than those of their own group, that jurors will listen to and consider all opposing points of view. For these five justices, representation on a jury meant nothing more than this minimum right to be heard.

By contrast, they saw proponents of unanimity as arguing for a more

radical theory of minority representation. Silently accusing their opponents of starting with the premise that justice is always group-specific,
they saw the dissenters as granting minorities a right to "block convictions," to veto them. The five-justice majority thought the situation was
not so dire as to require, under cover of unanimity, such a theory of
weighted or group representation. Although they didn't make this analogy, they might have referred to the UN Security Council, where each
permanent member nation has a veto. This scheme reflects a belief that
no nation can count on the others to represent its national interests. But
domestic relations among groups in the United States are not like foreign
relations among nations, the Court majority seemed to be suggesting.
Ultimately, we must presume that jurors will deliberate as impartial individuals, not group representatives. Because jurors could be trusted to dispense color-blind justice, there was no need to have any system of representation that depended on racially balancing the jury or on giving
minorities (through the impact of unanimous verdicts) a veto over the
majority.

Which side had the better of the argument? Missing on both sides was
genuine democratic faith in the collective wisdom that jurors achieve during deliberations, precisely because they draw on their differences in
defining common ground. The glaring shortcoming of the five-justice
majority was its resolute unwillingness to acknowledge the realities of
prejudice in American society. These justices fell back on an anachronis-
tic and hollow description of jury deliberation, where the group identity of
the individual juror simply disappeared inside the jury room. It was as if
jurors suddenly became disembodied pieces of reason, wholly uninfluenced by their own race, religion, or gender. The dissenting justices were
at their best in debunking this myth of disembodied deliberation, asking
law to take into consideration the undeniable ways jurors are partly the
product of their group background.

But the dissenters dug a hole for themselves by equating a juror's
group identity with a juror's baggage of prejudice and bias. Members of
the so-called liberal wing of the Court may have been more willing than
their conservative brethren to acknowledge the impact of race, gender,
and so forth on jury deliberation. But in the end they also lacked any
affirmative vision of how jurors could draw on their different, communal
backgrounds to inform rather than corrupt their conversation about a justice belonging to all communities. Indeed, all nine justices shared the
same mistaken ideal of disembodied deliberation, compared with which

the real-life influence of group identity on jurors co
as an invasion of prejudice and bias.

If anything, the dissenting justices surpassed
on the ubiquity of group-based bias in the jury
problem they wished to "solve" through the unanimity
being what they are, minority jurors will typically be heavily o_
bered by majority jurors. For instance, one sociologist estimates that a
minority group making up 10 percent of a county's population will have
three or more representatives on only 11 percent of that county's twelve-
person juries.[58] To the extent the subtleties of group bias reign, then, the
majority prejudice would be virtually unchecked in a state such as
Louisiana, which permitted nine persons to outvote three. The only solution, according to the dissenters, was to empower minority jurors to "protect," "represent," or be "spokespersons" for distinctive minority views.
Only the requirement of unanimity allowed minority jurors to achieve
effective representation for minority points of view.

The difficulty here is that the dissenters were led to invoke an "interest
group" model of representation for the jury that they themselves explicitly
rejected. Through unanimity, the juror representatives of each group get
to protect the particular interests of that group. It does not take much to
see that, were jurors to act on this theory, the very fabric of jury deliberation would unravel. Jurors would behave as if their primary obligation was
to mirror the interests of their section of the community, not to search for
common ground.

The dissents suggested such a representative role for jurors because
they so thoroughly equated jurors' drawing on the experiences of their
group with jurors' drawing on partisan bias. A better defense of the unanimous verdict requirement was available. To acknowledge that jurors
enter the jury room with views and values shaped in part by their creed,
race, or gender is not to accuse the jurors of bias in need of silencing. It is
to treasure the particularly rich conversations a democratic assembly
inspires, precisely because it brings into one communal conversation persons from different subcommunities. On a jury, these persons must, however, clearly understand that their goal is not to represent, to protect, or to
assert the interests of their own groups. It is to join with others in search
of the truth and shared justice, making a positive contribution to that
search by drawing on their own backgrounds when necessary but also listening to what others know better by virtue of their experiences.

The requirement of unanimity is indispensable to sending the right cue

...ors about what we expect of them. It surely contributes to an under-
...nding among jurors that their function is to persuade, not to outvote,
...ne another. When jurors behave in this way, they contribute knowledge
to the ongoing discussion. And the jury distinctively achieves collective
wisdom through deliberation, rather than collapsing into a body where
jurors behave as if their function were to represent the preconceptions
and interests of their own kind.

THE PRACTICAL EFFECTS OF ABOLISHING UNANIMOUS VERDICTS

Practically speaking, what difference would it make if juries were permitted to render 9–3 or 10–2 verdicts rather than unanimous verdicts? In
Apodaca and *Johnson*, the Court surmised that the effects would be minimal. Presumably, there would be some reduction in hung juries and thus
some gain in the efficiency of the system. But the Court thought neither
the prosecution nor the defense would gain an edge from the shift.[59]
Deliberation would proceed as before, and would be just as thorough,
reliable, and representative of opposing points of view.

THE CHICAGO JURY PROJECT

Even before the Court announced its decisions, social scientists were
busy studying the effects of unanimity on jury behavior. In 1955, the University of Chicago Jury Project undertook the most massive field study of
actual jury trials ever attempted in the United States. The project's original research plan called for secretly recording the actual deliberations of
juries. With the consent of the trial judge and counsel but without the
knowledge of the jurors, audio recordings were made in five civil cases in
federal district court in Wichita, Kansas. But when word of such recordings became public in the summer of 1955, the U.S. attorney general
publicly censured electronic "eavesdropping" on jury deliberations. Congress and more than thirty states responded by enacting statutes prohibiting jury taping.[60] Ever since, jury deliberations have been secret. A rare
exception occurred in 1986 when the Public Broadcasting System televised an authorized videotape of the actual deliberations of a Wisconsin
criminal jury.[61]

The Chicago Jury Project attempted to make a virtue out of its inability
to study "the real thing." In 1966, principal authors Harry Kalven, Jr.,

and Hans Zeisel published much of the project's findings in *The American Jury*, the most influential book ever written on the subject. Kalven and Zeisel dismissed deliberation as having no significant effect on the final verdict in nine of every ten cases. "With very few exceptions," they wrote, "the first ballot determines the outcome of the verdict. . . . [T]he real decision is often made before the deliberation begins."[62]

More precisely, *The American Jury* presented data showing that "where there is an initial majority either for conviction or for acquittal, the jury in roughly nine out of ten cases decides in the direction of the initial majority."[63] This suggests that in 90 percent of the cases, the shift from a unanimous verdict requirement to a majority verdict rule would not change the eventual outcome. Kalven and Zeisel were brutally frank in debunking the romance surrounding deliberation and the arrival at unanimity. In their view, deliberation changed votes less through the force of reason and more through the peer pressure and intimidation that the initial majority mustered against holdouts. In other words, the achievement of unanimity should not delude us into regarding the verdict as more reliable; intimidation, not rational discussion, was the tactic through which the initial majority almost always prevailed in a small group situation.

The American Jury's debunking of deliberation and unanimity set the stage intellectually for the Supreme Court's refusal in 1972 to grant constitutional protection to the unanimous verdict. Why should law insist that unanimous verdicts are essential to justice, when science shows that the initial majority almost always prevails anyway? If the ideals of unanimity and deliberation, so lofty in theory, are reduced in practice to the dirty dynamics of majority pressure on a few holdouts in a small room, then why protect the rule that fuels the pressure?

And yet the implications of *The American Jury* for unanimous verdicts were not entirely negative. Even by their own statistics, Kalven and Zeisel recognized that "the minority eventually succeed[ed] in reversing an initial majority" in roughly 10 percent of sampled cases. Though at times they trivialized this figure (calling the percentage "very few exceptions"), they conceded that they "must not push the point [about the unimportance of unanimity and deliberation] too far." Cases where a minority turned a majority around "may be cases of special importance." They were also likely to be cases where the minority did have the stronger arguments and so were able to resist the normal tide of peer pressure. In these cases, the requirement of unanimity arguably permitted deliberation to continue long enough for reasoned argument to prevail over initial opinions.

Kalven and Zeisel also appreciated that less than unanimous verdicts would change the frequency of hung juries. Their sample included a small number of hung juries, whose last vote was known. By looking at the percentage of hung juries that were deadlocked by one or two jurors, the authors concluded that hung juries could be reduced 42 percent by permitting 11–1 or 10–2 verdicts. They arrived at a similar estimate by studying the frequency of hung juries among cases reported to them from jurisdictions that permitted less than unanimous verdicts at the time. In these majority verdict jurisdictions, hung juries occurred 3.1 percent of the time—a reduction of 45 percent from the national average of 5.6 percent in unanimous verdict jurisdictions.[64]

Since *The American Jury* was published, these estimates have been roughly confirmed by a study of hung juries in Multnomah County (Portland), Oregon, under that state's 10–2 rule. From 1970 to 1972, juries hung in only 2.5 percent of 801 criminal trials—a reduction slightly over 50 percent from the national average.[65]

Does such a reduction in hung juries favor either the prosecution or the defense? This is a difficult question to answer empirically because it is hard to have accurate information about what eventually happens to a defendant whose jury hangs. The state may pursue a new trial—winning, losing, or hanging again. Or the state may forgo retrial altogether. With this warning in mind, Kalven and Zeisel's statistics indicated that the state gained at least an immediate advantage from the decline in hung juries. The reason was that, among juries deadlocked at 11–1 or 10–2, the holdouts were more than four times more likely to be holding out for acquittal than for conviction. Under a 10–2 rule, therefore, far more split juries return convictions than acquittals.[66]

Post-1972 Studies

The Supreme Court's decisions in *Apodaca* and *Johnson* spurred social scientists into a new round of empirical studies of unanimous versus majority verdicts. In general, these studies have shown that "jury verdicts do not differ as a function of decision-rule"; the ratio of convictions to acquittals remains the same, whether mock juries are instructed to return unanimous verdicts or verdicts down to a two-thirds majority.[67] The only major difference, as far as final verdicts go, is that unanimous juries are more likely to hang.[68] All of this basically confirms Kalven and Zeisel's findings.

But, although the product of deliberation does not significantly change under nonunanimous verdict conditions, the process of deliberation apparently does. One of the key factual assumptions the Court made in abandoning the unanimous verdict requirement was that the thoroughness of deliberation would remain unchanged. Specifically, the Court counted on the fact that a majority faction would continue earnest deliberation with holdouts and not simply cut off debate once the required number of votes for a verdict had been attained. Various recent mock jury studies dispute this conclusion, showing a marked tendency of juries to "stop. . . the deliberation when the required number was reached."[69]

In one simulation with names taken from actual jury lists, psychologist Reid Hastie and his colleagues studied the content of deliberation after eight jurors favored a verdict. On juries permitted to return an 8–4 verdict, "little occurs after the faction size reaches eight. . . . Deliberation continues for a few minutes, typically less than five." By contrast, on those juries required to reach unanimity, "approximately 20 percent of deliberation occurs after the largest faction contains eight or more members." Moreover, even if deliberation did continue on a jury that had reached the required eight-person majority, it never led to any desertions from the majority. And on seven of the twenty-three unanimous verdict juries studied, the largest faction reached eight but failed to render the final verdict.[70]

Such comparisons support the dissent of Justice Douglas in *Apodaca*, when he argued for the difference between "polite" debate (which a majority might deign to have with minority jurors whose votes are not needed) and "robust" argument (which takes place when the majority needs to persuade the minority jurors). As sociologist Michael Saks put it, the achievement of the minimum bloc of votes necessary for a verdict is "psychologically binding" on bloc members. The deliberation may continue but it continues as an option, not an obligation.[71]

Various subsidiary findings support the general conclusion that deliberation between majority and minority factions becomes weak and watery once the majority has enough votes for a verdict. Kalven and Zeisel found that, under unanimous verdict rules, juries were hung by one or two jurors in only 2.4 percent of all cases.[72] Yet, in Oregon, which allows juries to return 10–2 verdicts, the number of juries rendering verdicts with one or two holdouts is 25 percent of all juries. This provides evidence that Oregon juries conclude their work rapidly once they achieve the required ten votes rather than pursuing deliberation in hopes of convincing the holdouts.[73] It seems reasonable to assume that jurors, missing paychecks and family, will adjourn as soon as the law authorizes them to return a verdict, rather than continuing extra deliberation.

Mock studies back up this assumption by showing a decline in deliberation time involving less than unanimous verdict conditions. The Hastie study in Massachusetts showed unanimous juries deliberating on average 138 minutes, juries deliberating only 103 minutes under a ten out of twelve rule, and juries deliberating 75 minutes under an eight out of twelve rule.[74] It is not surprising that the shorter deliberation time on majority verdict juries translated into less time spent correcting errors of fact and fewer requests for clarification of the judge's instructions.[75]

Finally, and most important, the empirical studies showed that jurors returning nonunanimous verdicts felt far less certain of their conclusions than did their counterparts on unanimous verdict juries.[76] This is so intuitively plausible that we probably did not need fancy mock jury studies to prove it: jurors not voting in favor of the majority's verdict are hardly likely to think justice was done. What is perhaps not so obvious is that the holdouts left the trial feeling that the majority did not even listen to them seriously. According to the Massachusetts study, the style of deliberation under nonunanimous verdict instructions was likely to be more combative than under unanimous rules, with "larger factions in majority rule juries adopt[ing] a more forceful, bullying, persuasive style because their members realize that it is not necessary to respond to all opposition arguments when their goal is to achieve a faction size of only eight or ten members."[77] One consequence was that members of nonunanimous verdict juries corrected each other's errors of fact less frequently, with those in the minority apparently concluding that the effort was unproductive.[78]

These research findings suggest that the quality of jury deliberation is far more tied to the practice of unanimous verdicts than the Supreme Court allowed in 1972. Moreover, because "popular acceptance of the jury system is formulated, in part, by what former jurors say about it, jurors' satisfaction is not without its importance."[79] All studies to date verify that juror satisfaction sours under nonunanimous verdict conditions. To this extent, the unanimous verdict rule must be seen as a core ingredient underwriting the jury's ability to legitimate justice in the eyes of the community.

LEGITIMACY, JUSTICE, AND UNANIMITY

As a matter of partisan politics, the campaign to abolish unanimous verdicts predictably divides public opinion along conservative versus liberal lines. For conservatives, the unanimous verdict requirement is a "law and order" issue—one feature among many that makes the jury system inefficient, wasteful, and prodefendant to a fault. In England, the telling argument against the unanimous verdict was that it had permitted some notorious defendants to walk free after successfully bribing a juror or two.[80]

In the United States, instances of jury tampering have been rare. And removal of the unanimous verdict is hardly likely to accomplish the other political reforms sought. Even under unanimous conditions, juries convict more than two of every three felony defendants—hardly a sign that juries coddle criminals.[81] All studies confirm that the ratio of convictions to acquittals would not significantly change under 9–3 or 10–2 verdict rules.[82]

As to efficiency, there would be a reduction in the frequency of hung juries, but even here the gains would be minimal. As we saw earlier, under a 10–2 verdict rule Multnomah County, Oregon, juries hang less than half as frequently as the national average—2.5 percent of all jury trials versus 5.6 percent nationally.[83] But in calculating the economic savings from this reduction, jury scholar Jon Van Dyke reminds us that jury trials are such a small percentage of total criminal dispositions in the first place that a small reduction in the already small number of hung juries would not have much influence on the overall efficiency of the system in resolving cases.[84]

In noneconomic terms, is the unanimous verdict requirement inefficient because it leaves one out of every twenty juries deadlocked? It has long been part of Anglo-American legal culture to treasure the hung jury "because it represents the legal system's respect for the minority viewpoint that is held strongly enough to thwart the will of the majority."[85] Living with deadlocks in every twentieth case hardly seems too high a price to pay for the hesitancy we ought to feel in the face of doubts so strongly held.

The law and order attack on unanimous verdicts often assumes the old myth about hung juries—that one oddball, crank, or corrupt person can hang an entire jury. No doubt such a solitary, hanging jury does crop up now and again. But the central conclusion of Kalven and Zeisel's research on hung juries, confirmed many times since, is that one or two persons rarely hang juries in real life (only in movies such as Henry Fonda's *Twelve Angry Men*).[*]

If one or two persons manage to hold out in the end, they probably had company in the beginning. Thus, Kalven and Zeisel estimated that it takes a sizable minority faction on the first ballot—say, four or five persons—to produce the likelihood of a hung jury.[86] Such a factual finding takes much of the sting out of the conservative attack on the idiosyncratic or irrational behavior of hanging jurors. It turns out that we are dealing with a small subset of cases where a sizable number of jurors does entertain initial doubts about the majority view of the evidence. As Kalven and Zeisel put it in *The American Jury*, the primary cause of a hung jury is the "ambiguity of the case," not "an eccentric juror . . . refus[ing] to play his proper role."[87]

If conservatives exaggerate the gains from abolishing unanimous verdicts, liberals typically overstate the threats. Justice Douglas feared in his dissent in *Johnson* and *Apodaca* that attacks on the unanimous verdict would be followed by moves to abolish the presumption of innocence and the requirement of proof beyond a reasonable doubt.[88] All three of these procedural rights make the jury system slow to convict the guilty, and Douglas foresaw a rising "law and order" tide impatient with the inefficiency prized in the remark "Better to let 9 guilty persons go free than convict an innocent man."[89] But these worst-case scenarios have not been realized. In fact, over the last twenty years, no new state has accepted the Court's invitation to experiment with majority verdicts in felony cases. Politically, the unanimous verdict retains its appeal, very much a symbol of faith in the jury system.

The continuing popularity of the unanimous verdict is worthy of comment. One of the key functions of the criminal jury system is to legitimize, in the eyes of the community, the state's use of its coercive powers. The jury gives legitimacy to an accused's imprisonment, even execution,

---

[*]In the 1993 trial of three high school athletes from Glen Ridge, New Jersey, charged with raping a young, retarded woman, one juror initially held out from the decision of the eleven others to convict. Interviews after trial described how the eleven "went to work" on the lone holdout, who finally came into line. Jodi Enda, "Agonized Debate in Glen Ridge Case," *Philadelphia Inquirer*, March 18, 1993, p. S1. Similarly, in the 1994 trial of a Bucks County, Pennsylvania, woman for attempted murder, one juror held out for three days in favor of a not guilty by reason of insanity verdict. When she finally voted to convict, she said she was merely caving into pressure. She was "tired of being badgered, and she agreed to vote for a guilty verdict even though she had not changed her mind." Robert A. Farley, "Holdout Juror Said Pressure Was On," *Philadelphia Inquirer*, Jan. 13, 1994, p. A1.

because ordinary persons like ourselves give the verdict. But the jury's ability to maintain public confidence in the administration of justice is fragile. It depends in part on drawing the jury from the community at large so that all groups have a potential say in how justice is done. It depends also on public confidence that jury verdicts are just, accurate, and true. The strongest argument for retaining the unanimous verdict is that it is central to the legitimacy of jury verdicts.[90]

Common sense alone tells us that public confidence in the accuracy of verdicts is greater when the verdict is unanimous. Common sense also tells us that Justice Stewart was right to fret over the symbolic significance of replacing unanimous verdicts with majority verdicts.[91] In the best of circumstances, public confidence would erode whenever split verdicts resulted. In the worst cases, a crisis of legitimacy would greet verdicts split along racial or other group lines. Justice Stewart did not cite statistics about the probability of such group splits occurring. His point was that the very redesign of jury trials to permit such verdicts changed public attitudes toward the jury for the worst. It sponsored an ever present consciousness that majorities, if large enough, could rule absolutely on juries.

In the end, however, it must be admitted that there is a paradox behind the unanimous verdict's contribution to the jury's legitimacy. Unanimity inspires confidence because the public *believes* that requiring all jurors to agree promotes the search for truth. But, as Jacobsohn noted in his study of the unanimous verdict, this belief rests on at least a partial misconception.[92] Unanimity might inspire jurors to behave deliberatively—that is, to reason together across differences to reach a genuinely shared verdict. But, as Justice Powell pointed out, unanimity may prod jurors to behave more expediently, returning a compromise verdict that splits the difference between jury factions and has no rational basis.[93] To the extent that this happens, unanimity does not promote truth.*

But the public rarely learns of the compromises. The jury returns its unanimous verdict and does not explain how the result was reached. As far as the community is concerned, the unanimity reflects a genuine

---

*In the celebrated Menendez brothers trials that ended in deadlocked juries for each brother in January 1994, some jurors told television interviewers that they had considered a compromise verdict between those voting manslaughter and those favoring a murder conviction on charges that the brothers had killed their parents. The compromise would have convicted the brothers of first-degree murder of their mother but only manslaughter in the slaying of the father, whom the brothers said abused them. No compromise was reached.

meeting of the minds. It appears that the verdict must be right because all jurors agreed it was right.

The analysis so far suggests that unanimous verdicts contribute to the legitimacy of jury verdicts only so long as a certain fiction is maintained—that is, only so long as the public *mistakenly* believes that the more consensual the verdict, the more likely the verdict is correct. But is the public mistaken? Exactly how jurors "compromise" or harmonize during deliberations remains a mystery; studies of mock jurors are not likely to tell us how jurors behave when they bear actual responsibility for the decision.

No doubt there are cases where jurors strike a bargain simply to agree and go home, much like Justice Powell suggested. But jury compromises need not be of the expedient, horse-trading, split-the-difference, or flip-a-coin models.*

The alternative give-and-take model defines the democratic ideal of deliberation. On this model, jurors do not strike compromises between the different interests they represent. They each take seriously the goal of reaching the truth, earnestly seeking to harmonize their different understandings of the facts, their different assessments of an accused's culpability or responsibility for his acts. In the face of these differences, the conversation grows animated, intense, even angry. The unanimous verdict rule makes the deliberations all the more intense because the alternative of outshouting or outvoting opponents does not exist. In such circumstances, jurors certainly have incentives for compromising or harmonizing. But the cue we are giving jurors by requiring unanimity is that there are compromises and there are compromises. On the basic issue of whether an accused is guilty or not guilty, there can be no compromise,

---

*In February 1994 a jury rendered what was widely regarded as a compromise verdict in the trial of eleven Branch Davidians. The members were charged with murder in the notorious shootout that occurred when agents of the Federal Bureau of Alcohol, Tobacco and Firearms tried to serve a warrant on the group's compound in Waco, Texas, in 1993. The shootout left four agents and six Branch Davidians dead. At the outset of deliberations, according to one juror, "some thought it was outright murder on the part of the Branch Davidians. . . . [Others] thought it was outrageous murder on the part of the Federal Government." Eventually all jurors agreed that "there were a lot of dirty hands out there that day, on both sides." All twelve jurors agreed to acquit all Branch Davidians of murder charges but to convict seven of them on the lesser charge of voluntary manslaughter. According to the jury, murder was too harsh a sentence and the government bore some responsibility for its use of force. Sam Howe Verhovek, "Juror Says Doubts Determined Verdict in Sect Trial," *New York Times*, March 1, 1994, p. 21; Robert L. Jackson and Lianne Hart, "Waco Survivors' Trial to Open," *Philadelphia Inquirer*, Jan. 10, 1994, p. B3.

and even deadlocked jurors are carefully instructed that individual jurors should not "cave in" to achieve unanimity.

The whole point of having jurors deliberate face-to-face is to change people's preconceptions about a case through conversation with others. Unanimity empowers the conversation by signaling to jurors to put their opinions at risk. The ideal, which is often realized, is that power flows to the persuasive on the jury—that people change their minds not out of expediency but because their views actually have shifted through hearing the views of others. When deliberation works in this way, the achievement of unanimity speaks to the collection of wisdom, not the politics of compromise.

In Brazil, federal juries do not deliberate. At the close of evidence, jurors are individually polled in writing, a secret ballot is taken, and the majority prevails.[94] Such a procedure stands in stark contrast to our own, where deliberation is the essence of a juror's duty.

Replacing unanimous verdicts with majority verdicts would not obliterate deliberation altogether and import the Brazilian model. But it would alter the basic institutional design of our jury and the behavior promoted by that design. If they are instructed to return a unanimous verdict, jurors know their task is not to vote. For all their differences, they must approach justice through conversation and the art of persuading or being persuaded in turn. Majority verdicts signal an entirely different type of behavior, where jurors ultimately remain free to assert their different interests and opinions against one another. The distinctive genius of the jury system has been to emphasize deliberation more than voting and representation. Abolishing the unanimous verdict would weaken the conversations through which laypersons educate one another about their common sense of justice.

CHAPTER SIX

Race and the Death Penalty

THE JURY MAY be ancient, but the practice of recruiting jurors democratically from all walks of life is still in its infancy. As we have seen in previous chapters, the great reforms of jury selection in the United States occurred in 1968, when Congress legislated the cross-sectional requirement for federal juries; in 1975, when the Supreme Court extended the requirement to state juries; and in 1986 and 1994, when the Court prohibited prosecutors from using peremptory challenges to strike potential jurors solely because of their race or sex.[1] These reforms are still new—we do not yet know what difference it will make to the quality of jury deliberations that at long last serious efforts are being made to practice the democratic ideal of deliberation enriched by diverse perspectives.

In some areas of law, the enhancement of deliberation on cross-sectional juries is already encouraging. The most notable improvement has been in rape trials. Between 1961 and 1965, federal criminal juries convicted defendants of rape in only 38 percent of cases, a low conviction rate that stood out in comparison with an overall federal felony conviction rate during those years of nearly 70 percent.[*]

From 1985 to 1987, the rape conviction rate before federal juries rose to 73 percent, only slightly below the overall conviction rate at that time.[2] In and of itself, this dramatic rise in jury severity toward rape defendants does not tell us that the quality of deliberation or accuracy of verdicts

---

[*]Most rape trials occur in state courts. But federal case data is more complete and provides a better basis for tracing changes in jury verdicts over time.

improved. But contemporary accounts from the 1950s and 1960s describe jurors in those years as lenient toward rape defendants because they were prejudiced toward certain categories of rape victims; judges told the University of Chicago Jury Project that juries seemed to think a woman "assumed the risk" of rape through unconventional forms of behavior or provoked her own attack through some kind of contributory negligence.[3]

Today's shift away from such considerations is no doubt explained by many factors, including adoption of rape shield laws, the use of better forensic evidence, and changes in public attitudes toward rape (that it is about violence, not sex). But it hardly seems coincidental that the change in jury responses to rape occurred during the same period that sex-neutral selection procedures arrived in federal courts.[4]

In other areas, the capacity of jurors to live up to the hefty ideals of deliberation remains suspect. In this chapter, I turn to the death penalty as the most troubling instance where color-blind justice eludes us. But the question, not easy to answer, is how much responsibility juries bear for the continued racial pattern made by death-sentencing in the United States.

When the decisions of prosecutors, judges, and juries are considered together, the bottom line is that persons who kill white victims stand a substantially greater chance of receiving a death sentence than do persons who murder blacks. This race-of-victim bias in death sentencing is strong and consistent across many states; it does not disappear when the data are controlled for variables that seek a nonracial explanation for the pattern.[5] The influence of the victim's (white) race on prompting a death sentence is glaring when one considers that in the United States the risk of death by homicide is five times greater for nonwhites than for whites.[6] Yet death sentencing is distant from this reality, somehow discounting murders of blacks in comparison with the response to comparable white-victim murders.[*]

In an ideal world, the victim's race would be irrelevant to deliberations over whether a murderer should live or die. But as long as we

---

[*] Of course, not all murderers are eligible for punishment by death, under modern capital punishment laws. There is a limit, therefore, to how much we can learn about the fair application of the death penalty simply from raw data about the higher risks of nonwhites to homicide. As we shall see in this chapter, more exact assessments of racial disparities in death-sentencing depend on limiting the comparison to death-eligible cases and adjusting for legitimate case differences. Still, the great gulf between the locus of murder in this society and the death penalty response is worthy of comment.

inhabit a world where the odds of receiving the death penalty vary according to the skin color of the murdered victim, the morality of the death penalty is compromised and corrupted.

Although the jury is implicated in the bias, it is nowhere near primarily responsible for the race-specific ways capital punishment works. Studies consistently show that prosecutorial decisions—including the initial charging decision, the offer of a plea bargain that will permit a defendant to avoid risk of a death penalty, and the decision to seek the death penalty after a conviction—are the major points at which racial disparities skew the death sentencing process.[7] By comparison, the jury's effect on the death penalty's racial pattern is secondary.[8] Indeed, the jury system has evolved to a point where, if anything, jurors' death penalty decisions show a slight tendency to disadvantage white defendants.[9]

But jury death penalty decisions, like prosecutorial decisions, continue to show signs of race-of-victim bias that treats white-victim murderers as especially deserving of the death penalty.[10] This gives pause to those, like myself, who hold out the jury as a living example of the good that generally comes from empowering ordinary citizens to do justice. But, as I have stressed throughout this book, the jury's marriage of justice to democracy can work for better or for worse. In this chapter, I confront the death penalty record of juries as a sobering reminder of how far our aspirations for color-blind justice still surpass our practices.

The peculiar process of purging opponents of capital punishment from serving on juries in death penalty cases means that such "death-qualified" juries are unlike their counterparts in noncapital cases. If we are going to have a death penalty, the Supreme Court has found it only fair to permit the state to eliminate so-called nullifiers—persons who are so absolutely opposed to capital punishment that they could not abide by their oath to apply the law.[11] But this process of eliminating confirmed opponents of capital punishment from the jury excludes significantly more women than men and more blacks than whites.[12] There is also evidence, rejected by the Court, that persons who survive the "death-qualification" voir dire are more conviction-prone than the community at large.[13] All this indicates that the selection of a jury capable of deliberating impartially about death sentences has worked against the seating of a cross-sectional jury that would fairly bring all segments of the community together into the deliberations about who deserves to die.

Still, death-qualified jurors are not so different from other jurors that we can act as if they were recruited on Mars. And prosecutors presumably make decisions to seek or forgo the death penalty partly on the basis of their experience with juries in prior death penalty cases.[14] For these reasons, I believe we must acknowledge that the jury is implicated in the overall racial patterns traced out by the death penalty.

For a generation, the Supreme Court has struggled to define the permissible content for jury deliberations about death. But a consistent definition has escaped the Court. In 1987, the Court took the position that juries could not fairly deliberate over a death sentence if prosecutors introduced statements from the victim's family and friends about the impact of the murder on them.[15] Such victim-impact statements, the Court feared, would distract the jury with irrelevant factors that had nothing to do with what they should deliberate about—the character of the accused and the circumstances of the crime. But this was an extremely narrow approach to what is relevant to the death deliberation.

In 1991, a case came before the Court in which the prosecutor introduced a grandmother's statement of how a surviving three-year-old fared in the aftermath of the defendant's brutal killing of his mother and baby sister. The Court took this opportunity to overrule itself and permit victim impact statements once again to be introduced in the penalty phase of death penalty trials.[16] But this back and forth movement of the Court illustrates just how difficult it is to define satisfactorily the substance of deliberation over a death decision. To exclude consideration of the impact of the murder on the family would make the jury's conversation artificial, stilted, and hollow; to permit jurors to consider highly emotional appeals risks prompting death sentences based on factors that the defendant may not even have known about when committing the crime. This is just one important example of the difficulties courts have confronted when trying to draw a sensible line between what is and what is not relevant to jury deliberations about death sentences. I believe the time has come to admit that deliberation over death is beyond the jury's capacity.

THE DEATH PENALTY AS A "JURY QUESTION"

Thirty-nine jurisdictions authorize capital punishment today—thirty-seven states, the federal government, and the U.S. military. Between 1977, when executions resumed in the United States after a brief moratorium, and 1994, 226 persons were executed.[17]

The great majority of these jurisdictions place the death penalty decision in the hands of jurors rather than judges.* Why do states typically rely on juries to do death sentencing when they leave judges to do most other forms of sentencing? As a matter of constitutional law, the Supreme Court has approved both judge and jury death sentencing procedures.[18] But the Court has noted that jurors are "best able to express the conscience of the community" on the issue of whether imposition of the death sentence would constitute "cruel and unusual punishment."[19] The Supreme Court has said that a society's sense of what violates the Eighth Amendment ban on "cruel and unusual punishment" changes over time, reflecting "the evolving standards of decency that mark the progress of a maturing society."[20] Jury decision making on the death penalty provides a desirable "link between contemporary community values and the penal system."[21]

Several times, the Court has cited jury willingness to impose the death penalty, at least in extreme cases, as "a significant and reliable objective index" that capital punishment fits with prevailing moral sentiments about crime and punishment.[22] These citations of jury support for the death penalty are typically overstated. In 1991, 76 percent of the American people told a Gallup poll that they favored the death penalty for murder—only slightly down from the 1989 record high level of 79 percent.[23] But a leading death penalty study found that "the actual decisions made by . . . juries reflect much less enthusiasm for capital punishment in practice."[24] The relative lack of jury enthusiasm is all the more telling, given the state's right to exclude from the jury those persons absolutely opposed to the death penalty in all circumstances.[25] But the Court has generally treated the jury's record in death penalty trials as unambiguous evidence of continuing popular support for capital punishment.

In justifying the practice of leaving death decisions to juries, in 1984

---

*The statutes of twenty-nine states, as well as federal law, direct the jury to make the death penalty decision. In four states (Arizona, Idaho, Montana, and Nebraska), judges make the decision. In four other states (Alabama, Delaware, Florida, and Indiana), juries recommend but judges have the right to override a jury recommendation of life imprisonment and impose the death sentence. In Nevada, a panel of three judges may impose the death penalty in cases where the jury cannot agree. Michael L. Radelet and Michael Mello, "Symposium: Death-to-Life Overrides: Saving the Resources of the Florida Supreme Court," *Florida State Law Review* 20 (1992): 196, n. 2, updating *Spaziano v. Florida,* 468 U.S. 447, 463 (1984).

Justice John Paul Stevens called the death penalty "the one punishment that cannot be prescribed by a rule of law as judges normally understand such rules, but rather is ultimately . . . an expression of the community's outrage—its sense that an individual has lost his moral entitlement to live."[26] Justice Stevens went so far as to say that "capital punishment rests on not a legal but an ethical judgment—an assessment of . . . the 'moral guilt' of the defendant."[27]

Deliberating death, then, is the premier contemporary example where old invocations of the jury as the conscience of the community live on. But the invocations capture the familiar ambivalence about the jury as a forum for conscience that we have seen throughout this book. Justice Patrick E. Higginbotham, of the U.S. Court of Appeals for the Fifth Circuit, notes that the jury is the proper body to choose between a sentence of life or death because that choice is ultimately "visceral" and "uniquely laden with expressions of anger and retribution." Like Justice Stevens, Judge Higginbotham emphasizes that the death "decision must occur past the point to which legalistic reasoning can carry; it necessarily reflects a gut-level hunch as to what is just."[28] Such extralegal decisions fall best to a group of citizens who can share responsibility for the terrible decision and walk away from it, back to anonymity. But Judge Higginbotham notes that the jury's decisions on death are "inscrutable." Giving juries instructions on the death penalty will always be "at some point a charade," since the jury is designed to be "the blackbox of the judicial system."[29] Hence, Judge Higginbotham concludes, jury death sentencing brings with it the danger that irrational and capricious factors are the driving forces within the blackbox.*

Given the prevailing view that deliberating death is a process that goes beyond the legal expertise of judges, it is surprising that the Supreme Court has upheld the constitutionality of judge death sentencing at all. Consider the death penalty record of Florida, the only state where judges frequently override jury recommendations of life

---

*In 1990 and 1992, Hans Zeisel interviewed 238 persons selected for jury duty in capital trials in Cook County, Illinois. He found that as many as 75 percent of them did not understand key parts of death penalty instructions, including the meaning of mitigating circumstances, and the state's burden of proving that aggravating circumstances outweigh mitigating factors. Arthur S. Hayes, "Jurors' Grasp of Instructions May Stir Appeal," *Wall Street Journal*, July 16, 1992, p. B1; Helene Cooper, "Death Sentence Vacated Because Study Reveals Juror Misunderstanding," *Wall Street Journal*, Sept. 28, 1992 (federal judge relies on Zeisel study in ordering that death row inmate since 1979 be resentenced).

and impose the death penalty. From December 1972 through March 1988, 526 death sentences were imposed under Florida's current capital punishment law. Of these, 113 were death sentences imposed by the judge, overriding a jury recommendation of life. Thus, one in five convicts sentenced to die in Florida during those years actually received jury recommendations of life.[30] As of March 1992, the number of judicial overrides stood at 134.[31]

It is doubtful that such a death sentencing scheme would gain legitimacy in most other states. The irony in Florida is that juries are already among the most "death-prone" in the nation.[32] Permitting a state to execute a defendant whom the jury recommended for life raises deeply troubling questions about the Florida death scheme. On June 25, 1991, Bobby Ray Francis became the third Florida inmate executed despite a jury's recommendation of life.[33]

CALCULATING THE OVERALL DEATH SENTENCING RATE

Nationwide, as 1993 drew to a close, death row housed 2,785 prisoners. In absolute terms, this is a large number of persons to be under sentence of death. It will surprise no one that more than 98 percent of death row inmates are male, but it may be more surprising to learn, given the media portrait of prisons filled mostly with blacks, that a slight majority of those waiting execution are white.[34] Likewise, 54 percent of the 222 persons executed between 1977 and 1993 were white.[35] Later in this chapter I discuss disconcerting evidence that racial factors place African Americans at special risk when it comes to death penalty decisions, but it is the race of the victim, or a combination of victim race and defendant race, rather than the race of defendant standing alone that is at issue.[36] In fact, one leading study in Georgia found a reverse race of defendant factor at work, with 4 percent of black defendants charged with murder or voluntary manslaughter receiving the death penalty, as opposed to 7 percent of white defendants.[37] These numbers will help correct the mistaken popular image of prisons, and death row in particular, as filled mostly with blacks.

Each year, only a small percentage of defendants charged with capital crimes receives the death penalty. The Baldus study estimates that, in states authorizing capital punishment, the death penalty is imposed at a rate of 15.4 times per 1,000 homicides. The same study estimates that, from 1982 to 1984, some 2,000 to 4,000 defendants were indictable per year for a crime that made them eligible for the death penalty if convicted. Out of this initial pool of "death-eligibles," states imposed the death penalty in only 250 to 300 cases annually, producing a yearly death sentencing rate of 6–15 percent.[38]

In the 1990s, the average annual number of death sentences continues to be about 250. In 1990, 244 persons were sentenced to die; in 1991, the number was 266.[39] By comparison, 7,530 defendants were convicted of murder in state courts in 1990.[40] For further comparison, the number of persons arrested in 1990 for nonnegligent homicide was 22,990 (in 1992, the number was 23,760).[41] Clearly, death sentencing is an extremely selective process in the United States.

The death sentencing rate alone tells us more about the decisions of prosecutors than about jury death penalty decisions. This is because few persons indicted for murder ever make it all the way through to a jury determination on the death penalty. First, prosecutors have discretion to charge those arrested for a homicide with a murder punishable by death (so-called capital murder) or with a lesser degree of murder or even manslaughter. Second, prosecutors routinely enter into plea bargains, permitting great numbers of death-eligible offenders to escape the possibility of a death sentence by pleading guilty, frequently to a lesser included offense. For instance, according to studies in the 1980s, the proportion of death-eligible cases that ended in guilty pleas was 48 percent in Georgia, 49 percent in California, 58 percent in Colorado, 59 percent in Maryland, and 67 percent in North Carolina.[42]

Third, even after a defendant is convicted of murder at trial, prosecutors in many states have surprising discretion to waive the death penalty phase of trial and accept life imprisonment instead. In Georgia during the 1970s, prosecutors waived a jury hearing on the death penalty in 59 percent of cases where the jury had convicted the defendant of a capital crime. In California during the 1980s, the waiver rate was 50 percent; in South Carolina, it approached 64 percent.[43] The net effect of the prosecutor's role is that remarkable attrition occurs in the murder cases that ever make it all the way through to the death penalty phase of a jury trial. Presumably, those that do make it to that phase represent cases that prosecutors feel are the strongest candidates for imposition of the death penalty. It is not surprising that the jury death sentencing rate is relatively high in these prescreened cases. In Georgia, for instance, juries sentenced murderers to death in 55 percent of the penalty trials held between 1973 and 1978.[44] In dramatic comparison, only 5 percent (128 out of 2,484)* of persons indicted for murder and convicted of manslaughter or murder in Georgia during roughly the same years received the death penalty.[45]

Consider, for instance, this portrait of death penalty mechanics in Colorado from 1980 to 1984. During those years, the state indicted 179 persons for murder, charging all but 8 with capital murder. Prosecutors then accepted plea bargains from 61 percent (104 of 171) of the defendants indicted for capital murder. This left 39 percent (67 of 171) of those initially indicted for a capital crime to face trial. Three cases were dismissed. At trial, 56 of the remaining 64 were found guilty—43 of them for a capital crime that kept them eligible for the death penalty. But the prosecutor then waived the penalty phase of trial in 32 of the 43 capital murder conviction cases. The cases of 11 defendants (6 percent of those indicted for capital murder) made it to a penalty trial before a jury. Juries sentenced 4 of those 11 (36 percent) to death. Thus, although the jury sentenced a sizable percentage of those reaching a penalty trial to death, only 2 percent (4 of 171) of those indicted for capital crimes received the death penalty.[46]

THE PRE-1972 SITUATION: TOO MUCH JURY DISCRETION?

Because the death penalty is imposed infrequently, questions inevitably arise about whether arbitrary or discriminatory factors are at work in the sentencing. For more than a generation, the Supreme Court has overseen a vast rewriting of death penalty statutes, in an effort to save the death penalty from persistent charges about its uneven application. These reforms are directed primarily at juries, and the prosecutor's considerable discretion remains far more hidden as a potential source of discrimination. Indeed, the debate about the cruelty of the death penalty has

---

*In a conversation I had with Professor Baldus, he noted that not all 2,484 defendants were "death-eligible" under the terms of Georgia's post-*Furman* statute. In fact, there were no statutory aggravating circumstances present in 864 cases. See also David C. Baldus, George Woodworth, and Charles A. Pulaski, Jr., *Equal Justice and the Death Penalty: A Legal and Empirical Analysis* (Boston: Northeastern University Press, 1990), p. 650. If this number is subtracted from the total, then the adjusted death sentencing rate is 128 out of 1,620, or 7.9 percent.

turned—for practical and legal purposes—into a debate about the biases of juries and the arbitrariness of their decisions.

In 1972, in *Furman v. Georgia*, the Supreme Court placed what turned out to be a temporary moratorium on executions in the United States.[47] A majority of the Court was unwilling to go as far as declaring capital punishment to be "cruel and unusual punishment" in all circumstances. The Court's problem with capital punishment in 1972 was with the procedures involved, not the moral substance of the death sentence. Georgia law was typical of sentencing schemes in the thirty-nine capital punishment states in 1972: the laws left juries or judges with absolute discretion to pick and choose, among those convicted of capital crimes, who should be put under sentence of death. In making their selections, juries and judges did not have the benefit of any objective standards or legal guidelines. It was as if law simply did not exist in the death penalty phase of trials. California jurors, for instance, were instructed through 1971 that

> the law itself provides no standard for the guidance of the jury in the
> selection of the penalty, but rather commits the whole matter . . . to the
> judgment, conscience, and absolute discretion of the jury. . . . The law
> does not forbid you from being influenced by pity for the defendants and
> you may be governed by mere sentiment and sympathy for the defendants
> in arriving at a proper penalty in this case; however the law does forbid
> you from being governed by mere conjecture, prejudice, public opinion,
> or public feeling.[48]

By 1971, there were few other areas of law where the jury still received judicial blessing to function as the conscience of the community. As discussed in chapter 2, judges waged a long struggle to end the jury's right to nullify the law. But it is odd that well into our own times, juries in death penalty cases have enjoyed untrammeled discretion to show mercy or not to defendants eligible to be put to death. What was remarkable about the California instruction was its open acknowledgment that the jury's choice of death or life for a convict did not depend on formal legalisms of the kind that could be captured in a set of instructions. The jury was on its own because the death penalty judgment was so primal and raw, coming from a community's deepest sense about the dignity of life and the vileness of violent crime. No statute or instruction could possibly canvass for jurors all the factors—all the aggravating and mitigating circumstances— to be considered before making such an ultimate moral judgment.

The first time the Court reviewed this "unbridled discretion" instruction to juries in death penalty cases, it upheld the law in 1971.[49] The Court rested its approval of existing death penalty procedures on a historical review of the problems that discretionary death sentencing was supposed to solve. The foremost problem was that, under the older common law tradition of mandatory death sentences, juries preferred to nullify the law altogether and acquit defendants rather than send them to the gallows by conviction. Thomas Andrew Green's masterful study of the origins of the English jury shows that, in the fourteenth century, juries were already engaged in refusing to convict persons of capital crimes, rather than cooperate in their execution for crimes thought unworthy of death.[50] Even in 1791, the death penalty remained mandatory for more than two hundred offenses in England, and juries continued to nullify.[51] In the United States also, the Supreme Court noted, "at least since the Revolution, American juries have, with some regularity, disregarded their oaths and refused to convict defendants where a death sentence was the automatic consequence of a guilty verdict."[52]

In 1794, Pennsylvania responded to the nullifications triggered by mandatory death sentences by introducing degrees of murder.[53] But "juries continued to find the death penalty inappropriate in a significant number of first degree murder cases and refused to return guilty verdicts."[54] Thus, American law took the decisive step of recognizing the jury's absolute discretion to decide, in any case, that imposition of the death penalty would be inappropriate. Tennessee enacted the first jury discretionary sentencing statute in 1838, followed by Alabama in 1841 and Louisiana in 1846. By 1900, twenty-three states plus the federal government authorized juries to use their discretion to choose death or life for persons convicted of capital crimes. By the end of World War I, all but eight states had abolished the death penalty or converted to jury discretionary sentencing. As of 1963, the process was complete: in every state where juries had authority to impose a death sentence, they had discretion to spare the life of a defendant convicted of a capital crime.[55]

All this history was behind the Court's 1971 decision upholding California's "standardless" jury death sentencing system. Of course, California might have provided juries with some instructions on how to deliberate about death, without dictating executions. But the Court's position in 1971 was that judicial instructions could do little to harness the open-ended moral inquiry that history assigned to jurors deliberating on death sentences. Writing for the Court, Justice John Harlan thought that words did not yet exist that could clarify the jury's task in capital cases; in the end, juries "do little more—and must do nothing less—than express the conscience of the community on the ultimate question of life or death."[56]

But a scant thirteen months later, in *Furman*, the Court made a sudden turnaround and concluded that it could no longer constitutionally approve the arbitrary and capricious manner in which discretionary death sentencing worked in practice. Justice Byron White, for instance, could find "no meaningful basis for distinguishing the few cases in which [the death penalty] is imposed from the many cases in which it is not."[57] Justice Potter Stewart found that the death penalty was "cruel and unusual in the same way that being struck by lightning is cruel and unusual."[58] Justice Stewart went on to write the following:

> Of all the people convicted of [capital crimes], many just as reprehensible as these, the petitioners are among a capriciously selected random handful upon whom the sentence of death has in fact been imposed. . . . The Eighth and Fourteenth Amendments cannot tolerate the infliction of a sentence of death under legal systems that permit this unique penalty to be so wantonly and so freakishly imposed.[59]

If there was any logical basis for explaining what influenced the sentencer to choose the death penalty over life imprisonment, Justice Stewart noted, "it was the constitutionally impermissible basis of race." Justices William Douglas and Thurgood Marshall echoed the suspicion that racial bias was the crucial factor at work under any death penalty law that gave juries unchecked discretion to apply or not apply the death penalty. In their separate opinions, Douglas and Marshall cited evidence tending to show that capital punishment fell disproportionately on minority defendants.[60]

Because there were five separate opinions from the justices declaring the death penalty unconstitutional in *Furman*, it is difficult to state precisely what the fatal flaw in existing death penalty procedures was for the Court. But all five justices agreed that the death penalty had become cruel by 1972 precisely because it had become so unusual. Imposing the death sentence on just a handful of convicts had to be considered excessive punishment, in a state where prisoners convicted of basically indistinguishable crimes generally received life imprisonment terms.

POST-1972: THE NEW DEATH PENALTY
JURISPRUDENCE

If infrequency was the constitutional flaw in death penalty sentencing in 1972, then perhaps more regular or routine application of the death penalty might solve the problems of arbitrariness located by the *Furman* Court. Between 1972 and 1976, thirty-five states passed new death penalty statutes that aimed to make decisions routine rather than random.[61] Some states, such as North Carolina and Louisiana, attacked the problems in *Furman* by abolishing jury discretion and mandating the death penalty for specific categories of crimes, such as murder of a police officer, murder for hire, or murder committed during a simultaneous felony.[62] Other states, led by Georgia, Florida, and Texas, preserved the judge's or jury's discretion to make the final decision but attempted to narrow and channel the exercise of discretion by legislating standards for the death sentencer to apply.[63] The Supreme Court proved hostile to the idea of "mandatory death sentences" but receptive to a new era of "guided discretion" death penalty laws.

In a quintet of decisions handed down in 1976, the Supreme Court constructed a two-pronged "due process for death." One prong, still prominent today, was the requirement of "individualized sentencing" in death penalty cases.[64] Each death penalty case being unique, the Court stressed the need to consider defendants as individuals and to tailor the sentence to fit the particular circumstances of the person and the case. The Court thus struck down mandatory death sentences as inherently below constitutional thresholds.

Applying the principle of individualized sentencing in succeeding years, the Court has held that judge or jury must be free to consider any possible mitigating circumstance that a defendant wishes to offer.[65] It has also upheld death penalty instructions that inform jurors that they never *have* to sentence a person to death.[66]

The second prong of the Court's due process for death, which has receded in importance since 1976, was the principle of treating like cases alike. Following this maxim, the Court's focus shifted from individualized justice to consistent justice. The Court stressed the need for "objective symmetry," or "comparability," in death penalty decisions made by different judges or juries about defendants committing similar crimes. To achieve comparability, state laws needed to channel, without eliminating, juror and judge discretion during the death penalty phase of trials.[67] In

1976, the Court upheld the new death penalty statutes in Georgia, Texas, and Florida for striking a constitutional balance between the "pure discretion" schemes struck down in *Furman* and the mandatory laws struck down in North Carolina and Louisiana.[68]

The Supreme Court praised three particular features of the new Georgia capital punishment law. First, Georgia established bifurcated, or two-stage, trials for all capital crimes. In the first stage, the jury would decide only the issue of guilt or innocence. If the jury convicted the defendant of a capital crime, then a second, penalty, phase commenced. Prosecution and defense could introduce evidence of aggravating or mitigating circumstances during the penalty phase, going directly to the issue of punishment.[69]

Bifurcated trials offered one great procedural advantage over the prior one-stage trial process. Defendants were understandably reluctant to offer mitigating evidence before a jury had even convicted them. Indeed, such evidence was typically excluded as irrelevant at the guilt stage. But, under the one-phase procedure, defendants had no later opportunity to introduce evidence germane to penalty. Ironically, juries and judges making the death penalty decision were in possession of far less "raw material specifically relevant to penalty" than was available in most noncapital sentencing procedures. The bifurcated trial eliminated these difficulties.[70]

Second, and most important, Georgia reformed its law to specify objective standards or guidelines for the jury to follow in deliberating life versus death in the penalty phase of the trial. In cases where the defendant was convicted of murder, Georgia law specified that a jury could sentence the convict to death only if it found, during the penalty phase of the trial, that the state proved beyond a reasonable doubt that the murder involved at least one of ten "aggravating circumstances" listed in the death penalty statute.*

In Georgia, these ten statutory aggravating circumstances defined and

---

*These were the following: (1) offense committed by person with prior conviction for a capital felony or substantial history of serious assaultive criminal convictions; (2) offense committed during commission of another capital felony, aggravated battery, burglary, or arson in the first degree; (3) offender knowingly created great risk of death to more than one person in a public place by means of a weapon or other normally hazardous device; (4) offense committed for money or material of monetary value; (5) murder of specified judicial or prosecution officials, killed during or because of exercise of official duties; (6) offender hired another to murder or committed murder as agent of another; (7) murder was outrageously or wantonly vile, horrible, or inhuman in that it involved torture, depravity of mind, or an aggravated battery to the victim; (8) murder of a peace officer, corrections employee, or firefighter while engaged in the performance of official duties; (9) murder committed during escape from lawful custody or confinement; (10) murder committed to avoid or prevent lawful arrest or custody in a place of lawful confinement. 428 U.S. at 165–66, n. 9.

narrowed the pool of persons eligible to receive the death penalty. Once the jury determined that the murder involved one or more statutory aggravating circumstances beyond a reasonable doubt, then Georgia law permitted but did not require the jury to return a death sentence. Georgia jurors retained discretion to consider any other aggravating circumstances; they were absolutely entitled to consider any factor in mitigation, and they were not told how to weigh or balance aggravating or mitigating factors against one another. In other words, the Georgia law narrowed the jury's discretion in that it created a threshold judgment about who was death-eligible. But once juries made the positive judgment and crossed the threshold, they remained as free as in the days of *Furman* to pick and choose among the eligibles whom to send to prison and whom to send to death row.[71] Nonetheless, the Supreme Court considered the guidance given by the list of ten aggravating circumstances to be sufficient to cure the pre-*Furman* risks of "wanton and freakish" assignments of execution. Every murderer sentenced to die in Georgia would henceforth have committed a comparable crime, judged against the same statutory list of aggravating circumstances.

The third feature of Georgia's new death penalty law that the Court praised was provision for direct, expedited review of death sentences by the state's highest court. The Georgia Supreme Court was charged with undertaking a "proportionality review" of a defendant's death sentence, making sure it was not excessive to the crime in light of what other juries in Georgia did in similar cases. Such proportionality review, the Supreme Court noted, further reduced the pre-*Furman* dangers of arbitrary death sentences.[*]

THE PERSISTENCE OF RACIAL DISPARITIES IN DEATH SENTENCING

With the Court's approval, executions commenced again in the United States in 1977. Between 1977 and 1982, no more than two persons were executed in any given year. In 1984, the death penalty was carried out against twenty-one persons; over the last decade, the number of annual executions has ranged from a low of eleven to a high of thirty-eight in

---

[*]*Gregg v. Georgia*, 428 U.S. at 166–67. In subsequent cases, the Court has made clear that the Constitution does not require state death penalty laws to provide for proportionality review by a higher court. See *Pulley v. Harris*, 465 U.S. 37, 50–51 (1984).

1993.[72] But did the post-*Furman* generation of death penalty laws solve the problems of arbitrariness and discrimination that eviscerated the fairness of the death penalty prior to 1972? In 1987, in the case of *McCleskey v. Kemp*, the Supreme Court returned to Georgia to consider how the new death penalty procedures were working in practice.[73] Warren McCleskey was a black man convicted of killing a white police officer during an armed robbery of a furniture store. McCleskey did not argue (how could he?) that only a racially prejudiced jury could have sentenced him to death. Considered on its own terms, McCleskey's crime made him death-eligible twice over: he killed during an armed robbery and he killed a police officer answering the robbery alarm.

But McCleskey concentrated on the difference between his fate and that of defendants committing "similar crimes." The difference, McCleskey argued, reflected a racial trend that singled out those who murdered whites, especially black men who murdered whites, as the most frequent candidates for the death penalty. To support his claim of discrimination, McCleskey relied on a massive empirical study of Georgia death sentencing during the 1970s, under that state's revised and approved death penalty statute.[*]

Conducted by law school professors David C. Baldus and Charles A. Pulaski, Jr., and statistics professor George Woodworth, the so-called Baldus study was actually two different projects. The first study (the Procedural Reform Study) traced the fate of 594 persons who were arrested, tried, and convicted for murder in Georgia between 1973 and 1978.[74] A second, companion study (the Charging and Sentencing Study), covering 1973 through 1979, followed 2,484 defendants who were arrested and charged with homicide and eventually convicted of murder or voluntary manslaughter. Unlike the first study, the second study therefore collected data on those convicted by guilty plea as well as trial.[75]

---

[*]The Georgia data on race-of-victim effects on death sentencing have been duplicated in studies from a number of other states, including nonsouthern states. For Ohio, for example, see William J. Bowers and Glenn L. Pierce, "Arbitrariness and Discrimination Under Post-Furman Capital Statutes," *Crime & Delinquency* 26 (1980): 563–635; for Illinois and Oklahoma, see Samuel R. Gross and Robert Mauro, "Patterns of Death: An Analysis of Racial Disparities in Capital Sentencing and Homicide Victimization," *Stanford Law Review* 37 (1984): 54–68, 92–98. For further studies of southern states, see Sheldon Ekland-Olson, "Structured Discretion, Racial Bias, and the Death Penalty: The First Decade After Furman in Texas," *Social Science Quarterly* 69 (1988): 853–73; and William J. Bowers, "The Pervasiveness of Arbitrariness and Discrimination Under Post-Furman Statutes," *Journal of Criminal Law and Criminology* 74 (1983): 1067–100 (Florida).

The Baldus studies showed some (albeit not much) improvement in the fairness of death sentencing in Georgia from pre-*Furman* days. On the positive side, there had been a significant decline in the number of "excessive" death sentences—excessive in comparison to treatment of "similar crimes."[76] To deal with the problem of defining "similar crimes," the Baldus study ranked each case according to its relative culpability or blameworthiness. The authors arrived at six different levels of culpability, using a mix of a priori moral judgment and empirical analysis to identify factors that made cases comparable in their blameworthiness.[77] Criteria leading the authors to assign a murder to the least culpable level included evidence that the defendant was not the trigger person and had no intent to kill.[78] At the most culpable level, the murder took place during a contemporaneous rape, involved a stranger-victim or multiple victims, or was aggravated by mutilation, arson, or execution-style killing.[79]

Using these culpability levels, the Baldus authors found that juries applied the death penalty consistently at the extremes. In thirty-eight penalty trials involving the most culpable murderers, the jury imposed the death sentence in all cases.[80] These were the cases where, if there was to be a death penalty at all, juries found it fit to impose the ultimate judgment with regularity. One case summary will suffice to indicate the fact pattern that provoked juries across the board to pronounce the death sentence:

> The defendant, a 35-year-old male with a prior conviction for burglary and two convictions for nonviolent crimes, and three coperpetrators planned to burglarize a home. While the three coperpetrators were in the house, three male victims came home and the perpetrators shot them. Three more victims then arrived, two of whom were shot. The perpetrators took the remaining victim, the only female, to the woods, where she was raped and sodomized. They then shot her twice and mutilated her breasts. [81]

When it came to the least culpable level of murders, juries were almost as consistent in showing mercy. Georgia juries imposed the death sentence in only 7 percent (four of fifty-nine) of murders in this category.[82] Of course, the four death sentences had to be considered excessive, because so many "similar crimes" did not earn a death sentence. Here is a fact pattern that typified cases in which the jury refused the death penalty:

> The defendant is a 25-year-old male with a prior conviction for aggravated assault. The defendant and several friends, including the 24-year-old

male victim, were playing pool and drinking at a club. The defendant got into an argument with a friend over $2 and the victim tried to break it up. The defendant and his cousin went to the cousin's house to get a pistol. Upon returning to the club, the scuffle broke out again. When the victim approached the defendant, the defendant fired twice, shooting the victim in the chest and stomach. The defendant also shot another male, who was going toward the victim, in the shoulder.[83]

In the midrange of cases, any consistency or even-handedness of death sentencing fell apart. This was dramatically true for prosecutors, who become highly selective in sorting out which midrange cases to pursue all the way to a death penalty hearing (a finding confirmed by research in several other states).[84] But it was also true of jurors. In the midrange cases, juries neither routinely imposed nor regularly shunned the death penalty. Instead, as in pre-*Furman* days, one jury might select one defendant to die for committing a crime that seemed similar, in its level of culpability, to crimes typically punished by other juries with life imprisonment. For instance, at the second least culpable level, the jury death sentencing rate was 35 percent (fourteen of forty). At level three, the sentencing rate was 69 percent (eighteen of twenty-six).[85] What factors accounted for why some juries sentenced some midrange defendants to death, whereas other juries sentenced other similar defendants to life?

In part, the Georgia study found jurors and prosecutors influenced by a number of legitimate factors. The primary factor that explained upon whom the death penalty fell in these midrange cases appeared to be the number of statutory aggravating factors. "Indeed, of the more than 150 variables in the [Baldus] data, the number of statutory aggravating circumstances present played by far the major role in distinguishing between those defendants who received a death sentence and those who did not."[86] Juries also were influenced by such legitimate factors as whether the defendant was an underling and whether the murder involved multiple stabs, multiple victims, a young victim, or a police officer.[87]

All this was to the good. But in the end, the Baldus study found that legitimate factors alone could not account for jury or prosecution death sentencing decisions. Especially in the midrange of cases, the race of the victim emerged as a key factor explaining who received the death penalty. Baldus "collected data on every nonracial factor suggested as relevant by literature, case law or actors in the criminal justice system"—over 250 items in all. But, controlling for these factors, "race of victim disparities not only persisted in analysis after analysis . . . , but the race of the victim proved to be among the more influential determinants of capital sentencing in Georgia."[88] The authors soberly concluded that, even after all the reforms initiated by *Furman*, "defendants whose victims were white were nearly as disadvantaged after *Furman* as they were before."[89]

To isolate the influence of victim race—and combinations of victim and defendant race—on death sentencing, it will help to report on the two Baldus studies separately.

THE CHARGING AND SENTENCING STUDY

Baldus began with the raw numbers for the 2,484 persons initially charged with murder and convicted of murder or voluntary manslaughter in Georgia during the years studied. If no attempt were made to control for legitimate characteristics that differentiate cases, then the unadjusted data starkly showed a death penalty falling disproportionately on defendants convicted of killing whites. Overall, only 128 convicts, or 5 percent of the initial number, received a death sentence.[90] But defendants convicted of killing white victims were sentenced to death in 11 percent of cases (108/981), while defendants convicted of killing black victims received the death penalty in only 1 percent of cases (20/1,503).[91] In other words, white-victim murderers received the death penalty at a rate 8.3 times higher than black-victim murderers.[92]

The raw or unadjusted data for combinations of victim race and defendant race also called for some explanation. Even among those convicted of killing white victims, there was a far greater likelihood of receiving the death penalty if the defendant were black. Table 6.1 summarizes the racial disparities at work:

TABLE 6.1

Racial Combination	Death Sentencing Rate
Black defendant/white victim	.21 (50/233)
White defendant/white victim	.08 (58/748)
Black defendant/black victim	.01 (18/1443)
White defendant/black victim	.03 (2/60)

Note: Adapted from David C. Baldus, George Woodworth, and Charles A. Pulaski, Jr., *Equal Justice and the Death Penalty: A Legal and Empirical Analysis* (Boston: Northeastern University Press, 1990), p. 315.

TABLE 6.2

	Prosecutorial Decision to Seek Death Penalty	Jury Decision for Death Penalty
I. RACE OF DEFENDANT		
Black	.33 (125/274)	.54 (74/137)
White	.31 (103/333)	.57 (66/166)
Difference (B-W)	2 pts.	-3 pts.
II. RACE OF VICTIM		
White	.43 (186/437)	.58 (119/205)
Black	.15 (42/271)	.44 (21/48)
Difference (W-B)	28 pts.	14 pts.
III. DEFENDANT/VICTIM COMBINATION		
Black defendant/white victim	.70 (87/124)	.59 (55/93)
White defendant/white victim	.32 (99/312)	.57 (64/112)
Black defendant/black victim	.15 (38/250)	.43 (19/44)
White defendant/black victim	.19 (4/21)	.50 (2/4)

Note: Adapted from David C. Baldus, George Woodworth, and Charles A. Pulaski, Jr., *Equal Justice and the Death Penalty: A Legal and Empirical Analysis* (Boston: Northeastern University Press, 1990), p. 327.

The raw racial pattern made by the death penalty in Georgia was a combination of a number of discretionary decisions, from the prosecutor's initial decision as to whether to charge a suspect with a capital crime, to the jury's decision between life and death in those cases that made it to a penalty trial. For our purposes, it is significant that, even staying with the raw data, the jury was far less implicated in racializing the Georgia death penalty pattern than were prosecutors. To begin, prosecutors disposed of the majority of the 2,484 cases studied by accepting a guilty plea; at this stage, Baldus found that prosecutors were far more likely to accept voluntary manslaughter pleas (Georgia has no degrees of murder) in black-victim cases than in white-victim cases.[93] Moreover, Baldus compared prosecutorial decisions to seek a death sentence, for those convicted of murder, with jury decisions in penalty trials. The raw results, summarized in table 6.2, again indicate that the principal source of racial disparities in Georgia death-sentencing was the prosecutor, not the jury.

The fact alone that a convicted murderer was black did not correlate strongly with either a prosecutor's decision to seek the death penalty or a jury's decision to impose it. In fact, the unadjusted data placed white defendants at a slight disadvantage before (mostly white) juries. On the other hand, the fact that a person killed a white person rather than a black person did strongly correlate both with prosecutor decisions to seek the death penalty and jury imposition of it. But jury decisions did not show the same disparity, apparent in the prosecutorial data, between black defendant/white victim cases and white defendant/white victim cases.

Of course, all of this raw data does not control for legitimate nonracial variables that might explain what otherwise seems so suspicious a correlation between death sentencing rates and race of victim. The Baldus study therefore constructed a number of control models, grouping cases together according to the presence of aggravating and mitigating factors such as murder during armed robbery or another contemporary felony; prior record of the defendant; female victim; defendant under seventeen years of age; victim a police officer; multiple shots; killing to avoid arrest; victim was a stranger; rape involved; victim was tortured; and so on.[94] Much of this adjusted data did not aim at separating prosecutorial decisions from jury decisions.

In their central model—controlling for thirty-nine legitimate, nonracial variables—the authors found that the race of the defendant no longer had general statewide effects, to the detriment of blacks, on death sentencing in post-*Furman* Georgia. However, there were two principal exceptions— black defendants, such as McCleskey, were at a disadvantage when only the more aggravated white-victim cases were considered, and they remained at slight disadvantage in rural areas of Georgia.[95] Otherwise, there was marked improvement from the most blatant forms of racial discrimination characteristic of pre-*Furman* death sentencing.

However, the adjusted data told a different story about the continuing influence of a victim's race on death sentencing. In the thirty-nine-variable logistic control model, the odds that a defendant indicted for murdering a white would receive the death penalty were 4.3 times greater than the odds facing a defendant murdering a black in comparable circumstances.[96] Even when the study controlled for some 230 nonracial variables, in a linear regression analysis, the authors still found a statistically significant 6-percentage-point disparity in the death sentencing rates in white-victim and black-victim cases.[97]

Moreover, this 6-percentage disparity was an overall average. In the midrange of cases, where discretionary application of the death penalty was at its highest, the Baldus study estimated a 20-percentage-point disparity between the rates at which prosecutors sought, and juries imposed, the death penalty in black-victim and white-victim cases.*

One way to understand the significance of these numbers is to compare the influence of the victim's race on death penalty decisions with the influence of legitimate factors such as a defendant's prior record. The authors found that "the race of the victim has an importance of the same order of magnitude as 'multiple stabbing,' 'serious prior record,' and 'armed robbery involved.'" Indeed, race of victim was statistically more influential on death penalty decisions than the fact that the victim was a stranger.[98]

When the Baldus study analyzed the adjusted data, looking for the separate contributions of prosecutors and juries to the race-of-victim disparities, they found that the pattern was "attributable principally to prosecutorial decisions made both before and after trial."[99] Before trial, even when Baldus controlled for the most important, legitimate, nonracial case characteristics, prosecutors still were dramatically more likely to permit black-victim murderers than white-victim murderers to plead guilty to voluntary manslaughter.[100] After a trial producing a guilty-of-murder conviction, the odds of a prosecutor seeking the death penalty were 3.2 times greater if the victim was white.[101] This part of the Baldus study reached more tentative conclusions about race-of-victim discrimination in jury penalty trials. In McCleskey's Supreme Court brief, the Baldus study was relied on to show that "once cases become sufficiently aggravated so that juries begin imposing death sentences, the death-sentencing rate rises more sharply among white-victim cases than among black-victim cases." Thus, the brief continued, "at any particular level of aggravation, until the two bands finally converge at the upper levels of aggravation, a significantly higher percentage of white-victim cases receive the death sentence."[102]

The Baldus study, as published in book form in 1990, is consistent

---

*Baldus, et al., *Equal Justice*, p. 401. A 20-percentage-point difference is not the same as a 20 percent difference. As McCleskey's Supreme Court brief pointed out, if the death sentencing rate in black-victim cases was 14 percent (14 out of 100), then the death sentencing rate in white-victim cases would be 34 percent (34 out of 100). In other words, the death sentencing rate in white-victim cases would be more than twice as large (34/14) as the death sentencing rate in black-victim cases.

with this conclusion. But the authors are somewhat more conservative in assessing the overall race-of-victim effects on jury decision making. The authors found that, depending on the methodology used and background variables controlled for, the effect was statistically significant only in certain cases.[103] Given these inconclusive results about the jury's factoring of victim race, the authors stressed their general conclusion that the overall race-of-victim disparities at work were due mainly to prosecutorial decisions.[104]

THE PROCEDURAL REFORM STUDY

The second study (limited to the smaller number of cases that actually went to trial and resulted in murder convictions, plus the few cases where persons were sentenced to death after pleading guilty to murder) more or less confirmed the results reached in the Charging and Sentencing Study. As to race of defendants, after controlling for legitimate case differences, the authors found the "total absence of any race-of-defendant effect" disadvantageous to blacks. In fact, in urban Georgia, white defendants were at a slight disadvantage before mostly white juries; the pattern was reversed in rural areas but the authors did not find the slight disadvantage of black defendants to be statistically significant.[105]

The troubling story, once again, was race of victim. Unadjusted data showed that prosecutors sought the death penalty against persons convicted of murdering whites by a 3:1 margin over the rate at which Georgia prosecutors sought the death penalty for persons convicted of killing blacks. For juries, there was a 1.4 ratio between the rate at which death sentences were pronounced in white-victim cases versus black-victim cases.[106]

The importance of the victim's race remained high, through all models adjusting for the relative culpability of the crime. In fact, in one analysis, the "predicted death-sentencing rate for all of the white-victim cases exceeds the predicted level for all comparable black-victim cases."[107] By way of example, this part of the Baldus study looked at race-of-victim disparities in death sentencing rates among 188 armed robbery cases involving murder. Without any adjustments for the relative culpability of the crime, death sentences were 4.6 times more likely to occur in white-victim armed robbery cases than in black-victim armed robbery cases.[108] But, even after grouping cases according to relative culpability, the authors still found that armed robbers convicted of killing a white person were at least twice as likely to receive the death penalty as armed robbers found guilty of slaying a black.[109]

As in the other study, the authors found that the victim's race mattered most in the midrange of cases, where decisions often go either way. Among midrange cases, "the presence of a white victim increases the risk of a death sentence by a factor of two or more and by as much as 20 percentage points."[110]

The effect of a victim's race on death sentencing rates was more pronounced statistically than such legitimate factors as the following: the victim being a stranger, multiple victims, multiple stab wounds, hostage victim, and victim under twelve years of age.[111] Clearly, when the skin color of a murder victim correlated more closely with death penalty sentencing than did the victim's age being under twelve, something invidious and discriminatory was at large at least between 1973 and 1978 in Georgia.

Once again, it bears emphasis that these statistics were not the result of jury decisions alone but were also based on the selectivity of prosecutors in seeking the death penalty. Considering prosecutorial decisions on their own, the Baldus study found that "the presence of a white victim increased the odds that the prosecutor would seek a death sentence by a factor of 5.5." [112] At the prosecutorial level, "the race-of-victim-effect was more powerful statistically than any variable for a legitimate case characteristic."[113] The study's conclusions about discrimination and the jury were, as with the Charging and Sentencing Study, more muted. The authors found that at least five legitimate case characteristics had a larger practical impact on the jury's death penalty decision than did the victim's race.[114]

And, when using certain methodologies and controlling for main culpability differences in cases, the authors found the race-of-victim effect on jury decision making to be statistically insignificant.[115] Nonetheless, other estimates from this part of the Baldus study did show a statistically significant race-of-victim effect on jury penalty trial decisions.[116] Given these mixed conclusions, the Baldus authors remained cautious about the jury's particular role in discriminatory application of the death penalty.[117] They noted that "fewer pressures converge on juries to produce a race-of-victim effect; most important, they are not subject to the political, financial, and personal constraints under which prosecutors work."[118]

But the Baldus study documented that, even after adjusting for culpability levels, regression analysis revealed a 14.5-percentage-point disparity in jury death penalty decisions in white-victim cases and black-victim cases.[119] The presence of a white victim increased the odds that a jury would impose the death sentence by a factor of 7,[120] thus implicating jurors along with prosecutors in the overall discriminatory results. The authors noted that "juries are . . . subject to the influence of community sentiments and the greater identification of predominantly white jurors with white victims and their families."[121] And they showed that, for both juries and prosecutors, the race-of-victim effects were especially strong in the midrange of cases, when both juries and prosecutors have the greatest room to exercise discretion.[122] Thus, with a great deal of caution and far less certainty than they gave to their data on prosecutors, the Baldus authors concluded that race of victim played a role in explaining jury death sentencing patterns and was likely to remain a subtle factor so long as jurors were predominantly white.

THE SUPREME COURT RESPONDS

The Baldus study failed to convince the Supreme Court that Georgia's death penalty remained discriminatory in application. Warren McCleskey lost his appeal. On September 25, 1991, McCleskey became the 155th person executed in the United States since capital punishment resumed in 1977.

It is strange that, even as it authorized McCleskey's execution, the Court conceded the accuracy of the Baldus study and acknowledged a "discrepancy that appears to correlate with race" in the way Georgia was administering the death penalty.[123] But "apparent discrepancies in sentencing are an inevitable part of our criminal justice system."[124] To prove discrimination, McCleskey would have had to demonstrate that some state actor—the jury or the prosecutor—purposely discriminated against him on the basis of race. But, for the 5–4 Court majority, a person who killed a police officer during an armed robbery could hardly cry foul because a prosecutor sought and the jury imposed the death penalty on him. Legitimate, nonracial factors provided a full justification for the behavior of the prosecutor and jury toward McCleskey; there was no reason to suspect that race was a factor in his particular case.[125]

But what about the overall pattern? What about the fact that prosecutors and juries apparently, if unconsciously, use their discretion to be lenient toward defendants who commit crimes similar to McCleskey's, except that their victim was black or they were white? Here, the Court made two revealing responses. First, the pattern demonstrated by the Baldus study emerged "from the combined effects of the decisions of hundreds of juries that are unique in their composition."[126] No one intended the overall pattern and hence no one was legally responsible for it. Hundreds of different jury decisions did not add up to a consistent state "policy" to discriminate. Nor could any "inference [be] drawn from the general statistics" to any one jury's decision.[127] Each jury could be acting in good faith, and yet a discriminatory pattern could emerge that no one intended. To live with the jury system was to accept this possibility, in the Court's judgment.

Lurking within the majority opinion in *McCleskey* was a tired, somber mood of resignation, almost exhaustion, about the possibility of achieving color-blind application of the death penalty. The Court was frank in acknowledging that twenty years of reform had not succeeded in insulating death sentencing from the "risk" that race influenced selections for death row. The risk was inherent, the Court stressed, in any scheme that left the death sentencer with discretion to show mercy to some convicted murderers but not others. As the Court put it, the "'power to be lenient . . . is the power to discriminate.'"[128] But, given all the benefits that flow from permitting jury or judge to show mercy at the final moment, the risk that mercy will involve racial considerations is not "constitutionally significant."[129] For the Court, it was sufficient to note that there can be "no perfect procedure for deciding in which cases governmental authority should be used to impose death."[130]

In the closing pages of its opinion, the majority confided its secret fear about McCleskey's claim of discrimination. "Taken to its logical conclusion," McCleskey's argument "throws into serious question the principles that underlie our entire criminal justice system." After all, "we could soon be faced with similar claims [that racial bias had impermissibly tainted] other types of penalty." For instance, social scientists might next present evidence that race of defendant or victim correlated with length of prison sentence.*

Moreover, statistics could probably show that juries considered irrelevant factors other than race—for instance, the physical attrac-

---

*Under so-called habitual criminal statutes adopted by several states, prosecutors may seek enhanced prison terms for persons convicted three separate times of certain serious crimes. A study by the National Council for Crime and Delinquency reported that 22 percent of blacks who met the legal criteria were sentenced as habitual offenders, whereas only 12 percent of eligible whites were given added prison terms. Edward Felsenthal, "Life Terms Aren't Viewed as Big Deterrent," *Wall Street Journal*, Sept. 11, 1993, p. B12.

tiveness or even facial characteristics of a defendant or victim. In short, "there is no limiting principle to the type of challenge brought by McCleskey." Ultimately, the Court considered the complaint to be about the arbitrariness of American justice across its full spectrum, and not merely an attack on race and the death penalty.[131]

The Court's opinion reads as if the majority were desperately seeking to slam the lid on Pandora's box, for fear of what horrible news would follow any acknowledgment that race of victim and defendant impermissibly influence application of the death penalty. But I would offer two rebuttals to the Court's panic: race is different and death is different.

Let me turn first to why race is different. The Court makes the fatuous claim that, if it were to accept mere statistical correlations between race and the death penalty as evidence of invidious discrimination, then it would also have to accept, as adequate proof of discrimination, bald statistics showing a correlation between capital punishment and a victim's physical attractiveness. But there is a huge difference between the two demonstrations. In the case of race, history gives meaning to the statistics. Throughout the antebellum period, Georgia openly ran a dual death penalty system, differentiating between crimes committed by and against blacks and those committed by and against whites. For instance, the death penalty was automatic for murders committed by blacks, whereas juries might recommend life for anyone else convicted of murder. The state penal code specified that the rape of a free white female by a black "shall be" punishable by death. Rape by others of a free white female triggered a prison term of two to twenty years. Most telling is that if the rape was of a black woman, the law provided punishment "by fine or imprisonment, at the discretion of the court."[132]

The legacy of racial bias and the death penalty did not end with the official removal of racial categories from the law. Rape remained a glaring example of the "ongoing influence of history." Between 1930 (when the federal government began keeping statistics) and 1977, Georgia executed sixty-two men for rape; fifty-eight were black.[133]

In the 1950s, in national research that extended beyond the Deep South, the University of Chicago Jury Project detected race-of-victim effects on the death penalty similar to what the Baldus study would show forty years later. The project recounted the case of a defendant convicted of fatally stabbing his former lover to death on a public street, even as she fled from him. The judge would have sentenced to death but surmised that because it was a case of a "Negro killing a Negro . . . the jury did not attach enough importance to the value of a human life due to race."[134] In another case, a "Negro woman shoots and kills her husband"; the judge tells project researchers that he would have convicted her of first degree murder and given the death penalty. But the jury convicts only of manslaughter. In the judge's opinion, juries do not hold

> Negroes . . . to the same moral responsibility as white people. . . . Negroes kill each other without reason other than the immediate urge at the time. . . . Community regards the law as too severe for some Negro cases because of lack of moral sense.[135]

To take one final example, in a case of domestic violence where a man kills the woman with whom he is living, the judge attributes the jury's mercy "to the fact that juries give much more latitude to colored folks than to white. They know how liable colored folks are to act on impulse by shooting and cutting."[136]

It is difficult to know how much reliance should be placed on such reports by judges about the racial bias of juries. The reports themselves are worded in ways that often betray the judges' own prejudices and suggest the possibility that the judges are attributing their own intolerance to jurors. Still, the numbers bear out the unwillingness of jurors in the 1950s to impose the death penalty when the victim was black. What is so remarkable and troubling is that, after all the reforms of jury selection and substantive law that the civil rights years accomplished, the Baldus study found jurors reflecting the same prevailing social attitude about the death penalty and the victim's race.

Precisely because the historical connection between race and the death penalty runs so deeply and is so ugly, the *McCleskey* Court erred in characterizing racial disparities in Georgia death sentencing as "unexplained" but not "necessarily invidious."*

On the other hand, such an agnostic reaction might well be appropriate to some new social science study showing a correlation between defendants' facial characteristics and death penalty rates. In the absence of a history of legal discrimination against certain facial

---

*In 1994 the *New York Times* reported that retired Justice Lewis Powell now regrets casting a fifth vote to uphold McCleskey's death sentence. "Justice Powell's New Wisdom," *New York Times*, June 11, 1994, p. A20.

types, the numbers are not as important as those involved when the issue is race. In short, the Court's reasoning does not do justice to the special scourge—the special burden—that race and the death penalty place upon the land.

Likewise, the Court's fear is overblown that any admission of the death penalty's unfairness would open the door to attacks on the fairness of the criminal justice system as a whole. The peculiar winnowing of death penalty jury panels, which leaves eligible only those prepared to impose capital punishment in appropriate cases, creates problems of its own. Such death-qualified juries are more likely to convict a defendant of a capital crime in the first place.[137] And, because opposition to the death penalty is more prevalent among blacks and women, selection of juries to hear death penalty cases conflicts with the cross-sectional deliberations we count on elsewhere to protect the jury's integrity.[138]

GRUESOME MURDER, GRUESOME TRIAL

I close with a case that illustrates both the gruesome nature of murder and the awful possibility of executing the wrong person.[139] On August 23, 1980, Cheryl Ferguson, a sixteen-year-old white girl, was raped and murdered during a girls' volleyball tournament at Conroe High School in Montgomery County, Texas. Her body was discovered in a loft at the school, with blood on her clothing; an autopsy revealed semen in her vagina. In addition, a Caucasian pubic hair, not belonging to the victim, was found near her vagina. Analysis of the clothing identified type A blood. Although the victim's own blood type was type A, there were no lacerations on her body to indicate that the blood originated from her; presumably, it came from the perpetrator.

With school scheduled to open in a matter of days, Texas Ranger Wesley Styles promised an immediate arrest. Prior to interviewing any witnesses, Styles arrested Clarence Lee Brandley, a black janitor at the school. The day after the arrest, Styles conducted a "walk through" the school with three other janitors—Gary Acreman, Sam Martinez, and John Sessum—who implicated Brandley. A fourth janitor at the school, James Dexter Robinson, was not present. During the walk-through, it was concluded that the victim headed up a stairwell for a restroom. The janitors said they saw Brandley follow her up the stairs and heard screams.

Analysis revealed that Brandley had type O blood. Investigators made no attempt to obtain blood samples from the other janitors who had seen the victim moments before her death. The state also neglected to obtain pubic hair samples for comparison from the other janitors to compare with the Caucasian pubic hair found on the victim.[*]

At the time of Brandley's 1980 trial, the policy of the Montgomery County district attorney was "that all black persons were to be struck from the jury panel when there was a black defendant." An all-white jury ultimately deadlocked 11 to 1 for conviction. During deliberations, "the other jurors repeatedly called [the holdout] a 'Nigger [sic] lover.'" After mistrial was declared, the holdout received "thousands and thousands of harassing calls."

Brandley was retried in 1985, again before an all-white jury obtained through the use of peremptory challenges to strike all qualified blacks. The jury convicted Brandley and sentenced him to death. Execution was set for January 16, 1986.

A stay of execution was granted, and an evidentiary hearing was held on whether new evidence entitled Brandley to a new trial. At the evidentiary hearing, Sessum admitted that he lied at the first trial, out of fear of Gary Acreman. Sessum testified at the hearing that Acreman and Robinson followed the victim up the stairs. He heard the victim scream "No!" and "Don't!" and cry for help. Contradicting his trial testimony, Sessum now said that Brandley did not arrive until five or ten minutes after the girl was accosted.

Brenda Medina, who lived with Robinson at the time of the murder, testified at the hearing. She stated that Robinson arrived home around midnight the day of the murder and told her he had to leave because he had killed a girl. Robinson in fact left the state early the next morning, leaving his blood-stained tennis shoes. Medina first told her story to her lawyer in 1986, who informed the District Attorney's Office. However, the District Attorney's Office never informed Brandley's attorney of Medina's statement.

Two videotaped statements from Gary Acreman were also introduced at

---

[*]The exhibit containing the Caucasian hair disappeared after trial, while the record was being compiled for appeal. 781 S.W. 2d at 890. Many years after the trial, the state finally obtained blood samples from Acreman and Robinson. But the samples could not be compared with the blood on the victim's shirt because that, too, disappeared while the record for appeal was being compiled.

the evidentiary hearing. On tape, Acreman exonerated Brandley and implicated Robinson, stating that Robinson had threatened him into lying about the murder. However, Acreman appeared personally at the hearing and renounced his videotaped testimony.

Other evidence at the hearing indicated the state's total failure to investigate any leads inconsistent with Brandley's guilt. A student at Conroe High School at the time of the murder testified that she had passed the victim in the hallway between the restroom and the gymnasium. About a half hour later, she saw two white men rush through the gym—an event she remembered because there were no men attending the volleyball tournament. When the victim's body was discovered, this student told her coach about the men and her coach contacted the police, who were not interested.

On the basis of the evidence produced by the hearing, the Texas Court of Criminal Appeals set aside Brandley's conviction in 1989. It found the state's investigative procedures to border on "a subversion of justice."

The Brandley story combines outrage at a violent murder with outrage at the racism that almost sent Brandley to death by lethal injection in Texas. One trusts that the case is far from typical, but it is still a shock to find such a trial occurring in the 1980s.

A jury convicted and sentenced Brandley to death. But it was a jury selected under pre–*Batson v. Kentucky* rules that left prosecutors free to eliminate African-Americans and thus empower prejudice over evidence before an all-white jury. Today, the Montgomery County District Attorney's Office no longer has a manual directing trial lawyers to eliminate African-Americans. Nor would such a corruption of the jury be permissible. To this extent, the jury has evolved from the type that convicted Brandley. But the case is too recent, and the prospect of Brandley's execution is too ghastly, for us to rest comfortably with a death penalty that admits of human errors beyond correction.

Even without the overt racism exhibited against Brandley, the death penalty continues to exhibit a racial pattern in the 1990s. It is a good sign that the death penalty no longer falls disproportionately on black defendants per se; this shows that the jury evolves along with the culture. But the winnowing process still results in dramatic differences between the fate of those who kill whites and the fate of those who kill blacks. In an ideal world, perhaps concepts of moral retribution could justify capital punishment. But we are not citizens of such a time and place. Here and now, the racial disparities in the application of the death penalty compromise any moral argument on its behalf. We do not restore dignity to life by practicing capital punishment in ways that say white lives are worth more than black lives. The time has come to admit that the post-*Furman* procedures have not cured the problems that led the Supreme Court in 1972 to halt capital punishment as "cruel and unusual" in its application.

It is tempting to blame the jury alone for the discriminatory application of the death penalty. But, as the Brandley trial well illustrates, such blame would be mistaken on a number of grounds. First, as emphasized throughout this chapter, the evidence is clear that prosecutors bear major responsibility for the uneven toll the death penalty takes according to race. Juries are an easy target for the cynic who bemoans the irrationalities and prejudices of death sentencing. But the skepticism would be better directed at the politics of prosecutors who control when and against whom the death penalty is sought.

Second, although corroborating data are hard to come by, one study from Florida documented a more significant race-of-victim effect in the actual sentences imposed by trial judges than in the jury's sentencing recommendations in death penalty phase trials.[140] To be sure, Florida elects trial judges, so this may not be a fair test of judges' death sentencing merits. But it still should take some of the heat off juries to find that the Florida Supreme Court has vacated between two-thirds and three-fourths of all reviewed cases where a trial judge imposed the death sentence over a jury's life recommendation.[141]

Third and most important, jury death sentencing is not something the rest of us can simply disown—as if jurors were some groups of aliens infected with a strange racial virus unknown among the general population. Death penalty juries may be death-qualified in ways that skew their representativeness. But the gulf between those eligible to serve on capital punishment juries and those excluded is not so great that the community at large can disavow the death sentencing of juries. In fact, the death penalty decision remains the premier moment in contemporary trials when jurors are encouraged to deliver the conscience of the community. And though modern capital punishment statutes set out certain criteria for the jury to apply, ultimately the law tells jurors that they are free to show mercy or not. Jurors are given no official list of mitigating circumstances to consider, because no list could ever be complete or exhaust the factors that could legitimately sway jurors to stay the executioner's sword. In this sense, the death penalty decision is among the least mechanical and the most discretionary decision modern jurors make.

Are we surprised when jury mercy fails to be color-blind? Is the jury getting us wrong when it singles out black defendants murdering whites as the most fearsome of murder scenarios? I think not. Again, to study the jury is to study larger social failures in achieving color-blind justice.

Along with other state and local institutions, the jury has a troubled history of protecting local racism from national policies. Selection procedures that ensured all-white juries corrupted trials and turned juries into shelters for racial prejudice. In our own generation, reforms have begun to dismantle the all-white jury and, one hopes, sever the final threads connecting juries to racism. As I said before, some of these reforms, especially the end of race-based peremptory challenges, are still so new that their effect is not yet known. Perhaps, in time, they could enhance the fairness of jury deliberation on the death penalty. Perhaps genuinely cross-sectional juries could catch and mute the hidden biases that translate into the racial disparities in death sentencing we have studied in this chapter. Perhaps there is some way to solve the problems inherent in death-qualifying jurors and skewing the fullness of death deliberation.

In such a better future, we would then discuss the morality of the death penalty in and of itself. But for the present, color-blind justice eludes jurors, judges, and prosecutors when it comes to the death penalty. Those on death row and those about to be sentenced to it cannot wait for a better hour. To carry out executions in full knowledge that race remains a factor in the imposition of death sentences is to tolerate the most intolerable of constitutional violations. Even friends of the jury must acknowledge that the power to sentence to death is not one jurors can morally exercise on behalf of a community conscience that fails to live up to its own aspirations for color-blind justice.

Conclusion

AS THE TWENTIETH CENTURY draws to a close, jury trials in the United States bring to the fore one question above all others: In a multi-ethnic society, is there one justice for jurors to render, or are there different justices for different groups? In regard to race, the Rodney King trials put this question before the nation, but so too did a startling series of cases of interracial violence in recent years: the Bernhard Goetz trial, the Howard Beach and Bensonhurst attacks in Queens and Brooklyn, the trials of white police officers for slaying blacks in Detroit and Miami, the Crown Heights affair, and the Reginald Denny trial in Los Angeles. In all these cases, jury trials have been a window into our democratic soul. The jury system allows us to take a hard look at the conscience of the community and our inner doubts about the attainability of impartial justice.

The question of one justice versus many justices is sharpest when trials involve racial divisions, but the issue has life elsewhere. Consider four cases mentioned in this book. In 1994, the much publicized gender gap on Erik Menendez's jury (six men finding him guilty of murdering his parents, six women believing he was sexually abused and therefore guilty only of manslaughter) raised the issue of whether men and women respond in fundamentally different ways to cases involving allegations of sexual abuse.[1] In the trial of Lorena Bobbitt, on charges of maliciously wounding her husband by severing his penis, the jury of seven women and five men agreed unanimously that she was not guilty by reason of temporary insanity brought on by a history of abuse and rape. Nonetheless, the case raised concerns about different standards of justice for women defendants who claim that sexual abuse makes them not responsible for criminal acts.[2] In a 1992 Massachusetts trial of a Catholic priest for blocking access to abortion clinics, the prosecution used peremptory challenges to eliminate prospective jurors with Irish Catholic–sounding surnames, on the assumption that ethnicity and religion would control jurors' perspectives.[3] And in New York, specific community tensions between blacks and Jews seemed to be lived out on a mixed-race jury that acquitted an Egyptian-born defendant of murdering Jewish Defense League founder Meir Kahane, even while convicting the defendant of possessing the murder weapon during a shooting of another person.[4]

One case in particular captured the fragile reputation of jury justice in a society where the consuming issue is the racial or ethnic balance of power on the jury. In Miami, on Martin Luther King Day in 1989, William Lozano, a Hispanic police officer, shot and killed a black motorcyclist during a chase through the mostly black section of Overton; a passenger on the motorcycle died the next day of wounds suffered in the crash. Lozano claimed that he fired in self-defense at a speeding motorcycle heading in his direction, but the facts were unclear and the incident unleashed festering tensions between the African-American and Hispanic populations and led to three nights of rioting. Lozano was indicted for the slaying, and in December 1989, a Dade County jury of three whites, two blacks, and one Hispanic convicted him on two counts of manslaughter. But, in a decision emblematic of declining faith in the local geography of justice for which the jury has historically stood, a state appeals court reversed Lozano's conviction in 1991, finding error in the trial judge's refusal to move the trial from Miami and Dade County, where fears of further rioting may have unduly influenced jurors to convict.[5]

As Florida authorities searched for neutral turf for Lozano's retrial, there ensued a bizarre odyssey that acted out every issue about local justice, impartial justice, cross-sectional juries, and representative juries that this book has addressed. Black civic leaders balked at not permitting Miami citizens to judge the behavior of their own police, arguing that familiarity with police behavior in Miami was an indispensable element in any jury's ability to understand the case in context. But, if the trial had to be moved, they argued for a venue where the jury pool would include about as many African-Americans as would a jury pool in Dade County (the county pool is approximately 50 percent Hispanic, 30 percent white, and 20 percent African-American). Equally concerned about demographics, Lozano's lawyers stressed that he, too, as an immigrant from Colombia, was a member of an identifiable ethnic group and that his right to be tried by a cross-sectional jury meant that the venue for retrial should mirror the percentage of the Dade County population that was Hispanic.

The presiding judge, Thomas Spencer, first ordered the trial moved to mostly white Orlando, but, in the wake of the Rodney King trial, the judge countermanded himself, concerned that the percentage of African-Americans in the jury pool for Orange County (site of Orlando) was only half what it was in Dade County. Judge Spencer ordered the trial moved all the way to Tallahassee in Leon County, where the population, like that of Dade County, was approximately 20 percent African-American. The judge justified the long-distance shift as necessary to overcome the feeling of black Americans that they were "shut out from our judicial system." He vowed that "this court will insure that blacks will be on the jury that tries this case to the extent the law permits."[6]

Over the next few months, a demoralizing spectacle took place as various judges took turns ordering the trial back to Orlando, then back to Tallahassee, then finally back to Orlando again. In all, the proposed location for the trial shifted five times.[7] For the public, the impression had to be that choice of venue was crucial to the eventual verdict, that African-Americans and Hispanics could not trust one another to judge the case impartially, and that one side or the other would benefit from tilts in the racial percentages in the jury pool. In this way, the trial brought to life all the debates about racial and ethnic balancing and proportional representation Americans struggle with today.* The choice of venue became a "metaphor for every ethnic and racial issue that urban America has," remarked Abbe Smith of the Criminal Justice Institute at the Harvard Law School.[8]

In preferring Tallahassee over Orlando as an appropriate locale for retrial, Judge Spencer highlighted the closer demographic match with Miami as far as the African-American population went, but the judge seemed far less concerned that Hispanics accounted for only 2.5 percent of the Tallahassee population, compared with nearly half of Miami's population.[9] The defendant therefore objected that his right to trial by a cross-

---

*Likewise, in the 1994 retrial of Byron De La Beckwith for assassinating Medgar Evers, the judge ruled that pretrial publicity required a change of venue from Hinds County, site of the 1963 murder, but he moved the trial to Panola County, which had a racial composition similar to that of Hinds County. Timothy Noah and Helene Copper, "Defendant May Be Tried for Third Time in Death of Civil Rights Leader," *Wall Street Journal*, July 19, 1992, p. B1.

sectional jury was vitiated by the move from Miami to Tallahassee. "You can't change location to change jury complexion," Roy Black, Lozano's chief lawyer argued. "But if you're going to do it," Black continued, "you must take into account the right of the defendant, which just points out the problem with using quotas for juries. Somebody is always going to offend someone."[10] As constitutional law scholar Yale Kamisar noted, "The fact that both the defendant and victims are members of minority groups underscores the thicket we are getting into. You can't as a matter of principle favor one group over another, despite what this judge did."[11]

Concerned that the selection of Tallahassee was not evenhanded and might make any conviction vulnerable on appeal, the prosecution joined with the defense in asking that the trial be shifted back to Orlando, where African-Americans and Hispanics each made up about 10 percent of the jury pool.[12] This motion was granted; a last-ditch motion by the victims' families to return the trial to Tallahassee was denied, and trial finally commenced in Orlando in May 1993. A jury of three whites, two Hispanics, and one African-American acquitted Lozano of all charges on May 28.[13]

The Lozano case highlights the unresolved dispute in the United States about the demographics of justice and the way to make juries representative of the community. Judge Spencer was commendably sensitive to learning lessons from the Rodney King case, where moving the trial to mostly white Simi Valley led to a jury without African-Americans. The failure to have a racially representative jury left the not guilty verdicts without legitimacy—certainly in the black community but generally as well. During the search for an impartial venue to retry Lozano, many labeled Orlando the "Simi Valley" of Florida, and Judge Spencer thought that the appearance of injustice made a move to more racially mixed Tallahassee the wise course. But straightforward calculations of white versus black percentages of the jury pool did not work in a case with a Hispanic defendant. It was as if the judge did not fully follow through with his own theory that the best substitute venue for trying the case would be one that matched the mix of peoples in Miami.

There was no easy solution to the problems of impaneling the right kind of cross-sectional jury to try Lozano. Perhaps an elegantly simple answer would have presented itself if some other Florida city closely mirrored the population proportions of Miami. But because no city duplicated Miami's demographics, the choice of substitute venue was bound to be unsatisfactory from the point of view of representing groups in the same proportion that they would have been represented in the Dade

County jury pool. The eventual choice of Orlando rested more on compromise than on any discernible principle. And Miami authorities let out an audible sigh of relief when the peace held, despite Lozano's acquittal.

Behind the logistics of where to locate the Lozano trial lay broader issues about the democratic credentials of the jury. Throughout this book I have distinguished between two different ideals for jury democracy. The older ideal made deliberation, not representation, the key behavior we expected of jurors. The deliberative ideal was a demanding one, seeking to inspire jurors to put aside narrow group allegiances in favor of spying common ground. It was a model of democracy that believes that face-to-face meetings matter, that voting is secondary to debate and discussion, that power should ultimately go to the persuasive, that collective wisdom results from gathering people in conversation from different walks of life, that unanimity is practicable and desirable, and that there is a justice shared across the demographic divides of race, religion, gender, and national origin.

The new and competing ideal for the jury is a group-representation model, one that seeks to redesign the jury so that it basically fits the pluralist paradigm of democracy and interest group politics. This model is openly skeptical about whether deliberation inside the jury room matters; it insists, in the name of realism, that there is no one justice to share, that juries are not above the political fray but are a microcosm of the biases and prejudices, the bartering and brokering among group interests that dominate democratic deal making in general. According to this point of view, the key to jury verdicts becomes whom the jurors are, not what the evidence shows. Because jurors are seen as voting their demographics just as citizens do in elections, the crucial moment of trial is said to come during selection, and the highest aspiration we can have for jury democracy is to represent the perspectives of groups in some fair way, to balance the biases of jurors and therefore achieve an overall impartial jury.

The continuing power of group prejudice in American society gives point to the representative model of the jury and its correction of romantic myths about what goes on inside a jury room. But the correction goes too far when it discards the deliberative ideal entirely and turns instead to theories of proportional representation and the divisive notion that jurors are there to be allegiant advocates for their own kind. The Lozano trial illustrates just how difficult it would be to practice such a theory of representation—how balancing the jury on one axis may imbalance it on another. But the difficulties are more than practical. Any theory of proportional representation, applied to the jury, carries with it a suggestion that jurors are supposed to fill slots and to vote according to some predetermined perspective associated with those slots. Were real jurors to behave according to this theory, even the aspiration to deliberate to common ground would be gone. The whole jury enterprise would seem so precariously perched on achieving the right ethnic balance among jurors that enthusiasm for the jury as an instrument of justice would be lukewarm at best.

A contemporary defense of the deliberative ideal for the jury must acknowledge, as our predecessors did not, that the search for common justice starts with the different experiences attached to identity in America. We have learned the hard way that no ideal of deliberation fit for a multiethnic society can be naive about the conscience of "the" community and ignore the different subcommunities in which we live and that have obvious influence on the ways we perceive justice and injustice. But our differences need not be an obstacle to deliberation and rational persuasion; they can enrich conversation out of a commitment to the basic democratic norm that ordinary persons joined together can achieve the most complete assessment of events on trial—complete both in the sense of rendering the most accurate account of what happened and in the sense of judging its significance before the law.

I have argued that jury deliberation historically was compromised and corrupted by the discriminatory exclusions that allowed jurors to remain ignorant of the views of those excluded and to operate on the basis of narrow arguments persuasive only to their own kind. By putting an end to those exclusions, the reforms of the civil rights years made it possible for jury deliberations to be fully democratic, in the sense of creating collective wisdom through conversation across community lines. The key point here is that we should seek to inspire jurors not to represent their own kind but to use their different starting perspectives to educate one another, to defeat prejudiced arguments, and to elevate deliberations to a level where power goes to the most persuasive. Jurors in real cases may seldom practice this deliberative ideal perfectly. Egregious verdicts still occur, in an institution that requires us to risk much on the virtue of millions of citizens each year. But I think we sometimes forget just how much progress the jury in America has made from the abysmal record compiled by the all-white male jury during much of our history. It should be a cause of excitement and hope that we have done more to democratize jury selection and jury conversation in the last twenty years than in the previous two hundred.

And yet the constant drawing of attention to the ethnic background of jurors has taken its toll on public confidence in the ancient institution. The deliberative ideal continues to vanish, continuing many of the long-term historical trends I narrated in the early chapters of this book. If this ideal is once again to have the power to inspire, then it is imperative that certain reforms take place. I have argued in favor of preserving the unanimous verdict as a way of empowering arguments that resonate across group lines. For the same reason, I have argued for abolishing the peremptory challenge, which is so frequently wielded by lawyers to deprive a person from a place on the jury simply because of the person's religion, national origin, age, or occupation. The time has come to fully practice what we preach and to prohibit discriminatory, exclusionary practices from occurring under cover of the peremptory challenge. Too frequently, persons struck by peremptory challenge are left wondering why they were suspected of bias and whether the suspicion accused them of some level of inherent racism or prejudice.

Some of the reforms I have argued for in this book, in the name of enriching jury deliberation, are broader in scope and harder to achieve than those just mentioned. While acknowledging the dangers of jury nullification, I believe it necessary to instruct jurors that, as the conscience of the community, they may set aside the law to acquit a defendant. I say this because history indicates that we cannot eliminate jury nullification—we can only drive it underground. My preference is for a jury that does things aboveboard and is fully apprised of its choices. But I also believe that we impoverish jury deliberations by providing jurors with an overly mechanistic description of their function. The typical handbook warns the jury to leave the law to the judge, to accept the judge's instructions on the law whether they agree with them or not. What is left for the jury to do? Again, the handbooks say that jurors should merely find the facts, then produce a verdict by applying the judge's law to the facts as found. This is such a bland description that I fear it saps the intensity, independence, and passion we ought to be inspiring in jurors.

Worse, it is a description that displaces responsibility for the verdict from the jurors (reduced to mere law appliers) to the judge who pronounced the law. There is no room left for jurors to function openly as the conscience of the community that they are trying to create among themselves, to address any tensions that may exist between that conscience and the law. I am aware that restoring space for jury nullification runs the risk of unleashing bias in jurors, but this is a risk we must take if we are to preserve the jury as a forum where ordinary persons gain the power to reconcile law and justice in concrete cases.

Of all the reforms suggested in this book, the most difficult to achieve will be a reversal of jury selection trends that disqualify persons for over-exposure to pretrial publicity. These trends have been building for nearly two centuries, as stricter definitions of impartiality have made ignorance a virtue and knowledge a vice in would-be jurors. History has eclipsed the local knowledge model of the jury in irreversible ways; modern trial procedures leave no room for the older notion that jurors with personal knowledge of trial events, witnesses, or defendants are best equipped to hear the facts in context. But, even within contemporary legal standards for impartiality, judges need not disqualify media-following persons in quite the wholesale way they frequently do in highly publicized cases. In practice, jury selection needs to regain a sense of balance and to cease making the rabidly antidemocratic assumption that whole segments of the community are routinely unable to be fair-minded jurors. I suggest a regrounding of jury selection, considering that the open mind we desire in jurors is fully consistent with, perhaps even undergirded by, attention to leading stories of the day.

None of these reforms will protect our jury heritage unless accompanied by an even greater change. Most U.S. citizens strongly believe in their right to jury trial, but fewer feel responsibility to serve on juries when called. This imbalance between wanting individual rights and avoiding communal service is characteristic of contemporary democratic life across a number of issues, but it has a special urgency for juries. After all, no one can have the right to be tried before representative juries unless we all feel an obligation to accept jury duty in turn. Judges must do their part, by guarding against patterns of excuses and challenges that keep so many willing persons from serving. But more of us must be willing to serve.

Unfortunately, the numbers indicate that escaping jury service remains a favorite pastime of citizens. A 1988 Massachusetts report showed that 31 percent of jurors summoned for state jury duty in Massachusetts in 1988 were either disqualified or excused.[14] Twenty-five percent of qualified jurors found some way to cancel or postpone their jury duty; another 6 percent were simply absent.[15] These numbers, moreover, tell only part of the story of unwillingness to serve. Among those who do appear and are sent into a courtroom for voir dire, the art of getting excused is highly developed. Individuals accuse themselves of prejudice, students say they cannot afford to miss classes, and self-employed persons state they cannot afford to miss work.

Because so many prospective jurors will be excused, jury commissioners respond by summoning far more persons than will actually be needed on juries. A vicious cycle sets in when persons show up for jury duty only to find themselves warehoused for hours on end in waiting rooms, never even to be called into a courtroom (only 47 percent of those showing up for their first day of jury service were sent into a courtroom for questioning in Massachusetts). For anyone who has gone through the experience of discharging one's jury obligation by spending a day or more in a waiting room, the romance of the jury system is understandably fleeting.

These problems are not peculiar to our time. No-shows were enough of a problem in colonial Virginia that many of the colony's earliest jury statutes set out fines (given in pounds of tobacco) for those shirking jury duty.[16] Then as now, persons occupied elsewhere were not keen to interrupt their daily routines and travel to court. In short, we should not romanticize the virtues of the past or exaggerate the vices of modern life. The American jury survived the days when colonists were too busy to serve, and it will survive today's oft-expressed indifference to jury obligations.

Recently, many jurisdictions have eliminated statutory exemptions for various professionals (doctors, lawyers, judges, and teachers) that once sent the wrong message that some persons were too indispensable in their careers to serve as jurors. As a society, we are moving in the right direction by spreading the obligation to serve equally across all classes. And, for all the no-shows and excuses, the sheer number of citizens who do appear in court ready to serve is extraordinary, running into the many millions.[17]

In every waiting room for jurors in every court, the following story might be posted as a reminder of what the call to jury service has meant to the civil rights of Americans. Sometime between 1954 and 1955, a sanitation worker by the name of Mr. Cox (his first name is not recorded) received a summons to report for jury duty in federal court. Mr. Cox recalled being

extremely proud. . . . It was . . . one of the proudest moments of my life. Ever since I was a little kid . . . I've had a desire to serve. . . . Of course, [black] people [were] not permitted to serve. . . . I've read many books on the jury and when I was first called to serve I went to the library and read up on the jury system and what a fine institution it is. . . . When I got my summons . . . I got a sense of really belonging to the American community.[18]

But Cox's joy was short-lived. On the jury he was ignored or insulted; at lunchtime, he was no longer a legal equal but a black man who had to eat in a separate restaurant. "It was a terrible shock to me to know that I wasn't even permitted to eat in a white man's restaurant . . . when I was called upon to undertake an important public responsibility."[19]

Cox's experiences—both his initial exhilaration and his ultimate disappointment—should be in the minds of all us when the jury summons comes in the mail. It is a call to make history right at last.

By the time this book reaches print, there undoubtedly will be fresh jury trials splashed across the headlines and animating dinner conversations across the land. Once again, there will be villainous verdicts that convince many that the jury's grand experiment in democratic justice has reached the end of its tether. But there will also be heroic efforts by jurors that testify again to the importance of requiring government to make its proof to ordinary citizens. The ebb and flow of the jury's reputation is an old story, one that will continue so long as the jury remains the embodiment of nonelite, participatory ideals of democracy.

The direct and raw character of jury democracy makes it our most honest mirror, reflecting both the good and the bad that ordinary people are capable of when called upon to do justice. The reflection sometimes attracts us, and it sometimes repels us. But we are the jury, and the image we see is our own.

Epilogue to the Paperback Edition

"HOW WOULD FORREST GUMP vote were he on the O. J. jury?"

When a *Chicago Sun-Times* reporter asked me this question as jury selection got underway in the Simpson case, I was floored.[1] A case of this magnitude, I was convinced, would provoke a long overdue national conversation about juries—a conversation that would dare to ask whether money buys justice, how race does or does not affect jurors, and where to find impartial jurors in this age of massive pretrial publicity. But Forrest Gump on the jury? Looking back, I now appreciate the reporter's foresight in understanding that most persons expected entertainment from the trial, not justice.

By the time the jury was sequestered, I was less shocked to receive a call from *A Current Affair* asking if my book told any sex stories about jurors in hotel rooms. Over time, I became used to similar requests for inside stories about lawyers who marry jurors or jurors who marry sheriffs. Publishing a book on the jury on the eve of the Simpson trial turned out to be a mixed blessing. On the one hand, it was gratifying to find so much interest in the jury. On the other hand, my attempt to prompt a sober examination about the jury's role in a democracy was lost in a mania for titillating stories.

When it came to far-ranging questions, prospective Simpson jurors answered their fair share on a 75-page questionnaire covering 302 issues. No doubt the questionnaire saved court time by eliminating persons with clear biases. But it also permitted lawyers to go fishing for information only marginally relevant to weeding out prejudice ("Please name the three public figures you admire most"). Perhaps the most ingenious question was number 213: "Have you or anyone else close to you under-gone an amniocentesis?" Presumably, one side or both thought that jurors who trusted the accuracy of amniocentesis, a genetic test during preg-nancy for fetal defects, would automatically trust the accuracy of the genetic DNA tests so crucial to the prosecution's case against Simpson. For similar reasons, lawyers wanted to know how potential jurors felt about any tests performed on their blood or urine. It was as if the prosecu-tion's ideal juror was a naïve believer in the accuracy of all medical tests, while the defense was looking for people who knew little about medical technology and hated what they did know.

Although jury selection was exhaustive and consumed eleven weeks, it was not particularly effective in securing model jurors. As of this writing in June 1995, the Simpson trial threatens to set a record for the number of dismissed jurors with ten of the original twelve already removed for mis-conduct. Were this rate of dismissal to continue, Judge Lance A. Ito would run low on jurors and would have to consider declaring a mistrial. (California law permits trials to continue with less than twelve jurors when both sides agree. Less clear is whether a trial may proceed when the defense consents to a jury of less than twelve but the prosecution objects.) Despite these dangers, Judge Ito felt he had no choice but to boot jurors who failed to disclose episodes of domestic violence in their pasts, kept mum about having met Simpson once, made an open show of boredom by reading a book during trial, or appeared to be writing a book about the trial. In addition, there were unsubstantiated charges of racial infighting.

Concerns about juror book deals were particularly acute. Prior to the trial's start, the California legislature passed a law prohibiting jurors, for a period of ninety days following the discharge of the jury on which they served, from receiving more than fifty dollars for information about the trial. But Michael Knox, one of the first jurors to be dismissed, chal-lenged the constitutionality of the law. A federal judge found the law to violate the First Amendment, when applied to a person already off the jury.

So many jurors fell by the wayside that, irrespective of the final ver-dict, the jury system looked woeful at times. Part of the explanation lay with the extraordinary opportunities that this one jury had to turn their service into gold. But their misbehavior was not all that alarming, espe-cially when compared to other egregious cases in which jurors revealed themselves as God's messengers, deliberated while drunk or high on mar-ijuana, or sat in a corner and refused to deliberate at all.

What was unique about the Simpson jury was not the level of misconduct but the amount of surveillance it came under. On more than one occasion, Judge Ito received tips from anonymous sources that led to a juror's removal. Even if these tipsters were well meaning citizens, they opened up a new danger to jury trials. Interested parties could hire investigators to keep tabs on the jury, using or ignoring any discoveries according to how they felt about a particular juror.

The parade of dismissals threatened to rob the remaining jurors of any dignity, as they found themselves subject to searches and interrogations without the usual constitutional rights. But there was also a better and braver side to the Simpson jury. In one of the oddest moments in recent jury history, a majority of jurors shut down the trial for one day when they protested Judge Ito's removal of three sheriff's deputies accused by a dismissed juror of favoring white panel members. In defense of the deputies, thirteen of the then eighteen remaining jurors and alternates, including most black members, at first refused to leave their hotel rooms. When they finally did arrive in court, the thirteen conducted a "dress in" by wearing black or dark clothing. Later in the trial, the jurors again threatened revolt, this time to demand longer working hours and a speedier conclusion to the trial.

Clearly, these jurors were frustrated by trial delays, the purpose of which could rarely be explained to them. With silent gestures that could push jury reform in the right direction, they pointed accusing fingers at a trial process that wasted their time as it indulged every grandstanding gambit of lawyers. While we should not rush to abbreviate trials or to empower judges to silence lawyers, there was at least as much misconduct by the lawyers in this case as by the jurors. In addition, sidebars occurred so frequently that even attentive jurors could easily have lost the thread of argument. Virtually everyone played to the television cameras. In a celebrity's trial where money was no object, the adversary system ran amok. Jurors should not be made the scapegoats for a flawed process that implicated everyone.

The greatest doubt raised by the trial centered on the impact of race on jurors. District Attorney Gil Garcetti acted commendably (if politically) when he chose to hold the trial in the downtown district of Los Angeles, rather than nearer to the Brentwood area where the crimes occurred; that decision assured a jury pool, and eventually a jury, with a black majority.

The racial mix of the jury mattered because polls showed that whites overwhelmingly thought Simpson guilty, while a majority of blacks believed him innocent. The reasons for this sharp racial divide were not hard to divine: negative experiences with the police leave the minority community far more willing than the majority to believe that police stop, detain, arrest, and frame innocent persons. Of course, the militia movement in the United States and the Oklahoma City bombing show that significant numbers of whites are also hostile to law enforcement, so we should be cautious about such generalizations.

Until the Simpson jury renders its verdict or hangs, we will not know whether the jurors divide along the racial lines predicted by the polls. In this book, I review some of the recent New York cases—the Crown Heights affair and the Meir Kahane trial—in which suspicion of the police among minority jurors led to acquittals or partial acquittals. But I also review lesser-known cases, as well as mock-jury experiments, showing that race cannot be isolated from a host of other factors influencing each juror. Indeed, there is something deeply insulting about the claim that, once the race of a juror is known, you know everything you need to know about that juror. Historically, this was precisely the argument relied upon to exclude blacks from sitting as jurors in any case involving a black defendant.

Still, there is no denying that the Simpson trial became a rallying point for the black community, a vehicle for expressing hostility toward a criminal justice system thought to mistreat blacks in general, whether or not it treated Simpson fairly. We should not be surprised if representative juries reflect a basic "race gap" between whites, who tend to trust law enforcement, and minorities, who frequently do not. Once in the jury room, the intensity of face-to-face deliberation often bridges that gap by generating the kind of interracial conversation rare outside juries. But no matter how the Simpson case ends, it joins the Rodney King trials in putting the issue of race and the jury at center stage in our debates about justice in America.

Once the Simpson trial ends, proposals to reform the jury will begin in earnest. By way of epilogue to *We, the Jury*'s themes, I suggest some practical steps we should take to improve the quality of jury trials, even while recognizing the capacity of ordinary people to do justice.

We can begin by moving the juror from passive spectator to active participant. To this end, four proposals are noteworthy:

- *Permit jurors to submit questions*. State as well as federal trial courts are experimenting with juror questioning of witnesses.[2] This does not mean jurors get to pop off with a question whenever they want—judges need to screen the questions for compatibility with the rules of evidence. One way to do this is to have jurors submit questions in writing, to be reviewed in chambers with counsel present. The judge could then ask those questions deemed proper.

- *Let jurors take notes.* In most state and federal courts, notetaking is permissible at the discretion of the judge, but it ought to be an absolute prerogative of the juror.[3] Although Judge Ito permitted Simpson jurors to take notes, a 1988 study found that a sizeable majority of federal judges still prohibited jury notetaking.[4] To take a more recent example, a Kentucky judge permitted jurors to take notes during trial but then confiscated them before the jury began deliberations. The judge feared that "allowing notes into deliberations . . . permit[s] the best notetaker to dominate."[5] In an earlier time, when many jurors were illiterate, the ban on notetaking arguably served to equalize participation. But the hesitancy about notes has outlived its usefulness. Judges could deal with the fear of domination by instructing jurors not to defer to anyone else's notes when they conflict with their own memory of the testimony.[6] The claim that jurors will cease to pay attention to the testimony if they are busy taking notes is bogus—imagine preventing students from taking notes during a lecture or prohibiting attorneys or judges from consulting notes during trial.

- *Allow jurors to discuss the evidence during trial.* Perhaps the most controversial proposal for activating jurors is to permit them to talk to one another about the evidence during the trial.[7] Currently jurors are instructed not to talk to one another or anyone else about the evidence until the conclusion of each side's case. However, as the allegations of some dismissed Simpson jurors evidence, jurors disobey this rule during long trials. It flies in the face of human nature to swear persons to prolonged, total silence about the events consuming their lives.[8] Certainly, we should instruct jurors not to talk to anyone off the jury about the case; we should also instruct them to refrain from deliberating a verdict until all the evidence is in. But some amount of conversation about diverse reactions to a witness might do more to open than to close jurors' minds.

- *Jury Nullification.* In chapter 2, I review the long history of the jury's power to refuse to enforce criminal law against a defendant. That history records stirring victories for freedom, like antislavery jurors nullifying provisions of the Fugitive Slave Law that made it a crime to help slaves escape. It also includes nauseating triumphs of prejudice, as racist jurors acquitted the murderers of Emmett Till. Today, jury nullification remains as controversial a doctrine as ever: It figured prominently, if illicitly, in a Michigan jury's decision to acquit Dr. Jack Kevorkian of breaking that state's law against assisted suicide. In another recent case, a San Diego jury refused to enforce the marijuana laws against an AIDS sufferer who used the plant to combat nausea. And in 1995 a San Francisco jury convicted a defendant of assault and attempted carjacking, but when it was then asked to enforce the state's "three strikes" law by certifying that the defendant had two prior felony convictions, it was horrified to learn that certification would send the defendant away for twenty-five years to life. They refused to deliberate further and the judge declared a mistrial.

More troubling are cases in which jurors have been lobbied to excuse those who murder federal agents enforcing unpopular laws. In the 1994 trial of eleven Branch Davidians, charged with murdering Bureau of Alcohol, Tobacco and Firearms agents in Waco, Texas, advocates of jury nullification mailed leaflets to the (supposedly anonymous) jurors, urging them to nullify federal gun laws by acquitting the defendants. The jury convicted seven Davidians of manslaughter, but it did acquit all defendants of the more serious murder charges.

The ugly side of jury nullification is face up if it prompts jurors to treat murder as a permissible way to oppose law enforcement. In the present political climate, the venerable doctrine of nullification has become dangerous. However, I continue to believe that in the long run, we need to engage ordinary persons and not just experts, judges, and politicians in substantive deliberations about justice. The jury is an obvious forum in which to reengage lay persons in deliberations about justice, but only if jurors understand that their oath requires more of them than a mechanical application of the law. Ultimately, democratic justice asks the people to judge whether, in a concrete case involving a particular set of persons and facts, the law should be enforced. I emphasize that jury nullification empowers juries only to *acquit* defendants by refusing to enforce the law; it has nothing to do with the kind of lawlessness that would permit juries to convict against the law. Even when restricted to acts of mercy, jury nullification is risky business and I do not wish to minimize the gamble. But we should not complain about the people's lack of virtue as long as we isolate them from the responsibilties and activities that teach the sense of justice.

In addition to activating jurors, we need to educate them better about the law. The current system for instructing jurors is a charade and everyone knows it. We can make the law more comprehensible to jurors by enacting the following reforms:

- *Preinstruct juries.* It is standard practice to keep jurors in the dark about the law until the close of testimony. Some justify this tradition by arguing that jurors listen to the evidence more intently when they are not distracted by knowledge of its legal significance. I think this is flat-out wrong. It is telling that no one makes a similar argument about "distracted" judges when judges function as factfinders in bench trials. If anything, preinstruction might help jurors by providing them with a road map through the testimony.[9]

  A second objection to preinstruction is more substantial—judges may not know what instructions are proper until after the evidence is presented and frames the precise legal issues. True enough: judges may not be able to preinstruct on all substantive issues. But they should prod both sides during the pretrial conference to agree on areas for preinstruction.

- *Provide comprehensible, written instructions.* Scholars agree that current instructions come not only too late; they come in language that is often incomprehensible to lay persons.[10] To add insult to injury, jurors are not always provided with written copies of the instructions.

  Unfortunately, judges risk reversal on appeal if they experiment with modernizing instructions away from the stilted language approved in prior cases. Moreover, in states with officially approved written instructions ("pattern instructions"), the oddest scenario takes place whenever jurors ask for an explanation of what the pattern instruction means: the judge's hands are bound and the best he or she can do is to reread or resubmit the same officially approved instruction that the jurors say they do not understand.[11]

  Worse, a jury may find that even its simple request for a rereading of one instruction is denied. Appellate courts warn about the prejudicial effects of highlighting a particular instruction by rereading it out of context. Therefore, judges either deny the requested rereading or else swamp the jury a second time by redelivering whole sections of instructions.

  It is absolutely vital that trial courts be given the resources necessary to provide jurors with written copies of their instructions. Moreover, despite the risks involved, I would grant judges considerably more leeway than appellate courts now do to offer jurors alternative explanations of a legal concept they are having trouble grasping.[12]

•   •   •

An active and educated jury still needs to be a representative and impartial one. We have a long way to go before juries are true cross sections of the community. To attain that goal, I make the controversial suggestion in this book that we ought to abolish or scale back the peremptory challenge. The importance of this issue prompts me to add to what I say about jury selection in chapter 3.

Over the past decade, starting with the landmark *Batson v. Kentucky* decision, the U.S. Supreme Court has tried to preserve the peremptory challenge but prohibit its more discriminatory uses. Specifically, the Court has prohibited litigants from using a potential juror's race or sex as the sole grounds for exercising a challenge against him or her.[13] In the same spirit, lower courts have ruled that the Constitution does not tolerate peremptory challenges based on a person's religion, ethnicity, or national origin.[14] This extension of the Court's original rulings is crucial. At a minimum, peremptories should be disallowed whenever they target members of groups considered "suspect classes" entitled to heightened judicial protection under the Fourteenth Amendment's Equal Protection Clause.

But what about peremptory challenges against all people in the jury box under twenty-one, or all blue-collar workers? What if the prosecutor in a criminal case strikes a social worker on the belief that most members of that profession prefer treating people over punishing them?[15] What if the defense in a drug case peremptorily excuses a Drug Enforcement Administration (DEA) agent who happens to be in the jury box that day? Challenges such as these survive because age and occupation are not considered "suspect characteristics" triggering invidious discrimination on a par with race or sex discrimination.[16] Or, as the law professor Charles Ogletree points out, there is a more rational basis for generalizing about the bias of taxicab drivers in a suit involving a taxicab defendant than there is for generalizing about the bias of black jurors in a case involving a black defendant. Moreover, Ogletree adds, removing taxicab drivers from a jury panel does not undermine the impartiality of the remaining jury pool in quite the same way that striking all members of one race does.[17] For all these reasons, the Supreme Court has approved a modified peremptory challenge system: so long as lawyers can provide, if asked, an explanation for their peremptories that does not rest on race, gender, national origin, or religion, they are free to discriminate during jury selection on other grounds.

In certain situations, practitioners have a point when they defend peremptory challenges as a valuable tool for screening out suspected but unprovable bias.[18] In an ideal world, voir dire would be thorough and judges would rule correctly on each challenge for cause. But precisely because mistakes occur, peremptories serve as an important back-up. Suppose an accountant is called to serve as a juror in the trial of another accountant accused of fraud. There may be no way to prove to the judge that the accountant will be prejudiced in favor of the defense, but the plaintiff has good reasons to fear bias and to use a peremptory to remove that person. In this way, we safeguard against a jury selection process in which all power resides in judges making close judgment calls.

Practitioners also have a point when they defend peremptories as indispensable to serious voir dire examination of jurors. After all, harsh questions may antagonize a prospective juror. Unless litigants know they can exercise a peremptory against someone offended during voir dire, they may find it safer not to probe at all.[19]

I acknowledge all these legitimate uses of peremptory challenges. Yet I remain convinced that illegitimate uses so far outweigh proper ones that the time has come to eliminate peremptories or to curtail drastically their number. There are two separate reasons why peremptory challenges do more to inject bias into jury selection than to remove it.

First, *Batson* and its progeny have proven powerless to end racial, ethnic, religious, or sex discrimination during jury selection.[20] Instead, case law testifies to what the law professor Albert Alschuler aptly calls the remarkable "hydraulics" of discrimination.[21] *Batson* succeeded only in driving discrimination underground and into other channels. Once judges began asking lawyers to explain apparently race-specific or sex-specific uses of peremptory challenges, lawyers became skilled at explaining why their strikes had nothing to do with the race or sex of the persons challenged. In one case, prosecutors defended their repeated peremptories against black members of the jury pool by noting that all those struck lived in the same inner-city neighborhood as the defendant. In another trial, membership in the NAACP was cited as the reason for striking one of the few black men in the venire. In a third case, facial hair, not skin color, was offered as the reason for a pattern of peremptories that happened to eliminate more blacks than whites from the jury.[22]

Under current law, trial judges must accept such explanations, unless they find them to be implausible pretexts fabricated to mask discrimination. However, judges are understandably reluctant to charge lawyers with bad faith, and thus the modified peremptory system provides ample cover for conscious or unconscious forms of discrimination. In one reported case, a lawyer required several hours of rereading the voir dire transcripts before he "remembered" the neutral reasons motivating his disproportionate use of peremptories against minority venire members.

Some courts manage to put bite into *Batson* by insisting that any supposedly neutral reason for striking members of one race or one sex be used to strike members of other races or the opposite sex.[23] Hence prosecutors are on shaky ground if they strike blacks for belonging to the NAACP, but do not even ask whites whether they belong to civil rights groups. But there are limits to this way of enforcing neutrality. Challenged to explain why he struck unemployed black women but not unemployed white women, a Florida prosecutor satisfactorily explained that he was suspicious only of divorced, unemployed mothers without visible means of support.[24] Likewise, a lawyer need not strike all city residents but can state a narrower concern for the biases of residents of public housing projects troubled by gangs.[25]

In short, *Batson* has saddled trial judges with an "enforcement nightmare."[26] Conscientious trial judges in Massachusetts, for example, point out that it is difficult to charge a litigant with a racial pattern in the exercise of peremptories when there is only one minority member in the pool and the prosecutor or defense lawyer removes that single person. Moreover, judges report confusion as to what they are to do with the first minority or woman juror struck. Should they excuse that person immediately and send him or her back down to the jury waiting room, so the person can be called if needed for another trial? Or should they have the challenged person step down from the jury box but remain in the courtroom, in case it later becomes apparent that peremptories are being used in a discriminatory way? And what then? Should those jurors impermissibly struck because of their race or sex be reseated, as a way of punishing the side that abused their strikes? Or does an entirely new venire need to be brought into court—in which case a shrewd lawyer might think it worthwhile at least to try circumventing *Batson*, because the worst punishment is that jury selection starts over? All of these intricate procedural matters remain unresolved by *Batson*.[27]

But even if *Batson*'s antidiscrimination principle could be enforced, a second problem would remain. Outside the "suspect class" area, *Batson* leaves litigants as free as ever to skew the representativeness of juries. Peremptories may be used openly to eliminate an entire age, income, occupational, or geographical group from the jury. Worse, we still permit litigants to remove otherwise capable citizens from the jury on a mere hunch about demeanor, height, weight, dress, or body language. Why should we tolerate a jury selection system so at odds with the ideal of a randomly drawn and representative jury? I understand why the adversaries, whose prime interest is winning, want to defend their ability to fashion "designer juries" tailored to suit their clients' cases. But what public interest, with regard to the integrity and impartiality of juries, is served by post-*Batson* peremptories? Professor Alschuler marvelously captures the irony of the present system by imagining a conversation in which the prosecutor defends his peremptory strike against a black woman by explaining that he eliminated her because "she is handicapped and therefore might sympathize with someone's misfortune." The judge responds, "You did not strike her because she is black. That is good enough."[28]

But is it good enough? The costs of the modified peremptory system are considerable: capable citizens are summoned to court and then removed from juries on thin theories or thick stereotypes; public confidence in the jury erodes under constant pressure from the strategic gamesmanship; big money is spent on jury consultants who promise to win the battle of peremptories; the cross-sectional credentials of the jury are compromised; and already long trials become longer as judges conduct hearings to determine whether the peremptories fall on the permissible or impermissible side of the "neutrality" line.

Considerable though they are, these costs would be worth bearing if there were convincing evidence that peremptories did more to remove bias from the jury than to bring it in. I agree that we want impartial juries, even if this means a departure from the goal of representative juries. But one impressive empirical study of the pre-*Batson* era gave the peremptory challenge only a mixed review. Overall, it found the "collective performance of the attorneys . . . not impressive." Prosecutors were as likely to strike persons who ended up voting to convict as to acquit. Defense counsel did "slightly better." The researchers were mostly struck by the erratic benefits of peremptory challenges. Although on average the defense gained an advantage through peremptory challenges, that average was misleading because there was such disparity from case to case in the performance of counsel. These "adversarial inequities" did not paint a pretty picture of the larger public purposes served by peremptory challenges. The potential to imbalance the jury was great when one side was legally entitled to a greater number of peremptory challenges or simply had more luck or skill in using an equal number of them.[29]

Given the obvious costs but spotty benefits of peremptory challenges, I believe we can select juries in more democratic and efficient ways. By abolishing peremptory challenges, we end those strategies of jury selection that permit a lawyer's mere hunch (say, that thin people who frown are likely to favor conviction) to defeat a juror's right to serve. I do not hesitate to conclude that the equal protection rights of jurors, as well as the Constitutional mandate of representative juries, count for more than the litigants' partisan interest in excluding thin people who do not smile.

What about peremptories that rest on rational grounds for suspecting bias, but grounds that fall short of convincing a judge to strike the person for cause? We can compensate for the loss of these peremptories by expanding the current grounds for granting challenges for cause.[30] To refer back to earlier examples, judges should be willing to grant challenges for cause against a person obviously angered by one side during voir dire, or a person who clearly is not paying attention. The test should be less whether the judge personally finds the juror biased and more whether a litigant has reasonable, articulable grounds for suspecting bias.[31]

In an expanded for-cause system, lawyers would also have an opportunity to challenge would-be jurors on the basis of group bias. Examples of challenges reasonable enough to meet a lowered for cause standard might include defense objections to the DEA agent in a drug prosecution, or plaintiff's objections to the accountant in a suit against another accountant. In these situations, a litigant can articulate reasonable, case-specific grounds for suspecting that a person's occupation would unduly influence him or her. Suspecting persons for bias on these narrow grounds is far different than vague suspicions premised on global intuitions about, say, the antiestablishment attitudes of young people regardless of the case. Also too vague to support a challenge for cause is the prosecutor's stereotypical objection to social workers, that such an occupation makes them predisposed to oppose punishment.[32] In general, a judge should treat a social worker's promise of impartiality as conclusive, though there could be examples in which the social worker seems so hesitant in endorsing the legitimacy of punishment that a judge should grant the challenge for cause.

What I am proposing is that we modify the way challenges for cause are decided so as to permit lawyers to accomplish at that stage of jury selection most of what is good in peremptory challenges. I would entirely eliminate those challenges premised on arbitrary preferences that resist being put into words. Where else but in jury selection do we permit a public procedure to treat people differently according to their weight, whether they smile, how they dress, or the cut of their beard? Under current law, such reasons for striking jurors pass muster because they are neutral with respect to race, sex, religion, or national origin. But we should require more than neutral reasons before excusing a juror—we should require, in Alschuler's words, "good" and "sound" reasons suffi- cient to convince a reasonable person that the prospective juror harbors bias. After all, we can not expect people to take jury service seriously if we excuse them so arbitrarily. Just imagine telling the truth to a juror who is peremptorily removed after having rearranged work and family sched- ules and driven twenty miles to appear in court. "We thank you for com- ing. But you see, the defense has a theory about thin people who do not smile. Our system permits discrimination against you for this reason. Do not be offended; we sometimes discriminate against fat people who smile too much."

If peremptories are eliminated, ripples will be felt in other areas of the jury system. One issue likely to arise is whether to expand the scope of voir dire and to permit lawyers, rather than judges, to question the jury panel. Practitioners rightly argue that voir dire needs to be more exten- sive in peremptory-less trials, because they no longer will have the auto- matic right to remove a prospective juror whose bias was not sufficiently explored at the for-cause stage. At a minimum, this means encouraging judges to abandon the empty and insulting ritual often rehearsed during voir dire ("Are you or have you ever been a racist?") in favor of more probing and open-ended questioning.

A closer call is whether attorney-conducted voir dire is preferable to judge-controlled questioning. In a sizeable majority of federal courts, judges do the voir dire; by contrast, a majority of the states permit lawyers either to conduct the voir dire or to share questioning with the judge.[33] Studies confirm that voir dire is far more time-consuming when lawyers do the questioning.[34]

Much of the length of attorney-conducted voir dire has nothing to do with ferreting out bias. Every experienced trial attorney seizes the oppor- tunity presented by voir dire to indoctrinate the jury with certain precon- ceptions. One standard defense ploy in criminal cases is to ask prospec- tive jurors whether they can be fair and favor neither side at the start of the case. When the unsuspecting juror-to-be answers affirmatively, the lawyer then delivers a stirring lecture on the presumption of innocence and the requirement that a juror begin by favoring the defense.[35]

On the other hand, attorney-conducted voir dire must be given its due: lawyers probe for bias more thoroughly than judges typically do.[36] Lawyers have more incentive to challenge jurors, and they can be more casual in their approach than a judge's institutional role allows. Lawyers often get panel members to open up, for instance, by confessing some of their own shortcomings. It would be difficult for a judge to adopt a similar confessional style.

Attorney-conducted voir dire would be preferable were it not for the tortuous detours that consume time for no valid public purpose. One compromise position is to allow lawyers to conduct the voir dire but under tight judicial control, including perhaps outer time limits. New York is currently experimenting with such an approach in civil cases.[37] But it would also be worthwhile to experiment with making judicial questioning more open-ended and informal.

Abolishing peremptories would also have ripple effects on unanimous verdicts. Using social-choice theory, the political science professor Edward P. Schwartz and the law professor Warren F. Schwartz argue that more hung juries will occur in peremptory-less trials, because the range and extremes of opinions held by jurors will be greater.[38] If this prediction turns out to be correct, then the cost of eliminating peremptories may be too high to pay. But first we need to see in practice whether an expanded for-cause system can substitute for the peremptory system as a way of eliminating extremes of partisanship from the jury box.

To say we can make jury trials better is not to condemn what we have achieved. The only question that matters in the end is whether justice is purer, not just faster, in nations that dispense with our sort of jury. It is common today to hear praise for the efficiency of judge-dominated European trials. Praise is also bestowed on England for virtually abolishing the civil jury and for expediting criminal trials by stripping jury selection down to its bare bones (the first twelve persons called almost always become the jury) and by eliminating unanimous verdicts. But these reforms have stacked the deck in favor of the government and, in trials of accused Irish terrorists in the 1970s and 1980s, they led to an appalling number of erroneous convictions.

Before we import the English jury, we should remember that the jury is not meant to be an efficient means of trying cases. In criminal matters, the jury is designed for safety against oppressive government. In civil as well as criminal trials, the jury houses an ideal of popular or democratic justice. Sometimes, tension arises between safe justice and democratic justice. To live with the jury is to live with that tension, but to abandon the jury is to place all power in government, against history's warning.

Appendix

Following are some commonly cited statistics regarding jury trials in the United States.

NUMBER OF JURY TRIALS

It is surprising that no firm count of the total number of annual state jury trials is available. Approximately one-third of states do not provide information in their published annual reports about the number of cases that go to trial. Moreover, definitions of what counts as a jury trial vary from state to state, with some states starting their count once a jury is impaneled, others starting at introduction of evidence, and still others beginning their count only at verdict or decision.[1] Taking these difficulties into consideration, researchers for the National Center for State Courts estimate that the total number of state jury trials annually is in the vicinity of 150,000.[2]

Actual numbers are available for federal courts. In 1990 there were 9,826 jury trials in U.S. district courts, out of a total of 20,433 trials. Of the jury trials, 5,061 were criminal and 4,765 were civil.[3]

PERCENTAGE OF CASES THAT HAVE JURY TRIAL

Although large in absolute numbers, jury trials constitute only a small percentage of case dispositions annually. Relying on census data from the

1940s, Kalven and Zeisel estimated that 15 percent of all felony prosecutions reach a jury trial. A more recent estimate is that less than 5 percent of state felony criminal cases are disposed of through jury trial.[4] In 1990, in federal courts, the 5,061 criminal jury trials accounted for about 11.5 percent of the 44,295 criminal cases terminated that year.[5] On the civil side, jury trials account for roughly 1 percent of the more than nine million civil claims disposed of in state courts of general jurisdiction each year.[6] In federal courts in 1990, the 4,765 civil jury trials accounted for 2 percent of the 213,922 civil cases terminated over the preceding twelve months.[7]

NUMBERS OF JURORS ANNUALLY

Jury duty falls upon millions of Americans each year, making the jury system the most widespread example of participatory democracy in the United States today, despite all the loopholes that permit persons to escape service. As an example of state court jury utilization, Massachusetts summoned 905,795 potential jurors in 1988. Massachusetts courts use a "one day, one trial rule," where jurors who are not selected for trial during the first day of service are excused; those selected for a jury serve for one trial only. Of the number who received summonses, 314,343 were scheduled to appear for the first day of service; of these, 253,436 actually appeared. From this number, 47 percent (118,277) were actually sent to a courtroom, and 38,797 were impaneled.[8]

In federal district courts, over 400,000 persons were present for voir dire in jury trials during 1990. From this number, the total selected for actual jury service was 115,877.[9] The sum of individual days served by all federal trial jurors was 825,020.[10]

FEES

Fees for petit jury service vary considerably from states in which nothing is paid for the first three to five days and up to $50 thereafter (for example, Colorado, Connecticut, and Massachusetts), to states where the fee depends on whether one is selected for a jury (for example, Arkansas, Indiana, Michigan, Nevada, and South Dakota), to states that pay a high of $30 from day one (for example, Hawaii, New Hampshire, and Wyoming). Federal courts pay a daily fee of $40.[11]

CRIMINAL CONVICTION RATE (INCLUDING GUILTY PLEAS)

Of all criminal defendants whose cases were terminated in federal courts in 1990, 83 percent were convicted. In absolute numbers, cases involving 56,519 defendants were disposed of in 1990 in U.S. district courts; 46,725 were convicted; 9,794 had their cases dismissed or were found not guilty at trial.[12]

Guilty pleas or pleas of nolo contendere accounted for nearly 72 percent of all dispositions in federal courts.[13] Of all convictions, 86.5 percent were through guilty pleas or pleas of nolo contendere.

The National Center for State Courts estimates that in 1988, 66 percent of all criminal filings in state courts were disposed of by a guilty plea. But states differ widely, with California reporting that guilty pleas were entered in 87.2 percent of all criminal cases and Pennsylvania reporting guilty pleas in only 46.7 percent of all criminal cases.[14] In Massachusetts Superior Court, guilty pleas accounted for 64.1 of all dispositions in 1988.[15]

CONVICTION RATE OF CASES THAT GO TO TRIAL

Combining data for both bench and jury trials from nine states in 1988, the National Center for State Courts found that about two-thirds of all defendants who went to trial in those states' general jurisdiction courts in 1988 were convicted.[16] A study of felony cases tried in 1979 in thirteen local jurisdictions found that the conviction rate in eleven of the jurisdictions fell between 64 and 77 percent.[17]

The conviction rate in federal courts is higher, with 80 percent of defendants going to trial in 1990 being found guilty.[18]

JURY CONVICTION RATE VERSUS BENCH CONVICTION RATE

In federal courts in 1990, the jury conviction rate surpassed the conviction rate in bench trials. Juries convicted 84 percent (5,210/6,181) of the defendants who came before them. By contrast, the conviction rate in trials before judges was 62.7 percent (1,063/1,693).[19]

Recent, aggregate data for jury versus bench conviction rates in state courts is, not available. But after examining data through the 1970s for felony cases in six states, a large county in a seventh state, and the District of Columbia, the jury scholar James Levine found that juries in these jurisdictions convicted 74 percent of the time, while judges in bench trials convicted in 64 percent of cases. Another study of over 22,000 felony trials in 1978 found that juries convicted 72 percent of the time, and that judges deciding cases without juries convicted 58 percent of the time.[20] These numbers about jury severity throw into question one of the core conclusions Kalven and Zeisel came to in their classic 1950s study of the American jury. By comparing jury verdicts in 3,576 cases with the presiding judge's report of what verdict the judge would have rendered in a bench trial, Kalven and Zeisel found that judges disagreed with juries in approximately 22 percent of cases. But the disagreement was massively one-way—judges reported that they would have convicted in 19 percent of the cases where juries acquitted but would have acquitted in only 3 percent of the cases where juries convicted. On balance, therefore, Kalven and Zeisel found a net jury leniency factor of 16 percent.[21]

The more recent data comparing jury and bench conviction rates suggest that the common view of juries as more lenient than judges on defendants may no longer be true. However, it is difficult to know whether judges and juries are hearing the same kind of cases. It is possible that defendants with particularly strong legal defenses choose bench trials in disproportionate numbers.

Notes

INTRODUCTION

1. The case of Medgar Evers illustrates the way jurors can be either villains or heroes. On February 5, 1994, a generation after two all-white juries had deadlocked on charges that Byron De La Beckwith had murdered the Mississippi civil rights leader in 1963, a racially mixed jury finally convicted De La Beckwith of Evers's murder. See Ronald Smothers, "White Supremacist is Convicted of Slaying Rights Leader in '63," *New York Times*, Feb. 6, 1994, sec. 1, p. 1.

2. John Baldwin and Michael McConville, *Jury Trials* (Oxford: Clarendon Press, 1979), p. 94.

3. Leon F. Litwack, *North of Slavery: The Negro in the Free States 1790–1860* (Chicago: University of Chicago Press, 1961), p. 94.

4. *Taylor v. Louisiana*, 419 U.S. 522, 533 n. 13 (1975). However, women did serve on juries in the territory of Wyoming in 1870. See Carol Weisbrod, "Images of the Woman Juror," *Harvard Women's Law Journal* 9 (1986): 60, n. 2.

5. "The Jury Selection and Service Act," 28 U.S.C., secs. 1861–69.

6. *Taylor v. Louisiana*, 419 U.S. 522.

7. See, for example, George Priest, "Justifying the Civil Jury," in *Verdict: Assessing the Civil Jury System*, ed. Robert E. Litan (Washington, D.C.: Brookings Institution, 1993), pp. 124–27; and Peter H. Schuck, "Mapping the Debate on Jury Reform," in Litan, *Verdict*, p. 312.

8. Richard B. Schmitt, "Juries' Role in Patent Cases Reconsidered," *Wall Street Journal*, Feb. 18, 1994, p. B6.

9.   "Ford Attorney Decries $7 Million Jury Award," *Automotive News*, May 10, 1993, p. 28; "Ford Wins St. Louis Bronco II Case, Settles Another," *Automotive News*, March 29, 1993, p. 19. See also Amy Stevens, "Bronco II Verdict Affirmed," *Wall Street Journal*, June 21, 1993, p. B6, in which a New York federal jury awarded $1.2 million to injured plaintiff.

10. Diane Marder and Raoul Mowatt, "Bad Odds for the Innocent—Especially Blacks," *Philadelphia Inquirer*, Oct. 6, 1991, p. 1 (90 percent of eyewitness identification cases result in conviction); David Stipp, "The Insanity Defense for Violent Crime Cases Gets High-Tech Help," *Wall Street Journal*, March 4, 1992, p. 1 (insanity defense raised in only 1 percent of felony cases and succeeds in only a fourth of them); Heather S. Richardson, "Bobbitt: A Verdict that Kills Justice," *Wall Street Journal*, Jan. 24, 1994, p. A12; Diane Marder, "Defendants Test Limits in Making Excuses," *Philadelphia Inquirer*, Feb. 13, 1994, pp. 1, 3.

11. Darrow's remarks are quoted in E. H. Sutherland and D. R. Cressey, *Principles of Criminology*, 7th ed. (Philadelphia: Lippincott, 1966), p. 442.

12. Cookie Stephan, "Selective Characteristics of Jurors and Litigants: Their Influences on Juries' Verdicts," in *The Jury System in America*, ed. Rita Simon (Beverly Hills, Calif.: Sage Publications, 1975), p. 113.

13. Robert A. Wenke, *The Art of Selecting a Jury*, 2d ed. (Springfield, Ill.: Charles C. Thomas, 1988), p. 88.

14. Stuart Taylor, Jr., "Hinckley Cleared But Is Held Insane in Reagan Attack," *New York Times*, June 22, 1982, p. A1.

15. Marc Galanter, "The Regulatory Function of the Jury," in Litan, *Verdict*, p. 63.

16. National Center for State Courts, Court Statistics and Information Management Project, *State Court Caseload Statistics* (Williamsburg, Va.: National Center for State Courts, 1988), p. 57; and James Levine, *Juries and Politics* (Pacific Grove, Calif.: Brooks/Cole, 1992), p. 34.

17. See the appendix for a statistical profile of jury utilization in the United States.

18. *Batson v. Kentucky*, 476 U.S. 79 (1986). See chap. 3 for a full discussion of recent reforms of the peremptory challenge.

19. *J.E.B. v. Alabama ex rel. T.B.*, 114 S. Ct. 1419, 62 U.S.L.W. 4219 (1994).

CHAPTER 1: JURIES AND LOCAL JUSTICE

1.   *Irvin v. Dowd*, 366 U.S. 717, 722 (1961) ("The theory of our system is that the conclusions to be reached in a case will be induced only by evidence and argument in open court, and not by any outside influence, whether of private talk or public print"). See also *Patterson v. Colorado*, 205 U.S. 454, 462 (1907).

2.   *Mylock v. Saladine*, 1 Wm. Blackstone Rep. 480, 481 (1781).

3.   *United States v. Parker*, 19 F. Supp. 450, 458 (D.N.J. 1937), *aff'd. United*

States v. Parker, 103 F. 2d 857 (3d Cir. 1939), *cert. den.* 307 U.S. 642 (1939).

4. Jonathan Elliot, *The Debates in the Several State Conventions on the Adoption of the Federal Constitution* (New York: Burt Franklin, 1888), 3: 579.

5. *Flannelly v. Delaware & Hudson Co.*, 225 U.S. 597 (1912). For other examples where jurors used knowledge of local conditions to resolve factual questions, see Dale W. Broeder, "The Impact of the Vicinage Requirement: An Empirical Look," *Nebraska Law Review* 45 (1966): 99–118.

6. *Crawford v. Georgia*, 489 U.S. 1040 (1989), *reh. den.* 490 U.S. 1042 (Marshall, J., dissenting from denial of *cert.*).

7. Ibid., p. 1041. See also *Swindler v. Lockhart*, 495 U.S. 911 (1990) (Marshall, J., dissenting from denial of *cert.*), in which the defendant was granted a change of venue on retrial but only to a neighboring county where jury members knew that he had been previously convicted of murder and sentenced to death.

8. *Powell v. Superior Court*, 232 Cal. App. 3d 785, 789, 283 Cal. Rptr. 777, 779 (Cal. Ct. App. 1991). See also Barry Scheck, "Following Orders," *New Republic*, May 25, 1992, p. 17.

9. According to the 1990 U.S. census, 11.2 percent of the Los Angeles County population was black, compared with 2.3 percent of the population in Ventura County. Bureau of the Census, U.S. Dept. of Commerce, *1990 Census of Population and Housing: Summary Population and Housing Characteristics, California* (Washington, D.C.: U.S. Government Printing Office, 1991), p. 60.

10. Seth Mydans, "The Police Verdict: Los Angeles Policemen Acquitted in Taped Beating," *New York Times*, April 30, 1992, p. A1; Linda Deutsch, "Police Officer Acquitted in King Beating," *Philadelphia Inquirer*, April 30, 1992, p. A1; and Andrew Kull, "Racial Justice," *New Republic*, Nov. 30, 1992, p. 17.

11. See, for example, David Margolick, "As Venues Are Changed, Many Ask How Important a Role Race Should Play," *New York Times*, May 23, 1992, p. 7 (Margolick quoted a defense lawyer for one officer as saying, "I wouldn't say the case was won at that point, but if [the change of venue] hadn't been granted, the case would have been lost, no question"); "Out of the Frying Pan or into the Fire? Race and Choice of Venue After Rodney King," *Harvard Law Review* 106 (1993): 705–22; and S. Herman, "Justice Sees Through a Glass, Darkly," *Newsday*, May 4, 1992, p. 37.

12. See Newton N. Minow and Fred H. Cate, "Who is an Impartial Juror in an Age of Mass Media?" *American University Law Review* 40 (1991): 631–64; and Joseph M. Hassett, "A Jury's Pre-Trial Knowledge in Historical Perspective: The Distinction Between Pre-Trial Information and 'Prejudicial' Publicity," *Law and Contemporary Problems* 43 (1980): 155–68.

13. George Fletcher, *A Crime of Self Defense: Bernhard Goetz and the Law on Trial* (Chicago: University of Chicago Press, 1988), pp. 6, 85–90.

14. *United States v. North*, 713 F. Supp. 1444, 1445 (D.D.C. 1989), vacated 910 F. 2d 843 (1990), *mod.* and *reh'g. den.*, 920 F. 2d 940 (1990), *cert. den.*, 114 L. Ed. 2d 477 (1991). For a detailed account of the North jury selection, see text accompanying notes 135–43 for this chapter.

15. Michael Wines, "Selection of Jury Begins for North," *New York Times*, Feb. 1, 1989, p. A12.

16. Stephen Salisbury, "Graphic Questions: Potential Mapplethorpe Jurors Are Asked About Their Beliefs," *Philadelphia Inquirer*, Sept. 26, 1990, p. C1.

17. U.S. Constitution, art. 3, sec. 2, clause 3.

18. When the Norman Kings first invaded England, they were in need of some administrative device for discovering the traditional properties and privileges of the monarchy. They found what they were looking for in the Frankish Empire's practice of holding an inquest or inquisition on the local level and interrogating neighborhood notables for the desired information. From this sworn royal inquest, modern jury trial rose in the twelfth century. To enforce its authority and to bring matters within the jurisdiction of itinerant royal courts, the Crown relied on men of the neighborhood (originally the small local area of the vil or the hundred) to function first as a kind of grand jury making presentments about crimes in the neighborhood and those suspected of the crime. Here the jurors functioned more like neighbor-witnesses than impartial judges, "presumed to know before they come into court the facts about which they are to testify." Frederic W. Maitland and Francis C. Montague, *A Sketch of English Legal History* (New York and London: G. P. Putnam's Sons, Knickerbocker Press, 1915), pp. 45–60; Roger D. Groot, "The Jury of Presentment Before 1215," *American Journal of Legal History* 26 (1982): 1–24.

    Prior to 1215, those "presented" on suspicion of crime still customarily faced trial by ordeal. But in that year the Fourth Lateran Council forbade clergy from participating in the ordeal, thereby withdrawing its divine credentials. In the vacuum created by the loss of trial by ordeal, the presenting jury evolved into the trial jury. Theodore F. T. Plucknett, *A Concise History of the Common Law*, 4th ed.(London: Butterworth, 1948), pp. 104–21; John Marshall Mitnick, "From Neighbor-Witness to Judge of Proofs: The Transformation of the English Civil Juror," *American Journal of Legal History* 32 (1988): 201–35.

19. Sir William Blackstone, *Commentaries on the Laws of England* (Oxford: Clarendon Press, 1769), 4:344. The terms "venue" and "vicinage" should be but are not always distinguished. Venue refers to the place of trial, vicinage to the place where the jury comes from. Usually, the place of jurors and the place of trial will be the same, but it is possible to hold trial in one venue while summoning jurors from another vicinage. This was true of colonial Virginia practice, where serious cases were tried at the capital but jurors were summoned from the vicinage or county where the crime occurred. See Drew Kershen, "Vicinage," *Oklahoma Law Review* 29

(1976): 801, 831; William Wirt Blume, "The Place of Trial of Criminal Cases: Constitutional Vicinage and Venue," *Michigan Law Review* 43 (1944): 59–60.

20. Elliot, *Debates in Several State Conventions*, 2: 112 (Gore quoting Holmes).

21. Ibid., 3: 569.

22. Ibid., pp. 541–42.

23. Ibid., p. 569.

24. Ibid., pp. 545, 542, 541.

25. Ibid., p. 578 ("Your juries may be collected five hundred miles from where the party resides"); see also Herbert J. Storing, *The Complete Anti-Federalist* (Chicago: University of Chicago Press, 1981), 2:231, 3:61.

26. John M. Murrin and A. G. Roeber, "Trial by Jury: The Virginia Paradox," in *The Bill of Rights: A Lively Heritage*, ed. John Kukla (Richmond, Va.: Virginia State Library and Archives, 1987), pp. 110, 126.

27. Virginia Declaration of Rights, art. 8 (1776). For a detailed analysis of Virginia's commitment to jury trials in the seventeenth and eighteenth centuries, see Murrin and Roeber, "The Virginia Paradox," pp. 109–29 (as late as 1750, juries held a less conspicuous position in Virginia than any other mainland province, mattering mostly in trials for life).

28. The romantic defense of the jury given by the colonies on the eve of Revolution was not true to the history of every colony. In his study of early Connecticut, historian Bruce Mann documented a precipitous decline of the civil jury after 1700. At the beginning of the century, civil juries still decided most contested civil cases; by 1745, juries decided 20 percent or fewer cases, depending on the county. Mann connected the civil jury's decline to a general shift from communal ideals for law (where neighbors still judged one another on the basis of shared values) to a formal model for law (where technical rules aimed at predictable and uniform decisions). Bruce H. Mann, *Neighbors and Strangers: Law and Community in Early Connecticut* (Chapel Hill: University of North Carolina Press, 1987), pp. 75–81; Mann, "The Evolutionary Revolution in American Law: A Comment on J. R. Pole's 'Reflections'," *William and Mary Quarterly* 50 (3d series, 1993), p. 171.

In his study of seventeenth-century New England juries, historian John Murrin also found great contrasts. At one extreme were pro-jury colonies established without strong leadership from magisterial elites (for example, Rhode Island). At the other extreme were anti-jury colonies dominated by powerful magistrates (for example, New Haven Colony, which abolished juries even for capital cases). John M. Murrin, "Magistrates, Sinners and a Precarious Liberty: Trial by Jury in Seventeenth-Century New England," in *Saints and Revolutionaries: Essays in Early American History*, ed. David D. Hall, John M. Murrin, and Thad W. Tate (New York: W. W. Norton, 1984), pp. 152–206.

29. William E. Nelson, *Dispute and Conflict Resolution in Plymouth County*,

Massachusetts, 1725–1825 (Chapel Hill, N.C.: University of North Carolina Press, 1981), pp. 23–25.

30. John Phillip Reid, *In a Defiant Stance: The Conditions of Law in Massachusetts Bay, The Irish Comparison, and the Coming of the American Revolution* (University Park, Pa.: Pennsylvania State University Press, 1977), pp. 28–29.

31. Ibid., p. 29.

32. Ibid., pp. 45, 50–51.

33. Ibid., p. 32.

34. James Alexander, *A Brief Narrative of the Case and Trial of John Peter Zenger*, ed. Stanley Katz (Cambridge, Mass.: Harvard University Press, 1963).

35. *Penn and Mead's Case,* Howell's *State Trials* 6: 951 (1670).

36. See, for example, Elliot, *Debates in Several State Conventions*, 2: 112, 4: 150, 165; and Francis H. Heller, *The Sixth Amendment* (Lawrence, Kans.: University of Kansas Press, 1951) pp. 1, 27.

37. Heller, *Sixth Amendment*, p. 17.

38. Ibid., p. 20.

39. Kershen, "Vicinage," p. 831; Elliot, *Debates in Several State Conventions*, 4:150, 467. That there was no uniformity in the colonies in regard to holding trials in the county where the crime occurred can be seen by comparing provisions in the early constitutions adopted by the original thirteen colonies. Maryland (1776), Massachusetts (1780), and New Hampshire (1784) required "the trial of facts where they arise." Virginia (1776) specified a jury of "his [the accused's] vicinage." Pennsylvania (1776) required trial in the "country," changing "country" to "vicinage" in 1790. Georgia specified trial in the county. But none of the other colonies specified a venue in their early state constitutions. Blume, "Place of Trial of Criminal Cases," pp. 67–78.

40. Elliot, *Debates in Several State Conventions*, 2:112–13.

41. Ibid., 4:150.

42. Ibid., 3:537.

43. Kershen, "Vicinage," pp. 816–18 (Virginia, North Carolina, New York, and Rhode Island).

44. Blume, "Place of Trial of Criminal Cases," p. 68.

45. Elliot, *Debates in Several State Conventions*, 3: 578–79.

46. Storing, *Complete Anti-Federalist*, 4: 78.

47. Elliot, *Debates in Several State Conventions*, 3: 547.

48. Ibid., 2: 516.

49. Storing, *Complete Anti-Federalist*, 2: 249.

50. Ibid.

51. Ibid.

52. Ibid., pp. 142, 250.

53. Gordon S. Wood, *The Radicalism of the American Revolution* (New York: Alfred A. Knopf, 1992), pp. 258–59.

54. Storing, *Complete Anti-Federalist*, 2: 249.

55. Ibid., p. 320.

56. Heller, *Sixth Amendment*, pp. 16–24; Mann, *Neighbors and Strangers*, p. 78 (1715 compilation of long-standing practice that jurors were to own freehold worth forty shillings a year or have personal estate in the county of fifty pounds); Murrin and Roeber, "Virginia Paradox," pp. 120–24 (between 1705 and 1748 statutes required jurors in Williamsburg to possess "visible real and personal estate" of 100 pounds sterling and county jurors to possess estates valued at fifty pounds or more). As the Revolution approached and in its aftermath, several colonies or states lowered property qualifications for voters and jurors, by requiring that a man had only to be a taxpayer. See Willi Paul Adams, *The First American Constitutions: Republican Ideology and the Making of the State Constitutions in the Revolutionary Era*, trans. Rita and Robert Kimber (Chapel Hill, N.C.: University of North Carolina Press, 1980), pp. 196–207 and tables at pp. 293–311; Chilton Williamson, *American Suffrage: From Property to Democracy, 1760–1860* (Princeton: Princeton University Press, 1960), pp. 92–137; Merrill Jensen, *The New Nation: A History of the United States During the Confederation, 1781–1789* (New York: Alfred A. Knopf, 1950), p. 128. But in 1787 only the territory of Vermont had abolished tax-paying or property-owning qualifications for voters entirely. Adams, *First American Constitutions*, p. 196; Gordon S. Wood, *The Creation of the American Republic, 1776–1787* (Chapel Hill, N.C.: University of North Carolina Press, 1969), p. 168.

57. Nelson, *Dispute and Conflict Resolution*, pp. 25–26.

58. Adams, *First American Constitutions*, pp. 207–17.

59. Murrin and Roeber, "Virginia Paradox," p. 120; Albert W. Alschuler, "The Supreme Court and the Jury: Voir Dire, Peremptory Challenges and the Review of Judgments," *University of Chicago Law Review* 56 (1989): 153, 164.

60. See Cecilia M. Kenyon, "Men of Little Faith: The Anti-Federalists on the Nature of Representative Government," *William and Mary Quarterly* 12 (1955): 3, 43.

61. Letter of Jefferson to the Abbe Arnoux in *The Papers of Thomas Jefferson*, ed. Julian P. Boyd (Princeton, N.J.: Princeton University Press, 1958), 15: 283.

62. William E. Nelson, *Americanization of the Common Law: The Impact of Legal Change on Massachusetts Society, 1760–1830* (Cambridge, Mass.: Harvard University Press, 1975), p. 3.

63. Ibid.

64. *Diary and Autobiography of John Adams*, ed. L. H. Butterfield (Cambridge, Mass.: Harvard University Press, 1961), 2: 5.

65. Nelson, *Americanization of Common Law*, p. 3.

66. Ibid., p. 29.

67. Mann, *Neighbors and Strangers*, pp. 75, 71.

68. Ibid., p. 74. Other historians agree with Mann in seeing the loss of a connection between law and local community occurring well before the Revolution. See, for example, Konig, *Law and Community*, pp. 108ff.

69. Amasa M. Eaton, "The Development of the Judicial System in Rhode Island," *Yale Law Journal* 14 (1905): 148, 153. This source came to my attention through Shannon C. Stimson, *The American Revolution in the Law: Anglo-American Jurisprudence before John Marshall* (Princeton, N.J.: Princeton University Press, 1990), p. 49.

70. Mark DeWolfe Howe, "Juries as Judges of Criminal Law," *Harvard Law Review* 52 (1939): 582, 591.

71. Nelson, *Americanization of Common Law*, p. 29; see also Reid, *In a Defiant Stance*, pp. 27–64.

72. J. R. Pole, "Reflections on American Law and the American Revolution," *William and Mary Quarterly* 50 (3d series, 1993), p. 136. Pole also found the jury's role to be more political and representative than judicial. Ibid., p. 128. His conclusions have been criticized for exaggerating the jury's importance in shaping law. See Mann, "The Evolutionary Revolution," pp. 168–75; Peter Charles Hoffer, "Custom as Law: A Comment on J. R. Pole's 'Reflections'," and James A. Henretta and James D. Rice, "Law as Litigation: An Agenda for Research," *William and Mary Quarterly* 50 (3d series, 1993): 160–67; 176–80.

73. Quoted in Stimson, *American Revolution in the Law*, p. 88.

74. Storing, *Complete Anti-Federalist*, 2: 320.

75. Ibid.

76. Ibid., p. 321.

77. Ibid.

78. Ibid., p. 320.

79. *Diary of John Adams*, 2:5; Nelson, *Americanization of Common Law*, p. 26.

80. Ibid.

81. Storing, *Complete Anti-Federalist*, 2: 320.

82. Ibid., p. 250.

83. Ibid., 5: 39 (emphasis in original).

84. Edward Dumbauld, *The Bill of Rights and What it Means Today* (Norman, Okla.: University of Oklahoma Press, 1957), p. 183 (Virginia), p. 200 (North Carolina).

85. Kershen, "Vicinage," p. 817; Dumbauld, *Bill of Rights*, pp. 31–32 (Rhode Island); pp. 175–77 (Massachusetts); pp. 173–75 (Pennsylvania minority); p. 190 (New York).

86. Kershen, "Vicinage," p. 818, quoting *Annals of Congress of the United States*, 1st Cong., 1st sess., vol. 1, p. 435; Heller, *Sixth Amendment*, p. 30.

87. Kershen, "Vicinage," pp. 820–21; Dumbauld, *Bill of Rights*, p. 215.

88. Dumbauld, *Bill of Rights*, pp. 213–16.

89. Kershen, "Vicinage," p. 822; Dumbauld, *Bill of Rights*, p. 214.

90. *The Papers of James Madison*, ed. Charles F. Hobson and Robert A. Rut-

NOTES TO PAGES 34-39 277

land (Charlottesville, Va.: University of Virginia Press, 1979), 12: 419.

91. Kershen, "Vicinage," p. 822.

92. Ibid., p. 825.

93. *Annals of Congress,* vol. 1, p. 913.

94. Blume, "Place of Trial of Criminal Cases," p. 66.

95. Maeva Marcus, ed., *The Documentary History of the Supreme Court of the United States, 1789–1800,* (New York: Columbia University Press, 1992), 4:29.

96. Ibid., pp. 91–92; Charles Warren, "New Light on the History of the Federal Judiciary Act of 1789," *Harvard Law Review* 37 (1923): 49, 105–6.

97. Marcus, *Documentary History of Supreme Court,* 4: 92.

98. Compare *United States v. Hutchings,* 26 Fed. Cas. 440, 442 (case no. 15,429) (C.C.D. Va. 1817) (Marshall, J., instructing criminal jury that they were not bound to accept his opinion of the law) with *United States v. Battiste,* 24 Fed. Cas. 1042 (case no. 14,545) (C.C.D. Mass. 1835) (Story, J., denying that jury has any right to decide contested points of law). See chap. 2 for a fuller discussion of the jury's loss of lawmaking and law-nullifying authority.

99. *Georgia v. Brailsford,* 3 U.S. (3 Dall.) 1, 4 (1794).

100. *Sparf and Hansen v. United States,* 156 U.S. 51 (1895).

101. *United States v. Burr,* 25 Fed. Cas. 55, 87–88 (case no. 14,693) (C.C.D. Va. 1807); Albert J. Beveridge, *The Life of John Marshall* (Boston: Houghton Mifflin Company, 1919), 3: 274–387.

102. *United States v. Burr,* 25 Fed. Cas. 49 (case no. 14,692g) (1807).

103. Paul S. Clarkson and R. Samuel Jett, *Luther Martin of Maryland* (Baltimore, Md.: Johns Hopkins Press, 1970), p. 247, n. 6.

104. 25 Fed. Cas. at 55–56, 59.

105. Ibid. at 56, n. 2.

106. On June 24, 1994, a California state judge took the highly unusual step of dismissing a grand jury that was considering whether to indict O. J. Simpson for the murder of his ex-wife and her friend. The judge acted after both the prosecution and defense expressed a concern that grand jurors had been exposed to prejudicial pretrial publicity—most notably the release of 911 calls made by Nicole Simpson after her former husband broke down the back door to her house. Seth Mydans, "Citing News Deluge, Simpson Case Judge Excuses Grand Jury," *New York Times,* June 25, 1994, p. 1.

For federal courts, Fed. R. Crim. P. 6b(1) provides that a defendant may challenge "the array of jurors on the ground that the grand jury was not selected, drawn or summoned in accordance with law, and may challenge an individual juror on the ground that the juror is not legally qualified." An earlier draft of the rule did allow challenges for bias or prejudice, but this permission was omitted in the final draft. *Estes v. United States,* 335 F. 2d 609, 613, n. 7 (1964), *cert. den.,* 379 U.S. 964. See also Lester B. Orfield, *Orfield's Criminal Procedure under the Ferdeal Rules,* vol. 1 (Rochester,

N.Y. and San Francisco, Calif.: Lawyers Cooperative and Bancroft-Whitney, 1985), pp. 263–334 ("District Courts have asserted broadly that grand jurors may not be challenged for bias"); William W. Barron, *Federal Practice and Procedure* (St. Paul, Minn.: West Publishing, 1950), 4:44 (challenge for bias, "however appropriate in the selection of trial jurors, is wholly irrelevant and improvident in the case of members of the grand jury which prefers the charge and which of course should be scrupulously fair but not necessarily uninformed or impartial").

107. 25 Fed. Cas. at 56, n. 3.

108. Ibid. at 57.

109. Ibid.

110. Ibid.

111. Ibid.

112. Clarkson and Jett, *Luther Martin of Maryland*, p. 247, n. 7.

113. Beveridge, *Life of John Marshall*, 3:413, n. 1.

114. Ibid., p. 475.

115. 25 Fed. Cas. at 49.

116. Beveridge, *Life of John Marshall*, 3: 482.

117. 25 Fed. Cas. at 77.

118. Ibid. at 80.

119. *United States v. Callender*, 25 Fed. Cas. 239, 244–245 (case no. 14,709) (C.C.D. Va. 1800). See also 25 Fed. Cas. 55, 77. For an excellent analysis of the *Callender* case, see Kathryn Preyer, "*United States v. Callender*: Judge and Jury in Republican Society," in *Essays on the Judiciary Act of 1789*, ed. Maeva Marcus (New York: Oxford University Press, 1992), pp. 173–95.

120. 25 Fed. Cas. at 76.

121. Ibid. at 51.

122. Ibid. at 84–85.

123. Hawkins, quoted in Hassett, "Jury's Pre-Trial Knowledge," p. 162; 25 Fed. Cas. at 52. I am indebted to Hassett for the point made in the text about Hawkins and Marshall.

124. 25 Fed. Cas. at 52.

125. Ibid. at 77.

126. Ibid. at 51.

127. Hassett, "Jury's Pre-Trial Knowledge," pp. 162–63.

128. 25 Fed. Cas. at 81.

129. *The Papers of John Marshall*, ed. Charles F. Hobson (Chapel Hill, N.C.: University of North Carolina Press, 1993), 7:5, 8–9, 74–119.

130. Mark Twain, *Roughing It* (Hartford, Conn.: American Publishing Co., 1903), 2:75.

131. Minow and Cate, "Who is an Impartial Juror?" pp. 631, 636, n. 22.

132. *United States v. Anguilo*, 897 F. 2d 1169, 1180–83 (1st Cir. 1990), *cert. den.*, *Granito v. United States*, 498 U.S. 845 (1990); *United States v. Helms-*

ley, 737 F. Supp. 600 (1989); Paul Craig Roberts, "Leona May Be Guilty, But Not as Charged," *Wall Street Journal*, April 19, 1992, p. A14.

133. *Mu'Min v. Virginia*, 500 U.S. 415, 111 S. Ct. 1899, 1904 (1991) (details of alleged confession); *Patton v. Yount*, 467 U.S. 1025 (1984) (defendant objects to media reports of suppressed confession inadmissible on retrial); *Murphy v. Florida*, 421 U.S. 794, 798–99 (1975) (media barrage about defendant's prior convictions and notoriety as "Star of India" jewel thief).

134. Minow and Cate, "Who is an Impartial Juror?" pp. 646–47.

135. *Yount v. Patton*, 710 F. 2d 956, 972 (3rd Cir. 1983) (District Judge Stern concurring), *rev'd.*, *Patton v. Yount*, 467 U.S. 1025 (1984).

136. Jim Newton, "Prospective King Jurors Get Bias Questionnaire," *Los Angeles Times*, Feb. 4, 1993, p. A1.

137. *Yount v. Patton*, 710 F. 2d at 972.

138. *Patton v. Yount*, 467 U.S. at 1031, referring to *Irvin v. Dowd*, 366 U.S. 717, 725. See also *State v. Laaman*, 114 N.H. 794, 798, 331 A. 2d 354, 357 (1974), *cert. den.*, 423 U.S. 854 (1975) ("Inherent prejudice . . . exists when the publicity by its nature has so tainted the trial atmosphere that it will necessarily result in lack of due process").

139. *Rideau v. Louisiana*, 373 U.S. 723, 726–27 (1963).

140. *Irvin v. Dowd*, 366 U.S. at 725–28. In hindsight, the Court has rejected any suggestion that its decision in *Irvin* rested on "presuming" bias. Instead, the Court emphasized that *Irvin* turned on evidence of "actual bias" in eight of the twelve persons selected as jurors. See *Murphy v. Florida*, 421 U.S. at 798.

141. *Sheppard v. Maxwell*, 384 U.S. 333, 358 (1966); *Estes v. Texas*, 381 U.S. 532 (1965).

142. "Must Ignorance Be a Virtue in Our Search for Justice? Panel Two: Current Judicial Practice, Legal Issues, and Existing Remedies," *American University Law Review* 40 (1991): 573, 581.

143. *Murphy v. Florida*, 421 U.S. at 799 (no presumption of prejudice from pervasive reporting of famous jewel thief's prior convictions).

144. *Patton v. Yount*, 467 U.S. 1025.

145. *Mu'Min v. Virginia*, 111 S. Ct. at 1904. The defendant complained that the publicity was especially prejudicial because it compared his crime with that of Willie Horton, made famous during the 1988 presidential election.

146. David Johnston, "North Guilty on 3 of 12 Counts; Vows to Fight Til 'Vindicated'; Bush Denies a Contra Aid Deal," *New York Times*, May 5, 1989, p. A1.

147. Richard Moran and Peter d'Errico, "An Impartial Jury or an Ignorant One?" *Boston Globe*, Feb. 12, 1989, p. A18.

148. *United States v. North*, 713 F. Supp. 1444, 1445 (D.D.C. 1989).

149. Dennis Bell, "North Jury Selection Begins; Effect of Iran-contra Hearings at Issue," *Newsday*, Feb. 1, 1989, p. 7.

150. Fred Kaplan, "North Jurors Won Seats with Blissful Ignorance," *Boston Globe*, April 22, 1989, p. 3.

151. Bell, "North Jury Selection Begins," p. 7; Kenneth Winkler, "A Verdict on the Jurors," *Newsday*, March 21, 1989, p. 56.

152. Winkler, "Verdict on Jurors," p. 56.

153. Hassett, "Jury's Pre-Trial Knowledge," p. 156. See also Bruce Fein, "Face-Off: Picking the Oliver North Jury," *USA Today*, Feb. 9, 1989, p. 8A.

154. Johnston, "North Guilty," p. A1; David E. Rosenbaum, "Jurors See North as a Scapegoat for His Superiors," *New York Times*, May 6, 1989, p. A1.

155. The accounts of jury selection come from my own observations of the process. Because of my status as an assistant district attorney, I have cleared the use of this information with the Massachusetts Criminal History Systems Board.

156. Steven Brill, *Trial by Jury* (New York: American Lawyers Books/Touchstone, 1989), p. 230.

157. William Raspberry, "The Verdict for Barry and a Verdict for the City," *Washington Post*, Aug. 11, 1990, p. C1.

158. Mydans, "Police Verdict," p. A1.

159. Seth Mydans, "Jury Acquits 2 on Most Charges in Beatings in Los Angeles Riots," *New York Times*, Oct. 19, 1993, p. A1.

160. Jack Lagguth, "Ruby Case: Who is a Witness," *New York Times*, March 1, 1964, sec. 4, p. 6E; *Jack Rubenstein, alias Jack Ruby v. The State of Texas*, 407 S.W. 2d 793, 794 (Tex. Crim. App. 1966).

161. Lagguth, "Ruby Case," p. 6E.

162. Homar Bigart, "Ruby Sentenced to Death Speedily by Dallas Jury; Oswald Killer to Appeal," *New York Times*, March 15, 1964, p. 1.

163. Gary Wills and Ovid Demaris, *Jack Ruby* (New York: New American Library, 1967), p. 202.

164. *Nebraska Press Ass'n v. Stuart*, 427 U.S. 539, 549, n. 3 (1976).

CHAPTER 2: JURIES AND HIGHER JUSTICE

1. Michael Granberry, "Abortion Protest Juries Told to Ignore Nullification Ad," *Los Angeles Times* (San Diego County edition), Jan. 27, 1990, p. B1, and "NOW Urges Advertisers to Drop Reader," *Los Angeles Times* (San Diego County edition), Feb. 3, 1990, p. B1. See also Alan W. Scheflin and Jon M. Van Dyke, "Merciful Juries: The Resilience of Jury Nullification," *Washington and Lee Law Review* 48 (1991): 165–83.

2. Granberry, "Juries Told to Ignore Ad," p. B1.

3. Ibid.

4. Katherine Bishop, "Diverse Group Wants Juries to Follow Natural Law," *New York Times*, Sept. 27, 1991, p. B16.

5. *United States v. Dougherty*, 473 F. 2d 1113 (D.C. Cir. 1972).

6. *United States v. Anderson*, 356 F. Supp. 1311 (D.N.J. 1973). See also Donald Janson, "17 of Camden 28 Found Not Guilty," *New York Times*, May 21, 1973, p. 1.

7. The judge at first told the jury it did not have the power to nullify. But, after hearing arguments from counsel, he changed his mind and told the jury that his earlier comment was wrong. Apparently, the judge decided to permit defendants to argue for nullification, given evidence that FBI informants supplied the antiwar protesters with the tools used in their draft raids. The judge instructed the jury that if it found that the conduct of government agents and informants was "offensive to the basic standards of decency, and shocking to the universal sense of justice," it might acquit any defendant "to whom this defense applies." Quoted in Alan W. Scheflin and Jon M. Van Dyke, "Jury Nullification: The Contours of a Controversy," *Law and Contemporary Problems* 43 (1980): 51, 53; Jon M. Van Dyke, *Jury Selection Procedures: Our Uncertain Commitment to Representative Panels* (Cambridge, Mass.: Ballinger Publishing, 1977), pp. 238–39. Legal scholars agreed that "never before had a judge given any jury such an instruction." Donald Janson, "Judge Instructs 'Camden 28' Jury," *New York Times*, May 18, 1973, p. 13.

8. Defense counsel David Kairys, quoted in Scheflin and Van Dyke, "Jury Nullification," pp. 52–53, n. 2, and Van Dyke, *Jury Selection Procedures*, pp. 239–40.

9. *United States v. Dougherty*, 473 F. 2d at 1137–38, n. 54.

10. *United States v. Spock*, 416 U.S. F. 2d 165 (1st. Cir. 1969).

11. Jessica Mitford, *The Trial of Dr. Spock* (New York: Alfred A. Knopf, 1969), pp. 220–35.

12. See text accompanying notes 28–35 of this chapter.

13. George Fletcher, *A Crime of Self-Defense: Bernhard Goetz and the Law on Trial* (Chicago: University of Chicago Press, 1988), p. 155 (nullification "completes" the law by recognizing principles of justification beyond the written law).

14. Gunnar Myrdal, *An American Dilemma: The Negro Problem and Modern Democracy* (New York: Harper & Brothers Publishers, 1944), pp. 524, 551–52.

15. Jennie Rhine, "The Jury: A Reflection of the Prejudices of the Community," *Hastings Law Journal* 20 (1969): 1417, 1439, n. 52.

16. Hiroski Fukurai, Edgar W. Butler, and Richard Krooth, *Race and the Jury: Racial Disenfranchisement and the Search for Justice* (New York: Plenum Press, 1993), pp. 5–6; Caroline Rand Herron, Carlyle C. Douglas, and Michael Wright, "The Acquittals," *New York Times*, April 22, 1984, sec. 4, p. 4.

17. Gary J. Simpson, "Jury Nullification in the American System: A Skeptical View," *Texas Law Review* 54 (1976): 488, 514.

18. California Jury Instructions, Criminal (CALJIC) (St. Paul, Minn.: West Publishing, 1989), no. 1.00.

19. Office of Jury Commissioner, *Trial Juror's Handbook*, 9th ed. (Boston: Office of the Jury Commissioner, 1991), pp. 4–6 (emphasis in original).

20. *Handbook for Jurors* (Montgomery County, Pa.: Court of Common Pleas, 1993), pp. 7–10.

21. *Manual of Modern Criminal Jury Instructions for the Ninth Circuit,* nos. 1.01 and 3.01 (1992).

22. Mark DeWolfe Howe, "Juries as Judges of Criminal Law," *Harvard Law Review* 52 (1939): 582–616; "The Changing Role of the Jury in the Nineteenth Century," *Yale Law Journal* 74 (1964): 170–92; William E. Nelson, *Americanization of the Common Law: The Impact of Legal Change on Massachusetts Society, 1760–1830* (Cambridge, Mass.: Harvard University Press, 1975), pp. 3–35; John D. Gordan III, "Juries as Judges of the Law: The American Experience," *Law Quarterly Review* 108 (1992): 272–79; J. R. Pole, "Reflections on American Law and the American Revolution," *William and Mary Quarterly* 50 (3d series, 1993): 123–59.

23. "The Trial of William Penn and William Mead, at the Old Bailey, for a Tumultuous Assembly," Howell's *State Trials* 6: 951 (1670).

24. James Alexander, *A Brief Narrative of the Case and Trial of John Peter Zenger,* ed. Stanley Katz (Cambridge, Mass.: Harvard University Press, 1963).

25. See Stanley Campbell, *The Slave Catchers: Enforcement of the Fugitive Slave Law, 1850–1860* (Chapel Hill, N.C.: University of North Carolina Press, 1968), pp. 148–69.

26. See Scheflin and Van Dyke, "Jury Nullification," pp. 85–114.

27. *United States v. Dougherty,* 473 F. 2d at 1133–37.

28. For similar use of the Barry and North cases as examples of possible jury nullification, see Scheflin and Van Dyke, "Merciful Juries," p. 175, n. 51.

29. David Margolick, "Jurors Acquit Dr. Kevorkian in Suicide Case," May 3, 1994, *New York Times,* p. A1; Jack Lessenberry, "Michigan Jury Acquits Kevorkian," *Boston Globe,* May 3, 1994, p. A1; Richard Knox, "Verdict Touches Off Deliberations," *Boston Globe,* May 3, 1994, p. A10.

30. Michael York and Tracy Thompson, "Barry Guilty on 1 Count, Cleared on 1; Mistrial Declared on 12 Other Charges . . . ," *Washington Post,* Aug. 11, 1990, p. A1.

31. "Four Jurors Biased Toward Barry, Judge Says," *New York Times,* Nov. 1, 1990, p. A20.

32. Quoted in Scheflin and Van Dyke, "Merciful Juries," p. 175, n. 51.

33. William Raspberry, "The Verdict for Barry and a Verdict for the City," *Washington Post,* Aug. 11, 1990, p. C1.

34. David Johnston, "North Guilty on 3 of 12 Counts; Vows to Fight Til 'Vindicated'; Bush Denies a Contra Aid Deal," *New York Times,* May 5, 1989, p. A1.

35. David E. Rosenbaum, "Jurors See North as a Scapegoat for his Superiors," *New York Times,* May 6, 1989, p. A1.

36. Ibid.

37. See note 22 from this chapter and text accompanying notes 52–63 from chapter 1.

38. See Alan W. Scheflin, "Jury Nullification: The Right to Say No," *Southern California Law Review* 45 (1972): 168, 169, n. 2.

39. Modern advocates of jury nullification typically seek to defend the doctrine even while rejecting the jury's general right to decide questions of law. See, for example, Scheflin, "Jury Nullification," p. 169, n. 2.

40. Thomas Andrew Green, *Verdict According to Conscience: Perspectives on the English Criminal Trial Jury, 1200–1800* (Chicago: University of Chicago Press, 1985), pp. 153–236; John Phillip Reid, *In a Defiant Stance: The Conditions of Law in Massachusetts Bay, The Irish Comparison, and the Coming of the American Revolution* (University Park, Pa.: Pennsylvania State University Press, 1977), pp. 27–64.

41. Green, *Verdict According to Conscience*, pp. 221–22; Catherine Owens Peare, *William Penn: A Biography* (Philadelphia, Pa.: J.B. Lippincott, 1957), pp. 109–10.

42. Howell's *State Trials* 6: 954–55.

43. Ibid. at 957.

44. Green points out that these details are not included in the official transcript of the trial published in the *State Trials*, which derives from an account of the trial written by Penn and Mead themselves (*The People's Ancient and Just Liberties Asserted*). It is included in the account published by the Lord Mayor of London who presided over the trial. Sir Samuel Starling, *An Answer to the Seditious and Scandalous Pamphlet, entitled The Trial of W. Penn and W. Mead* (London, 1671), p. 15. See Green, *Verdict According to Conscience*, p. 223, n. 97.

45. Howell's *State Trials* 6: 957.

46. Ibid. at 958.

47. Ibid. at 959.

48. Green, *Verdict According to Conscience*, quoting Starling, *Answer to the Seditious Pamphlet*, p. 18.

49. Howell's *State Trials* 6: 959–60.

50. "An Appendix by way of DEFENCE for the PRISONERS as what might have been offered against the Indictment and illegal Proceedings of the Court thereon, had they not violently over-ruled and stopped them," Howell's *State Trials* 6: 970–71 (1670).

51. Howell's *State Trials* 6: 960–61.

52. Ibid. at 961–62.

53. Ibid. at 963–64.

54. Ibid. at 964–68.

55. Green, *Verdict According to Conscience*, p. 225.

56. Ibid.

57. "Case of the Imprisonment of Edward Bushel for Alleged Misconduct as a Juryman," Howell's *State Trials* 6: 999–1026; Vaughn's Reports 35, 124 Eng. Rep. 1006 (1670).

58. Howell's *State Trials* 6: 1015–16.

59. Shannon C. Stimson, *The American Revolution in the Law: Anglo-American Jurisprudence before John Marshall* (Princeton, N.J.: Princeton University Press, 1990), p. 23, quoting Sir William Blackstone, *Commentaries on the Laws of England* (Oxford: Clarendon Press, 1769), vol. 4, chap. 2, pp. 150–51.

60. Alexander, *Brief Narrative*, pp. 99–100.

61. Ibid., p. 78.

62. Ibid., p. 93.

63. Ibid., p. 99.

64. Ibid., p. 96.

65. Ibid., p. 29.

66. William W. Van Alstyne,"*Congressional Power and Free Speech*: Levy's Legacy Revisited," *Harvard Law Review* 99 (1988): 1089, 1093.

67. *Georgia v. Brailsford*, 3 U.S. (3 Dall.) 1, 4 (1794).

68. Howe, "Juries as Judges," pp. 587n, 597n.

69. Robert Green McCloskey, *The Works of James Wilson* (Cambridge, Mass.: Harvard University Press, 1967), 2:540.

70. Howe, "Juries as Judges," p. 595.

71. "Changing Role of the Jury," pp. 174–75.

72. *Commonwealth v. Blanding*, 20 Mass. 304 (1825), quoted in ibid.

73. Howe, "Juries as Judges," p. 592, citing *State v. Croteau*, 23 Vt. 14 (1849), overruled *State v. Burpee*, 65 Vt. 125 (1892).

74. *Sparf and Hansen v. United States*, 156 U.S. 1, 169 (1895), citing *United States v. Hutchings*, 26 Fed. Cas. 440, 442 (case no. 15,429) (C.C.D. Va. 1817).

75. *United States v. Hodges*, 26 Fed. Cas. 332, 334–35 (case no. 15,374) (C.C.D. Md. 1815).

76. Lucius Manlius Sargent ("Sigma"), *Reminiscences of Samuel Dexter (1857) 60-61*, quoted in Scheflin, "Jury Nullification," p. 176, n. 31. The case is *United States v. The William*, 28 Fed. Cas. 614 (case no. 16,700) (D.C. Mass. 1808).

77. Howe, "Juries as Judges," p. 606.

78. 24 Fed. Cas. 1042 (C.C.D. Mass 1835) (case no. 14,545).

79. Ibid. at 1043–44.

80. Ibid. at 1044.

81. Ibid. at 1043.

82. Ibid.

83. Ibid.

84. Campbell, *Slave Catchers*, pp. 24–25.

85. 26 Fed. Cas. 1323 (case no. 15, 815) (C.C.D. Mass. 1851).

86. Campbell, *Slave Catchers*, pp. 148–50.

87. 26 Fed. Cas. at 1331.

88. Ibid. at 1331, 1336.

89. Ibid. at 1332, 1334, 1336.

90. Ibid. at 1336.

91. My attention was first drawn to the rich debates over the jury at the Massachusetts Constitutional Convention of 1853 by "The Changing Role of the Jury in the Nineteenth Century," *Yale Law Journal* 74 (1964): 170–92. I have since read the *Official Report of the Debates and Proceedings in the State Convention to Revise and Amend the Constitution* (Boston: White and Potter, Printers to the Convention, 1853), 3:430–517. This volume is available at the Massachusetts State Archives. Page references will be given directly to the *Debates and Proceedings*, but I remain heavily indebted to the *Yale Law Journal* article for highlighting crucial moments during the debates.

92. *Debates and Proceedings*, pp. 442 (delegate Hillard), 443–44 (delegate Keyes referring to unlikelihood that Boston juries would enforce Fugitive Slave Law; impossibility of finding local juries willing to enforce liquor prohibition laws), 455 (delegate Allen). "Changing Role of the Jury," p. 177.

93. *Commonwealth v. Porter*, 51 Mass. 263, 274–75, 287 (1845).

94. *Debates and Proceedings*, pp. 430–31.

95. Ibid., p. 443 (delegate Keyes).

96. Ibid., p. 462 (delegate Gray).

97. Ibid., p. 455.

98. Ibid., p. 458.

99. Ibid., p. 445.

100. Ibid., pp. 431–32, 515–17.

101. "Changing Role of the Jury," pp. 182–83.

102. Ibid., p. 183.

103. 71 Mass. 185 (1855).

104. Ibid. at 187, 228–36.

105. 156 U.S. 51 (1895).

106. Ibid. at 59–60 (emphasis in original).

107. Ibid. at 61–62, n. 1 (emphasis in original).

108. Ibid. at 64.

109. Ibid. at 101–2.

110. Ibid. at 102–3.

111. *Sparf and Hansen v. United States*, 156 U.S. at 173 (Gray, J., dissenting).

112. *Diary and Autobiography of John Adams*, ed. L. H. Butterfield (Cambridge, Mass.: Harvard University Press, 1961), 2:4–5; Pole, "Reflections," p. 132; Stimson, *American Revolution in the Law*, p. 79.

113. Stimson, *American Revolution in the Law*, p. 59, quoting *The Papers of Thomas Jefferson*, ed. Julian Boyd (Princeton, N.J.: Princeton University Press, 1950), 1:134.

114. Ibid., quoting Perry Miller, *Life of the Mind in America* (Garden City, N.Y.: Anchor Books, 1962), p. 66.

115. Nelson, *Americanization of Common Law*, pp. 4, 165–66, 174.

116. Gary Cohn, "Simone Jurors Queried," *Philadelphia Inquirer*, March 23, 1993, p. B1.

117. Jerome Frank, *Courts on Trial* (Princeton, N.J.: Princeton University Press, 1949), p. 110–14 .

118. *McCleskey v. Kemp*, 481 U.S. 279, 312 (1987).

119. Civil Liberties Union of Massachusetts position paper on file with author.

120. Scheflin and Van Dyke, "Jury Nullification," pp. 84–85.

121. Scheflin and Van Dyke, "Merciful Juries," pp. 173–75.

122. *People v. Dillon*, 34 Cal. 3d 441, 491–92 (1983) (Kaus, J., concurring).

123. Green, *Verdict According to Conscience*, pp. 42–43.

124. Richard O. Lempert, "Why Do Jury Research," in *Inside the Juror*, ed. Reid Hastie (Cambridge, Mass.: Cambridge University Press, 1993), pp. 252–53.

CHAPTER 3: JURY SELECTION AND THE CROSS-SECTIONAL IDEAL

1. *Smith v. Texas*, 311 U.S. 128, 130 (1940).

2. *Report of the Judicial Conference Committee on the Operation of the Jury System*, 26 F.R.D. 409, 421–22 (1960).

3. Charles A. Lindquist, "An Analysis of Juror Selection Procedures in the United States District Courts," *Temple Law Quarterly* 41 (1967): 32, 44.

4. "The Jury Selection and Service Act," 28 U.S.C., secs. 1861–69.

5. *Taylor v. Louisiana*, 419 U.S. 522, 528 (1975). It is not unconstitutional per se for a state to compile a jury list that is a cross section only of the "intelligent and upright citizens of the community." Shirley S. Abrahamson, "Justice and Juror," *Georgia Law Review* 20 (1986): 257, 262 (Georgia). See also *Carter v. Jury Comm'n*, 396 U.S. 320, 323 (1970) (finding no facial constitutional violation in Alabama statute that limited jury eligibility to those who "are generally reputed to be honest and intelligent and are esteemed in the community for their integrity, good education, and sound judgment").

6. *Coke upon Littleton*, 155b (1832). Blackstone similarly spoke of the need for jurors to be "indifferently chosen." Sir William Blackstone, *Commentaries on the Laws of England* (Oxford: Clarendon Press, 1769), 4: 343.

7. *United States v. Wood*, 299 U.S. 123, 145–46 (1936).

8. Jennie Rhine, "The Jury: A Reflection of the Prejudices of the Community," *Hastings Law Journal* 20 (1969): 1417, 1429 ("a proportional representation of all biases is a practical possibility"); Roger S. Kuhn, "Jury Discrimination: The Next Phase," *Southern California Law Review* 41 (1968): 235–328.

9. *People v. Wheeler*, 583 P. 2d 748, 755 (1978) ("overall impartiality"); *Commonwealth v. Soares*, 377 Mass. 461, 480 (1979), *cert. den.*, *Massachusetts v. Soares*, 444 U.S. 881 ("diffused impartiality").

10. See the discussion of *Ballard v. United States*, 329 U.S. 187 (1946), in text of notes 81–87.

11. See, for example, "Out of the Frying Pan or into the Fire? Race and Choice

of Venue After Rodney King," *Harvard Law Review* 106 (1993): 705, 709; "Developments: Race and the Criminal Process," *Harvard Law Review* 101 (1988): 1472, 1559 ("without the broad range of social experiences that a group of diverse individuals can provide, juries are often ill-equipped to evaluate the facts presented").

12. "Developments: Race and the Criminal Process," p. 1559 ("unconscious prejudice"); Sheri Lynn Johnson, "Unconscious Racism and the Criminal Law," *Cornell Law Review* 73 (1988):1016, 1022 ("subtle, unconscious alteration of judgment" due to racism); *People v. Wheeler*, 583 P. 2d at 755 (unrealistic to expect jurors to be devoid of deep-rooted biases); *Commonwealth v. Soares*, 377 Mass. at 487, n. 30; Rhine, "The Jury," p. 1430.

13. For example, Andrew Kull, *The Color-Blind Constitution* (Cambridge, Mass.: Harvard University Press, 1992).

14. For example, T. Alexander Aleinikoff, "A Case for Race-Consciousness," *Columbia Law Review* 91 (1991): 1060–1125.

15. See, for example, Sam J. Ervin, Jr., "Jury Reform Needs More Thought," *ABA Journal* 53 (February 1967): 132, 134.

16. Sheri Lynn Johnson, "Black Innocence and the White Jury," *Michigan Law Review* 83 (1985): 1611–1708; Johnson, "Unconscious Racism," pp. 1016–37; "Note: The Case for Black Juries," *Yale Law Journal* 79 (1970): 531–50.

17. Andrew Kull, "Racial Justice," *New Republic*, Nov. 30, 1992, p. 17; see also "Out of the Frying Pan," p. 708; Donna St. George, "Fairness, Race, and the Jury System," *Philadelphia Inquirer*, April 11, 1993, p. 1. For the retrial of King's assailants and the conviction of two of the four officers, see chapter 1.

18. "Female Jurors Assert Sexism Hurt Menendez Deliberations," *New York Times*, Jan. 31, 1994, p. A13; Mary B. W. Tabor, "Stereotyping Men, Women and Juries by Trial and Error," *New York Times*, Feb. 6, 1994, sec. 4, p. 3.

19. For recent reviews of the impact of race on juries, see Nancy J. King, "Postconviction Review of Jury Discrimination: Measuring the Effects of Juror Decisions," *Michigan Law Review* 92 (1993): 63; "Out of the Frying Pan," p. 709; "Developments: Race and the Criminal Process," pp. 1557–61; Johnson, "Unconscious Racism," p. 1016; Johnson, "Black Innocence and White Jury," pp. 1696–98; Hiroski Fukurai, Edgar W. Butler, and Richard Krooth, *Race and the Jury: Racial Disenfranchisement and the Search for Justice* (New York: Plenum Press, 1993); Jon Van Dyke, *Jury Selection Procedures: Our Uncertain Commitment to Representative Panels* (Cambridge, Mass.: Ballinger Publishing, 1977), pp. 33–35. For a study that finds socioeconomic status, not race, to be the major determinant of juror response, see James M. Gleason and Victor A. Harris, "Race, Socio-Economic Status and Perceived Similarity as Determinants of Judgements by Simulated Jurors," *Journal of Social Behavior and Personality* 3 (1975):

175, 178. For recent studies and surveys of gender and jury verdicts, see Shirley S. Abrahamson, "Justice and Juror," *Georgia Law Review* 20 (1986): 257–98; Nancy S. Marder, "Gender Dynamics and Jury Deliberations," *Yale Law Journal* 96 (1987): 593–612; Reid Hastie, Steven Penrod, and Nancy Pennington, *Inside the Jury* (Cambridge, Mass.: Harvard University Press, 1983), pp. 140ff; Edmond Costantini, Michael Mallery, and Diane M. Yapundich, "Gender and Juror Partiality: Are Women More Likely to Pre-judge Guilt?" *Judicature* 67 (1983): 120–33; Hubert S. Feild and Leigh B. Bienen, *Jurors and Rape* (Lexington, Mass.: Lexington Books, 1980), pp. 95–150; Carol J. Mills and Wayne E. Bohannon, "Juror Characteristics: To What Extent Are They Related to Jury Verdicts," *Judicature* 64 (1980): 22–31; Van Dyke, *Jury Selection Procedures*, pp. 41–42; Charlan Nemeth, Jeffrey Endicott, and Joel Wachtler, "From the '50s to the '70s: Women in Jury Deliberations," *Sociometry* 39 (1976): 293–304. For the impact of age and occupation on jurors, see Van Dyke, *Jury Selection Procedures*, pp. 25–28, 35–39.

20.   Harry Kalven, Jr., and Hans Zeisel, *The American Jury* (Chicago: University of Chicago Press, 1970), p. 456.

21.   "Out of the Frying Pan," p. 709.

22.   As part of the University of Chicago Jury Project of the 1950s, Prof. Dale Broeder reported on striking instances of racial prejudice, told to him by jurors in posttrial interviews. In one case, despite the presence of a black woman on the jury, other jurors openly argued for conviction on the theory that "niggers are just no good." In another interview, a white juror justified convicting a black defendant even where the evidence was not clear, by arguing that "niggers have to be taught to behave. I felt that if he hadn't done that, he'd done something else probably even worse and that he should be put out of the way for a good long while." Dale W. Broeder, "The Negro in Court," *Duke Law Journal* (1965): 19, 23.

23.   *Strauder v. West Virginia*, 100 U.S. 303, 305 (1880).

24.   *Virginia v. Rives*, 100 U.S. 313, 315 (1880).

25.   According to the court, de jure exclusion of blacks from jury service vio-lated the rights of black citizens to be considered equally worthy with whites to serve as jurors. De jure exclusion of blacks from the jury also vio-lated the rights of the black defendant to be treated by the law the same as a white defendant. The violation gave the white defendant the right to trial before a jury on which members of his own race could serve but denied the reciprocal right to a black defendant.

26.   *Virginia v. Rives*, 100 U.S. at 322.

27.   Ibid. at 315.

28.   Van Dyke, *Jury Selection Procedures*, pp. 10–11. The colonists brought the mixed jury with them to Plymouth colony, involving natives in passing on disputes between settler and native. Throughout the eighteenth century and into the nineteenth, a jury of six aliens and six citizens continued to be

used. For example, Pennsylvania courts in 1783 granted the motion of four Italian defendants for a mixed jury. In 1823, Virginia courts similarly resorted to a mixed jury to try an alien on charges of piracy. Lewis LaRue, "A Jury of One's Peers," *Washington and Lee Law Review* 33 (1976): 841–76. One of the most fascinating examples of the mixed jury is its use in nineteenth-century Hawaii to resolve disputes between natives and foreigners. Peter J. Nelligan and Harry V. Ball, "Ethnic Juries in Hawaii: 1825–1850," *Social Process in Hawaii* 34 (1992): 113–63. For a study of the mixed jury that appeared too recently to be consulted for this book, see Marianne Constable, *The Law of the Other: The Mixed Jury and Changing Conceptions of Citizenship, Law, and Knowledge* (Chicago: University of Chicago Press, 1994).

29. *Virginia v. Rives*, 100 U.S. at 323.

30. See Benno Schmidt, Jr., "Juries, Jurisdiction, and Race Discrimination: The Lost Promise of *Strauder v. West Virginia*," *Texas Law Review* 61 (1983): 1401, 1429–41; Martha Craig Daughtrey, "Cross-Sectionalism and Jury-Selection Procedures after *Taylor v. Louisiana*," *Tennessee Law Review* 43 (1975): 1, 2–19.

31. *Gibson v. Mississippi*, 162 U.S. 565, 569, 584 (1896).

32. *Brownfield v. South Carolina*, 189 U.S. 426, 429 (1903).

33. *Martin v. Texas*, 200 U.S. 316, 320–21 (1906).

34. Van Dyke, *Jury Selection Procedures*, p. 53.

35. *Norris v. Alabama*, 294 U.S. 587, 592, 596–97 (1935).

36. Ibid. at 592, 594, 596–97.

37. Daughtrey, "Cross-Sectionalism," p. 17.

38. Van Dyke, *Jury Selection Procedures*, p. 54.

39. *Hale v. Kentucky*, 303 U.S. 613–14 (1938).

40. *Pierre v. Louisiana,*, 306 U.S. 354 (1939).

41. *Patton v. Mississippi*, 332 U.S. 463 (1947).

42. *Avery v. Georgia*, 345 U.S. 559 (1953).

43. See *Turner v. Fouche*, 396 U.S. 346, 354 (1970) (Georgia confined jury duty to persons deemed "discreet," "upright," and "intelligent"); *Carter v. Jury Comm'n*, 396 U.S. at 323 (similar in Alabama—see note 5). In the federal courts, as we saw earlier, the view as late as 1960 was that the "jury list should represent as high a degree of intelligence, morality, integrity, and common sense as possible." *Report of the Judicial Conference Committee on the Operation of the Jury System*, 26 F.R.D. at 421.

44. The commissioner testified that "my acquaintance is generally predominantly, of course, with the White Race . . . so, if there were any errors here, they certainly are of omission and not of commission. No effort was made to exclude anyone." *Rabinowitz v. United States*, 366 F. 2d 34, 40–41 (5th Cir. 1966).

45. Ibid. Just how long-lived was the career of this rationalization of the absence of blacks from juries can be seen by comparing the 1959 remarks

of the jury commissioner quoted in note 44 with these words from the chief justice of the Delaware Supreme Court in 1881: "That none but white men were selected is in nowise remarkable in view of the fact—too notorious to be ignored—that the great body of black men residing in this State are utterly unqualified by want of intelligence, experience, or moral integrity. The exceptions are rare." *Neal v. Delaware*, 103 U.S. 370, 393–94 (1881).

46.   Broeder, "The Negro in Court," p. 24 (in a case where a black defendant was tried for transporting his wife and girlfriend across state lines to engage in prostitution, the jurors wanted to know whether "many Negroes engage in such conduct? Is it fair to make Negroes conform to the white man's notion of what is proper?").

47.   Ibid.; see also note 22.

48.   Gunnar Myrdal, *An American Dilemma: The Negro Problem and Modern Democracy* (New York: Harper & Brothers Publishers, 1944) pp. 524, 552–53.

49.   *Powell v. Alabama*, 287 U.S. 45 (1932). The Supreme Court reversed the convictions on the ground that it was a denial of due process in a capital case not to provide effective assistance of counsel to indigent and illiterate defendants. The supposed ringleader, Haywood Patterson, was tried again and sentenced to death, but the trial judge set the verdict aside. At a third trial, Patterson and Clarence Norris were again sentenced to death, but the Supreme Court reversed these convictions because, as we saw, blacks had systematically been excluded from their juries. *Norris v. Alabama*, 294 U.S. 587 (1935); *Patterson v. Alabama*, 294 U.S. 600 (1935). Between 1935 and 1937, Alabama quashed the indictments against five of the original nine defendants but obtained convictions against the other four, including a death sentence against Norris. That sentence was commuted. By 1946, all convicted defendants in the case had been paroled, except for Patterson, who escaped successfully to Michigan in 1948. See James Goodman, *Stories of Scottsboro* (New York: Pantheon, 1994); Dan T. Carter, *Scottsboro: A Tragedy of the American South* (Baton Rouge: Louisiana State Univerity Press, 1969), pp. 3–50; Anthony Lewis, *Gideon's Trumpet* (New York: Vintage, 1966), pp. 245–46.

50.   Stephen J. Whitfield, *A Death in the Delta* (Baltimore, Md.: Johns Hopkins University Press, 1991), p. 42.

51.   Blackstone, *Commentaries*, 3: 362.

52.   Carol Weisbrod, "Images of the Woman Juror," *Harvard Women's Law Journal* 9 (1986): 59, 60, n. 2; Deborah L. Rhode, *Justice and Gender: Sex Discrimination and the Law* (Cambridge, Mass.: Harvard University Press, 1989), p. 48.

53.   William Waller Hening, *Laws of Virginia*, (Charlottesville, Va.: University Press of Virginia, 1969 [facsimile reprint]), 1:209; Susie M. Ames, *Studies of the Virginia Eastern Shore in the Seventeenth Century* (New York: Russell and Russell, 1940), pp. 176, 178.

54. John Demos, *Entertaining Satan: Witchcraft and the Culture of Early New England* (New York: Oxford University Press, 1982), p. 180.

55. Elizabeth Cady Stanton, Susan B. Anthony, and Matilda Joslyn Gage, eds., *History of Woman Suffrage, 1876–1885* (Rochester, N.Y.: Susan B. Anthony, 1886), 3: 731–38.

56. Daughtrey, "Cross-Sectionalism," p. 52; Weisbrod, "Images of the Woman Juror," p. 60, n. 2; Rhode, *Justice and Gender*, p. 49.

57. Stanton, Anthony, and Gage, *History of Woman Suffrage*, p. 735.

58. Weisbrod, "Images of the Woman Juror," p. 66; Rhode, *Justice and Gender*, p. 49.

59. See Weisbrod, "Images of the Woman Juror," pp. 66–67.

60. Abrahamson, "Justice and Juror," p. 263.

61. Daughtrey, "Cross-Sectionalism," p. 53 .

62. Weisbrod, "Images of the Woman Juror," pp. 60–61.

63. *Taylor v. Louisiana*, 419 U.S. 522 (1975).

64. See, for example, *Bradwell v. Illinois*, 83 U.S. (16 Wall) 130, 141–43 (1873) (Bradley, J. concurring); Daughtrey, "Cross-Sectionalism," pp. 59–61; Weisbrod, "Images of the Woman Juror," pp. 65–67.

65. *Hoyt v. Florida*, 368 U.S. 57, 61–62 (1961).

66. *Taylor v. Louisiana*, 419 U.S. 522.

67. Kalven and Zeisel, *The American Jury*, pp. 249–50.

68. *Hoyt v. Florida*, 368 U.S. at 64.

69. *Smith v. Texas*, 311 U.S. at 130.

70. Ibid. at 129, 131.

71. Judicial Conference of the United States, *Report to the Judicial Conference of the Committee on Selection of Jurors* (1942), p. 15.

72. Jerome Frank, *Courts on Trial: Myth and Reality in American Justice* (Princeton, N.J.: Princeton University Press, 1949), pp. 109–45.

73. See, for example, Robert S. Redmount, "Psychological Tests for Selecting Jurors," *Kansas Law Review* 5 (1957): 391 (urging use of tests "to minimize the threat to rational juridical process . . . that comes from incompetent jurors").

74. *Thiel v. Southern Pacific Co.*, 328 U.S. 217, 223–24 (1946).

75. *Fay v. New York*, 332 U.S. 261 (1947). Whereas the Supreme Court can rely on its supervisory powers to impose a requirement on federal courts, the Court can impose the same requirement on state courts only by finding that it was mandated by the Constitution itself.

76. Ibid. at 291.

77. 28 U.S.C. secs. 1861–69.

78. Ibid., sec. 1863(b)(2).

79. Ibid., secs. 1863–1866.

80. *Taylor v. Louisiana*, 419 U.S. at 528.

81. Daughtrey, "Cross-Sectionalism," p. 56, n. 246.

82. *Ballard v. United States*, 329 U.S. 187, 191 (1946).

83. See, for example, Carol Gilligan, *In a Different Voice: Psychological Theory and Women's Development* (Cambridge, Mass.: Harvard University Press, 1982); Abrahamson, "Justice and Juror," p. 271.

84. Weisbrod, "Images of the Woman Juror," pp. 70–82.

85. *Ballard v. United States*, 329 U.S. at 193–94.

86. Ibid. at 194–95.

87. For a similar discussion, see Weisbrod, "Images of the Woman Juror," pp. 79–81. Weisbrod points out that Carol Gilligan's "different voice" argument is reminiscent of the *Ballard* Court's sense that men and women each bring a different moral calculus to jury deliberations.

88. *Taylor v. Louisiana*, 419 U.S. at 524.

89. Ibid. at 528.

90. Ibid. at 529, n. 7, quoting H.R. Report No. 1076, 90th Cong., 2d sess. 8 (1968), *U.S. Code Congressional and Administrative News* (St. Paul, Minn.: West Publishing, 1968), p. 1797.

91. Ervin, "Jury Reform Needs More Thought," p. 134.

92. Van Dyke, *Jury Selection Procedures*, p. 18.

93. *People v. Wheeler*, 583 P. 2d at 755.

94. 419 U.S. at 529.

95. Hon. Irving R. Kaufman, "Foreward: Jury Selection in the Fifth Circuit," *Mercer Law Review* 20 (1969): 347–48.

96. Johnson, "Black Innocence and White Jury," pp. 1611, 1655 ("All the venire selection cases stress that the exclusion of minorities impairs the impartiality and legitimacy of the jury system; one might assume that this reasoning would lead the Court to hold that a defendant's jury—and not simply the panel from which the jury is selected—must include minorities. Certainly bias can only manifest itself in individual cases").

97. *Batson v. Kentucky*, 476 U.S. 79, 86, n. 6 (1986) ("It would be impossible to apply a concept of proportional representation to the petit jury in view of the heterogeneous nature of our society").

98. See, for example, *McCleskey v. Kemp*, 481 U.S. 279, 316, n. 39 (1987) ("the national 'majority' is composed of various minority groups . . . and the ethnic composition of the Nation is ever-shifting").

99. See Van Dyke, *Jury Selection Procedures*, p. 17–18.

100. *Bradley v. Super. Ct. for Los Angeles Cty.*, 531 F. 2d 413, 416, n. 9 (9th Cir. 1976).

101. Van Dyke, *Jury Selection Procedures*, p. 18.

102. See, for example, Lani Guinier, "The Triumph of Tokenism: The Voting Rights Act and the Theory of Black Electoral Success," *Michigan Law Review* 89 (1991): 1077–154.

103. 28 U.S.C., sec. 1863(b)(2). In 1992, Congress amended this section to permit Massachusetts federal courts to draw names of prospective jurors from resident lists compiled by each town and city.

104. 28 U.S.C. 1863(b)(2) ("The plan shall prescribe some other source or

sources of names in addition to voter lists where necessary to foster the policy and protect the rights secured by sections 1861 and 1862 of this title").

105. "The voting list need not perfectly mirror the percentage structure of the community, but any substantial percentage deviations must be corrected by the use of supplemental sources. The committee would leave the definition of 'substantial' to judicial decision. "Federal Jury Selection Act," H. Report 1076, *Congressional Record*, 90th Cong., 2d. sess. (1968), vol. 114, pt. 4, p. 3990.

106. Ibid.

107. Van Dyke, *Jury Selection Procedures*, p. 90, quoting Senate testimony of Judge Irving R. Kaufman.

108. Hon. Walter P. Gewin, "An Analysis of Jury Selection Decisions," appended to *Foster v. Sparks*, 506 F. 2d 805, 811 (5th Cir. 1975) ("We are aware of no case in which exclusive reliance on voter registration lists has been invalidated"). For an update of Judge Gewin's conclusion, see *United States v. Cecil*, 836 F. 2d 1431, 1447 (4th Cir. 1988) (conclusion of Judge Gewin supported by all reported decisions since).

109. *United States v. Afflerbach*, 754 F. 2d 866, 869–870 (10th Cir. 1985), *cert. den.*, 472 U.S. 1029; *United States v. Warinner*, 607 F. 2d 210, 214 (8th Cir. 1979), *cert. den.*, 445 U.S. 927 (1980); *United States v. Brady*, 579 F. 2d 1121, 1134 (9th Cir. 1978), *cert. den.*, 439 U.S. 1074 (1979); *United States v. Freeman*, 514 F. 2d 171 (8th Cir. 1975); *United States v. Lewis*, 472 F. 2d 252, 256 (3rd Cir. 1973); *Camp v. United States*, 413 F. 2d 419, 421 (5th Cir. 1969), *cert. den.*, 396 U.S. 968 (1969); *United States v. Caci*, 401 F. 2d 664, 671 (2d Cir. 1968), *vacated and remanded on other grounds*, 394 U.S. 310 (1969).

110. *United States v. Biaggi*, 909 F. 2d 662 (2d Cir. 1990), *cert. den.*, *Simons v. United States*, 499 U.S. 904 (1991).

111. *United States v. Freeman*, 514 F. 2d 171 (8th Cir. 1975).

112. National Center for State Courts, *State Court Organization*, preliminary draft (Williamsburg, Va.: National Center for State Courts, forthcoming), table 4.

113. Abrahamson, "Justice and Juror," p. 273.

114. *Brooks v. Beto*, 366 F. 2d 1, 23 (5th Cir. 1966).

115. Kull, "Racial Justice," p. 18.

116. For a sampling of numerous law review articles on the subject, see Douglas L. Colbert, "Challenging the Challenge: The Thirteenth Amendment as a Prohibition Against the Racial Use of Peremptory Challenges," *Cornell Law Review* 76 (1990): 1–128; "Note: Affirmative Selection: A New Response to Peremptory Challenge Abuse," *Stanford Law Review* 38 (1986): 781–812; Toni M. Massaro, "Peremptories or Peers?—Rethinking Sixth Amendment Doctrine, Images, and Procedures," *North Carolina Law Review* 64 (1986): 501–64; James H. Druff, "The Cross-Section Requirement and Jury Impartiality," *California Law Review* 73 (1985): 1555–96; "Peremptory Challenges and the Meaning of Jury Representation," *Yale Law Journal* 89

(1980): 1177–98; "Limiting the Peremptory Challenge: Representation of Groups on Petit Juries," *Yale Law Journal* 86 (1977): 1715–40.

117. For the history of the peremptory challenge, see Colbert, "Challenging the Challenge," pp. 9–13; *Swain v. Alabama*, 380 U.S. 202, 212–220 (1965).

118. *Swain v. Alabama*, 380 U.S. at 219.

119. Blackstone, *Commentaries*, 4: 347.

120. *McKinney v. Walker*, 394 F. Supp. 1015, 1018 (D.S.C. 1974).

121. *People v. Wheeler*, 583 P. 2d at 761.

122. Ibid. at 761–62.

123. Ibid. at 762.

124. *Duncan v. Louisiana*, 391 U.S. 145 (1968) (applying Sixth Amendment to states); *Taylor v. Louisiana*, 419 U.S. 522.

125. *Swain v. Alabama*, 380 U.S. at 223.

126. *Commonwealth v. Soares*, 377 Mass. at 487–88.

127. *Batson v. Kentucky*, 476 U.S. at 103–4 (Marshall, J., concurring).

128. *Ex Parte Clarence Lee Brandley*, 781 S.W. 2d 886, 926 (Tex. Crim. App. 1989), *cert. den.*, *Texas v. Brandley*, 498 U.S. 817 (1990).

129. Judge Newman held that the pattern of race-based peremptory challenges called for the exercise of his supervisory powers to prevent continued exclusion of blacks from juries. However, the Second Circuit Court of Appeals vacated his decision. *United States v. Robinson*, 421 F. Supp. 467 (D. Conn. 1976), *revd. sub nom. United States v. Newman*, 549 F. 2d 240 (2d Cir. 1977).

130. Robert Blauner, *Racial Oppression in America* (New York: Harper and Row, 1972), p. 225.

131. The state supreme court eventually found the peremptory challenge improper and reversed the conviction. *Commonwealth v. Harris*, 409 Mass. 461 (1991). For another description of a prosecutor's successful rebuttal of a prima facie case, see Johnson, "Unconscious Racism," p. 1024.

132. *J.E.B. v. Alabama ex rel. T.B.*, 114 S. Ct. 1419, 62 U. S. L.W. 4219 (1994).

133. *Holland v. Illinois*, 493 U.S. 474, 484 (1990).

134. Holland apparently relied on the Sixth Amendment, rather than the Fourteenth Amendment's equal protection clause, because he was not of the same race as the excluded prospective jurors. However, subsequent to *Holland*, the Supreme Court ruled that *Batson*'s prohibition of race-based peremptory challenges applies even in situations where the struck jury venire members are not of the same race as the defendant. *Powers v. Ohio*, 499 U.S. 400 (1991).

135. *Holland v. Illinois*, 493 U.S. at 484.

136. Ibid. at 488.

CHAPTER 4: SCIENTIFIC JURY SELECTION

1. See, for example, Robert A. Wenke, *The Art of Selecting a Jury*, 2d ed. (Springfield, Ill.: Charles C. Thomas, 1988), pp. 61–90.

2.   Hiroshi Fukurai, Edgar W. Butler, and Richard Krooth, *Race and the Jury: Racial Disenfranchisement and the Search for Justice* (New York: Plenum Press, 1993), p. 156.

3.   Thomas B. Metzloff, "Resolving Malpractice Disputes: Imaging the Jury's Shadow," *Law and Contemporary Problems* 54 (1991): 43, 119–20.

4.   Ronald Sullivan, "Kahane Trial Lawyer Ordered to Prove No Bias in Juror Choices," *New York Times*, Nov. 13, 1991, p. B2.

5.   Bill Berkeley, "Murder Trial Draws Passions of Middle East," *National Law Journal*, Dec. 30, 1991, p. 8.

6.   Sullivan, "Kahane Lawyer Ordered to Prove No Bias," p. B2.

7.   Berkeley, "Murder Trial Draws Passions," p. 8.

8.   Selwyn Raab, "Jury Selection Seen as Crucial to Verdict," *New York Times*, Dec. 23, 1991, p. B8.

9.   Laurie Goodstein, "Kahane Jurors Explain Acquittal on Main Counts; Verdict is Surprise in Extremist's Killing," *Washington Post*, Dec. 23, 1991, p. A4.

10. Numerous recent studies call into question the effectiveness of scientific jury selection. See Phoebe C. Ellsworth, "Some Steps Between Attitudes and Verdicts," in *Inside the Juror: The Psychology of Juror Decision Making*, ed. Reid Hastie (Cambridge, Mass.: Cambridge University Press, 1993), pp. 42–64; Robert MacCoun, "Decisionmaking by Civil Juries," in *Verdict: Assessing the Civil Jury System*, ed. Robert Litan (Washington, D.C.: Brookings Institution, 1993), p. 151; Solomon M. Fulero and Steven D. Penrod, "The Myths and Realities of Attorney Jury Selection Folklore and Scientific Jury Selection: What Works?," *Ohio Northern University Law Review* 17 (1990): 229–53; Shari Seidman Diamond, "Scientific Jury Selection: What Social Scientists Know and Do Not Know," *Judicature* 73 (1989): 178–83; Saul M. Kassin and Lawrence S. Wrightsman, *The American Jury on Trial: Psychological Perspectives* (New York: Hemispheres Publishing, 1988), pp. 60–62; Michael J. Saks, "Social Scientists Can't Rig Juries," in *In the Jury Box: Controversies in the Courtroom*, ed. Lawrence S. Wrightsman, Saul M. Kassin, and Cynthia E. Willis (Beverly Hills, Calif.: Sage Publications, 1987), pp. 48–62; Michael J. Saks, "Book Review: Blaming the Jury," *Georgetown Law Journal* 75 (1986): 693, 710–11; Valerie P. Hans and Neil Vidmar, *Judging the Jury* (New York: Plenum Press, 1986), pp. 89–93; Reid Hastie, Steven Penrod, and Nancy Pennington, *Inside the Jury* (Cambridge, Mass.: Harvard University Press, 1983), pp. 124ff; John Baldwin and Michael McConville, "Does the Composition of an English Jury Affect its Verdict," *Judicature* 64 (1980): 132, 137–39; John Baldwin and Michael McConville, *Jury Trials* (Oxford: Clarendon Press, 1979), pp. 88–105.

11. C. W. Heyl, "Selection of the Jury," *Illinois Bar Journal* 40 (1952): 328–41; J. A. Appleman, *Successful Jury Trials: A Symposium* (Indianapolis: Bobbs-Merrill, 1952), quoted in Hastie et al., *Inside the Jury*, p. 122.

12. S. W. McCart, *Trial by Jury* (New York: Chilton Press, 1964), quoted in

Cookie Stephan, "Selective Characteristics of Jurors and Litigants: Their Influences on Juries' Verdicts," in *The Jury System in America*, ed. Rita Simon (Beverly Hills, Calif.: Sage Publications, 1975), p. 98.

13. Appleman, *Successful Jury Trials*, p. 122; M. J. Bloomstein, *Verdict: The Jury System* (New York: Dodd, Mead Co., 1968), p. 71, quoted in Edmond Costantini, Michael Mallery, and Diane M. Yapundich, "Gender and Juror Impartiality: Are Women More Likely to Prejudge Guilt?" *Judicature* 67 (1983): 125, n. 9.

14. L. S. Katz, "The Twelve Man Jury," *Trial* (Dec./Jan. 1968–69), pp. 39–40, 42, quoted in Hastie et al., *Inside the Jury*, p. 122.

15. Bloomstein, *Verdict*, p. 98.

16. F. Lee Bailey and H. Rothblatt, *Fundamentals of Criminal Advocacy*, quoted in Jeffrey T. Frederick, *The Psychology of the American Jury* (Charlottesville, Va.: Michie Co., 1987), p. 44.

17. Clarence Darrow, "Attorney for the Defense," *Esquire* (May 1936), quoted in Hastie et al., *Inside the Jury*, pp. 122–23.

18. I. Goldstein, *Trial Technique* (Chicago: Callaghan Publishing, 1935), quoted in Hastie et al., *Inside the Jury*, p. 122.

19. Murray Sams, Jr., "Persuasion in the Voir Dire: The Plaintiff's Approach," quoted in Frederick, *Psychology of American Jury*, p. 4.

20. Melvin Belli, *Modern Trials*, abridged ed. (Indianapolis, Ind.: Bobbs-Merrill, 1963), pp. 310–11.

21. Russ Herman, "Juror Selection in Civil Litigation," *Trial* 25 (January 1989): 71, 75. See also Wenke, *Art of Selecting a Jury*, pp. 75–76.

22. Wenke, *Art of Selecting a Jury*, p. 77. See also Dale W. Broeder, "The University of Chicago Jury Project," *Nebraska Law Review* 38 (1959): 744, 748; Stephan, "Selective Characteristics of Jurors and Litigants," p. 113.

23. *Ex Parte Clarence Lee Brandley*, 781 S.W. 2d 886, 926 (1989). This practice is now prohibited by *Batson v. Kentucky*, 476 U.S. 79 (1986).

24. Wenke, *Art of Selecting a Jury*, p. 78.

25. *United States v. Ahmad*, 347 F. Supp. 912 (M.D. Pa. 1972), *modified sub. nom. United States v. Berrigan*, 482 F. 2d 171 (3rd Cir. 1973). See Jay Schulman, Phillip Shaver, Robert Colman, Barbara Emrich, and Richard Christie, "Recipe for a Jury," in Wrightsman et al., *In the Jury Box*, pp. 13–47.

26. Morton Hunt, "Putting Juries on the Couch," *New York Times*, Nov. 28, 1992, sec. 6, pp. 70, 78, 82.

27. Ibid.; *United States v. Anderson*, 356 F. Supp. 1311 (D.N.J. 1973) (Camden 28); *United States v. Briggs*, 366 F. Supp. 1356 (M.D. Fla. 1973) (Gainesville Eight); Hans and Vidmar, *Judging the Jury*, pp. 81–83 (jury selection in Gainesville Eight); *Davis v. Lindsay*, 321 F. Supp. 1134 (S.D.N.Y. 1972); Fukurai et al., *Race and the Jury*, p. 158 (Angela Davis); John B. McConahay, Courtney J. Mullin, and Jeffrey T. Frederick, "The Uses of Social Science in Trials with Political and Racial Overtones: The Trial of Joan Little," *Law and Contemporary Problems* 41 (1977): 205–29;

Steven Brill, "Inside the Jury Room," in *Trial by Jury*, ed. Steven Brill (New York: American Lawyer/Touchstone, 1989), pp. 201–65; Jay Mathews, "New Courtroom Consultants; DeLorean Jury Selected with Expert Help," *Washington Post*, Aug. 17, 1984, p. A1.

28. *United States v. Mitchell*, 372 F. Supp. 1239 (S.D. N.Y. 1973); Hans Zeisel and Shari Seidman Diamond, "The Jury Selection in the Mitchell-Stans Conspiracy Trial," *American Bar Foundation Research Journal* (1976): 151–74.

29. Tamar Lewin, "Business and the Law: Jury Research, Ethics Argued," *New York Times*, March 9, 1982, p. D2 (IBM); Hunt, "Putting Juries on the Couch," pp. 70–72 (MCI); Hans and Vidmar, *Judging the Jury*, p. 88 (General Motors); Stephen J. Adler, "Consultants Dope Out the Mysteries of Jurors for Clients Being Sued," *Wall Street Journal*, Oct. 24, 1989, pp. A1, 10 (Penzoil, National Football League, IBM).

30. Hunt, "Putting Juries on the Couch," pp. 70–72; Adler, "Consultants Dope Out Mysteries," pp. A1, 10; Wade Lambert, "Jury Consultants Lose Mystique as Firms Tighten Belts," *Wall Street Journal*, Feb. 4, 1994, p. B1.

31. Cathy E. Bennett and Robert B. Hirschhorn, "Voir Dire in Criminal Cases," *Trial* (October 1992), pp. 68–78.

32. Philipp M. Gollner, "Consulting by Peering into Minds of Jurors," *New York Times*, Jan. 7, 1994, p. A23.

33. Ibid.

34. Hunt, "Putting Juries on the Couch," p. 72; Adler, "Consultants Dope Out Mysteries," p. A1.

35. Adler, "Consultants Dope Out Mysteries," p. A1.

36. Ibid.

37. Ibid.

38. Lewin, "Business and the Law," p. D2.

39. Amitai Etzioni, "Science: Threatening the Jury Trial," *Washington Post*, May 26, 1974, p. C3.

40. Ibid.

41. Hans and Vidmar, *Judging the Jury*, p. 84.

42. Ibid., p. 83; Lewin, "Business and the Law," p. D2; Hunt, "Putting Juries on the Couch," p. 86.

43. John H. Kennedy, "Pretrial Studying of Jurors Becomes a Key to the Case," *Boston Globe*, Feb. 19, 1990, Metro sec., p. 1.

44. David Margolick, "At the Bar: For a Pioneer in Jury Selection, a Case for New Inspiration," *New York Times*, Nov. 22, 1991, p. A2.

45. Bennett and Hirschhorn, "Voir Dire in Criminal Cases," p. 68.

46. Ibid., pp. 70, 76–77.

47. Ibid., p. 75.

48. See Walter F. Abbott, *Surrogate Juries* (Philadelphia, Pa.: American Law Institute–American Bar Association Committee on Continuing Professional Education, 1990).

298

NOTES TO PAGES 152–73

49. Adler, "Consultants Dope Out Mysteries," p. A10; Lewin, "Business and the Law," p. D2.
50. Hans and Vidmar, *Judging the Jury*, p. 80.
51. Adler, "Consultants Dope Out Mysteries," p. A1; Kennedy, "Pretrial Studying of Jurors," p. 1.
52. Adler, "Consultants Dope Out Mysteries," p. A10.
53. Ibid.
54. Ibid.
55. Ibid.
56. Hunt, "Putting Juries on the Couch," p. 85, quoting an interview with Donald Vinson in the magazine *Litigation*.
57. Adler, "Consultants Dope Out Mysteries," p. A10.
58. Hunt, "Putting Juries on the Couch," p. 70.
59. Fed. R. Crim. P. 24 (b) provides that if the offense charged is punishable by greater than one year in prison, then the normal allotment of peremptory challenges is ten for the defense and six for the government. If the offense is punishable by death, then each side gets twenty peremptories. If the offense is punishable by fine or a prison term of not more than one year, then each side is entitled to three challenges. In case of multiple defendants, the judge has discretion to enlarge the numbers.
60. The most important article, published days after the verdict and on the basis of interviews with some jurors, was Martin Arnold, "How Mitchell-Stans Jury Reached Acquittal Verdict," *New York Times*, May 5, 1974, p. A1.
61. Zeisel and Diamond, "Jury Selection in Mitchell-Stans Trial," p. 167.
62. Kalven and Zeisel, *The American Jury*, p. 488.
63. Jay Matthews, "New Courtroom Consultants: DeLorean Jury Selected with Expert Help," *Washington Post*, Aug. 18, 1984, p. A1.
64. *People v. Lee Edward Harris*, 36 Cal. 3d 36, 43–45, 679 P. 2d 433 (1984).
65. Jeff Rosen, "Jurymandering," *New Republic*, Nov. 30, 1992, pp. 15–16.
66. Fukurai, *Race and the Jury*, p. 208.
67. Timnick and McGraw, "McMartin Verdict: Not Guilty," *Los Angeles Times*, Jan. 19, 1990, p. A1.
68. Saks, "Social Scientists Can't Rig Juries," p. 52.
69. Saks, "Blaming the Jury," pp. 695–96, 711.
70. Diamond, "Scientific Jury Selection," p. 181.
71. Ellsworth, "Steps Between Attitudes and Verdicts," p. 61.
72. Kassin and Wrightsman, *American Jury on Trial*, p. 28.
73. Ellsworth, "Steps Between Attitudes and Verdicts," p. 61.
74. Baldwin and McConville, "Composition of an English Jury," p. 134.
75. Ellsworth, "Steps Between Attitudes and Verdicts," p. 42.
76. Saks, "Social Scientists Can't Rig Juries," p. 52.
77. See, for example, Nancy S. Marder, "Gender Dynamics and Jury Deliberation," *Yale Law Journal* 96 (1987): 593, 597–601.
78. David Margolick, "Lorena Bobbitt Acquitted in Mutilation of Husband,"

New York Times, Jan. 22, 1994, p. A1.

79. See Baldwin and McConville, *Jury Trials,* pp. 88–105 (gender composition does not influence jury verdicts in England); Rita Simon, *The Jury and the Defense of Insanity* (Boston: Little, Brown, 1967), p. 109 (differences between working women and housewives); A. P. Sealy and W. R. Cornish, "Jurors and Their Verdicts," *Modern Law Review* 36 (1973): 496–508 (no difference in two theft cases and one rape case; some association between sex and verdict in one simulated rape case); Mills and Bohannon, "Juror Characteristics," pp. 22, 30 (no difference in murder and one rape case; women more likely to convict in robbery case); Hastie et al., *Inside the Jury,* p. 141 (little gender influence on verdicts outside rape); Peter J. Nelligan, "The Effects of the Gender of Jurors on Sexual Assault Verdicts," *SSR* 72 (1988): 249–51 (number of males and females on rape-case juries in one district in Hawaii from 1955 to 1977 did not correlate with propensity to acquit or convict of rape).

80. Hastie et al., *Inside the Jury,* p. 141; see also Michael G. Rumsey and Judith M. Rumsey, "A Case of Rape: Sentencing Judgments of Males and Females," *Psychological Reports* 41 (1977): 459–65 (trend for female undergraduates to express greater certainty of guilt than males); Ronald E. Smith, John P. Keating, Reid K. Hestner, and Herman E. Mitchell, "Role and Justice Considerations in the Attribution of Responsibility to a Rape Victim," *Journal of Research in Personality* 10 (1976): 346–57 (men more likely to think certain kinds of women encouraged the rape).

81. Gary D. Lafree, Barbara F. Reskin, and Christy A. Visher, "Jurors' Responses to Victims' Behavior and Legal Issues in Sexual Assault Trials," *Social Problems* 32 (1985): 389–407 (personal characteristics of jurors do not affect decisions; juror judgments on rape vary according to the legal issues disputed); Hubert S. Feild and Leigh B. Bienen, *Jurors and Rape* (Lexington, Mass.: Lexington Books, 1980), chap. 4 generally, pp. 95–150 (racial bias a factor in rape verdicts); Hubert S. Feild, "Juror Background Characteristics and Attitudes Toward Rape," *Law and Human Behavior* 2 (1978): 73, 82–84 (statistically significant correlation between sex and attitudes toward rape, but "relatively low"; sex of juror showed no correlation with sentencing of defendant by mock jurors; individual attitudes toward rape more important than juror's background in explaining response to rape cases); Nelligan, "Effects of Gender of Jurors," pp. 249–51.

82. Charlan Nemeth, Jeffrey Endicott, and Joel Wachtler, "From the '50s to the '70s: Women in Jury Deliberations," *Sociometry* 39 (1976): 293–304 (no significant difference in verdicts given by male and female jurors); Mills and Bohannon, "Juror Characteristics," p. 30 (no difference in murder case); Sealy and Cornish, "Jurors and Their Verdicts," pp. 496–508 (no difference in theft case); Simon, *Jury and Defense of Insanity,* (no consistent gender influence). Some studies do conclude that women jurors are more likely than their male counterparts to prejudge a defendant's guilt. See, for example, Costantini et al., "Gender and Juror Partiality," pp. 120–33.

83. Mills and Bohannon, "Juror Characteristics," p. 31.

84. Ibid., p. 27.

85. Ellsworth, "Steps Between Attitudes and Verdicts," p. 61.

86. Robert Blauner, *Racial Oppression in America* (New York: Harper and Row, 1972), p. 247.

87. Hunt, "Putting Juries on the Couch," p. 70.

88. *Batson v. Kentucky*, 476 U.S. 79 (1986); *J.E.B. v. Alabama ex rel. T.B.*, 114 S. Ct. 1419 (1994).

89. Marianne Constable, "What Books About Juries Reveal About Social Science and Law," *Law and Social Inquiry* 16 (1992): 366.

90. Ibid.

91. Ibid., pp. 367, 365.

CHAPTER 5: THE UNANIMOUS VERDICT

1. Anonymous Case, 41 *Lib. Assisarum* 11 (1367). See also Philip B. Kurland and Gerhard Casper, *Landmark Briefs and Arguments of the Supreme Court of the United States* 71 (1972): 827, 862.

2. Frederick Pollock and Frederic W. Maitland, *History of English Law* (Cambridge, Mass.: Cambridge University Press, 1959), 2:626.

3. Majority verdicts were permitted in the Carolinas, Connecticut, and Pennsylvania in the seventeenth century. *Apodaca v. Oregon*, 406 U.S. 404, 408, n. 3. (1972). See also Francis H. Heller, *The Sixth Amendment* (Lawrence, Kans.: University of Kansas Press, 1951), pp. 16–18.

4. *Johnson v. Louisiana*, 406 U.S. 356, 369 (opinion of Powell, J.) (1972).

5. *Thompson v. Utah*, 170 U.S. 343, 353 (1898). For other cases treating unanimity as essential in federal criminal jury trials, see *Andres v. United States*, 333 U.S. 740, 748–49 (1948); *Patton v. United States*, 281 U.S. 276, 288–90 (1930); *Hawaii v. Mankichi*, 190 U.S. 197, 211–12 (1903); *Maxwell v. Dow*, 176 U.S. 581, 586 (1900).

6. *American Publishing Co. v. Fisher*, 166 U.S. 464, 467–68 (1897).

7. *Criminal Justice Act of 1967*, chap. 80, sec. 13(1), quoted in Jon M. Van Dyke, *Jury Selection Procedures: Our Uncertain Commitment to Representative Panels* (Cambridge, Mass.: Ballinger Publishing, 1977), p. 206, n. 65.

8. *Johnson v. Louisiana*, 406 U.S. 356; *Apodaca v. Oregon*, 406 U.S. 404. The requirement that federal jury verdicts must be unanimous is codified at Fed. R. Crim. Proc. 31(a).

9. *Apodaca v. Oregon*, 406 U.S. at 410.

10. *Johnson v. Louisiana*, 406 U.S. at 359–63.

11. *Apodaca v. Oregon*, 406 U.S. at 412–14.

12. *Williams v. Florida*, 399 U.S. 78 (1970) (six-person jury permissible in state criminal jury trials); *Colgrove v. Battin*, 413 U.S. 149 (1973) (six-person jury permissible in federal civil jury trials).

13. *Ballew v. Georgia*, 435 U.S. 223 (1978). For federal civil jury trials, the

rules now provide that the minimum number is six. Fed. R. Civ. Proc. 48.

14. *Burch v. Louisiana*, 441 U.S. 130 (1979).

15. National Center for State Courts, *State Court Organization*, preliminary draft (Williamsburg, Va.: National Center for State Courts, forthcoming), table 7.

16. *Proffit v. Florida*, 428 U.S. 242, 249 (1976).

17. See, for example, *Copeland v. State*, 241 Ga. 370, 245 S.E. 2d 642 (1978); *State v. Ruppert*, 54 Ohio St. 2d 263, 375 N.E. 3d 1250 (dictum), *cert. den.*, 439 U.S. 954 (1978); *Ashton v. Commonwealth*, 405 S.W. 2d 562 (Kentucky, 1965) (in misdemeanor trials), *rev'd on other grounds*, 384 U.S. 195 (1968). Federal courts consider the unanimous verdict to be too important to be waived in nonpetty criminal jury trials. *United States v. Morris*, 612 F. 2d 483 (10th Cir. 1979); *United States v. Gipson*, 553 F. 2d 453 (5th Cir. 1977). See also Elizabeth F. Loftus and Edith Greene, "Twelve Angry People: The Collective Mind of the Jury," *Columbia Law Review* 84 (1984): 1427–28.

18. J. Roland Pennock, "Majority Rule," in *International Encyclopedia of the Social Sciences*, (New York: Macmillan, 1968), 9:536.

19. *Apodaca v. Oregon*, 406 U.S. at 407, n. 2.

20. M. V. Clarke, *Medieval Representation and Consent: A Study of Early Parliaments in England and Ireland* (New York: Russell and Russell, 1964), p. 251.

21. *Apodaca v. Oregon*, 406 U.S. at 407, n. 2.

22. Ibid.

23. Aristotle, *Politics*, bk. 3, sec. 1281, ed. Benjamin Jowett (London: Oxford University Press, 1921).

24. Willmoore Kendall, *John Locke and the Doctrine of Majority-Rule* (Urbana, Ill.: University of Illinois Press, 1959), pp. 109–10.

25. John Calhoun, *A Disquisition on Government* (Indianapolis, Ind.: Bobbs-Merrill, 1979), pp. 23–25.

26. Ibid., pp. 27–31.

27. Ibid., p. 51.

28. John Locke, "The Second Treatise on Government," in *Two Treatises of Government*, ed. Peter Laslett (New York: Mentor Books, 1965), chap. 8, para. 96, pp. 375–76.

29. Kendall, *John Locke*, pp. 120ff; Pennock, "Majority Rule," p. 536.

30. Lani Guinier, "The Triumph of Tokenism: The Voting Rights Act and the Theory of Black Electoral Success," *Michigan Law Review* 89 (1991): 1077, 1112, 1116. After President Clinton nominated Guinier to head the civil rights division of the Justice Department, critics labeled her a "quota queen" and other derogatory terms for her views in this article on how to enhance the legislative process so as to give effective voice to minority and marginalized groups. Among other things, Guinier proposed a theory of "proportionate interest representation," where "the harshness of majority rule" would be softened by permitting candidates who were getting a specified minority of votes to still be elected. Ibid., pp. 1138ff.

31. *Apodaca v. Oregon*, 406 U.S. at 412–14. In 1934, Oregon voters amended their state constitution to permit 10–2 split verdicts in all criminal cases except first-degree murder cases. Kurland and Casper, *Landmark Briefs* 71: 571–77.

32. *Duncan v. Louisiana*, 391 U.S. 145 (1968), made the right to jury trial in criminal cases specified in the Sixth Amendment applicable to the states through the due process clause of the Fourteenth Amendment.

33. *Johnson v. Louisiana*, 406 U.S. at 359–63; *Apodaca v. Oregon*, 406 U.S. at 411–12. Since 1898, the Louisiana Constitution has permitted criminal juries to return nonunanimous verdicts in all noncapital cases. The Louisiana Code of Criminal Procedure requires twelve jurors to be unanimous in capital cases; ten of twelve to agree on a verdict in cases where conviction necessarily results in confinement at hard labor; and unanimous agreement of six jurors in cases where a convicted defendant may be confined to hard labor. Louisiana Code Crim. Proc., art. 782 (1992).

34. *Apodaca v. Oregon*, 406 U.S. at 409–10.

35. Ibid. at 410–11.

36. Ibid. at 410.

37. Ibid. at 411.

38. Kurland and Casper, *Landmark Briefs* 71: 872.

39. For example, *Smith v. Texas*, 311 U.S. 128 (1940) and other cases cited in *Apodaca v. Oregon*, 406 U.S. at 412.

40. In 1968, Congress legislated the requirement that federal jury pools be composed to represent a cross-section of the community. "The Jury Selection and Service Act," 28 U.S.C., secs. 1861 et seq.

41. Kurland and Casper, *Landmark Briefs* 71: 872.

42. Ibid., p. 935.

43. *Johnson v. Louisiana*, 406 U.S. at 398 (Stewart, J., dissenting).

44. Ibid.

45. *Johnson v. Louisiana*, 406 U.S. at 389 (Douglas, J., dissenting).

46. *Apodaca v. Oregon*, 406 U.S. at 413–14.

47. *In re Winship*, 397 U.S. 358, 363–64 (1970).

48. *Johnson v. Louisiana*, 406 U.S. at 363.

49. Ibid. at 361.

50. *Allen v. United States*, 164 U.S. 492, 501 (1896), partly quoted in *Johnson v. Louisiana*, 406 U.S. at 361–62.

51. *Johnson v. Louisiana*, 406 U.S. at 377 (opinion of Powell, J.).

52. I have profited immensely, in puzzling over unanimity's contribution to the legitimacy of jury verdicts, from Gary C. Jacobsohn, "The Unanimous Verdict: Politics and the Jury Trial," *Washington Law Quarterly* 39 (1977): 39, 48–57.

53. Ibid.

54. *Johnson v. Louisiana*, 406 U.S. at 369–78.

55. Ibid., at 399–403 (Marshall, J., dissenting).

56. Ibid., at 388–89 (Douglas, J., dissenting).

57. Ibid., at 396 (Brennan, J., dissenting).

58. Hans Zeisel, ". . . And Then There Were None: The Diminution of the Federal Jury," *University of Chicago Law Review* 38 (1971): 711, 722.

59. *Johnson v. Louisiana*, 406 U.S. at 374, n. 12 (opinion of Powell, J.)

60. Harry Kalven, Jr., and Hans Zeisel, *The American Jury* (Chicago: University of Chicago Press, 1970), pp. xv, 487, n. 12.

61. "Inside the Jury Room," "Frontline," April 11, 1986.

62. Kalven and Zeisel, *The American Jury*, p. 488 (emphasis omitted).

63. Ibid.

64. Ibid., pp. 460–61.

65. Van Dyke, *Jury Selection Procedures*, p. 209.

66. Kalven and Zeisel, *The American Jury*, p. 460.

67. Jeffrey T. Frederick, *The Psychology of the American Jury* (Charlottesville, Va.: Michie Co., 1987), p. 283; Michael J. Saks, *Jury Verdicts: The Role of Group Size and Social Decision Rule* (Lexington, Mass.: Lexington Books, 1977), pp. 95–98; Charlan Nemeth, "Interactions Between Jurors as a Function of Majority vs. Unanimity Decision Rules," in *In the Jury Box: Controversies in the Courtroom*, ed. Lawrence S. Wrightsman, Saul M. Kassin, and Cynthia E. Willis (Beverly Hills, Calif.: Sage Publications, 1987), pp. 241, 246, 250, 253.

68. Reid Hastie, Steven D. Penrod, and Nancy Pennington, *Inside the Jury* (Cambridge, Mass.: Harvard University Press, 1983), p. 60.; Saks, *Jury Verdicts*, p. 99; Nemeth, "Interactions Between Jurors," p. 241.

69. Nemeth, "Interactions Between Jurors," p. 250; Hastie et al., *Inside the Jury*, pp. 76, 90, 94–98; Guinier, "Triumph of Tokenism," p. 1122.

70. Hastie et al., *Inside the Jury*, pp. 94–98.

71. Saks, *Jury Verdicts*, p. 94.

72. Kalven and Zeisel, *The American Jury*, p. 460.

73. "The Supreme Court, 1971 Term," *Harvard Law Review* 86 (1972): 1, 153; Van Dyke, *Jury Selection Procedures*, p. 211.

74. Hastie et al., *Inside the Jury*, p. 60.

75. Ibid., pp. 88, 90.

76. Ibid., pp. 76–78; Nemeth, "Interactions Between Jurors," p. 244; Saks, *Jury Verdicts*, p. 95; John Guinther, *The Jury in America* (New York: Facts on File Publications, 1988), p. 83.

77. Hastie et al., *Inside the Jury*, p. 112.

78. Guinther, *Jury in America*, p. 81.

79. Ibid., p. 83.

80. Van Dyke, *Jury Selection Procedures*, p. 209.

81. For instance, under unanimous verdict rules, federal criminal juries convicted 82 percent of defendants in 1990. Bureau of Justice Statistics, U.S. Department of Justice, *Compendium of Federal Justice Statistics, 1990*, p. 31.

82. See n. 67.

83. Van Dyke, *Jury Selection Procedures*, p. 209.

84. Ibid.

85. Zeisel, ". . . And Then There Were None," p. 719, n. 42.

86. Kalven and Zeisel, *The American Jury*, p. 462.

87. Ibid.

88. *Johnson v. Louisiana*, 406 U.S. at 392–94 (Douglas, J., dissenting).

89. Ibid. at 393.

90. See Jacobsohn, "The Unanimous Verdict," pp. 48–57.

91. *Johnson v. Louisiana*, 406 U.S. at 397–99 (Stewart, J., dissenting).

92. Jacobsohn, "The Unanimous Verdict," p. 50.

93. *Johnson v. Louisiana*, 406 U.S. at 377 (opinion of Powell, J.).

94. Herman G. James, *The Constitutional System of Brazil* (Washington, D.C.: Carnegie Institution of Washington, 1923), p. 122.

CHAPTER 6: RACE AND THE DEATH PENALTY

1. "The Jury Selection and Service Act," 28 U.S.C. 1861 et seq.; *Taylor v. Louisiana*, 419 U.S. 522 (1975); *Batson v. Kentucky*, 476 U.S. 79 (1986); *J.E.B. v. Alabama ex. rel. T.B.*, 114 S.Ct. 1419, 62 U.S. L.W. 4219 (1994).

2. James Levine, *Juries and Politics* (Pacific Grove, Calif.: Brooks/Cole, 1992), p. 110–11.

3. Harry Kalven, Jr., and Hans Zeisel, *The American Jury* (Chicago: University of Chicago Press, 1970), pp. 249–57.

4. By force of the Civil Rights Act of 1957, Congress for the first time qualified women for federal jury service, irrespective of whether women were eligible for jury service in the state in which the federal court sat. Jury scholar Jon Van Dyke undertook a survey of women on federal court juries during the early 1970s. His work showed that women were still underrepresented on juries, but in comparison with a generation earlier the numbers were up. Jon Van Dyke, *Jury Selection Procedures: Our Uncertain Commitment to Representative Panels* ((Cambridge, Mass.: Ballinger, 1977), pp. 350–71.

5. General Accounting Office, *Death Penalty Sentencing: Research Indicates Pattern of Racial Disparities* (Washington, D.C.: Government Printing Office, 1990). The most complete empirical study of the death penalty documenting racial disparities is of Georgia in the mid- to late 1970s. See David C. Baldus, George Woodworth, and Charles A. Pulaski, Jr., *Equal Justice and the Death Penalty: A Legal and Empirical Analysis* (Boston: Northeastern University Press, 1990), pp. 42–46, 140–97, 306–69. Studies in other states have confirmed or anticipated the basic finding in the Baldus study that white-victim murders are more likely than black-victim murders to result in death sentences. See Samuel R. Gross and Robert Mauro, "Patterns of Death: An Analysis of Racial Disparities in Capital Sentencing and Homicide Victimization," *Stanford Law Review* 37 (1984): 27, 55, 63, 93–98, 105 (Arkansas, Florida, Georgia, Illinois, Mississippi, North Carolina, Oklahoma, and Virginia); William Bowers and Glenn L. Pierce, "Arbitrariness

and Discrimination under Post-Furman Capital Statutes," *Crime & Delinquency* 26 (1980): 563–635 (Florida, Georgia, Ohio, and Texas).

6. Gross and Mauro, "Patterns of Death," p. 55, quoting a 1981 FBI study of the lifetime risk of death by homicide, controlled for race and sex. This study found that one nonwhite baby male out of every twenty-eight born in the United States is likely to be a victim of homicide.

7. See Baldus et al., *Equal Justice*, pp. 164, 327–28, 403; Gregory D. Russell, *The Death Penalty and Racial Bias: Overturning Supreme Court Assumptions* (Westport, Conn.: Greenwood Press, 1994), p. 82; Michael L. Radelet and Glenn L. Pierce, "Race and Prosecutorial Discretion in Homicide Cases," *Law and Society Review* 19 (1985): 587–621.

8. Baldus et al, *Equal Justice*, pp. 168–69, 327–28, 403.

9. Ibid., pp. 161–62, 185, 327, 401.

10. Ibid., pp. 162, 164, 327, 357.

11. *Lockhart v. McCree*, 476 U.S. 162 (1986); *Wainwright v. Witt*, 469 U.S. 412 (1985); *Witherspoon v. Illinois*, 391 U.S. 510 (1968).

12. Russell, *Death Penalty and Racial Bias*, pp. 86–87; Michael Finch and Mark Ferraro, "The Empirical Challenge to Death-Qualified Juries: On Further Examination," *Nebraska Law Review* 65 (1986): 21, 44–50; Robert Fitzgerald and Phoebe C. Ellsworth, "Due Process v. Crime Control," *Law and Human Behavior* 8 (1984): 31, 46; Claudia L. Cowan, William C. Thompson, and Phoebe C. Ellsworth, "The Effects of Death Qualification on Jurors' Predisposition to Convict and on the Quality of Deliberation," *Law and Human Behavior* 8 (1984): 53, 67 (excluded jurors are more likely to be women). See also Denise-Marie Santiago and Richard Burke, "Life Term in Killing of Officer," *Philadelphia Inquirer*, April 12, 1991, p. A1 (lone female stands against death penalty for slayer of police officer).

13. See *Lockhart v. McCree*, 476 U.S. at 168–73 (citing but rejecting studies purporting to show death-qualified juries are unconstitutionally conviction-prone).

14. Gross and Mauro, "Patterns of Death," pp. 109–10.

15. *Booth v. Maryland*, 482 U.S. 496 (1987); *South Carolina v. Gathers*, 490 U.S. 805 (1989).

16. *Payne v. Tennessee*, 111 S. Ct. 2597 (1991).

17. NAACP Legal Defense Fund, *Death Row, U.S.A.* (Fall 1993): 1, 4.

18. *Spaziano v. Florida*, 468 U.S. 447, 460–65 (1984).

19. Ibid. at 470 (Stevens, J., dissenting).

20. *Witherspoon v. Illinois*, 391 U.S. at 519, n. 5.

21. *Gregg v. Georgia*, 428 U.S. 153, 190 (1976).

22. *McCleskey v. Kemp*, 481 U.S. 279, 300 (1987).

23. For 1991, see Bureau of Justice Statistics, U.S. Department of Justice, *Sourcebook of Criminal Justice Statistics— 1992* (Washington, D.C.: Government Printing Office, 1992), p. 205 (Tables 2.53, 2.54). For 1989, see *The Gallup Report* (Princeton, N.J.: The Gallup Poll, January 1989), pp.

27–28. Polling on the death penalty shows all the weaknesses of polling in general. When the question was phrased "Are you in favor of the death penalty for persons convicted of murder?" the response was 76 percent in favor in 1991. But when the question was "What do you think should be the penalty for murder—the death penalty or life imprisonment with absolutely no possibility of parole?" the number favoring the death penalty dropped to 53 percent. *Sourcebook*, p. 205 (Table 2.53). The latter question may be closer to the one jurors have to answer.

24. Baldus et al., *Equal Justice*, p. 130.

25. *Wainwright v. Witt*, 469 U.S. 412; *Witherspoon v. Illinois*, 391 U.S. 510.

26. *Spaziano v. Florida*, 468 U.S. at 468–69 (opinion of Stevens, J.).

27. Ibid. at 481.

28. Patrick E. Higginbotham, "Juries and the Death Penalty," *Case Western Reserve Law Review* 41 (1991): 1047, 1048–49.

29. Ibid., pp. 1048–49, 1056.

30. Michael Mello, "Article: The Jurisdiction to Do Justice: Florida's Jury Override and the State Constitution," *Florida State Law Review* 18 (1991): 924, 925–26.

31. Radelet and Mello, "Death-to-Life Overrides," p. 196.

32. Mello, "Jurisdiction to Do Justice," p. 926.

33. Ibid.; Radelet and Mello, "Death-to-Life Overrides," p. 196; NAACP Legal Defense Fund, *Death Row, U.S.A.*, pp. 17–20 (Florida).

34. Of the 2,785 death row inmates in October 1993, 50.20 percent (1,398) were white, 39.57 percent (1,102) were black, 7.32 percent (204) were Hispanic, 1.76 percent (49) were Native American, 0.68 percent (19) were Asian, and 0.47 percent (13) were of unknown background. NAACP Legal Defense Fund, *Death Row, U.S.A.*, p. 1.

35. Ibid., p. 4.

36. See the fourth section of this chapter for the data regarding racial disparities and the death penalty.

37. *McCleskey v. Kemp*, 481 U.S. at 286, relying on the Baldus study cited in appellant's brief. See also Baldus et al., *Equal Justice*, p. 315. Much of the explanation for the apparent advantage of being a black defendant in death-eligible murders is rooted in the race-of-victim bias that keeps prosecutors from seeking, or juries from imposing, the death penalty in cases involving black defendants and black victims. Once this is understood, the apparent anomaly of the conclusions regarding race and defendant disappears.

38. Baldus et al., *Equal Justice*, p. 235. On the basis of more recent research, Professor Baldus still finds 6–15 percent to be a good estimate of the yearly death sentencing rate. Estimates of the death-sentencing rate depend on how one defines the pool of "death-eligible" cases. The authors of the study quoted in the text included in the category of death-eligible offenders not only those convicted of capital murder but also "defendants whom juries could have found to be death-eligible, based on the applicable statute, but

who were actually convicted of a lesser offense than capital murder." Ibid.; telephone conversation with author, March 23, 1994.

In their monumental study of Georgia death sentencing during the 1970s, Professor Baldus and his coauthors provided two different calculations of that state's death sentencing rate. Out of 2,484 persons indicted for murder from 1973 through 1979 and convicted of murder or voluntary manslaughter, only 128 (5 percent) received the death penalty. Baldus et al., *Equal Justice*, p. 314. The low rate reflected the fact that large numbers of defendants avoided facing trial and a possible death sentence by pleading guilty. The authors therefore calculated a higher death sentencing rate by considering only how often persons *tried and convicted* of murder receive the death penalty. From March 1973 through June 1978, a total of 606 cases resulted in murder convictions following a trial; 112 of these defendants received the death penalty, resulting in a death sentencing rate of 19 percent. Moreover, only 483 of the 606 defendants convicted of murder were eligible for execution under the terms of Georgia's death penalty law. The overall death sentencing rate was therefore 23 percent (112 out of 483 cases). Baldus et al., *Equal Justice*, pp. 43–44, 89.

39. Bureau of Justice Statistics, U.S. Department of Justice, *Prisons and Prisoners in the United States* (Washington, D.C.: Government Priniting Office, 1992), p. xv; *Sourcebook of Criminal Justice Statistics* (1992), p. 672.

40. *Sourcebook of Criminal Justice Statistics* (1992), p. 527 (Table 5.49).

41. Federal Bureau of Investigation, U.S. Department of Justice, *Uniform Crime Reports* (1992), p. 13.

42. Baldus et al., *Equal Justice*, p. 233, collecting studies.

43. Ibid., pp. 106, 234.

44. Ibid., p. 233.

45. Ibid., p. 314.

46. Ibid., pp. 233–34.

47. *Furman v. Georgia*, 408 U.S. 238 (1972). Active efforts by the Legal Defense Fund and others had kept states from executing anyone since 1967. There were more than 600 prisoners waiting on death row for the Court's decision in *Furman*.

48. *McGautha v. California*, 402 U.S. 183, 189 (1971). The order in which juries were given the instructions has been inverted in the text accompanying this note.

49. Ibid. The *McGautha* decision also upheld Ohio's similar "standardless" jury discretion procedures. At the time, the *McGautha* decision was consistent with the decisions of every state court of last resort to have considered the issue, as well as decisions of every federal court of appeals that had reached the issue. See Higginbotham, "Juries and the Death Penalty," p. 1055.

50. Thomas Andrew Green, *Verdict According to Conscience: Perspectives on the English Criminal Trial Jury, 1200–1800* (Chicago: University of Chicago Press, 1985), pp. 28–64.

51. *Woodson v. North Carolina*, 428 U.S. 280, 289 (1976).

52. Ibid. at 293.

53. Ibid. at 290.

54. Ibid. at 291.

55. Ibid. at 292.

56. *McGautha v. California*, 402 U.S. at 202.

57. *Furman v. Georgia*, 408 U.S. at 313 (White, J., concurring).

58. Ibid. at 309 (Stewart, J., concurring).

59. Ibid. at 309–10.

60. Ibid. at 249ff (Douglas, J., concurring); at 364–66 (Marshall, J., concurring).

61. *Gregg v. Georgia*, 428 U.S. 153, 179, n. 23 (1976).

62. *Woodson v. North Carolina*, 428 U.S. 280; *Roberts v. Louisiana*, 428 U.S. 325 (1976).

63. *Gregg v. Georgia*, 428 U.S. 153; *Proffit v. Florida*, 428 U.S. 242 (1976); *Jurek v. Texas*, 428 U.S. 262 (1976).

64. *Woodson v. North Carolina*, 428 U.S. at 304 (striking down mandatory death sentencing for not allowing consideration of "the character and record of the individual offender").

65. *Lockett v. Ohio*, 438 U.S. 586, 604–5 (1978). The Court has also made clear that each individual juror has the right to consider any mitigating factor, whether or not the jury unanimously finds such a factor to be present. *Mills v. Maryland*, 486 U.S. 367 (1988).

66. *Zant v. Stephens*, 462 U.S. 862, 871 (1983) (in Georgia there exists "an absolute discretion in the fact finder to . . . not impose death"). States differ in their instructions to juries. California, for instance, instructs jurors that "if you conclude that the aggravating circumstances outweigh the mitigating circumstances, you *shall impose* a sentence of death." *Boyde v. California*, 494 U.S. 370, 374 (1990). The italicized language appears to make it mandatory upon the jury to impose the death penalty if aggravating circumstances outweigh mitigating circumstances. But the Supreme Court has upheld the constitutionality of California procedures. Juries still retain discretion to engage in "individualized sentencing" and to show mercy whenever they find mitigating factors outweigh the aggravating circumstances. Ibid. at 375. See also *Walton v. Arizona*, 497 U.S. 639, 651 (1990).

67. *Gregg v. Georgia*, 428 U.S. at 189.

68. See notes 62 and 63.

69. *Gregg v. Georgia*, 428 U.S. at 197.

70. Vivian Berger, "'Black Box Decisions' on Life or Death—If They're Arbitrary, Don't Blame the Jury: A Reply to Judge Patrick Higginbotham," *Case Western Reserve Law Review* 41 (1991): 1067, 1070–71.

71. *Zant v. Stephens*, 462 U.S. at 871–72, 874. See also Berger, "'Black Box Decisions,'" pp. 1073, 1076.

72. Executions per year have been as follows: 1985 (18); 1986 (18); 1987 (25); 1988 (11); 1989 (16); 1990 (23); 1991 (14) 1992 (31); 1993 (38). NAACP Legal Defense Fund, *Death Row, U.S.A.*, p. 4.

73. 481 U.S. at 279.

74. Baldus et al., *Equal Justice*, pp. 42–44. There were 594 different offenders but 606 total cases in the study because there were two penalty trials in twelve instances.

75. Ibid., p. 45.

76. Ibid., pp. 88–98.

77. Ibid., pp. 46–59.

78. Ibid., p. 49.

79. Ibid., p. 50.

80. Ibid., p. 115.

81. Ibid., p. 609.

82. Ibid., p. 115.

83. Ibid., p. 602.

84. Ibid., pp. 160–69, 327–28, 403; Russell, *Death Penalty and Racial Bias*, p. 82; Radelet and Pierce, "Race and Prosecutorial Discretion," pp. 587–621.

85. Baldus et al., *Equal Justice*, p. 115.

86. Ibid., pp. 89–90.

87. Ibid., p. 157.

88. Brief for Petitioner, *McCleskey v. Kemp*, no. 84-6811 (Sept. 3, 1986).

89. Baldus et al., *Equal Justice*, p. 150.

90. Ibid., pp. 314–15.

91. Ibid., p. 315.

92. Ibid., p. 314.

93. Ibid., p. 327–28, 361, n. 47.

94. Ibid., pp. 319–20.

95. Ibid., pp. 319, 328, 401.

96. Ibid., pp. 316, 326.

97. Ibid., pp. 317, 344, 620 (Schedule 3).

98. Ibid., p. 318.

99. Ibid., p. 328.

100. Ibid., p. 361, n. 47.

101. Ibid.

102. Brief for Petitioner, *McCleskey v. Kemp*, no. 84-6811.

103. Baldus et al., *Equal Justice*, pp. 327, 355 (linear analysis not statistically significant), 403, 644 (logistic analysis statistically significant).

104. Ibid., p. 328.

105. Ibid., pp. 150, 185.

106. Ibid., p. 162.

107. Ibid., p. 150.

108. Ibid., p. 152.

109. Ibid., pp. 151–52.

110. Ibid., p. 160.

111. Ibid., p. 155.

112. Ibid., p. 164.

113. Ibid., p. 167.

114. Ibid., pp. 167–69, 596–98.

115. The crucial data is summarized in Ibid., p. 187 (Table 44).

116. Ibid., p. 403.

117. Ibid., pp. 168–69, 186, 403.

118. Ibid., p. 184.

119. Ibid., p. 163.

120. Ibid., p. 164.

121. Ibid., p. 184.

122. Ibid., p. 185.

123. *McCleskey v. Kemp*, 481 U.S. at 291, n. 7, 312.

124. Ibid. at 312.

125. Ibid. at 296–99.

126. Ibid. at 295, n. 15.

127. Ibid. at 294.

128. Ibid. at 312.

129. Ibid. at 313.

130. Ibid.

131. Ibid. at 314–15.

132. Ibid. at 329–30 (Brennan, J., dissenting).

133. Ibid. at 332.

134. Kalven and Zeisel, *The American Jury*, p. 442.

135. Ibid., pp. 340–41.

136. Ibid., p. 341.

137. Finch and Ferraro, "Empirical Challenge," pp. 51–60; Cowan, Thompson, and Ellsworth, "Death Qualification," pp. 67ff; Fitzgerald and Ellsworth, "Due Process," pp. 41–46.

138. Finch and Ferraro, "Empirical Challenge," pp. 44–50; Fitzgerald and Ellsworth, "Due Process," pp. 31, 46; Russell, *Death Penalty and Racial Bias*, p. 86.

139. *Ex Parte Clarence Lee Brandley*, 781 S.W. 2d 886 (Tex. Crim. App. 1989), *cert. den.*, *Texas v. Brandley*, 498 U.S. 817 (1990).

140. Baldus et al., *Equal Justice*, p. 256, quoting a study of twenty-one Florida counties between 1972 and 1978.

141. Michael Mello, "Taking Caldwell v. Mississippi Seriously: The Unconstitutionality of Capital Statutes That Divide Sentencing Responsibility Between Judge and Jury," *Boston College Law Review* 30 (1989): 283, 290.

CONCLUSION

1. "Female Jurors Assert Sexism Hurt Menendez Deliberations," *New York Times*, Jan. 31, 1994, p. A13.

2. David Margolick, "Lorena Bobbitt Acquitted in Mutilation of Husband," *New York Times*, Jan. 22, 1994, p. A1.

3. Patricia Nealon, "Conviction Overturned of Priest Who Blocked Boston Abortion Clinic," *Boston Globe*, March 1, 1994, p. 19. As noted in chapter 3, a Massachusetts appeals court overturned the conviction in 1994, finding the prosecutor's use of peremptory challenges to be a violation of the defendant's right to a cross-sectional jury.

4. Selwyn Raab, "Jury Selection Seen as Crucial to Verdict," *New York Times*, Dec. 23, 1991, p. B8. See also chap. 4, notes 4–9.

5. Larry Rohter, "Miami Police Officer is Acquitted in Racially Charged Slaying Case," *New York Times*, May 29, 1993, sec. 1, p. 1; Neil Weiner, "Inner-City Riots Have Followed a Pattern of Police Abuse, " *Philadelphia Inquirer*, May 3, 1992, p. C7.

6. Larry Rohter, "Florida Trial Odyssey Ends for an Officer Charged in 2 Killings," *New York Times*, May 9, 1993, sec. 1, p. 16; Larry Rohter, "The Nation: Lozano Case Tests How Racially Balanced a Jury Must Be," *New York Times*, May 16, 1993, sec. 4, p. 3; Larry Rohter, "Mixed Jury Picked to Try Policeman," *New York Times*, May 15, 1993, p. A6; "Miami Officer's Retrial Moved Yet Again," *New York Times*, May 11, 1993, p. A18; Milo Geyelin and Martha Brannigan, "Jury Selection in Racially Charged Cases Becomes More Difficult after Rioting," *Wall Street Journal*, May 5, 1992, p. 31.

7. Rohter, "Miami Police Officer is Acquitted," p. 1.

8. Rohter, "Lozano Case," p. 3.

9. Rohter, "Mixed Jury," p. 6.

10. William Booth and Joan Biskupic, "Balancing Race and Rights in Jury Box; Sensitive Trials Pose Question: Just What is a Panel of One's Peers," *Washington Post*, May 11, 1993, p. A1.

11. Rohter, "Lozano Case," p. 3.

12. Booth and Biskupic, "Balancing Race and Rights," p. A1; Rohter, "Florida Trial Odyssey Ends," p. 16; "Miami Officer's Retrial Moved Yet Again," p. A18.

13. Rohter, "Miami Police Officer is Acquitted," p. 1.

14. Trial Court Department, *Annual Report, 1988*, p. 200. In 1993, the Philadelphia jury commissioner estimated that, as of mid-March, his office had mailed 158,000 questionnaires to prospective jurors; 71.8 percent did not respond. By contrast, the courts of Pittsburgh County mailed out approximately 75,000 questionnaires in 1992; only nine persons failed to respond.

15. Ibid., p. 200.

16. Susie M. Ames, *Studies of The Virginia Eastern Shore in the Seventeenth*

Century (New York: Russell and Russell, 1940), pp. 177–78 (1664 record that Timothy Coe "for his obstinate and perverse behavior as a Grand Jury-man" was fined 500 pounds of tobacco).

17. James P. Levine, *Juries and Politics* (Pacific Grove, Calif.: Brooks/Cole, 1992), p. 36.

18. Dale W. Broeder, "The Negro in Court," *Duke Law Journal* (1965): 26.

19. Ibid, p. 27.

EPILOGUE TO THE PAPERBACK EDITION

1. Judy Markey, "So How About Gump for the Simpson Jury?" *Chicago Sun-Times,* September 29, 1994, sec. 2, p. 32.

2. Georgia, Nebraska, and Texas are the only states that prohibit juror ques-tioning of witnesses. For examples of procedures approved in other states, see *State v. LeMaster,* 669 P. 2d 592 (Ariz. 1983) (written questions); *Scheel v. State,* 350 So. 2d 1120, 1121 (Fla. 1977) (direct questioning); *Common-wealth v. Urena,* 632 N.E. 2d 1200, 1203–4 (Mass. 1994) (written question-ing the better procedure); *State v. Howard,* 360 S.E. 2d 790 (N.C. 1987) (written questioning "better practice" but direct questioning allowed); *State v. Barrett,* 297 S.E. 2d 794 (S.C. 1982), *cert. den.,* 460 U.S. 1045 (1983) (written questions "safer practice"). For federal courts that permit juror questions, see *United States v. Sutton,* 970 F. 2d 1001, 1005 (1st Cir. 1992); *United States v. Lewin,* 900 F. 2d 145 (8th Cir. 1990). See also Brookings Institution, *Charting a Future for the Civil Jury System: Report from an American Bar Association–Brookings Symposium* (Washington, D.C.: Brookings Institution, 1992), p. 20; Arizona Supreme Court Commit-tee on More Effective Use of Juries, *Juries: The Power of 12: Report of the Arizona Supreme Court Committee on More Effective Use of Juries* (Phoenix: Arizona Supreme Court Committee on More Effective Use of Juries, 1994), pp. 90–91; Hon. B. Michael Dann, "'Learning Lessons' and 'Speaking Rights': Creating Educated and Democratic Juries," *Indiana Law Journal* 68 (1993): 1229, 1253–55; Hon. Curtis Von Kann, "Reinventing the Jury Trial," *Legal Times,* January 2, 1995, p. 21; William W. Schwarzer, "Reforming Jury Trials," 132 F.R.D. 575, 591–93 (1990); Lis Wiehl, "After 200 Years, the Silent Juror Speaks," *New York Times,* July 7, 1989, p. B5; Larry Heuer and Steven Penrod, "Increasing Jurors' Participation in Trials: A Field Experiment with Jury Notetaking and Question Asking," *Law and Human Behavior* 12 (1988): 231; Leonard B. Sand and Steven Allen Reiss, "A Report on Seven Experiments Conducted by District Court Judges in the Second Circuit," *New York University Law Review* 60 (1985): 423.

3. See, for example, *United States v. Wild,* 47 F. 3d 669 (4th Cir. 1995); *Clem-mons v. Sowders,* 34 F. 3d 352, 356 (6th Cir. 1994); *Poole v. State,* 650 So. 2d. 541 (Ala. 1994); *People v. Mayfield,* 852 P. 2d 331 (Cal. 1993); *Jackson v. State,* 641 So. 2d. 1369, 1370 (Fla. 1994); *Commonwealth v. Urena,* 632

N.E. 2d 1200, 1203–4 (Mass. 1994); *State of Ohio v. Sweet*, 1993 Ohio App. Lexis 492 (Ohio 1993). See also *Civil Jury System*, pp. 18–19; Arizona Supreme Court Committee, *Juries*, pp. 83–85; Dann, "Learning Lessons," pp. 1251–52; Schwarzer, "Reforming Jury Trials," 132 F.R.D. at 591; John Guinther, *The Jury in America* (New York: Facts on File, 1988), pp. 68–69; Sand and Reiss, "A Report on Seven Experiments," pp. 448–49.

4. Saul M. Kassin and Lawrence S. Wrightsman, *The American Jury on Trial: Psychological Perspectives* (New York: Hemispheres Publishing, 1988), pp. 128–29.

5. *Clemmons v. Sowders*, 34 F. 3d at 357.

6. See *United States v. Wild*, 47 F. 3d 669 (1995).

7. Arizona Supreme Court Committee, *Juries*, pp. 96–99; Dann, "Learning Lessons," pp. 1262–68; Von Kann, "Reinventing the Jury Trial," p. 21; Schwarzer, "Reforming Jury Trials," pp. 593–95.

8. Elizabeth F. Loftus and Douglas Leber, "Do Jurors Talk?" *Trial* (January 1986): 59–60 (finding 11 percent of jurors disobeyed instruction not to talk about evidence); Thomas L. Grisham and Stephen F. Lawless, "Note: Jurors Judge Justice: A Survey of Criminal Jurors," *New Mexico Law Review* 3 (1973): 352, 358 (44 percent of surveyed jurors talked about evidence during trial).

9. *Civil Jury System*, pp. 23–24; Arizona Supreme Court Committee, *Juries*, pp. 80–83; Dann, "Learning Lessons," pp. 1249–50; Schwarzer, "Reforming Jury Trials," 132 F.R.D. at 583–85; Special Committee on Jury Comprehension of the American Bar Association Litigation Section, *Jury Comprehension in Complex Cases* (Chicago: American Bar Association, 1989), pp. 49–52; Valerie Hans and Neil Vidmar, *Judging the Jury* (New York: Plenum Press, 1986), pp. 122–23.

10. Von Kann, "Reinventing the Jury Trial," p. 21; Dann, "Learning Lessons," p. 1256; Schwarzer, "Reforming Jury Trials," 132 F.R.D. at 582; Hans and Vidmar, *Judging the Jury*, pp. 120–22.

11. Lawrence J. Severance and Elizabeth F. Loftus, "Improving the Ability of Jurors to Comprehend and Apply Criminal Jury Instructions," *Law and Society Review* 17 (1982): 153, 161.

12. Brookings Institution, *Charting a Future for the Civil Jury System*, p. 24.

13. *Batson v. Kentucky*, 476 U.S. 79 (1986) (race); *J.E.B. v. Alabama ex rel. T.B.*, 114 S.Ct. 1419 (1994) (gender).

14. *Casarez v. Texas*, 1994 Tex. Crim. App. Lexis 140 (Pentecostals); *United States v. Biaggi*, 853 F. 2d 89 (2d Cir. 1988), *cert. den.*, 489 U.S. 1052 (1989) (Italian-Americans); *Commonwealth v. Carleton*, 36 Mass. App. Ct. 137 (1994) (Irish-Americans).

15. Barbara D. Underwood, "Ending Race Discrimination in Jury Selection: Whose Right Is It, Anyway?" *Columbia Law Review* 92 (1992): 725, 762.

16. See, for example, *Ford v. Seabold*, 841 F.2d 677 (6th Cir. 1988), *cert. den.*, 488 U.S. 928 (1988) (young adults and college students not entitled to

Batson-style protection); *Anaya v. Hansen*, 781 F. 2d 1 (1st Cir. 1986) (same result for blue-collar workers or less-educated individuals as a group); *United States v. Canfield*, 879 F. 2d 446 (8th Cir. 1989) (same result for city residents).

17. Charles Ogletree, "Just Say No!: A Proposal to Eliminate Racially Discriminatory Uses of Peremptory Challenges," *American Criminal Law Review* 31 (1994): 1099, 1134–35.

18. Underwood, "Ending Race Discrimination," pp. 762ff; Ogletree, "Just Say No!" pp. 1137–51; Barbara Allen Babcock, "A Place in the Palladium: Women's Rights and Jury Service," *University of Cincinnati Law Review* 61 (1993): 1139, 1174–80.

19. Babcock, " A Place in the Palladium," pp. 1175–76; Underwood, "Ending Race Discrimination," pp. 762–71; Ogletree, "Just Say No!" pp. 1137–51.

20. See *People v. Bolling*, 582 N.Y.S. 2d 950, 956 (Bellacosa, J., concurring) (N.Y. 1992).

21. Albert W. Alschuler, "The Supreme Court and the Jury: Voir Dire, Peremptory Challenges, and the Review of Jury Verdicts," *University of Chicago Law Review* 56 (1989): 153, 199.

22. For examples such as these, see *Higginbotham v. State*, 428 S.E. 2d 592 (Ga. 1993) (permissible to strike blacks within same neighborhood as defendant or witnesses); *United States v. Payne*, 962 F. 2d. 1228 (6th Cir.), *cert. den.*, 113 S.Ct. 306 (1992) (NAACP); *State v. Butler*, 731 S.W. 2d 265, 271–72 (Mo. 1987) (elderly).

23. See, for example, *Whitsey v. State*, 796 S.W. 2d 707, 714 (Tex. 1989) (suspicious to use peremptories to strike blacks but not whites of a given age); Ogletree, "Just Say No!" pp. 1124–25 (discussing North Carolina "all or nothing" rule).

24. *Files v. State*, 613 So. 2d 1301 (Fla. 1992).

25. *Burgess v. Georgia*, 450 S.E. 2d 680 (Ga. 1994).

26. William Pizzi, "*Batson v. Kentucky*: Curing the Disease But Killing the Patient," *Supreme Court Review* (1987): 97, 134.

27. These observations were brought to my attention by trial judges in Massachusetts during a seminar discussion of my book sponsored by the Flaschner Judicial Institute, held at Boston College on April 27, 1995. I wish to thank all the judges who attended.

28. Alschuler, "The Supreme Court and the Jury," p. 200.

29. Hans Zeisel and Shari Seidman Diamond, "The Effect of Peremptory Challenges on Jury and Verdict: An Experiment in Federal District Court," *Stanford Law Review* 30 (1978): 491, 513, 517–19, 528–29.

30. Professor Ogletree, among others, has made similar suggestions, although he would preserve at least defense peremptories. See Ogletree, "Just Say No!" pp. 1132–37.

31. Ibid., p. 1134.

32. Underwood, "Ending Race Discrimination," p. 762.

33. Reid Hastie, "Symposium Issue on the Selection and Function of the Modern Jury: Is Attorney-Conducted Voir Dire an Effective Procedure for the Selection of an Impartial Jury?" *American University Law Review* 40 (1991): 703.

34. Alschuler, "The Supreme Court and the Jury," p. 157, n. 13, quoting Marci Chambers, "Who Should Pick Jurors, Attorneys or the Judge," *New York Times,* June 13, 1983, p. B4. In January 1995, New York state judges began overseeing civil voir dire in four state counties; their oversight power included imposition of severe time limits. Jan Hoffman, "Favorable Verdict for Jury Changes; Lawyers Are Unhappy; Other Signs Are Hopeful, Too," *New York Times,* April 12, 1995, p. B1.

35. Hastie, "Attorney-Conducted Voir Dire," p. 704; Alschuler, "The Supreme Court and the Jury," pp. 158–60.

36. Barat McClain, "Note: Turner's Acceptance of Limited Voir Dire Renders *Batson*'s Equal Protection a Hollow Promise," *Chicago-Kent Law Review* 65 (1989): 273, 300; Robert Rodriguez, "Comment: *Batson v. Kentucky,* Equal Protection, the Fair Cross Section Requirement, and the Discriminatory Use of Peremptory Challenges," *Emory Law Journal* 37 (1988): 755, 794.

37. Hoffman, "Favorable Verdict," p. B1.

38. Edward P. Schwartz and Warren F. Schwartz, "The Challenge of Peremptory Challenges," preliminary draft of paper prepared for presentation at the Annual Meeting of the Public Choice Society, Long Beach, Calif., March 24–29, 1995 (cited with permission).

APPENDIX

1. National Center for State Courts, *State Court Caseload Statistics: Annual Report* (Williamsburg, Va.: National Center for State Courts, 1988), p. 66.

2. Telephone interviews with Brian Ostrom and Thomas Munsterman of the National Center for State Courts, February 16, 1994. For a larger estimate of three hundred thousand, see James P. Levine, *Juries and Politics* (Pacific Grove, Calif.: Brooks/Cole, 1992), p. 36.

3. Administrative Office of the U.S. Courts, *Annual Report of the Director of the Administrative Office of the United States Courts* (1990), p. 161 (Table C7).

4. Harry Kalven, Jr., and Hans Zeisel, *The American Jury* (Chicago: University of Chicago Press, 1970), pp. 17–18; Levine, *Juries and Politics,* p. 34. See also National Center for State Courts, *State Court Caseload Statistics,* p. 56 (Table 4) (in thirteen reported jurisdictions, percentage of felony cases resolved by jury trial ranged from low of 2.1 percent in Texas to high of 6.9 percent in Alaska). For thirty-two states providing appropriate data in 1988, the National Center for State Courts calculated that jury trials constituted 2.9 percent of all criminal dispositions, including felony, misdemeanor, or drunk driving charges. Ibid., p. 55 (Table 3).

5. Administrative Office of the U.S. Courts, *Annual Report* (1990), pp. 10, 161 (Tables C7 and D).

6. Marc Galanter, "The Regulatory Function of the Civil Jury," in *Verdict: Assessing the Civil Jury System*, ed. Robert E. Litan (Washington, D.C.: Brookings Institution, 1993), p. 63; Levine, *Juries and Politics*, p. 34; National Center for State Courts, *State Court Caseload Statistics*, pp. 60, 67–69.

7. Administrative Office of the U.S. Courts, *Annual Report* (1990), p. 133 (Table C4).

8. Trial Court Department (Massachusetts), *Annual Report* (1988), p. 200.

9. Administrative Office of the U.S. Courts, *Annual Report* (1990), p. 17 (Table 11).

10. Ibid., pp. 16–17.

11. Steven W. Hays and Cole Blease Graham, Jr., *Handbook of Court Administration and Management* (New York: Marcel Dekker, 1993), pp. 415–16; Bureau of Justice Statistics, *Sourcebook of Criminal Justice Statistics* (1992), p. 91 (Table 1.92).

12. Administrative Office of the U.S. Courts, *Annual Report* (1990), p. 12 (Table 9). Numbers provided by the Department of Justice for 1990 are slightly different. According to these figures, the number of defendants convicted (47,486) accounted for 80.9 percent of all defendants (58,696) whose cases were disposed in federal district courts in 1990. Bureau of Justice Statistics, U.S. Department of Justice, *Compendium of Federal Justice Statistics, 1990*, p. 31.

13. Ibid. A total of 40,452 defendants entered pleas of guilty or nolo contendere, out of a total of 56,519 defendants whose cases were terminated.

14. National Center for State Courts, *State Court Caseload Statistics*, p. 57. See also Bureau of Justice Statistics, U.S. Department of Justice, *Report to the Nation on Crime and Justice* (1983), p. 65.

15. Trial Court Department (Massachusetts), *Annual Report* (1988), p. 97.

16. National Center for State Courts, *State Court Caseload Statistics*, pp. 56–57 (Table 5).

17. Bureau of Justice Statistics, U.S. Department of Justice, *Report to the Nation on Crime and Justice 1983*, p. 65.

18. Administrative Office of the U.S. Courts, *Annual Report* (1990), p. 204 (Table D7); 6,273 defendants were convicted by jury or judge, whereas 1,691 were acquitted.

19. Ibid. Similar, but not exactly the same figures, are reported by the Bureau of Justice Statistics, *Compendium of Federal Justice Statistics, 1990*, p.31.

20. Levine, Juries and Politics, p. 124. Levine cites his own study and the study of Robert Roper and Victor Flango, "Trial before Judges and Juries, "*Justice System Journal* 8 (1983): 186–98; and Levine, "Using Jury Verdict Forecasts in Criminal Defense Strategy," *Judicature* 66 (1983): 448–61.

21. Kalven and Zeisel, *The American Jury*, pp. 56–59.

Index